HP Network Node Manager 9: Getting Started

Manage your network effectively with NNMi

Marius Vilemaitis

[PACKT] enterprise 器

PUBLISHING   professional expertise distilled

BIRMINGHAM - MUMBAI

HP Network Node Manager 9: Getting Started

First published: January 2011

Production Reference: 1201210

Published by Packt Publishing Ltd.
32 Lincoln Road
Olton
Birmingham, B27 6PA, UK.

ISBN 978-1-849680-84-4

www.packtpub.com

Cover Image by Dan Anderson (Dan@CAndersonAssociates.com)

Credits

Author
Marius Vilemaitis

Reviewers
Lance Ecklesdafer
Eran Maor

Acquisition Editor
Amey Kanse

Development Editors
Dhiraj Chandiramani
Hyacintha D'Souza

Technical Editors
Gaurav Datar
Erika Fernandes

Copy Editors
Neha Damle
Leonard D'Silva
Janki Mathuria

Indexer
Rekha Nair

Editorial Team Leader
Gagandeep Singh

Project Team Leader
Priya Mukherji

Project Coordinator
Srimoyee Ghoshal

Proofreaders
Kelly Hutchison
Samantha Lyon

Graphics
Geetanjali Sawant

Production Coordinators
Shantanu Zagade
Arvindkumar Gupta

Cover Work
Shantanu Zagade

About the Author

Marius Vilemaitis is an implementation and integration professional with 10 years of experience in IT infrastructure monitoring tools. He has worked in various roles during this period, including System Administrator, Analyst, Engineer, and Implementation and Integration Consultant. Marius has worked in projects for mid-and large-size companies from various industries such as internet service providers, telecom companies and mobile operators, government departments and agencies, electrical and retail chain companies, among others. Marius has accomplished stunning results during his role in the designing and testing of Customs Management Systems (CMS), as well as leading a team of developers to accomplish the designing tasks.

Here is what he has to say about his experience with IT infrastructure monitoring tools:

> *The IT infrastructure monitoring is just about switching between red and green light. All that you need for your success is to find the magic moment to trigger a right color indicator at the right place. And this is the moment when you recognize that the most complicated and challenging thing is to have a right team, whichever stage you are in − development, implementation, or operations.*

Marius also provides training in IT infrastructure monitoring and management tools, which includes network, server, application, and premises monitoring, as well as configuration management.

This book wouldn't have been published without the help of many people, who contributed ideas and helped find solutions. It would be hard to list all of the names, but these people are my co-workers, partners, customers, and friends; all of them are part of this book. All these people are the source of my experience as well.

A special thanks to my family for infinitive support and living all these days without seeing their husband and dad. This book wouldn't have happened without you.

About the Reviewer

Lance Ecklesdafer is a Cisco certified Network Associate and experienced Microsoft Professional with more than 25 years of experience in Information Technology. He has experience in designing, planning, installing, managing, and supporting small to enterprise level networks and computer systems. He also has experience in designing, implementing, managing, and troubleshooting client networks, security solutions, and system applications.

During his career in IT, Lance has provided leadership to help select technology direction along with supplier and network services for Fortune 100 companies. He has participated not only in day-to-day operations, but also in project work. Any moves, changes, or adds of equipment was under his responsibility to not only design and plan, but also to implement at client's location. He also has experience in designing and building of midrange hosting environments.

Lance has extensive network monitoring background, which includes HP Openview Operations, Network Node Manager, Nagios Groundwork, Cacti, and WhatsUp Gold Professional, just to name a few. With the help of these tools, he has been able to provide information related to performance issues, incident and problem management, and root cause analysis.

Lance lives in Grand Blanc, Michigan, with his wife of 15 years, Christine. Besides Information Technology, Lance also studies Archaeology, Egyptology, and Archaeoastronomy.

www.PacktPub.com

Support files, eBooks, discount offers and more

You might want to visit www.PacktPub.com for support files and downloads related to your book.

Did you know that Packt offers eBook versions of every book published, with PDF and ePub files available? You can upgrade to the eBook version at www.PacktPub.com and as a print book customer, you are entitled to a discount on the eBook copy. Get in touch with us at service@packtpub.com for more details.

At www.PacktPub.com, you can also read a collection of free technical articles, sign up for a range of free newsletters and receive exclusive discounts and offers on Packt books and eBooks.

http://PacktLib.PacktPub.com

Do you need instant solutions to your IT questions? PacktLib is Packt's online digital book library. Here, you can access, read and search across Packt's entire library of books.

Why Subscribe?

- Fully searchable across every book published by Packt
- Copy and paste, print and bookmark content
- On demand and accessible via web browser

Free Access for Packt account holders

If you have an account with Packt at www.PacktPub.com, you can use this to access PacktLib today and view nine entirely free books. Simply use your login credentials for immediate access.

Table of Contents

Preface

This book guides you through the whole network monitoring implementation process. It covers all NNMi features and gives you hints to adapt this management software to your specific needs. It also describes how to use built-in features and adapt them in the most efficient way. It stitches the gap between technical personnel and management, covering subjects in both technical and business language.

What this book covers

Chapter 1, Before we Manage with NNMi, introduces NNMi 8.x as well as NNMi 9.x software, and describes the role of this software within the whole picture of infrastructure management. It describes what versions, modules, and smart plugins are and should be chosen when designing NNMi.

Chapter 2, Discovering and Monitoring Your Network, describes how to plan discovery scope and deal with network discovery issues, troubleshoot discovery results, and manage which nodes and interfaces should be monitored.

Chapter 3, Configuring and Viewing Maps, provides information about map configuration and map views, and describes what can be achieved while configuring maps, groups, and views.

Chapter 4, Configuring Incidents, is a key factor to successful monitoring, where accuracy is essential in selecting which events should be threaded as an incident and how operators should be notified. The chapter covers technical incident configuration, including a description of the business processes involved.

Chapter 5, Controlling Access to NNMi, describes how to control access to NNMi using embedded access control, integration with LDAP, or a combination of these two methods.

Chapter 6, Troubleshooting, Security, and Backup, provides a list of troubleshooting tools and ways on how find an issue and fix it. Knowing troubleshooting techniques and being familiar with the provided troubleshooting tools is a must for the system administrator. The chapter also covers the main security considerations that should be taken into account, while working with NNMi. The chapter ends with a description of the built-in backup and recovery tools, which can speed up the backup and recovery application. It covers the steps to be taken for backing up an application and recovering from it. It also describes how system configuration can be migrated from one NNMi application to the other.

Chapter 7, Application Failover and High Availability Solutions, describes the ability of NNMi to configure failover and to run on High Availability (HA) equipment. The chapter also provides the failover configuration process and the HA configuration steps.

Chapter 8, Navigating Console and Learning Network Inventory, starts a new section of the book, where several of the following chapters are mainly dedicated to operators. It explains how to navigate the NNMi console, going through menu items, different tabs, and views.

Chapter 9, Monitoring Your Network, continues to improve the operator's knowledge to be successful. The chapter covers several monitoring approaches. It also explains the incident management lifecycle and problem investigation issues.

Chapter 10, Extending NNMi, provides the capability to extend functionality. The administrator may want to monitor device custom attributes or extend NNMi features using URLs. This chapter covers the main features available for NNMi extension. The chapter also describes NNMi's major smart plugins that expand the functionality in a particular area.

Chapter 11, Integrating NNMi with Other Management Tools, as the name suggests, covers integration with the most common tools. A Large Network Operation Center may have more management tools that cover other infrastructure areas or management features than NNMi does. Integration with a different management system boosts infrastructure management. Integration can increase functionality and improve management processes as well.

Appendix A, Upgrading from NNM 6.x/7.x, covers the steps for upgrading NNM from earlier 6.x/7.x versions to NNMi 8.x.

Appendix B, Upgrading from NNMi 8.1x, provides a description on how to make an upgrade to NNMi 9.00.

Appendix C, What's Next..., brings the reader outside NNMi, and gives a vision on the next steps to be taken to keep improving the Network Operations Center.

What you need for this book

You will need to have HP Software NNMi 8.x or NNMi 9.x installed on your server. If you are working in a lab or practicing at home, you can install NNMi trial software, which is valid for 30 days and can be downloaded from the HP website (http://openview.hp.com).

The book provides a few links on the Internet, so you may need an internet connection to access the pages referred to. In case you are having trouble with your NNMi installation or configuration, you may refer to the HP forums at the following web address: http://itrc.hp.com.

Who this book is for

The book is written, keeping in mind the following audience:

- Monitoring solution designers, who plan how to implement NNMi
- Network engineers, who plan to start managing their network
- System administrators, who start administering NNMi
- Network monitoring operators, who want to learn how to use NNMi

If you belong to any one of these professions, then this book is for you. It's also for professionals who describe themselves as beginners, or intermediate level professionals. The book is also useful to the old version NNM users who wish to switch to NNMi.

Conventions

In this book, you will find a number of styles of text that distinguish between different kinds of information. Here are some examples of these styles, and an explanation of their meaning.

Code words in text are shown as follows: "Here we make an assumption that our node names follow the naming convention as <hostname>.<country_abbreviation>.<company_name>.com".

A block of code will be set as follows:

```
nnmloadnodegroups.ovpl -? | -u <user> -p <password> -f <CSV_file> [ -r
true|false ]
 Example:
       nnmloadnodegroups.ovpl -u myadminusername -p myadminpassword
-f /tmp/nnmconfig.csv
```

Any command-line input or output is written as follows:

Name	PID	State	Last Message(s)
OVsPMD	3654	RUNNING	-
nmsdbmgr	3655	RUNNING	Database available.
ovjboss	3669	RUNNING	Initialization complete.

New terms and **important words** are shown in bold. Words that you see on the screen, in menus or dialog boxes for example, appear in our text like this: "Click **Save and Close** to close Syslog Servers Node Group configuration window".

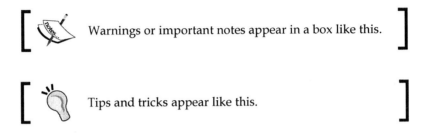

[　Warnings or important notes appear in a box like this.　]

[　Tips and tricks appear like this.　]

Reader feedback

Feedback from our readers is always welcome. Let us know what you think about this book—what you liked or may have disliked. Reader feedback is important for us to develop titles that you really get the most out of.

To send us general feedback, simply send an e-mail to feedback@packtpub.com, and mention the book title via the subject of your message.

If there is a book that you need and would like to see us publish, please send us a note in the **SUGGEST A TITLE** form on www.packtpub.com or e-mail suggest@packtpub.com.

If there is a topic that you have expertise in and you are interested in either writing or contributing to a book, see our author guide on www.packtpub.com/authors.

Customer support

Now that you are the proud owner of a Packt book, we have a number of things to help you to get the most from your purchase.

Downloading the example code for this book

You can download the example code files for all Packt books you have purchased from your account at http://www.PacktPub.com. If you purchased this book elsewhere, you can visit http://www.PacktPub.com/support and register to have the files e-mailed directly to you.

Downloading the color images of this book

We also provide you a PDF file that has color images of the screenshots used in this book. The high resolution color images will help you better understand the changes in the output. You can download this file from https://www.packtpub.com/sites/default/files/0844EN_HPNetworkNodeManager.pdf.

Errata

Although we have taken every care to ensure the accuracy of our content, mistakes do happen. If you find a mistake in one of our books—maybe a mistake in the text or the code—we would be grateful if you would report this to us. By doing so, you can save other readers from frustration and help us improve subsequent versions of this book. If you find any errata, please report them by visiting http://www.packtpub.com/support, selecting your book, clicking on the errata submission form link, and entering the details of your errata. Once your errata are verified, your submission will be accepted and the errata will be uploaded on our website, or added to any list of existing errata, under the Errata section of that title. Any existing errata can be viewed by selecting your title from http://www.packtpub.com/support.

Piracy

Piracy of copyright material on the Internet is an ongoing problem across all media. At Packt, we take the protection of our copyright and licenses very seriously. If you come across any illegal copies of our works, in any form, on the Internet, please provide us with the location address or website name immediately so that we can pursue a remedy.

Please contact us at copyright@packtpub.com with a link to the suspected pirated material.

We appreciate your help in protecting our authors, and our ability to bring you valuable content.

Questions

You can contact us at questions@packtpub.com if you are having a problem with any aspect of the book, and we will do our best to address it.

Before we Manage with NNMi

1

If you are planning to implement a network management tool where Network Node Manager (NNMi) is one of the items in your shopping list, or you are thinking of upgrading your system or expanding it, this chapter is a good starting point.

Before we go into the technical details, it's important to understand what NNMi is in general, and how it fits into infrastructure management's big picture.

NNMi brings value by not only monitoring a network as a standalone management tool, but it is also valuable because of its ability to integrate with other infrastructure management tools like server and application management, end user experience monitoring, or service desk tools. The ability to integrate NNMi with other tools and making it part of a big puzzle makes NNMi an enterprise-level management tool. Let's take two companies as an example: **Internet Service Provider (ISP)** and a retail chain company. The only thing these companies have in common is a large network and a long list of network devices to be managed. Both of them may choose NNMi as a network management tool. The difference is about what role NNMi will play in their whole infrastructure management umbrella. NNMi for ISP would play a major (if not solo) role in the whole infrastructure, as the network for ISP is a major business asset. For the retail chain company, NNMi will only be a part of the management tools used, as the network is only one media, and it's a small piece of a list of services which are involved in doing business. The network is only a part in the whole IT infrastructure chain. Server and application monitoring are as important as the network, or any other part of IT. One company will demand a long list of advanced feature monitoring, while the other will demand smooth integration with other monitoring tools. As you see, both of them can use NNMi as a network management tool.

The following topics will be covered in this chapter:

- What HP Software NNMi can do for us
- Choosing the right edition
- Understanding iSPIs
- Server sizing considerations
- How NNMi will impact my infrastructure
- License policy
- Installing software
- Summary

What can HP SW NNMi do for us?

A fool with a tool is still a fool

-author unknown

This old adage tells everything about what a management tool can do for us. NNMi can make life easier, but it can't do so without our carefully planned and prepared effort.

Network Node Manager is a tool which can help us to keep an eye on our network, find issues, recognize outages related to network, and help us improve our network availability and performance. Even so, it's a tool. NNMi, as any other tool, will not replace your network administrator, but will help him/her instead.

This book is designed in order to show you how to use NNMi, to share best practices, and to demonstrate use cases.

Network Node Manager — the name itself denotes that this tool is dedicated to managing networks. But let's make it clear and find out what exactly *network* and *manage* mean.

Listed here are examples of unrealistic expectations that people can have of NNMi:

- A network administrator installs NNMi and expects that his job is taken care of, and that he can lie on a chair and wait for another paystub.
- The manager that has approved the purchase of NNMi expects NNMi to instantly resolve all issues relating the network without any human effort.

One question that people with limited management tool knowledge may have is "why do I need these management tools if I already have a management tool for servers and another for databases"? The answer is, each tool is positioned for one specific purpose, and there is no tool for everything so far. Tool positioning is made by an activity, which tool makes and the infrastructure type it is designed for.

For such positioning, a very good example is a matrix of functionality and infrastructure coverage, where matrix columns define the infrastructure's area and rows define functionality.

In most cases, infrastructure can be divided into the following parts:

- Peripheral devices (UPS, temperature and humidity sensors, door switches, and fluid detectors)
- Network devices (routers and switches)
- Firewalls and other security device servers (Hardware and OS)
- Applications (Oracle, SQL, Web or Mail Server, CRM, ERP tools, and so on)
- Service (e-Shop, Stock Exchange trade platform, e-Magazine, and such others)

Each part of the infrastructure can be divided into the following management areas by activity:

- Configuration management
- Fault and problem management
- Performance and capacity management
- Security management
- Knowledge management
- Service management

According to this tool positioning philosophy, NNMi can be positioned as a fault and performance management tool.

 NNMi 8.x is fault monitoring tool, because it doesn't have performance data collection and graphing capability.

To clarify few of the other HP Software management tools are positioned in the following table:

	Peripheral	Network	Servers	Applications	Services
Service					
Knowledge					
Security					
Performance/ capacity	OVPI	Partly NNMi OVPI	OVPI	OVPI	Business Availability Center
Fault		NNMi	OV Operations	OV Operations	Business Availability Center
Configuration		Partly NNMi HP SW NAS			

NNMi can automatically discover a network, recognize network devices and their configuration, and draw an IP map accordingly. As NNMi *recognizes* discovered devices, it can show what the impact for a network would be if one of the devices goes down, the interface gets disconnected, or the performance parameters (like latency) exceed set limits (threshold). Network state is mapped by NNMi using two types of information sources:

- Messages sent from managed devices (SNMP traps)
- Regular polls that check for device state or configuration changes

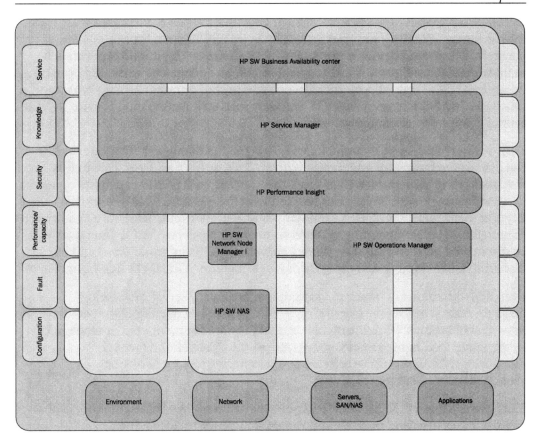

NNMi can monitor performance parameters such as interface utilization, interface errors, CPU load, or almost any other performance information that is provided by device SNMP agent. NNMi can generate a message to an incident browser if some performance parameters exceed expected limits (thresholds), or if a fault occurs in a managed device. At the same time, NNMi can't be treated as a capacity management tool. NNMi 8.x cannot collect any performance data, store it for a long time, or present an advanced performance or capacity report. NNMi 9.0 already has features such as performance data graphing and custom poller, which send incidents based on SNMP object ID or their combination. But NNMi standalone tool cannot have following features:

- Flexible data storage
- Performance data advanced analysis

NNMi also provides network inventory detailed data about devices that were either loaded during discovery or input manually by an NNMi operator as a custom attribute. Discovered device reports, as well as device configuration reports such as interface list, configured VLANs, serial numbers, or contact information, can be presented. NNMi cannot perform network device configuration backup or restore functions. In addition, unlike the HP Software Network Automation Service, NNMi cannot change device configuration.

On the other hand, even though NNMi is designed to manage network devices, it can discover and monitor any device with an IPV4 or IPV6 address. Due to this, workstations or servers, as well as any other devices with SNMP capability or agents designed to work with NNMi, can be used with the product. NNMi cannot be called a server management tool, as it cannot monitor server-specific hardware or software parameters of server operating systems software or hardware. All IP interfaces will be discovered on servers, but no other hardware specific information would be discovered, like number and capacity of disks, memory, CD/DVD-ROMs, and so on.

Even if NNMi cannot do much in terms of workstation or server monitoring, there are cases when server monitoring by NNMi may be valuable. Some servers or workstations must be permanently on, and they are not monitored or managed by any other tool. In such a case, nodes can be added into NNMi for state monitoring. NMMi should be selected as a monitoring tool for Server or Workstation monitoring exclusively.

Thus, we can expect NNMi to help us solve network outage issues, monitor paths, identify root cause, and monitor and report some performance issues.

Choosing the right edition

NNMi is sold in two editions:

- Starter
- Advanced

This allows you to choose what best suits your particular infrastructure management needs. Less complex networks do not require as many features as management tools do, such as complex networks with advanced technologies and solutions.

In order to make a decision regarding which version you should utilize, you should answer the following questions:

- Do you need to monitor trunks and port aggregations?
- Do you need to monitor router redundancy groups, such as HSRP or VRRP?
- Do you need to monitor IPv6?

- Do you plan to implement global network management solution (for example, one NNMi works as collection station and reports to another NNMi, which is a primary manager)?
- Do you need to integrate NNMi to RAMS tool?"

If your answers to the previous questions are *NO*, then NNMi Starter edition is just right for you.

Also, don't forget that you can upgrade your starter edition to an advanced edition anytime as a later date. Technically, it's about entering a new license key into the software. It may be a more complicated challenge to get approval from management spending on licenses later on. This should also be taken into account when you plan which version to acquire.

So, if you are satisfied with the starter edition features for now, but think that you may need the advanced features in the future, I would recommend that you begin with the starter edition for now and upgrade later on. The following table gives you a brief comparison between starter and advanced editions:

Features	NNMi	NNMi Advanced
L2 and L3 discovery	+	+
Custom SNMP data collection (no storage)	+	+
Dynamic RCA	+	+
Management by exception	+	+
iSPI support	+	+
MPLS*	+	+
Multicast*	+	+
VoIP*	+	+
Performance based event correlation	+	+
Integration with OVPI	+	+
Integration with RAMS		+
Root Cause Analysis (RCA)	+	+
Trunks/ Port aggregation (Support for: PaGP, SMLT, MLT - protocols)		+
Router redundancy groups (HSRP, VRRP)		+
Path View visualization extension		+
MPLS WAN Clouds (RAMS)		+
Global Network Management (GNM)		+
IPv6 (on Unix)		+
Virtualized Server management		+

*— if according iSPI is used
+— the mentioned feature is supported on that edition

Understanding Smart Plug-ins (iSPI)

iSPI is a Smart Plugin, which can be installed on top of the Network Node Manager for feature expansion.

NNMi has a pretty long list of features, especially when we consider the information it provides in regards to network topology and all other information related to it. Every network is unique in terms of technologies it uses and purposes it is designed to. For example, carrying voice over IP, where voice converges with IP networks. MPLS is another unique technology, which in some terms can be treated as a separate science and needs additional management approach. Multicast is another story, with its own features and headaches from an operations perspective.

All these technologies and features are not rocket science, but it is really an additional effort to be developed as a management tool. Most of NNMi users have hardly any of these technologies, so why should they pay for features they never use?

Mostly, SPIs use NNMi's discovered nodes and their configuration as a primary source of information. Also, iSPI provides some information back to NNMi, that is, additional features or technology configuration, configuration changes, performance parameters, or alarms.

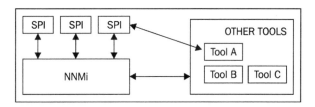

Here is a list of major SPIs:

- **iSPI for MPLS**: Allows users to discover and monitor MPLS-specific objects and parameters. For example, L2/L3 VPNs, MVPN, Pseudo wire VC, VRF, PE-CE, PE-PE links, and so on.

- **iSPI for IP Telephony**: This iSPI discovers and monitors VoIP-specific objects and parameters. It supports VoIP monitoring from Avaya, Cisco, and Nortel vendors.

- **iSPI Network Engineering toolset**: This iSPI is a set of additional tools, which allows NNMi operator to initiate some routine actions, which helps in troubleshooting issues.

- **iSPI for Performance**: After NNMi version 8.11, this iSPI has been divided into two separate iSPIs: iSPI Performance for Metrics and iSPI Performance for Traffic. These iSPIs collect and report performance specific data—**Network Engineering Toolset (NET)**. This iSPI provides additional troubleshooting and diagnostics tools for network engineers.

- **iSPI for Multicast**: This iSPI provides multicast network specific features, such as discovering and monitoring IP multicast routing topology, multicast enabled nodes, PIM interfaces and neighbors, and so on.

Questions such as *"Do I need SPI? If so, which one of these to choose? Will it do what I expect?"* are ones commonly asked while designing NNMi. Let's take a look at the major SPIs.

iSPI for Performance

Before NNMi 8.11, there was iSPI Performance, which was introduced as two separate iSPIs on later NNMi versions. Legacy iSPI performance was collecting performance metrics based on SNMP queries on managed nodes. Later on, HP introduced the ability to collect data from flows, as flow data has a different list of features than performance data collected by SNMP. These iSPIs are:

- **iSPI Performance for Metrics**: Legacy iSPI performance with few improved features.

- **iSPI Performance for Traffic**: iSPI, which collects, analyzes, stores, and presents flow data.

Let's take a look at both in detail.

iSPI Performance for Metrics

The iSPI Performance for Metrics adds the performance management capability to NNMi by analyzing, processing, and aggregating metrics collected by NNMi from different network elements. This release of the iSPI Performance for Metrics includes the following features:

- Path health reports
- Component health reports
- Interface health reports
- Custom polled reports

Also, unlike in previous NNM versions (7.x and earlier), we cannot trigger alerts based on performance data in basic NNMi versions. That is, we need to receive alarms when the device CPU load exceeds 95%, the interface utilization exceeds 70% or comes below 5% for longer than one hour. Default NNMi can't handle it. iSPI performance brings this feature into NNMi. Now, we can say that NNMi and iSPI Performance both together cover fault and performance monitoring areas.

The network performance data adds more functionality for network management. It improves your network management by:

- Allowing operators to retrieve more data during investigations
- Enriching your monitoring by providing alerts based on performance data
- Providing information to network planners and analysts, where they can see long-term statistics, which makes future planning more accurate

iSPI Performance collects, stores, arrays data, and presents it in drill-down reports. Using data mining in reports, we can drill down until we reach the node or interface, which causes issues.

Users have relative flexibility in creating their own reports, as custom SQL queries can be created on reports by user-specific needs, such as a report with custom time period, or metrics, which are monitored. iSPI reports are reached from the NNM console, and no additional logins and passwords are needed as iSPI recognizes usernames or passwords used by NNMi. Reports running after they are selected and take up to 15 to 20 seconds. To eliminate this query at runtime, you can schedule the report to run in advance, as the scheduled report is displayed immediately.

All monitored metrics can trigger threshold alarms, so operators can be notified before real impact occurs. Performance-based alarms also reflect the status of the nodes, which makes the map status more accurate for monitoring.

 Previous NNM versions (7.x and earlier) represented node status only based on status poller results.

Earlier NNM versions used to cause a lot of confusion when performance-based alarms indicated possible outages or upcoming service impacts, and map icons remained in a normal (green) state.

NNMi iSPI Performance for Metrics may be licensed to monitor a smaller number of nodes than its corresponding NNMi. Consider, if you are a service provider and only a small part of your managed nodes has a requirement to be monitored features, which are supported by iSPI performance for metrics. Buying licenses for all the nodes would be a waste of money. Another wasteful example would be, if your NNMi, except routers and switches, also monitors a Users have relative flexibility in creating their own reports, large number of workstations or servers which don't need to be covered by iSPI Performance for Metrics.

As HP changes licensing policy on a regular basis, please contact your HP representative to check the most current licensing policy, as it may be changed by the time the book is read. Please refer to `http://support.openview.hp.com/selfsolve/manuals`.

NNMi can be configured to poll vendor proprietary MIBs, issue a threshold incident, set status on the map to alert operations, report on values and with NNMi iSPI performance for metrics.

iSPI is not a replacement to HP Performance Insight (OVPI), but depending on particular requirements, sometimes iSPI Performance for Metrics may be used as an alternative to OVPI. The following table provides *high-level* comparison of iSPI Performance for Metrics and OVPI:

NNMi iSPI Performance for Metrics	Open View Performance Insight
Tightly integrated with NNMi	May be integrated into NNMi as well as can be a separate product
Short to medium term data is stored	Long-term data is stored
Collects MIB data using SNMP	Customized data collection methods can be used, that is, Operations Manager or Performance Manager agent
Designed to be used for proactive monitoring and generating alarms	Designed for long-term reporting
Tool very handy for operations	Tool for operations, analysis, planning, and reporting to management

If you are, or plan to be an NNMi system administrator, you should be prepared to be asked whether or not iSPI Performance for Metrics loads a network with extra ICMP or SNMP traffic. Although the answer is yes, iSPI queries extra information, but on the other hand, it wouldn't load a network as much as it would separate a tool from a third party vendor, because iSPI uses the same SNMP process to collect performance and status information. It means that it eliminates extra polling, as the data is queried and responded using same packet bulks.

iSPI Performance for Traffic

By introducing this iSPI, NNMi took a step into network service monitoring. This iSPI uses flow data and can detect reports such as performance issues, like separate traffic types HTTP, mail, and FTP traffic. It can report about top sources or destinations, and so on. So now, the NNMi operator can take a look on what's happening inside IP traffic, as iSPI Performance for Traffic analyzes flow data. The following flow versions and vendors are supported:

- NetFlow: version 5, version 9
- S-Flow: version 5

iSPI Performance for Traffic is very useful for troubleshooting network issues, such as:

- What kind of traffic utilizes my bandwidth most or fills it up?
- What sources or targets generate most traffic?

These issues are a headache not only for operators, but for network or service analysts and planners as well. If your data channel is divided into traffic classes based on traffic type (that is, 20% of traffic for HTTP, 30% for mail, and so on), this iSPI will also tell you about your traffic classic behavior.

Example: Why is my HTTP browsing is so slow, while my interface utilization is below 70%? Answer: HTTP traffic is configured to take max 30% of your bandwidth, and HTTP takes all of it while other traffic classes are less loaded, which makes total bandwidth utilization less than 100%. So, instead of constant questions and unclear situations, iSPI Performance for Traffic gives a clear answer, with evidence, that it is time to change traffic class allocation limits. This can be seen in the following diagrams:

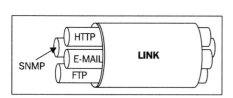 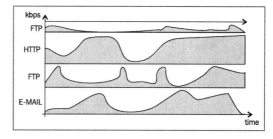

This iSPI can be used in conjunction with iSPI Performance for Metrics, which provides navigation between Metric and Traffic data.

 iSPI Performance for Traffic cannot trigger an alarm.

Traffic generates performance reports from the IP flow records as follows:

- Aggregates the IP flow record.

- Correlates obtained IP flow records with NNMi topology for context-based analysis.

- Enriches the IP flow records by providing the ability to add or update the available fields in the flow records. For example, DNS name resolution and application mapping.

Flow data is collected using flow collectors, which can be designed as two tier collectors: local and master. NNMi supports either of the two scenarios: co-located and non-co-located deployment of leaf, master collectors, and NNMi, as well as NNMi iSPI Performance server. The following figure represents the two-tier, hierarchical flow collection and processing:

- **Leaf collectors**: They are responsible for flow filtering, application mapping, DNS name resolution, and summary data feed to master collector.

- **Master collector**: This collector is responsible for collecting and correlating all summary records as central point from all leaf-level collectors.

- **Common NNMi iSPI Performance Reporting Server**: This server is responsible for building traffic analysis reports, which are done on the same server as iSPI Performance for Metrics.

Multiple leaf collectors per physical machine can be supported.

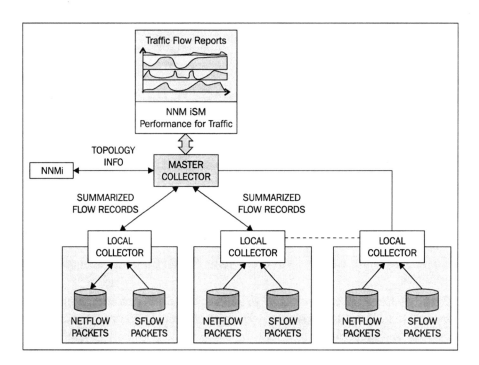

Can this iSPI be used as a replacement to OVPI? General answer is no. However, there may be some cases when iSPI Performance for Traffic may cover the required features. The following table provides a general comparison between iSPI and OVPI:

iSPI Performance for Traffic	Open View Performance Insight
Tightly integrated with NNMi	May be integrated into NNMi as well as can be separate product
Short to medium term data is stored	Long-term data is stored
No alarms can be triggered	Alarms can be triggered based on threshold settings
Focused on flow collection	Focused on long term trending, forecasting and capacity planning
Tool, very handy for operations	Tool for operations, analysis, planning and reporting to management
Supports Net Flow (v5, v9) and sFlow (v5)	Supports Net Flow (v5) and sFlow (v5, with IUM collector)

iSPI Network Engineering toolset

When an issue on the network occurs, the operator needs to troubleshoot the issue and often a sequence of additional action is required, such as checking the current status of interface, getting node configuration, evaluating outage impact, or collecting information about end nodes connected to switch.

Another headache for system administrators and operators is constant and meaningless SNMP traps, which floods the message browser and cause event storms. This can be caused by some improperly configured settings on group of nodes, or constant and frequent event generation on one node.

All these issues are solved by iSPI NET. It is a set of tools, which helps in troubleshooting network issues. In general, there are three major features in this iSPI:

- Diagnostics
- Troubleshooting tools, attached switch port troubleshooting
- Trap analytics

iSPI diagnostics

iSPI diagnostics helps to collect additional configuration data from network devices, such as:

- Current configuration for Cisco router, Cisco switch, or Nortel switch
- Diagnostic checks on a specified interface on Cisco router
- Gather routing information

To configure this automatic diagnostics gathering, you need to complete following steps in **SNMP Trap Configuration, Remote NNMi 6.x/7.x Event Configuration**, or **Management Event Configuration** forms:

- Specify node group in *Configuration Per Node Group* form
- In the *Diagnostic Selection*, select which diagnostics you want to use

Diagnostic must be valid for a node which runs diagnostics. That is, Cisco configuration can run only on Cisco devices.

Incident's lifecycle state must match state which was configured. That is, if lifecycle state is *closed*, then diagnostics will run only when incident's state would be *closed*.

Troubleshooting tools

This tool examines switches, detects and maps switch ports with end nodes connected to them. End nodes don't need to be discovered by NNMi, as this data is queried from the switch's ARP table. Using this data collection method, the troubleshooting tool provides the following information:

- Which switch port the node is connected to. It can be searched by IP address, node name, or MAC address.
- All nodes attached to switch.

This functionality is very useful for troubleshooting LAN issues. Many NNMi users were complaining about the lack of this feature in previous NNMi versions (7.x and earlier).

Trap analytics

By default, NNMi measures the rate of incoming traps (incoming trap rate for each device and rate of each incoming trap for each trap OID). If the rate of incoming traps exceeds the defined threshold, NNMi blocks such traps until the rate decreases below the minimum threshold limit.

 Thresholds can be configured by the administrator using `nnmtrapsconfig.ovpl` script.

SNMP trap analytics allows you to get reports based on this trap information, by the following criteria:

- Amount of traps within a specific time period
- Trap amount for specified node
- Trap amount to a specific trap identifier—OID

All data is logged to `trapanalytics.0.0.log` file. This file provides following data for specific time intervals:

- Traps per second
- TOP 10 trap generator sources
- TOP 10 generated traps

This data is useful in making analysis of SNMP traps, which allows us to optimize messages from your managed network. Many administrators are complaining that they receive too many messages. In many cases, administrators say they have no idea where to start. So, start from the largest troublemakers—TOP 10 OIDs and TOP 10 sources. If you fix at least TOP 5 OIDs, you will reduce the amount of alarms by 40-80%. So, even if the situation looks hopeless, there is a small and easy way to make the step between a messy and shining browser.

iSPI IP Telephony

HP NNMi Smart Plug-in for IP Telephony extends the functionality of NNMi, providing more detailed information about the VoIP telephony infrastructure. iSPI for VoIP discovers, monitors, and presents additional views of VoIP specific parameters, such as:

- IP address, hostname, version, model, type, and status of device
- Phone model, registration state, extension number, and supported protocol controller
- VoIP network health

First of all, your VoIP devices will be discovered automatically and presented on a map as VoIP-specific devices, so that you can easily recognize VoIP phone, PBX, or voice gateway on a map.

The NNMi SPI for IPT provides comprehensive monitoring for an IP telephony service. It includes features, which are VoIP specific: voice gateway, calls, and path control.

Using iSPI for IPT monitoring is more detailed than IP generic monitoring, and gives an advantage for VoIP-specific issues against plain NNMi monitoring of IP network. iSPI for IPT helps detect outages in their early stage.

The quality of calls has been reduced, so more calls are dropped or being provided with long voice delays. Using plain NNMi, you wouldn't recognize such behavior and you would have *green* map with no incidents regarding this issue, while your IPT users are struggling and complaining about poor quality. iSPI for IPT would notify you about such (and even more) service decreases, so the only thing you should take care of is to fix a problem.

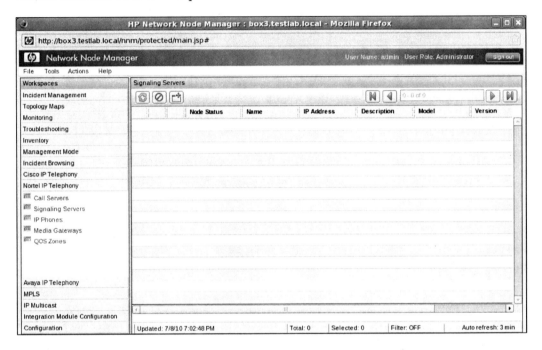

The following list provides a detailed feature list, which is supported by iSPI IPT:

- Infrastructure management:
  - Call Manager 5.x, 6.x inventory, detail views, and status/incident.
  - Cisco GK inventory, detail views, and status/incident.
  - Cisco ICT inventory, detail views, and status/incident.
  - Nortel CS 1000, Nortel SS, and Nortel VGMC/MGC/MC inventory, detail views, and SNMP trap-based alarm status.

- IP phone management:
  - Inventory and detail view of Cisco IP phones (SCCP/SIP), their registration status and their relationship to Call Managers.
  - Inventory and detail view of Nortel IP phones, their relationships to Nortel CS.

- Detailed Cisco Voice Gateway management:

    ° Cisco DS0 channel inventory, detail view, alarm status, usage status.

    ° Cisco DS1 (T1/E1 CAS/PRI/BRI, E&M, FXS, and FXO) Circuit Switched interface inventory and detail view, alarm status/incident, and usage incident/status.

    ° Cisco VGW inventory and detail view, alarm status/incident, usage status/incident, H323 and MGCP support.

- Voice quality monitoring and diagnostics:

    ° CDR/CMR-based Jitter, latency, delay, MOS monitoring for calls in Cisco IPT networks and incidents.

    ° Nortel QoS zone inventory, detail view with 32 QoS metric values for Nortel QoS zones and incidents.

    ° Nortel QoS SNMP trap-based monitoring of quality of calls in Nortel IPT network and incidents.

    ° Voice path draws L2/L3 path between two Cisco IP Phones for media.

    ° Control path draws L2/L3 path between a Cisco IP Phone and its Call Manager.

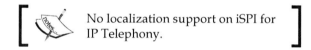

No localization support on iSPI for IP Telephony.

iSPI for MPLS

iSPI for MPLS helps to monitor MPLS-specific parameters. It uses NNMi's node inventory and provides MPLS-specific, real-time data for MPLS-enabled devices:

- MPLS **Virtual Private Networks (VPN)** on provider edge devices.

- MPLS Pseudo Wire **Virtual Containers (VC)**.

- **Traffic Engineering (TE)** tunnels.

- Monitors status and displays VPNs, VRFs, TE tunnels, and Pseudo Wire VCs attributes.

- Generates incidents for the MPLS-specific faults or changes in the topology.

The following figure represents the difference between managing MPLS-enabled network using plain NNMi (left-hand side picture) and using iSPI MPLS (right-hand side picture):

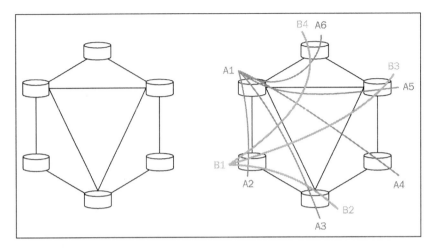

iSPI MPLS automatically discovers MPLS devices and presents MPLS-specific data like L3-VPN/VRF, L2VPN (Pseudo Wire), and MPLS traffic engineering. MPLS specific views and implemented correlation are provided on MPLS specific incidents.

 MPLS is supported only on Cisco IOS, IOS XR.
iSPI MPLS does not support localization.

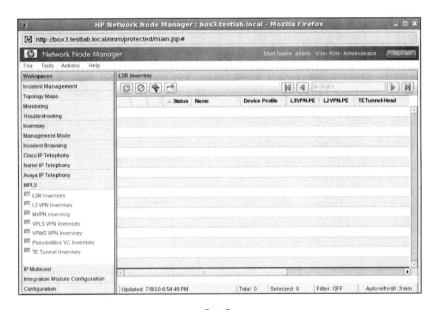

The detailed feature list of iSPI for MPLS is as follows:

- L3-VPN Management:
    - ° Inventory view of L3-VPNs.
    - ° Details views for an L3-VPN including VRFs, VRF-details.
    - ° Monitoring of VRF state and incident/status-propagation for L3-VPNs.

- **Label Switched Router (LSR) views:**
    - ° LSR core view.
    - ° Launch from LSR view to other views showing node-centric MPLS-services.

- Traffic Engineering management:
    - ° Inventory view of TE Tunnels.
    - ° TE Tunnel details view.
    - ° Monitoring of TE tunnel status and incidents.

- Pseudo-wire management:
    - ° Inventory view of pseudo-wires.
    - ° Monitoring of pseudo-wire status and incidents.
    - ° As any other iSPI, it can be installed at any time, even if your deployment is completed a long time ago.

iSPI multicast

IP multicast is a technique for one-to-many communications over an IP infrastructure in a network. It scales to a larger receiver population by not requiring prior knowledge of who or how many receivers there are. Multicast uses network infrastructure efficiently by requiring the source to send a packet only once, even if it needs to be delivered to a large number of receivers. Multicast mostly is used for services such as video or audio broadcasting, when many users may be watching/listening for the same content. The nodes in the network take care of replicating the packet to reach multiple receivers only when necessary. The most common low-level protocol to use multicast addressing is **User Datagram Protocol (UDP)**. By its nature, UDP is not reliable—messages may be lost or delivered out of order. Reliable multicast protocols such as **Pragmatic General Multicast (PGM)** have been developed to add loss detection and retransmission on top of IP multicast (source—Wikipedia).

The following figures represent Multicast's graphical presentation:

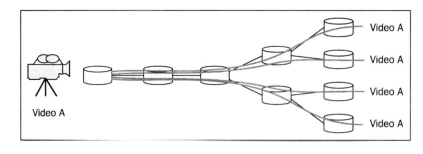

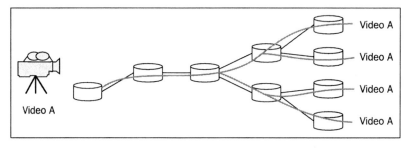

iSPI Multicast allows monitoring multicast networks. It automatically detects multicast configuration, shows multicast-specific views, and monitors multicast-specific parameters. iSPI Multicast allows the user to diagnose issues in early stage, which leads to the reducing of MTBF. iSPI Multicast provides information like Multicast Node/Interface inventory, including a designated router, discovers Multicast neighbors and provides Multicast neighbor's status.

 iSPI Multicast is supported only on Windows.
iSPI Multicast supports only Cisco IOS.

The following screenshot provides iSPI for Multicast window in NNMi:

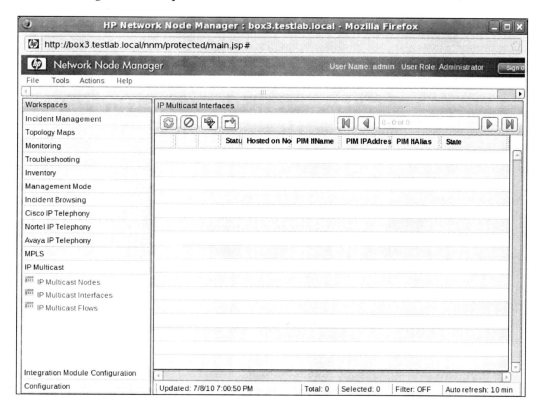

Server sizing considerations

NNMi server sizing depends on many parameters, which sometimes cannot be precisely measured and, more importantly, doesn't give a straight answer as to which server hardware should be selected. This is a list of parameters which should be taken into account when you start sizing an NNMi server:

- Number of managed nodes
- Number of managed interfaces
- Number of managed networks
- Number of managed segments
- Number of managed VLANS
- Number of managed HSRP groups
- Number of connected ports

- Number of simultaneous users
- What iSPIs are planned to be used?

HP representatives use server sizing calculator, which is based mostly on the parameters listed previously. Calculation output, however, is not accurate. HP provides several configuration examples on their website, which were tested, and regarded this as the best source for server sizing. In the following table, there are three server sizings taken from HP NNMi documentation. According to these examples, you may decide what server hardware should be ordered for your infrastructure.

Parameter	Small	Medium	Large
Number of nodes	Up to 3K	3K - 8K	8K - 18K
Number of discovered interfaces	Up to 120K	Up to 400K	Up to 900K
Number of polled interfaces	Up to 10K	Up to 50K	Up to 70K
Number of polled node components	40K	60K	80K
Number of concurrent users	Up to 10	Up to 25	Up to 40
CPU	4 CPU cores (2.5GHz for x64, 1.4GHz for IPF or RISC)	4 CPU cores (2.5GHz for x64, 1.4GHz for IPF or RISC)	8 CPU cores (2.5GHz for x64, 1.4GHz for IPF or RISC)
RAM	8 GB	16 GB	24 GB
Java heap size	4 GB (-Xmx 4096m)	6 GB (-Xmx 6g)	10 GB (-Xmx 10g)
Disk space for application installation	5 GB	5 GB	5 GB
Disk space for database	60 GB	140 GB RAID 1+0 or 5/6 with write cache recommended (4 disk)	300 GB RAID 1+0 or 5/6 with write cache recommended (4 disk)

 Remember, memory is never enough. So if you have an opportunity, size your server with more memory than you see in sizing recommendations.

Question: Which Operating System should we choose?

Answer: Personally, I have neither done detailed tests on NNMi performance, nor have I met anybody who has neglected the commonly that RISC or IPF architecture servers perform better than Intel architecture servers. Also, when you make your decision about OS, consider maintenance costs. Hardware is only a part of all your costs and I would say not the largest one. Your headache may increase if you choose OS which you are not familiar with, or have no professionals who are familiar with it. If you are a Windows guy, go for Windows. If you are more experienced with Linux, choose Linux instead. All of them work and having your favorite OS on operations will reduce **MTTR** (**Mean Time To Repair**) and probably **MTBF** (**Mean Time Between Failures**), and will increase your satisfaction working with NNMi as well.

When choosing an OS, also takes into account the iSPI you plan to use. Some of them are OS-specific and you may be forced to choose a specific OS. For example, iSPI for Multicast works only on Windows OS. Read iSPI latest release notes before you make a decision.

How NNMi will impact my infrastructure

Designing management tools, such as NNMi, are not only about sizing a server. The following are important issues as well:

- Traffic consumption by the monitoring tool
- Security policy changes in your infrastructure
- Data storage space for system backups
- Infrastructure device naming convention

Traffic consumption by the monitoring tool

When you design an NNMi system, you should also take into consideration the system impact to the whole infrastructure. For example, NNMi polls devices on a regular basis and receives SNMP traps as well. Depending on your monitored infrastructure size, polling cycle, and SNMP trap flow, you can overload your network bandwidth. Due to this, you should estimate if you can afford such traffic consumptions during system design stage.

There is no accurate traffic load calculator, as NNMi optimizes its polls grouping into SNMP query bulk reads. Using this method, it is hard to estimate traffic load. The only way to get a real number is to try it in a lab or operational environment. Traffic generated by NNMi depends on:

- Number of polled interfaces
- Polling frequency
- Data collection objects (if iSPI Performance for Metrics is used)
- Data collection polling intervals (if iSPI Performance for Metrics is used)

So, if you notice that NNMi consumes too much traffic, try reducing one or more parameters listed previously.

Security policy changes in your infrastructure

Before you start NNMi implementation, make sure your firewall has following ports opened:

- TCP Ports 80, 443, 1098, 1099, 3873, 4444, 4445, 4446, 4447, 4457, 4458, 8083, 8086, and 8087
- UDP Ports 161, 162, 696, and 45588

Antivirus software slows NNMi performance or even stops some of the functionalities. So before you start NNMi implementation, make sure that you have disabled your antivirus. This is a very important point. If you have any issues launching your NNMi server, the first thing that should be checked (after you checked whether all services are up and running) — is if you have antivirus running.

Data storage space for system backups

You will also probably design an NNMi with regular backups, which have to be stored in some external data storage. Consider a dedicated safe data storage place for your backups. *Chapter 6, Troubleshooting, Security, and Backup*, describes backup processes in more detail.

Infrastructure device naming convention

Another recommended, but not necessary, task is to make sure that your managed nodes follow your infrastructure's naming convention. There is no technical limitation and NNMi will work in either of the following ways:

- No naming convention at all
- Device names were changed after NNMi completed node discovery
- Naming convention was applied before NNMi implementation

This recommendation is about your own convenience. First of all, you will need to make sure that node names have changed in NNMi after you changed them on managed devices. Then, if you have used some long-term data for analysis, name changes will make a mess in your reports. If you have implemented some integration with third party tools on your own, you may have some integration issues if your API wasn't designed to be ready for node name changes.

Licensing policy

NNMi is licensed by discovered nodes. One node-one license and it doesn't matter whether it is a switch with several dozens of interfaces or just a workstation with one network interface. It is a good practice to design the network discovery to discover only nodes which are needed to monitor and avoid any additional nodes as much as possible, for the following reasons:

- You may reach your license limit very fast. Please be aware that unlike NNMi 7.x and its previous versions, NNMi 8.x and newer do not discover any additional nodes when the license limit is reached.

- The more devices that are being polled, the more the server is loaded. In other words, by monitoring unnecessary nodes, either the server works slower, or extra hardware is purchased for upgrades to maintain system performance.

Also, keep in mind that NNMi counts nodes that are discovered. So even if you have set a node to an unmanaged mode, it is still counted against licensing policy.

NNMi installation comes with a 250 nodes license for 30 days, and it includes NNMi Advanced and NNMi iSPI NET features for the same period of time. You don't need to reinstall NNMi if you have decided to add your permanent license on top of the trial version, even if your permanent license has the standard edition.

To check what license is installed currently, go to **Help | About HP Network Node Manager i-series**:

Product Name:	HP Network Node Manager Software Product				
License class:	Unknown				
Capacity:	0				
Advanced Enabled					
Expiration Date:	January 9, 2010 11:59:59 PM EST				
Days Remaining:	Expired				
License Type:	Instant-On				
Consumption:	3				
Status of licenses:					
Type	Capacity	Expiration Date	Start Date	Valid	State
Instant-On	250	Jan 9, 2010 11:59:59 PM EST	Started	No	Expired

HP Network Node Manager Software Product: license expired on 1/9/10 11:59 PM					
Product Name:	HP Network Node Manager iSPI Network Engineering Toolset Software				
License class:	Unknown				
Capacity:	0				
Expiration Date:	January 9, 2010 11:59:59 PM EST				
Days Remaining:	Expired				
License Type:	Instant-On				
Consumption:	3				
Status of licenses:					
Type	Capacity	Expiration Date	Start Date	Valid	State
Instant-On	250	Jan 9, 2010 11:59:59 PM EST	Started	No	Expired

Close

Licenses are sold by 50 node incremental, that is, if you monitor 125 nodes, you need 3 by 50 nodes licenses. As soon as the amount of your discovered nodes is over 150, you will need additional 50 nodes licenses (even if you have just one node over; that is, 151 nodes require 200 nodes licenses).

iSPIs are licensed separately and each of them has its own licensing policy. Read each iSPI's release note when you size your system or contact HP representatives if you need assistance counting required iSPI license capacity.

Installing software

I assume that you already have hardware for your NNMi. The installation consists of three major parts:

- Prerequisite check
- Installation process
- Post installation tasks

Prerequisite check

Before you start installing NNMi, make sure that you have fulfilled following requirements:

- NNMi server has a **Fully Qualified Domain Name (FQDN)** and it has to be resolvable to NNMi server.
- If SNMP trap service is installed on NNMi server, it has to stopped.
- You have installed and configured your web browser .

 Firefox and latest version of IE are not supported.

- If your server has DHCP enabled, make sure that NNMi server is consistently assigned the same IP address.
- Antivirus (if any) is disabled.
- Following ports are available on NNMi server (TCP: 443, 1098, 1099, 3873, 4444, 4445, 4446, 4447, 8083, 8086, and 8087 and UDP port 696).
- Your NNMi server is configured to support your desired locale.

Installation process

To install NNMi, complete following steps (screen shots about installation for version NNMi 8.x may differ):

1. Download HP NNMi software from HP website (`http://www.openview.hp.com/`). If you did that already or have NNMi installation in media, proceed to the next step.
2. Copy installation files or insert the media into a server.
3. Run the installation file:
    - Unix: `setup.bin`
    - Windows: `setup.exe`

 You have to run the installation file with root (Unix type OS) or administrator (Windows OS) privileges.

4. Follow instructions on installation guide window:

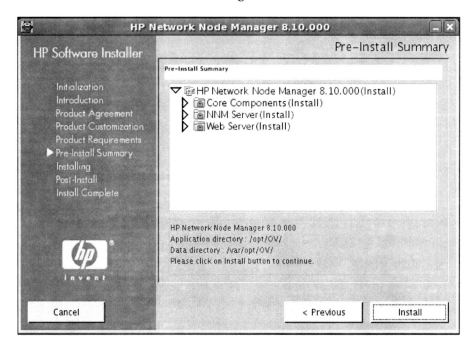

Software installation is intuitive and mostly is **Next, Next, Finish** process. It has the following steps:

1. Initialization.
2. Introduction.
3. Product agreement.
4. Product customization.
5. Product requirements.
6. Pre-Install summary.
7. Installation.

8. Post-Install.

9. Install complete. If you see this message window, you have completed your installation. Now you can start managing your infrastructure and follow the description given in the next chapters.

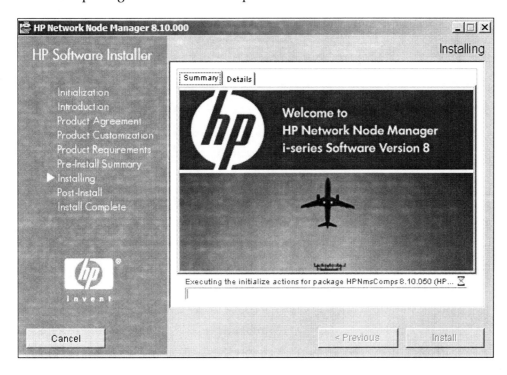

NNMi also supports silent installation mode. This is very useful for remote installations or installations using remote configuration tools, like RADIA, MS **System Center Configuration Manager (SCCM)**, and so on.

> If your NNMi management server has more than one domain name, NNMi chooses one during the installation process. To determine which fully-qualified domain name NNMi is using, run the nnmofficialfqdn.ovpl script. See the nnmofficialfqdn.ovpl reference page, or the Unix main page, for more information.

Post installation tasks

When you are done with installation, check if NNMi is installed successfully:

1. Check if NNMi processes are running:

    ```
    ovstatus -c
    ```

     NNMi services and processes are described in more detail in *Chapter 6*.

2. Check log files for installation errors or warnings:

    Unix:

    `$NnmDataDir/log/nnm/nnm-install-config.log`

    `$TMP/nnm-install-config_vbs.log`

    `$TMP/nnm-preinstallcheck.log`

    Windows:

    `%NnmDataDir%\log\nnm\nnm-install-config.log`

    `%TMP%\nnm-install-config_vbs.log`

    `%TMP%\nnm-preinstallcheck.log`

3. Check if NNMi console is opening. By default, NNMi can be accessed by the following URL:

    If https communication is configured, then the URL is as follows:

    `https://<server_name_or_ip_address:<port_number>`

    By default, port 8080 and HTTP connection is used in NNMi 8.x version. NNMi 9.x uses HTTPS by default.

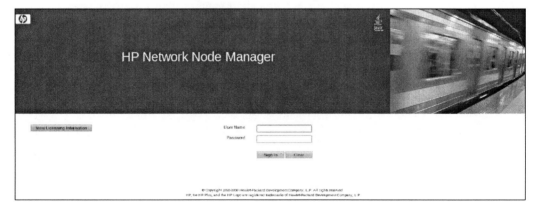

4. Login as user `system`. Default *system* user credentials are:

    Username: system

    Password: system

[

Please change the **system** user password after installation and create a new user with administrator privileges, which should be used by the NNMi administrator. It's not the best practice to use the **system** user for logging into NNMi. *Chapter 5, Controlling access to NNMi* describes how users can be created.
]

5. Navigate through workspaces. If you can navigate through workspaces and you don't receive any errors, that's the sign that the GUI part of NNMi has been installed correctly.

Summary

As you see, there is a list of issues that we have to solve before implementing NNMi. If we follow a *task list*, all tasks are achievable. But the most important task is to understand the NNMi role in your whole infrastructure. All other tasks may be completed easily.

Now you are ready to find a place for NNMi in your infrastructure and designing this tool so that it works for you, and not you for it.

2
Discovering and Monitoring Your Network

This chapter describes the following topics:

- Planning and implementing network discovery
- NNMi and managed node communication
- Boosting your network discovery
- Limiting your network discovery
- Discovery examples
- State poller

Discovery in NNMi

Discovery is an activity which takes care that the nodes included in discovery boundaries are discovered by NNMi and loaded into the NNMi database, with detailed information about the inventory and configuration of the discovered device. It also takes care that the detailed node configuration is discovered, which is the key for topology map drawing and overall further monitoring.

The very first step when the management tool is installed is to discover your network. It's very important to have a well-designed and configured discovery, as it directly affects the system performance, licensing costs, and monitoring efficiency.

How discovery works

NNMi uses a list of protocols and techniques to discover the network. It discovers nodes and their configuration, including interfaces and connection information (including Layer 2 and Layer 3 information). This spiral discovery accurately checks for new devices in a network, their configuration, and configuration changes. It also gathers object status information and tracks their changes. It also places them on an NNMi map, which is stored in an NNMi database.

Layer 2 (the Data Link Layer) is the protocol layer, which transfers data between adjacent network nodes in a wide area network (http://en.wikipedia.org/wiki/Wide_area_network) or between nodes on the same local area network (http://en.wikipedia.org/wiki/Local_area_network) segment. The Data Link Layer provides the functional and procedural means to transfer (http://en.wikipedia.org/wiki/Transfer) data between network entities, and it may provide the means to detect and possibly correct errors that may occur in the Physical Layer (http://en.wikipedia.org/wiki/Physical_Layer). Examples of data link protocols are Ethernet (http://en.wikipedia.org/wiki/Ethernet) for local area networks (multi-node), and the **Point-to-Point Protocol** (**PPP**) (http://en.wikipedia.org/wiki/Point-to-Point_Protocol), HLDC (http://en.wikipedia.org/wiki/HDLC), and ADCCP (http://en.wikipedia.org/wiki/ADCCP) for point-to-point (dual-node) connections.

Layer3 (the Network Layer) is responsible for routing packets delivery (http://en.wikipedia.org/wiki/Packet_forwarding) including routing (http://en.wikipedia.org/wiki/Routing) through intermediate routers, whereas the Data Link Layer (http://en.wikipedia.org/wiki/Data_Link_Layer) is responsible for Media Access Control, Flow Control, and Error Checking (Layer 2 and Layer 3 definition source: Wikipedia).

This process is continuous. Discovery is never completed. If anything changes in a network, NNMi spiral discovery updates these changes instantly. Change notification accuracy depends on configured polling cycles.

There are two discovery modes in NNMi:

- **List-based discovery**: This mode uses seeds to tell NNMi exactly which nodes should be discovered. This is a seed file replacement from NNM 7.x and earlier versions.

- **Rule-based discovery**: This mode uses rules for node discovery, such as IP address range, system object ID range, excluded IPs, and so on.

We will provide a few examples about how to configure each of these discovery methods in this chapter.

A combination of these two modes can be used as well. Initial discovery adds seed nodes into the topology database and spiral discovery takes care of the accuracy of the network discovery.

As soon as a node is discovered, the following actions are taken by NNMi automatically:

- **Layer 3 data is discovered**: Information such as node identification (IP address and hostname) is determined. Detailed node information discovery is made. The following protocols are used to determine the node's inventory and configuration: ARP, BGP, OSPF, HSRP, and VRRP.
- **Layer 2 data is discovered**: Discovery protocols, such as Cisco, Enterasys, Foundry, and Cabletron are used. Link aggregation groups are determined and Forwarding data is collected. Group information is collected as well, such as FDB and VLAN.

The following diagram graphically describes how spiral discovery works:

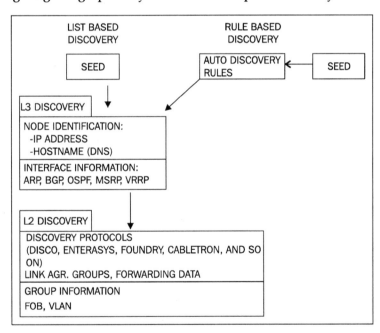

If any changes in the node configuration appear, NNMi automatically initiates a device and device's neighbor rediscovery. There is only one exception—node rediscovery is not initiated if some internal device data has changed (that is, contact information or firmware version).

The administrator can set rediscovery intervals, which can vary from one hour to few days. By default, it's 24 hours. A rediscovery interval should be chosen according to network dynamics (how often network changes). If the network is pretty stable, rediscovery can be set to 24 or even 48 hour cycles. If your network is dynamic, consider lower rediscovery cycles.

To change the rediscovery interval, complete the following steps:

1. Select **Discovery Configuration** in the **Configuration** workspace.
2. Enter a new value in the **Rediscovery interval** field.
3. Click **Save and close**.

The following list shows the advantages and disadvantages of list-based and rule-based discoveries:

- List-based discovery:
  - Strictly defined list of nodes
  - Good for stable networks
  - NNMi does not discover new nodes if they are added into the network
  - Easy to control node amount against a license

- Rule-based discovery
  - Not strictly defined list of nodes
  - Good for dynamic networks, often with new node installation
  - Easy to control node amount against a license

SNMP is a key protocol for accurate discovery of nodes and their connections. As soon as a node is discovered, sysObjectID (which is a key for further device discovery) is retrieved from a device. Devices are profile based on their sysObejctID, which is queried using SNMP (SNMP OID 1.3.6.1.2.1.1.2).

NNMi has over 3600 device profiles at the time of release. NNMi admin can create a new device profile based on the new sysObjectID.

NNMi does not perform any out of the box discovery, unless the system administrator configures what needs to be discovered. Also, it is important to know that by default, only routers and switches are discovered. Each discovered node counts against license, no matter what state it is in. In other words, even if the node is set as *not managed*, it is counted against license. If you are short on license, please make sure that you monitor only important devices. All others should be deleted.

To see how many nodes are discovered and how are you doing against a license, complete the following steps:

1. Select **Help** | **About HP Network Node Manager i** from the main menu.

2. The window with the main NNMi status information opens, and it also provides information about the number of discovered nodes and license capacity.

To check nodes, which are discovered, complete the following steps:

1. Select **Inventory** workplace.

2. Select **Nodes.**

2. Investigate nodes, which are already discovered.

This chapter will tell us how to delete nodes. It may not be straightforward, because if a node was discovered already, it means that it passed some of the discovery filters, or was seeded. Before you delete a node, you should modify your discovery rules accordingly.

The discovered node name is selected using the following sequence:

*   Short DNS name is used

*   If this name cannot be resolved using DNS, short sysObjectID name is used

*   If this name is not provided on the device, then IP address is used as a node name

If you don't have DNS, or for some reason you don't want or are not allowed to make records in DNS server, you can use hosts files. A host file is an alternative to DNS and makes name resolution inside a node. It is still recommended to use DNS, if available. This is because the hosts file only resolves names for requests from a node where the hosts file is. If there are many records in the hosts file (hundreds or even thousands), it makes an impact on the system performance.

 If you have thousands of devices, the hosts file may decrease name resolution performance.

Example of hosts file syntax: Assume we need to add box1 and box2 nodes into a hosts file, which are in `testlab.local` domain. The hosts file records would look like this:

```
10.10.1.1    box1.testlab.local box1
10.10.1.2    box2.testlab.local box1
```

The hosts file is located in following path:

Unix: `/etc/hosts`

Windows: `c:\Windows\System32\drivers\etc\hosts`

 NNMi version 8.0x has selected the highest loopback address as a primary management address. Starting from NNMi 8.10, the lowest IP address is taken as a primary management address. An exception is Cisco devices, which loopback IP address with the lowest IP selected as a primary management address.

How node configuration is discovered:

- If a device supports SNMP, then the interface table is read and all interfaces of that node are represented on a map.
- If a device does not support SNMP, then DNS (or hosts file) is queried and such a node is loaded into the inventory database. If a node with the same node name, but different IP address, is already in inventory database, then the discovered interface is added into the already discovered node. The following screenshot represents the discovery configuration window:

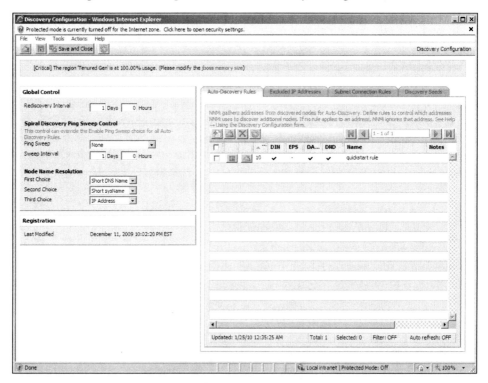

Discovery configuration was improved since NNM7.x and the earlier versions. NNMi has a more intuitive configuration, which is placed on one window instead of several windows and configuration files.

Discovery can be configured using the Discovery Configuration Form. A Communication Configuration Form is used to configure communication about how devices should be polled or queried. The discovery engine uses discovery rules and/or seeds. All discovered data is stored in RDBMS. Previous NNM versions have had several binary databases. The following diagram represents the main discovery configuration elements:

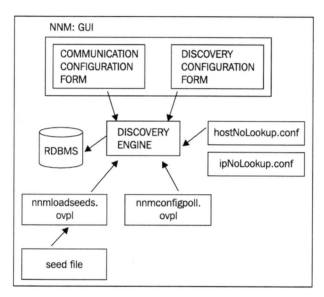

Configuring communication protocols

In order to manage a network, management tools use several communication protocols, which assure accurate and detailed information. The challenge for the management tool is to know which protocol to use, and how it should be configured so that it could communicate with the managed nodes. This section describes two communication protocols, which are used in NNMi: ICMP and SNMP.

What is a communication in NNMi?

NNMi uses ICMP ping and SNMP management protocol for network monitoring. ICMP may be used for initial device discovery and availability checks (if configured to use ICMP) and the remaining part is done by SNMP management protocol. SNMP management protocol is key in network management; including query device configuration, routing tables, interface status, and so on. NNMi works with SNMP version 1, 2c, and 3. In order to communicate with NNMi and managed devices via SNMP, NNMi needs to know which community names to use for accessing devices. In general, NNMi needs to have configured the following communication data:

- **ICMP**: It needs to be configured if ICMP pings are used for monitoring
- SNMP community names
- Delay and the number of retries

The section entitled *Configuring SNMP community name in NNMi* describes how to configure SNMP community names in NNMi, change delays and the number of retries.

What is the role of ICMP in NNMi?

By default, SNMP protocol is used for communication between the management server and a managed node, but NNMi can also be configured to make a status poll for some, or all, IP addresses using ICMP ping. Be cautious using ICMP, as ICMP is not as powerful as SNMP. For example:

- Some addresses may not be reachable from an NNMi server.
- ICMP can be used only for interfaces, which have an IP address only.
- ICMP can only tell if an IP address is reachable, while SNMP can also determine the reason, whether the interface is administratively or operationally up or down. Also, SNMP can determine the status of all interfaces on the node by reading their SNMP OIDs without polling every interface.

In short, ICMP only pings IP addresses, while SNMP gets full configuration and monitors interfaces whether or not they have an IP address assigned.

Example: Assume NNMi needs to poll the status of all interfaces on node A. The following figure shows how the node is reached by NNMi.

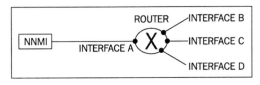

NNMi can reach router A via interface A. NNMi can also reach interface B, but NNMi has no route to interfaces C and D.

If you are using a status polling via ICMP, then NNMi can reach only interfaces A and B, and has no status information about interfaces C and D (they will be considered unreachable).

If you are using SNMP status polling, NNMi queries the node's SNMP **MIB** (**Management Information Base**) on node A for information about all interfaces via interface A, and, device responds to NNMi about a list of all interfaces on router A (during configuration check polls) and reports status of all interfaces (during status polling).

What is the role of SNMP in NNMi?

For SNMP, in order to communicate with NNMi server and the managed node, the following needs to be done:

- Managed node has SNMP enabled and SNMP community name set or username and password if it's SNMPv3.

- NNMi server has to know that SNMP community's name (SNMP configuration).

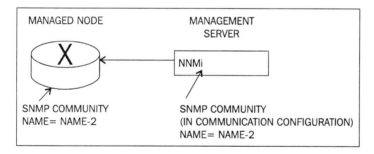

As SNMP protocol was improved over the time, protocol versioning was introduced. Now there are three major SNMP versions used:

- **SNMPv1**: This is the first version of protocol. It is described by RFC 1155 and RFC 1157.

- **SNMPv2c**: This is an updated version of SNMPv1, and is described by RFC 1901, RFC 1905, RFC 1906, and RFC 2578. This version expanded 64bit counter support. Getbulk operation was introduced, which allows sending messages in bulk and saving network resources. snmpinform command was introduced, which allows us to send a confirmed notification.

- **SNMPv3**: This version was created for improvements in security. The following features were introduced:
    - ° Authentication
    - ° Privacy
    - ° Authorization and access control

It is also very important that all traffic sent by this version of SNMP is encrypted, so passwords cannot be read using network analyzers (for example, WireShark).

Main difference between SNMP versions from a security point of view is that SNMPv1 and v2c sends information through a network as plain text, while SNMPv3 uses encryption. SNMPv1 and v2c security is organized using SNMP community names (can be considered as a password), which is also sent via the network in plain text. SNMPv3 uses usernames and passwords, which are allowed to control which OIDs can be accessible to users and usernames. Passwords are also sent via the network as encrypted.

If you are not sure which version you should use, my recommendations are:

- Use SNMPv3 whenever your devices support this version.
- If not, use read-only community names for SNMPv1 and v2c, as NNMi doesn't make any changes to managed devices, but only reads and collects data and NNMi has no need for writing community names.

There can be configured SNMP communities in three ways using NNMi SNMP communication settings:

- **Node specific settings**: Here you can set community names for specific nodes.
- **Region settings**: Community names for address ranges can be set using this tab.
- **Default community settings**: A default community name is set for all other devices, which are not in the previous lists.

It is recommended to use region settings as much as possible, and to use specific node settings only when you cannot define a node's community without using a combination of the *region* and *default* settings.

How NNMi deals with overlapping SNMP community configuration

Because NNMi has three ways to define SNMP community names for managed nodes (node specific, region, and default), it is obvious that community settings for some nodes may overlap. That is, we have node 192.168.1.1, which has the SNMP community name *Secret-123*. This node is configured in NNMi's **Communication Configuration** view as node specific, and the rest of these subnet nodes have SNMP community names *Secret-000* and that's configured in region settings. At the same time, the default community name in NNMi **Communication Configuration** view is set as *public*. So, looks like node 192.168.1.1 passes all these three zone community configurations. This is how NNMi decides which community name to use.

Region settings supersede default community settings and node specific supersedes region settings. This gives us flexibility in configuring communities and avoids the hassle of configuring every device separately.

So, as described in our example, NNMi will use the *Secret-123* (node specific) SNMP community for node 192.168.1.1.

Best practices when configuring SNMP communities

To make your life easier, it is recommended that you follow the SNMP community naming convention, however if you decide to create your own naming conventions, I can give the following suggestions:

- Don't set read-write community for NNMi—it uses only read-only.
- Avoid special symbols in your community names, such as: @,:,&,%,$,#,",; (semicolon), and (comma). Not only does NNMi not support the @ symbol, but you may have some other software in your environment which uses SNMP for communication and application code. These special characters may cause communication problems, bugs, or software hangs. Even if you don't have any additional software for now, don't forget that you may have it in future.

- Give common names for node groups, which are administered by the same staff. That is, if your backbone and distribution network is administered by different groups and the access network is administered by remote groups, depending on the location you may want to configure the following SNMP community names: one name for all backbone network devices, another for distribution network devices, and each access network device would have a community name based on branch office to which it belongs. Then you don't have to worry, as distribution network staff won't mess with the backbone or access network devices, and access network engineers won't mess with the backbone or distribution network devices.

- Give different community names for separate nodes only if you have specific security requirements for particular device/devices. Otherwise, I would consider it when changing names more frequently.

- Change community names periodically. Frequency should be chosen based on security requirements and the effort required to change names. If you have a configuration management tool (like Cisco Works, HP ProCurve Manager, or HP SW Network Automation Service), it doesn't take too long to change names. If this is the case, changing names once every three months would be a reasonable. If you have dozens or even hundreds of devices, and the entire configuration has to be done manually, I would say once a year would be great. Honestly, I've met only a few companies where community names are changed more frequently than once a year.

Configuring SNMP community names in NNMi

To configure SNMP community names in NNMi, go to the **Configuration** workspace and select **Communication Configuration…**:

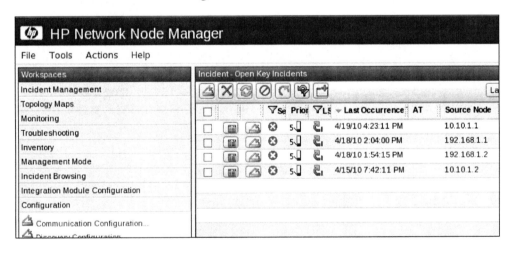

In the main window, you can set the following parameters:

- Enable SNMP Address discovery.

- **SNMP timeout**: The time that determines how long NNM should wait for the SNMP messages' reply (in milliseconds). Maximum timeout can be 59 seconds and 999 milliseconds.

- **SNMP retry count**: It describes how many times NNMi should try sending packets if timeout comes. If zero is set, then no retries will be initiated.

- **SNMP port**: Default is port 161. You can change it if required.

- **SNMP proxy address and port**: If SNMP proxy is used to reach a device, then you need to set SNMP proxy address and port number for communication.

- **SNMP minimum security level**: Here you can set which security level NNMi should consider while communicating with a node. SNMP version preferences are given in the next paragraph.

- **ICMP timeout**: Represents how long NNM should wait for ICMP messages reply (in milliseconds). Maximum timeout can be 59 seconds and 999 milliseconds.

- **ICMP retries count**: It describes how many times NNMi should try sending packets after SNMP timeout. If zero is set, then no retries will be initiated.

Your network devices may support various versions of SNMP, starting from v1, v2c, and SNMPv3. You can set the minimum security level that is acceptable to NNMi. However, if you set your minimum security level, NNMi makes queries and automatically selects appropriate security levels using the following assumptions:

- If there is one or more SNMP community strings configured, use SNMPv2 for communication.

- If no response was received, use SNMPv1.

- If there are one or more SNMPv3 users configured, security level is selected by following rules:
    - Use **No Authentication, No Privacy** if any users are configured.
    - Use **Authentication, No Privacy** if any users are configured.
    - Use **Authentication, Privacy** if any users are configured.

- If no SNMP response was received, the device is not discovered. The NNMi administrator can override this and the device would be discovered with **NO SNMP** profile.

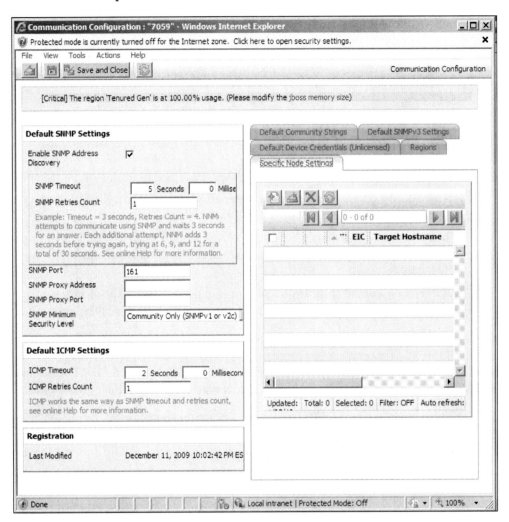

Be careful with timeouts and retry counts, as timeout is doubled for every subsequent retry. You may have polling loops with slow networks or accidental network bottlenecks. For example, if you set timeout for 2 seconds and retry count 3, the first packet sent will have a 2 second timeout. If it doesn't respond, the second packet will have a 4 second timeout, and the third will have 8 seconds. So, there is a total 14 seconds timeout.

The community name order in the **Default Community Settings** doesn't matter. NNMi takes all names simultaneously and the community name, which responds to the query, is selected as primary for that device.

A large number of default SNMP communities will affect the performance in a negative way.

The right part of the window has SNMP configuration tabs for node specific, zone, and default SNMP community configuration.

When the initial discovery is completed, it's good practice to check whether all devices were discovered and if the correct information is shown in NNMi. This may happen, because of several reasons:

- **Device is not accessible**: Firewall or access lists blocks traffic, device is down, routing issues
- **Device cannot communicate with NNMi**: Device is wrong or does not have SNMP configured, wrong SNMP settings on NNMi
- **Neighbor device is not configured properly**: That is, wrong or missing SNMP settings

First of all, you can check if all nodes have SNMP configured properly by selecting **Inventory View | filter Device Profile** column and check if you have any **No SNMP** records. If so, do one (or both if needed) of the following:

- Configure SNMP settings on NNMi
- Check if managed device has SNMP configured and have connectivity

Here is a list of symptoms, which may help to troubleshoot:

- **Device not discovered**:
  - Check if the device is accessible by ICMP
  - Check if the device is accessible by SNMP
  - Check if the correct SNMP settings are configured
  - Check if the neighbor device is discovered properly
- **Device is shown as generic**:
  - Check whether the device is accessible by SNMP
  - Check if the device has SNMP configured properly

The following diagram represents the SNMP communication troubleshooting workflow:

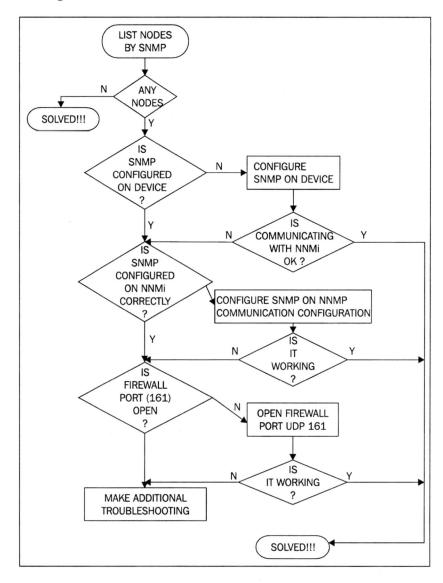

You can take control over the network load configuring polling cycles.

If your firewall is blocking the communication to some of your devices, you can do one of the following:

- Talk to the security personnel and agree to open the required ports, so that you could monitor devices blocked by the firewall

- Configure NNMi to exclude these nodes from the discovery and status polling scope

This is recommended to avoid poller polling unreachable devices and improving poller performance in that way. There are two protocols you can disable for specific node or some group of nodes:

- **ICMP traffic**: Disabling ICMP traffic will affect your network monitoring in the following way:
    - Auto discovery will not discover such nodes, unless nodes are seeded, queried through ARP cache, or queried through SNMP MIB entries (that is, CDP and EDP).
    - State polling cannot determine the state, although you can configure ICMP fault polling groups.
    - Ping action (using **Actions | Ping**) cannot be used.

- **SNMP traffic**: Disabling SNMP will affect your network monitoring in the following way:
    - Device will have **No SNMP** profile and will not show any other interface but itself. It means that you will see a generic device with one IP interface.
    - Discovery will not learn anything about the neighbor devices. So they must be seeded in order to have them discovered and this will affect connectivity information, so these devices will be shown as unconnected.
    - State poller will use only ICMP pings to determine device status. No performance data will be collected.
    - Causal engine cannot locate the root cause of incidents.

The following screenshot represents Autodiscovery Rules window:

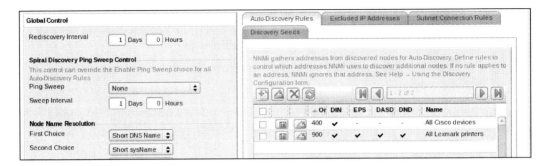

If you have Cisco devices using loopback addresses, consider un-checking the **Enable SNMP Address Discovery** box. That way, the loopback address is the only address that will ever be used for SNMP communication.

Boosting up discovery with seeds

Sometimes, NNMi may have difficulties discovering some nodes. For example, nodes that are far away from NNMi in terms of number of hops. In such cases, we may want or even need to boost a discovery, forcing NNMi to load some devices automatically. This can be done using seeds. This section describes how to work with seeds.

What are seeds?

A seed is a list of nodes which has to be loaded into the NNMi topology. Technically, it's a simple part of NNMi—the administrator lists IP addresses or hostnames, which have to be forced into NNMi's topology. But on other hand, it's very important to understand its meaning and influence on the whole deployment and operation process. Seeds are very handy when devices cannot be discovered by auto discovery rules.

How can discovery be boosted with seeds?

For NNM 7.x and earlier the versions, seeds were text files, which were read by netmon process. NNMi needs to have seeds loaded into a database and there are two ways to do so:

- Entering manually using NNMi GUI
- Loading from seed file using `nnmloadseeds.ovpl` command

The following is the syntax for these files:

```
IP_Address          #       node_name
```

That is:

```
192.168.1.1         #       dnsserver01.companydomain.local
```

Number sign (#) is used as a comment sign and anything after it in the line are taken as **Notes** (see the screenshot in the section *Example 2: Create a seedfile for batch load*) in **Discovery Seed** configuration tab in **Discovery Configuration**. It is always a good practice to keep notes about the nodes you are adding, so the next time you open a **Discovery Seed** configuration window you can remember why each of the nodes were added. It is even more important to keep notes if you have more than one NNMi administrator, so that each of them can know what is going on in the network management. The IP address found in the seed is determined as a primary management address. If it has a hostname, then NNMi takes the IP address that is resolved by DNS.

> For Cisco devices, the loopback address should be used for discovery. Make sure that the DNS is correctly configured to resolve the name by loopback addresses.
>
> It is good practice to have one seed file. If you add new devices into the seed file, they will be loaded into NNMi topology. If you delete any node from the seed file, they will not be deleted automatically from NNMi topology and vice versa, if you delete a node from topology, it will not be deleted from the seed and it will be discovered again.

The following screenshot displays discovery configuration by providing discovery seeds (**Discovery Seeds** tab on **Discovery configuration** window).

Only the name or IP address is required in seeds. No subnet masks are required.

How to load seeds in NNMi

There are two ways in which you can seed nodes into NNMi discovery:

- Adding nodes using the seed configuration tab window
- Creating a seedfile and load it using the `nnmloadseeds.ovpl` command

Let's examine one of these two options using an example.

Example 1: Adding nodes using seed configuration tab window

We have two nodes with IP addresses 10.10.1.1 and 192.168.1.1 and we will seed them using configuration window. Complete the following steps:

1. Select **Configuration workspace**.
2. Select **Discovery Configuration** view.
3. Select **Discovery Seeds** tab.

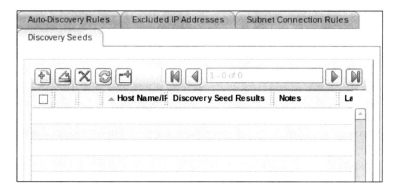

4. Select the **New** button in the top left corner of the **Discovery Seeds** tab.
5. Enter `10.10.1.1` in **Host Name/IP** field and click **Save and Close**:

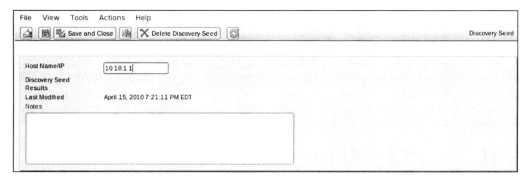

6. Repeat step 4 and 5 for the IP address **192.168.1.1**.

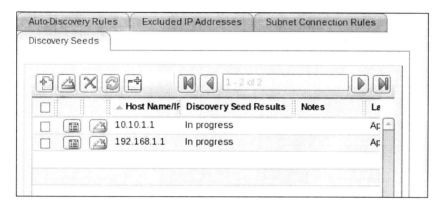

Congratulations! You have loaded two nodes into the seed window, which you can see in the previous figure. Your nodes are being discovered now and in a couple of seconds, you will see all the information regarding these nodes.

Example 2: Create a seedfile for batch load

Now, using batch load command (nnmloadseeds.ovpl), let's load two more devices, which have IP addresses **10.10.1.2** and **192.168.1.2**. Complete the following steps to load nodes using batch command:

1. Create a file with a list of IP addresses and save it (we chose filename /tmp/seedfile in our example), as follows:

```
10.10.1.2        #seededbox1.testlab.local
192.168.1.2      #seededbox2.testlab.local
```

Text after number sign (#) will go as comments in **Discovery Seed Results** window.

2. Run nnmloadseeds.ovpl command with file pass parameter as follows:

```
nnmloadseeds.ovpl -f /tmp/seedfile
```

You should get a response about seed results. In our example, two seeds were added and no duplicate or invalid seeds were provided (output example is shown as follows):

```
[root@box1 bin]# ./nnmloadseeds.ovpl -f /tmp/seedfile
2 seeds added
0 seeds invalid
0 seeds duplicated
[root@box1 bin]#
```

3. Make sure that nodes were added. Open seed configuration window by selecting **Configuration** | **Discovery Configuration** | **Discovery Seeds**:

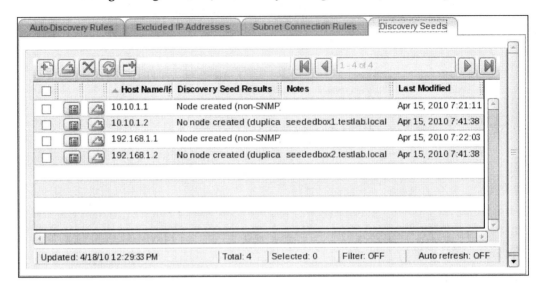

 As you see in the preceding figure, nodes from `seedfile` were loaded with comments provided in a file into **Notes** field.

Limiting discovery with filters

Discovery configuration in NNMi not only requires methods for discovery boosting (seeds and auto-discovery rules), but limitations as well. So NNM has boundaries where discovery should be stopped. This section describes the discovery filters used in NNMi.

What are discovery filters?

Discovery filters are rules within NNMi, which define discovery boundaries and control so that NNMi wouldn't discover anything outside these boundaries. In other words, that's a tool to limit NNMi's discovery.

Why do we need discovery filters?

Proper discovery planning can save you a lot of:

- **Money**: Save expenses on purchasing licenses, not important nodes excluding from discovery.

- **Time**: This can be done by dealing with unimportant nodes later on, trying to solve issues based on received alarms, or trying to delete unimportant nodes later on.

- **System performance**: The fewer nodes you manage, the better is the performance.

If you choose list-based discovery, then the only way to control the amount of discovered devices are seeds.

If you choose rule-based auto-discovery, then dealing with rules makes you a manager in selection of choosing which devices need to be discovered. Mistakes made in rules can make you run out of license limits very quickly, or can decrease system performance that is overloading your system. On the other hand, mistakes can make you discover too few nodes and leave a part of your network undiscovered.

The following screenshot represents the Auto-discovery configuration window:

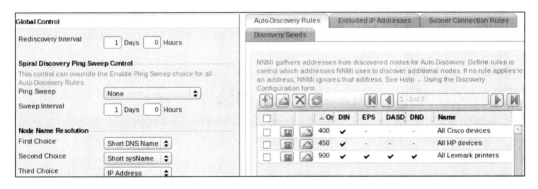

Auto-discovery rule ordering number affects the discovery in the following ways:

- **IP address ranges**: If the device complies with two or more auto-discovery rules, the rule with the lowest ordering number is applied.

- **System Object ID (sysObjID) ranges**: If no IP address has complied with the auto-discovery rules, then system object ID setting applies to all auto-discovery rules with higher numbers. In the case that the IP address is included in the auto-discovery rule, then system objects ID is applied only within that particular auto-discovery rule.

Starting from NNMi 8.10, you can use ping sweep to help the auto-discovery process discover nodes on listed IP address ranges. It is very handy on networks that NNMi does not have control of, for example, ISP networks.

Ping sweep works only if your subnet mask is 16 bit or smaller, that is, 192.168.*.*.

 It is good practice to enable ping sweep on small network ranges. If you have a firewall between NNMi and a node which you plan to monitor, please check that the firewall is not blocking ping sweep packets.

Discovery seeds may be used in auto-discovery rules. It's recommended to provide at least one seed per rule.

You can also set IP address ranges to exclude an addresses from discovery.

There might be overlapping auto-discovery rules. That is, range *A* is configured as the range to be discovered and range *B* is configured as the range not to be discovered:

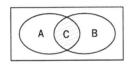

Range *C* is covered by both rules, but will comply only with the rule which has the lowest rule-ordering number.

Filter configuration example

The section entitled *Discovery examples* provides an example about how to configure the discovery filter by an IP address and system object ID.

Examining discovery results

Discovery is a continuous process. After the initial discovery is completed, the devices are periodically discovered for configuration changes so that NNMi can display the most accurate map. However, you may want to check the discovery status. There is no straight green or red indicator telling you if everything was discovered by NNMi, as it's not only about the amount of discovered nodes, but it is also about the device configuration and their connections with each other, including Layer 2 and Layer 3 connections.

The following table describes the main issues that can be caused by discovery and their possible solutions:

Result	Solution
Too many devices have been discovered	See seeds and auto-discovery filters.
Missing device or devices	See auto-discovery filters.
	Check connection to device (devices).
	Add into seed.
Discovered device/devices is/are not accurate	Check if SNMP traffic is not limited to device (devices).
	Rediscover the node.

There are several places where you can examine your discovery results:

- The overall situation can be found by selecting **Help | About HP NNMi**. Here you will find general information about the management server state, including state poller data. As you will see later on, this window may help you recognize some primary issues on NNMi performance.

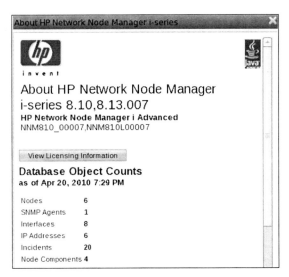

- Node discovery state: Every node shows their discovery state in the inventory tab. It has three status states:

    ○ **Newly created**: This state indicates that the node is in the NNMi's database, but more information needs to be collected to determine the node's state and status.

     ◦ **Discovery completed**: This state shows that node discovery is completed and all the information needed is already collected.

     ◦ **Rediscovery in process**: This state shows that NNMi is updating the information about the node.

To see in which state node discovery is, make the following changes (here is one of possible ways):

Inventory | **Nodes** | select a node | **Open** (it is a small icon on the top left window corner)

- **Seed success**: There is an option to check whether seeds were discovered. To verify, navigate to **Configuration** | **Discovery Configuration** | **Discovery Seeds**. **Discovery Seed Result** presents the result of the seed discovery. If you find **Node created**, that indicates that the seed was discovered. The following table presents all possible values of **Discovery Seed Results**.

The following table provides a list of Discovery Seed Result status values:

Result	Description
New seed	This state is shown when a new seed is entered. As soon as the discovery begins, this is changed to **In progress**.
	Troubleshooting: If this state doesn't change, please make sure that the discovery process is running. Try restarting the discovery process.
In progress	This state is shown while discovery is in progress.
Node created	Discovery seed is discovered.
Node created (non-SNMP device)	Discovered device doesn't support SNMP. The device is added into the database, but doesn't provide any SNMP information.
Node not created (duplicate seed)	The address or hostname provided in the seed is already in the database.
Node not created (DNS resolution failed)	The hostname provided in the seed cannot be resolved by DNS. Please add records into DNS or check if any mistakes are in setting the hostname.
Node not created (license expired)	NNMi rejects new discovered nodes after the license limit is reached. Please expand your license or review existing discovery, if any node can be deleted to make space in the license pool.
Failed	Some NNMi internal error has happened. For more details, please check discovery log file.
	Unix: $OV_LOG/nnm/disco.0.0.log
	Windows: %OV_LOG%\nnm\disco.0.0.log

- **Overall inventory**: A list of discovered devices. Check discovered devices in NNMi's discovery inventory table. To verify, navigate to **Inventory | IP Addresses**. Verify that nodes that you expected to be discovered are listed in this inventory table. The following is a screenshot of the inventory window:

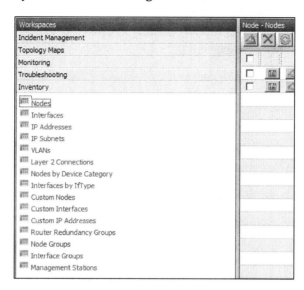

- **Layer 2 and Layer 3 results**: Layer 2 and Layer 3 views are separated. Layer 2 represents traffic across physical links in the network. It also provides information such as MAC address, VLANs, and its related information; while Layer 3 represents traffic routed by address and its related information, such as IP address. To be generic, Layer 2 is switch-related information and Layer 3 is router or switch router related information.

Layer 2 shows the physical network's connection inventory. This can be checked by following these steps:

1. Click on the **Inventory** workspace.

2. Click on **Nodes** and select the node in which you are interested.

3. Go to **Actions | Layer2 Neighbor View** and change the **Number of hops** accordingly, to expand or reduce number of hops that you want to be shown on a map.

VLAN information is also part of the Layer 2 inventory. You can check VLAN results by doing the following:

1. Click on the **Inventory** workspace.
2. Click on **VLANs** and select the VLAN in which you are interested.
3. Click on **Open** (icon on top left corner) to open the VLAN form and check the VLAN discovery results.

Layer 3 inventory results can be checked by following these steps:

1. Click on the **Inventory** workspace.
2. Click on **Nodes** and select the router.
3. Go to **Actions | Layer3 Neighbor View** and change the number of hops to expand or reduce map area.

If the results are not exactly what you expected, try one or more of the following:

- Check ordering of your Auto-Discovery rules.
- Check poll node for rediscovering inventory by clicking on **Actions | Configuration Poll**.
- Verify whether IP addresses are not listed in the **Excluded IP Address** filter.
- Manually add or remove the connection.

If the discovery results are not something you have expected and you need some adjustments, there are several ways to modify discovery accuracy. An example in real life could be if you are missing some devices, which have to be discovered, or a device that was reconfigured, displays the old configuration information. The following is a list of suggested solutions:

- **Spiral discovery**: As NNMi also uses information collected from neighbor devices, some information may be not accurate until the neighbor devices are polled and configuration data is collected. So, if you see some data that is inaccurate, which was recently discovered, be patient and allow NNMi to collect it. Depending on network size, 10-30 minutes would be a reasonable time.
- **Scheduled discovery**: NNMi periodically makes discovery in scheduled time intervals. If changes in your network appeared after your last scheduled discovery, you may want to wait for the next scheduled discovery. To check what intervals are configured on your system, go to **Discovery Configuration** and see the **Global Control** window for **Rediscovery Interval** and **Sweep Interval** (if any other option than **None** is selected in Ping Sweep configuration).

- **Delete node**: If you delete a node, NNMi forces node rediscovery. One of the ways in which we can use this method is that the IP address, which was assigned to one of the discovered devices, should be reassigned to some other device (no matter whether or not it was discovered before). If you have both devices discovered, it is a good idea to delete both of the devices and let NNMi rediscover them with updated information.

- **Add or delete discovery seeds**: Whenever a seed is added or deleted, NNMi forces the rediscovery of nodes in the seed list.

- **Accurately detect interface changes**: If your device doesn't show all interfaces or interfaces are not accurate, this can be because the node has interface renumbering and NNMi does not have accurate information. To fix this issue, follow the steps that need to be done are listed as follows:

- **Add or delete connections**: If you are using Frame Relay, ATM, or MPLS links between your WAN, your map may need a manual edition of connections. Connections can be added or deleted by the following sequence:

  ° `nnmconnedit.ovpl` command with option `-t` should be initiated to generate an XML template.

  ° The XML template is modified according to what connection needs to be modified.

  ° `nnmconnedit.ovpl` command with option `-f` is initiated to load configuration into the NNMi database.

Example 1: If the connection between interface `Customer_ABC`, which is in `Router_1` and interface `WAN_LINK`, which is in `Customer_ABC_Router` needs to be added, we do it as follows:

1. Run this command to create `add.xml` file:

   nnmconnedit.ovpl -t add

2. Open `add.xml` file, which was created after completion of this command, and modify the file accordingly:

```
<connectionedits>
  <connection>
    <operation>add</operation>
    <node>Router_1</node>
    <interface>Customer_ABC</interface>
    <node>Customer_ABC_Router</node>
    <interface>WAN_Link</interface>
  </connection>
</connectionedits>
nnmconnedit.ovpl -f add.xml
```

Example 2: If the connection between interface `Customer_ABC`, which is in `Router_1` and interface `WAN_LINK`, which is in `Customer_ABC_Router` needs to be deleted, we do following:

1. Run this command to generate the `delete.xml` file:

    nnmconnedit.ovpl -t delete

2. Open the `delete.xml` file, which was created after completion of this command, and modify the file accordingly:

```
<connectionedits>
  <connection>
    <operation>delete</operation>
    <node>Router_1</node>
    <interface>Customer_ABC</interface>
    <node>Customer_ABC_Router</node>
    <interface>WAN_Link</interface>
  </connection>
</connectionedits>
nnmconnedit.ovpl -f delete.xml
```

Stopping/starting managing of nodes, cards, or interfaces

There are cases when the discovered node (nodes) needs to be stopped from being polled by NNMi for sometime. That is:

*   You want a node to be displayed on a map, but no status changes need to be monitored.

*   The node is under maintenance works and needs to be stopped being monitored to avoid fault-positive incidents in a browser.

What is a stop managing object?

NNMi allows configuring for a specific object management mode. That is, to set some nodes, cards, interfaces, or addresses into managed, unmanaged, or out of service state.

Why we need to change the management mode?

This gives a flexible adjustment tool for administrators to comply with complex management requirements. It also allows improvement of system performance, including only objects that need to be managed. There might be cases when some nodes are discovered, but not managed. Also, there might be cases when maintenance is applied to a part of the network and the administrator wants to exclude following alarms to be displayed to operators. That is, firmware upgrade for some switches or specific model of routers, and so on. In that case, there is an option to temporarily set a group of objects to the **Out Of Service** state.

How does it work?

There are two management modes used in NNMi:

- **Management mode**: This mode can be set on node. Interface and address modes are calculated based on node settings. Mode on interface is set based on mode-on-node, and mode-on-address is calculated based on mode-on-interfaces associated to that address. Possible values are:
    - Managed
    - Not managed
    - Out of service

- **Direct management mode**: This mode is set on the interface or address by the user and it computes interface or address values as following:
    - Inherited
    - Not managed
    - Out of service

One of the ways to see the management of mode-for-node, interface, or address is using node view, interface view, or IP address view.

The following screenshot represents management mode in node view:

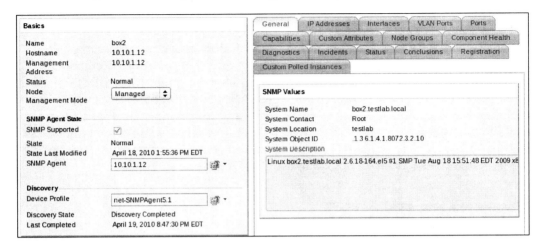

To change management mode you can use:

- `nnmmanagementmode.ovpl` script
- Use the form

If you set the object to **Not Managed** or **Out of Service** mode, the following features would be affected:

- **Management Mode**: For nodes, setting the **Management Mode** to **Not Managed** or **Out of Service** has the following effects:
  ○ No incidents are generated for the node
  ○ The status of a node is set to **No Status**
  ○ The node's SNMP agent is excluded from fault polling
  ○ The node's interfaces or addresses are excluded from fault and performance polling
  ○ Traps related to the node, interface, or address are not stored
  ○ NNMi quits gathering component health data about the node
  ○ NNMi deletes all polled instances associated with the **Not Managed** or **Out of Service**, and the node stops being monitored.
  ○ The node is removed from any associated Router Redundancy groups
  ○ The node is excluded from the discovery
  ○ **Actions | Configuration Poll** is no longer available for the node or incident related to that node

- **Direct Management Mode**: For interfaces, setting the **Direct Management Mode** to **Not Managed** or **Out of Service** has the following effects:
  - ° No incidents are generated for the interface
  - ° No incidents are generated for the address
  - ° The status of the interface is set to **No Status**
  - ° The state of the address is set to **Not Polled**
  - ° The address is excluded from fault and performance polling
  - ° The interface and any related addresses are excluded from fault and performance polling
  - ° The Administrative State and Operational State of the interface are set to **Not Polled**
  - ° Traps related to interface will not be stored

If the address or interface is set to **Not Managed** using Direct Management Mode, NNMi calculates the management mode for all associated objects. The following table provides a list of possible values on every object.

The table provides a list of management modes for interfaces, where the first column represents a node's management mode, and the second and third columns show the interfaces management mode, depending whether interface is set as direct management mode or not:

Node – Management Mode	Interface – Direct Management Mode	Interface – Management Mode
Managed	Inherited	Managed
Not Managed	Inherited	Not Managed
Out of Service	Inherited	Out of Service
Managed	Not Managed	Not Managed
Not Managed	Not Managed	Not Managed
Out of Service	Not Managed	Not Managed
Managed	Out of Service	Out of Service
Not Managed	Out of Service	Out of Service
Out of Service	Out of Service	Out of Service

The following table provides a list of dependencies of management mode for addresses:

Node — Management Mode	Interface — Direct Management Mode	Address — Direct Management Mode	Address — Management Mode
Managed	Inherited	Inherited	Managed
Not Managed	Inherited	Inherited	Not Managed
Out of Service	Inherited	Inherited	Out of Service
Managed	Not applicable	Inherited	Managed
Not Managed	Not applicable	Inherited	Not Managed
Out of Service	Not applicable	Inherited	Out of Service
Managed	Not Managed	Inherited	Managed
Not Managed	Not Managed	Inherited	Not Managed
Out of Service	Not Managed	Inherited	Not Managed
Managed	Not Managed	Not Managed	Not Managed
Not Managed	Not Managed	Not Managed	Not Managed
Out of Service	Not Managed	Not Managed	Not Managed
Managed	Not applicable	Not Managed	Not Managed
Not Managed	Not applicable	Not Managed	Not Managed
Out of Service	Not applicable	Not Managed	Not Managed
Managed	Out of Service	Inherited	Out of Service
Not Managed	Out of Service	Inherited	Out of Service
Out of Service	Out of Service	Inherited	Out of Service
Managed	Out of Service	Out of Service	Out of Service
Not Managed	Out of Service	Out of Service	Out of Service
Out of Service	Out of Service	Out of Service	Out of Service
Managed	Not applicable	Out of Service	Out of Service
Not Managed	Not applicable	Out of Service	Out of Service
Out of Service	Not applicable	Out of Service	Out of Service

Management mode change examples

We have a scheduled maintenance window on site A and B and we, as NNMi administrators, don't want operators to receive any messages from these sites during maintenance window. The best way to achieve this requirement is to change management mode to Out of Service on the nodes that are under the maintenance window. Assuming that site A and B are nodes with IP addresses 10.10.1.1 and 192.168.1.1.

Complete following steps in order to set nodes into **Out of Service** mode:

1. Select **Inventory** workspace.
2. Select **Nodes** view.
3. Select nodes **10.10.1.1** and **192.168.1.1**.

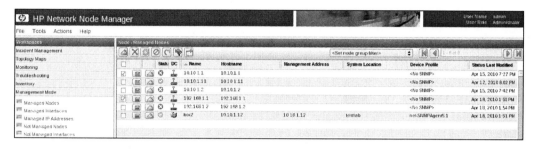

4. Select **Actions** from top menu.
5. Select **Out of Service**.

Congratulations! You have set nodes to **Out of Service** mode. To make sure they are in this mode, you may refresh **Nodes** view or open **Out Of Service Nodes** in same **Management Mode** workspace:

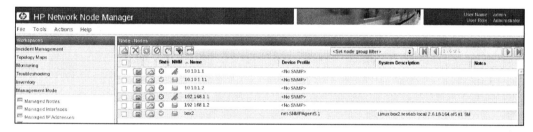

After maintenance is complete, we may need to set these nodes back to **Managed** mode. Complete the following steps to set nodes back to **Managed** mode:

1. Select **Management mode** workspace.
2. Select **Out of Service Nodes** view.
3. Select nodes **10.10.1.1** and **192.168.1.1**.

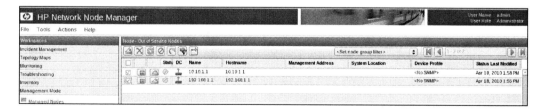

4. Select **Actions** from top menu.

5. Select **Managed**.

Congratulations! You set nodes back to **Managed** mode.

Discovery examples

Here, we provide few real life examples which may be familiar to you.

Example 1: Seed module

Assume that we have a network that has to be managed. We have the IP addresses of all devices that need to be managed, and our network is stable. New devices are rarely installed and we have control over them.

According to such requirements, the fastest and most accurate way would be to seed all devices for discovery, as shown in the diagram below:

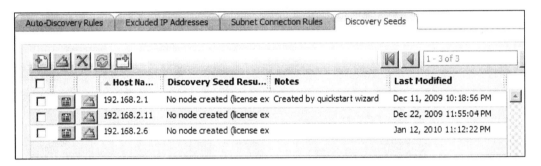

When seeding a list of nodes that need to be discovered, we make sure that we load all nodes we need to, and which make our discovery configuration more simple. If you have a list of nodes and it's more than few nodes, you'd rather load seeds from the file using the `nnmloadseeds.ovpl` command. The previously mentioned filter configuration example provides steps on how to configure seeds using the batch file.

Example 2: Discover by IP address range and system Object ID

An ISP network consists of three networks: backbone, distribution, and access network. The ISP only wants to monitor the backbone and distribution networks, with only few devices from the access network, which have a specific service level agreement with customers. The backbone consists only of Cisco routers; the distribution network uses only Cisco equipment. Both networks have strictly dedicated IP address ranges. The access network has many vendors' equipment and NOC staff has the IP addresses of the devices, which have a specific service level agreement (VIP customers).

The following is a network diagram:

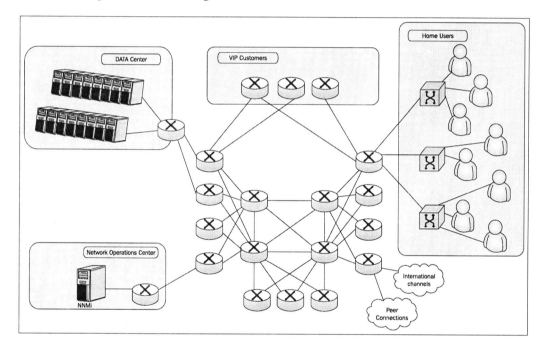

In this case, one of solutions to create discovery could be achieved by creating the following discovery rules:

- Devices that have SNMP system object ID .1.3.6.1.4.1.9... and are from following IP address range.

  The following diagram represents Auto-discovery by system object ID:

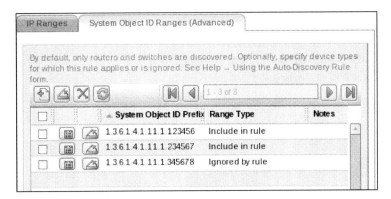

- Seed GOLD SLA devices (VIP): This would assure that you don't miss any device from your VIP list.

  The following diagram represents Auto-discovery by IP addresses:

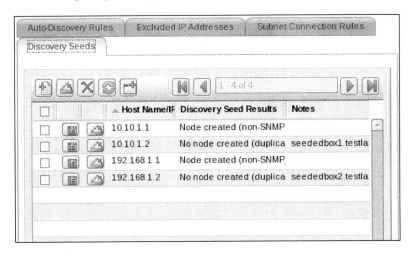

Now you need to wait for a couple of minutes to see the discovery results. If the number of devices which need to pass the discovery filter is large, you may need to wait for more than a couple of minutes.

If you don't see some of the nodes even after waiting for a long time, try the following:

- Review your discovery filter and make sure you didn't miss anything

- Make sure these nodes are configured for SNMP and NNMi has that SNMP community set in **Communication Configuration** view

- If you are sure you did the previous steps correctly, you can enter node (nodes) into seed

Rediscovering your network from scratch

Sometimes, when your discovered network looks far from what you expected, it is easier to wipe the whole NNMi database and start discovery from scratch. It is very common during implementation, when the initial discovery filters don't work as they were supposed to.

If you decide to delete existing NNMi inventory and start discovery all over again, you should proceed with following steps:

1. Stop NNMi services:

   `ovstop -c`

2. Optional: Backup existing database:

   `nnmbackup.ovpl -type offline -target <backup_directory>`

3. Optional: Save current NNMi configuration (exports into XML file):

   `nnmconfigexport.ovpl`

4. Optional: Save existing incidents:

   `nnmtrimincidents.ovpl`

5. Drop and create the NNMi database from scratch:

   `nnmresetembdb.ovpl -nostart`

    For an Oracle database, the database should be dropped using Oracle native tools or commands.

6. If you have iSPIs installed, or third party application integration, follow this product integration documentation to check whether some additional actions should be taken.

7. Start NNMi services:

    ```
    ovstart -c
    ```

8. Start NNMi configuration and discovery.

State poller

This section describes state poller, which is used in NNMi.

What is state poller?

There are nodes or interfaces in a network, which need more accurate monitoring (more frequent polling). It is not performance effective to set polling intervals for a whole network, based on most frequent polling demand.

How does it work?

State poller allows for the setting of polling intervals and types for classes, interface types, or node types. Configuration is organized by groups, which allows flexibility in maintaining state poller, especially if the network is dynamic and new discoveries need specific polling configuration.

The following screenshot represents the State poller configuration window:

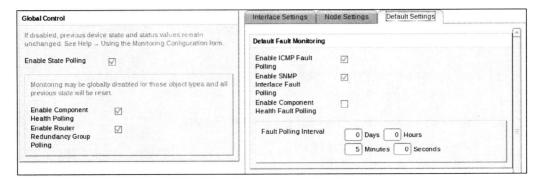

State poller can be configured to use ICMP or SNMP status checks and can be configured for interface or node. This type of configuration is very flexible, but simultaneously complicated, as overlapping may occur. It is OK as long as we know how overlapping works. There are few rules about how NNMi evaluates objects for state polling:

- If the object is interface, then the interface group is evaluated starting from the lowest group number to the highest. The first matched group is applied. No more evaluation is done.

- If the object was not found in the interface group, node groups are evaluated. Again, evaluation is done starting from the group with the lowest group number to the highest. The first matched group is applied. No more evaluation is done. Any interface that didn't match any interface group inherits settings from its node's group settings, which were applied to the node.

- If any object in the device didn't match any state polling rule, default settings are applied.

The following diagram represents the State poller setting evaluation flow:

Group	Group ID	
Interface groups	10 20 30 40 50 60	Evaluation
Node groups	10 20 30 40 50 60	Evaluation
Default Settings		

How to plan state polling

Initially, it may look like a very tricky and difficult task to understand how the NNMi administrator will know what polling settings to set on every single node, and on every interface in a network. Especially when NNMi monitors hundreds, if not thousands of devices, and thousands if not tens of thousands interfaces.

So, forget about the amount of nodes and interfaces. Let's get answers to following questions first:

- Which devices do we plan to monitor?

- What parameters do we want to monitor?

- What maximum delay is tolerated for notifying a state change?

Answers to these questions will give us a pretty clear picture about what the state poller settings should look like. Will we use ICMP or SNMP? Should we care more about traps, or do we plan to poll devices proactively?

As an example, let's take a very generic ISP network that has a backbone network, VIP customers, home users, international links, and peer connections with other ISPs:

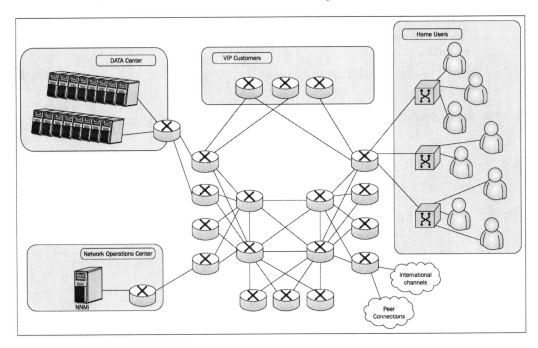

It's obvious that not all devices or interfaces have the same demand for polling. VIP customers, international, and peer connections are probably in the top list that ISP most care about in terms of monitoring. These sites will have more frequent polling cycles, while home users will have less frequent polling cycles. So, we already have a rough state polling design. If we analyze each segment more accurately, we could continue increasing a state polling configuration list.

Such assessment as shown in the previous example will be your starting point for decision input about what interface or node groups should be created.

It is good practice to create simple and short groups, which later would be combined into hierarchical levels for monitoring or visualization purposes.

State poller can use ICMP or SNMP queries. Before you decide which one you want to use, it is important to know what each of them does:

- ICMP ping is used to check the availability of each IP address
- SNMP queries nodes for status information, and as SNMP can query data from nodes about more specific parameters, these queries can also be used for fault monitoring or performance data collection (if iSPI for performance is used)

It is hard to estimate how much SNMP traffic will load the network, as polling is designed to use optimized queries. Every time the configuration is saved, state poller recalculates objects, which can be grouped and optimized for common polling groups.

Polling intervals can be set for each group and can be selected from a wide interval range, from as short as one minute to as long as a day or two. Setting polling intervals is pretty tricky, as by setting too short intervals you can heavily decrease the system performance, and by setting too large intervals you will lose accuracy on monitoring.

State poller operations can be checked at any time using the **Help | About Network Node Manager i-series** table from the main window menu:

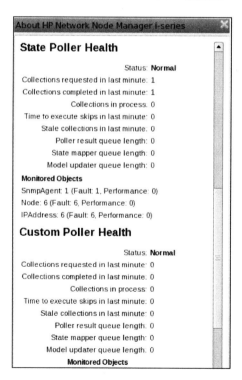

The following table describes some presented parameters.

Result	Description
Status	Overall state poller status:
Poll Counters	• Collections requested in the last minute • Collection completed in the last minute • Collections in process
Time to execute skips in the last minute	The number of scheduled polls that did not complete within the polling cycle. Excellent if it's zero. If it's more than zero, then it is recommended to monitor this number and if it keeps increasing, it means that NNMi's poller cannot poll properly and more of the scheduled polls are behind schedule. Recommendation: • Check whether all processes are running • Fine tune the polling periods and make them less frequent
Stale connections	Are the connections which have not received a response for longer than 10 minutes. Excellent if this number is zero. Otherwise, this parameter needs monitoring and if it keeps increasing, it means that there are problems with polling engine.
Poller result queue length	Excellent if poller result queue length is equal to zero or close to it. Otherwise ovjboss is running out of memory.
State mapper queue length	Excellent if state mapper queue length is equal to zero or close to it. Otherwise, system performance and database should be checked.

Example

As a state poller configuration example, let's take the previously described network (the diagram in the section entitled *How to plan state polling*), and configure state poller to fulfill the following requirements:

- All nodes need to be polled using SNMP every five minutes, except the objects described as follows:
  - ° All interfaces with the name DataCenter should be polled every one minute using SNMP.
  - ° There are two HP printers in the NOC subnet, which are connected to a network but do not support SNMP, so they need to be polled using ICMP every five minutes.

Complete the following steps to configure state polling according to requirements:

1. Set global monitoring settings by completing following steps:
    i.   Select **Monitoring Configuration** in **Configuration** workspace.
    ii. Select the **Default Settings** tab.

iii. Set **Fault Polling Interval** to **5** minutes.

iv. Make sure **Enable SNMP interface Fault Polling** is checked and **Enable ICMP Management Address Polling** is unchecked.

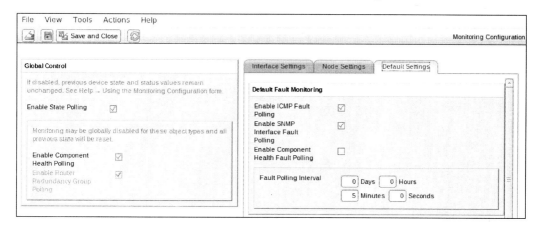

2. Configure all interfaces with the interface name **Data Center** to be polled every one minute using SNMP:

i. Select **Interface Settings** tab:

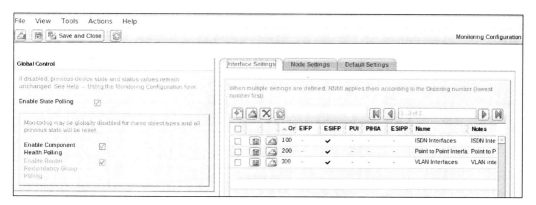

ii. Select **New** on **Interface group** field.

iii. Name the interface group, that is, **Datacenter interfaces**.

iv. Select **Additional filters** tab.

v. Select the following values: **Attribute** = **IfAlias**, **Operator** = **=**, and **Value** = **Data Center**.

vi. Click **Append**.

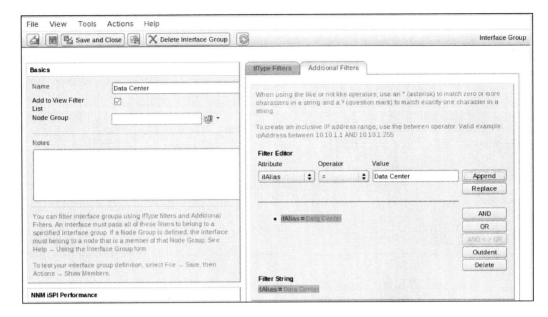

vii. Click **Save and Close**.

viii. Make sure **Enable SNMP Interface Fault Polling** is selected and **Enable ICMP Management Address Polling** is unchecked.

ix. Set ordering number, that is, 150.

x. Set **Fault Polling Interval** to **1** minute.

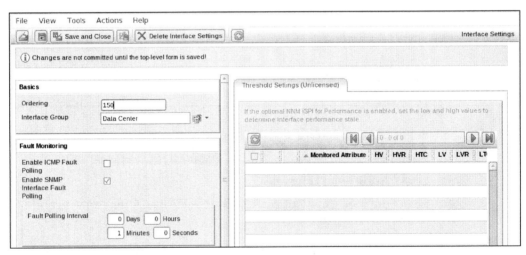

xi. Click **Save and Close**.

3. Configure HP printers to be polled every five minutes using ICMP:

   i. Select **Node Settings** tab.

   ii. Select **New**.

   iii. Set ordering number, that is, `150`.

   iv. Set **Enable ICMP Fault Polling**.

   v. Uncheck **Enable SNMP interface Fault Polling**.

   vi. Make sure that **Fault Polling interval** is set to **5** minutes.

   vii. Select **New** in **Node group**.

   viii. Enter name in **Name** field, that is, **Printers**.

   ix. Select **Device Filters** tab.

   x. Select **New**.

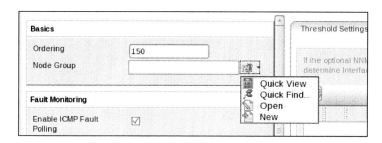

   xi. Select the following value in the device filter window: **Device Category = Printer, Device Vendor = Hewlett-Packard**.

   xii. Click **Save and Close**.

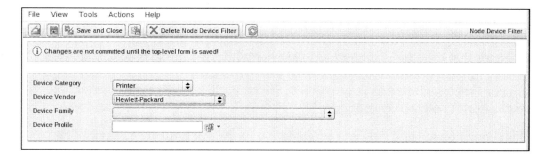

xiii. Select **Save**.

xiv. Select **Actions | Show Members** to see whether devices are included in your filter.

 You won't see printers if you don't have them in your discovered topology. In a real life scenario, you can always use **Show member** to check whether you have properly configured the filter scope.

xv. Click **Save and Close**.

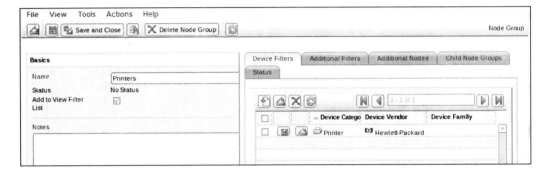

Summary

As you see from this chapter, a lot of improvements were made in the discovery configuration compared to NNM 7.x and earlier versions. User interface is more intuitive and easier to understand. But the main challenge remains the same. No matter how easy to use a tool is, it's the discovery strategy that makes it work correctly. As you see from the examples used in this chapter, no matter whether your network is huge, with thousands of devices, or relatively small, there are standard questions that the administrator has to answer while designing discovery strategy. As long as these questions are answered, there is no such thing as a network is too large or too complicated to be monitored. There might be a discussion about how much effort it will take to configure NNMi, building rules, exceptions, and so on.

This chapter completed building a foundation for NNMi implementation. When all devices are discovered, the next step is setting up maps so that they would be intuitive and easy to understand.

3
Configuring and Viewing Maps

Every network is unique and every network operations center has its own requirements for monitoring. There are a lot of system configuration and maintenance issues, which need to be solved in order to have a nice and easy-to-use tool.

Object grouping makes system configuration more flexible. This feature also makes big networks smaller. Imagine a map with 100 nodes and another map with containers where each container represents a group of nodes (location).

This feature makes monitoring more intuitive. Operators can monitor objects grouped by visual domains. As an example, we can compare a company's network, which has hundreds of network devices located all around the country. Monitoring these devices listed in a table makes monitoring more confusing than effective. The visual location of devices instantly allows operators to understand the impact of every issue that occurs in a network.

This chapter covers the following topics:

- Node groups
- Node group map configuration and viewing
- Path views
- User interface configuration
- Web browser-specific settings
- Symbols

We will also find examples to explain most of these topics, which will help us to easily understand each topic and how it can be applied in real life.

Node groups

This section describes what node groups are and how they can be configured. Node grouping knowledge will help us optimize the monitoring setting configuration and improve Node Group Map configuration.

What are node groups?

A node group is a set of nodes, which have common attributes such as device category, vendor, host name, IP address, and contact information, among others within the same group. It can be a group of devices at the same location, the same manufacturer or model, devices belonging to a particular group or dedicated for specific functionality, belonging to the same defined range of IP addresses, and so on. Node groups are configured by the NNMi administrator. Node groups in NNMi are used for:

- Defining and monitoring configuration, which allows us to configure monitoring settings flexibly regarding node groups.

- Working with the NNM Performance metrics and Traffic SPI Filters options to create a report.

- Creating custom view filters to help operators quickly navigate through monitored data. There are few view types where node groups can be used as a view filter in NNMi:

   - **Browsing incidents**: Browsing incidents only for a selected node group will make an incident list shorter, easier to navigate, and easier to recognize the issues.

   - **Listing nodes**: We don't need to list all our discovered nodes while using filters. Instead, we can filter nodes by the specific group we need to work with, that is, by device location, function, and responsibility, among others.

   - **Filtering IP addresses**: Node groups can be created based on IP address ranges as well. As an example, this can be useful when our staff have divided responsibility by IP address.

The next section describes how to configure node groups.

By default, NNMi has the following preconfigured node groups:

- **Microsoft Windows Systems**: This node group includes any device manufactured by Microsoft.

- **Non-SNMP Devices**: This node group includes any device that does not respond to SNMP.

- **Important Nodes**: This node group is used by the Causal Engine. Any devices in this group receive special treatment. When a current member of this group stops responding, the Causal Engine generates a "Node Down" incident and sets the device status to Critical. For example, when a WAN Edge Device is in the shadow of another problem, NNMi generates a "Node Down" incident because the router is listed in the Important Nodes group. This node group is empty by default. Consider populating this group with critical servers that run important applications and critical WAN routers.

[**Caution**: Do not delete the Important Nodes group.]

- **Networking Infrastructure Devices**: This node group is populated with a list of categories for network devices. Any device within our management domain that matches these categories is automatically included in this node group. Devices in this group are automatically monitored for Component Health fault metrics.

- **Routers**: This node group is populated with a list of categories for network devices that represent routers. Any router, switch-router, or gateway within our management domain is included in this node group.

- **Switches**: This node group is populated with a list of categories for network devices that represent switches. Any switch, be it an ATM switch or switch-router within our management domain, is included in this node group.

The administrator can modify these groups to reflect your own needs.

Configuring node groups

This section describes how to configure node groups in NNMi.

Node groups are configured in the **Node Group** window of the **Configuration** workspace. There are several rules to be considered while configuring node groups:

- The same device can belong to more than one group.
- Node groups can be constructed into node hierarchies.

- Node groups can be created using any of the following tabs (either alone or as a combination): device filters, additional filters, additional nodes, child node groups, and status.

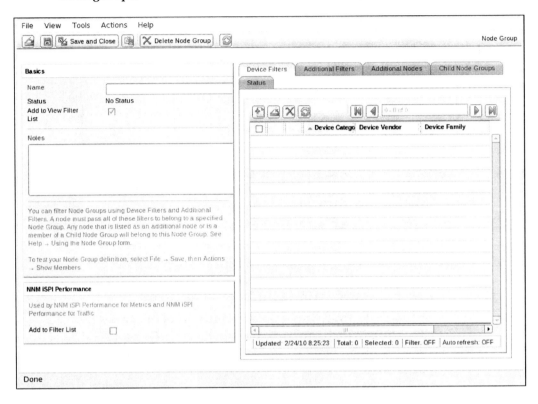

Here is a description of these tabs:

- **Device Filters**: Nodes can be filtered by their attributes, including the following:
    - **Device category**: Category assigned to device, that is, router, switch, personal computer, and so on.
    - **Device vendor**: Device vendor assigned to a device based on device's system object ID, that is, Cisco, HP, Juniper, and so on.
    - **Device family**: Device family assigned to a device based on device's system object ID, that is, Cisco catalyst 6500 Series Switches, Cisco 500 Series Content Engines, and so on.
    - **Device profile**: Device profile is assigned to a node based on device system object ID.

These attributes are configured in NNMi, based on the device system object ID. The system object ID is assigned by manufacturer as the device identifier, for example, HP switch 2400 has a system object ID .1.3.6.1.4.1.11.2.3.7.11.10 and HP switch 2424 has a system object ID .1.3.6.1.4.1.11.2.3.7.11.11.

Based on the system object ID, NNMi assigns the node to a predefined category, vendor, family, and profile. It's done to help NNMi identify the device type and to help the user filter devices as well.

These device attributes can also be modified or created by NNMi administrator (**Configuration | Device Profiles**).

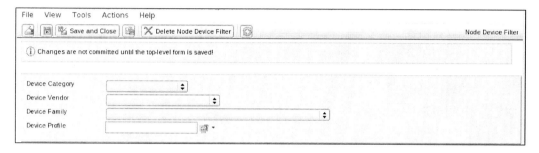

- **Additional Filters**: This is where expressions of filter attributes can be used. The following is the list of attributes, which can be used in filter expressions:

  ○ Sysname: System name, assigned to a device during configuration

  ○ sysLocation: System location assigned to a device during configuration

  ○ sysContact: System contact information assigned to a device during configuration

  ○ Hostname: Is the device hostname

  ○ hostedIPAddress: Is the IP address of a device

  ○ island

  ○ mgmtIPAddress: IP address that is threaded as management by NNMi

  ○ customAttrName: The name of custom attribute

  ○ customAttrValue: The value of custom attribute

  ○ Capability: Device capability, assigned by NNMi, based on device system object ID

Filters are created by the administrator. Attributes are assigned to nodes based on their configured data, or data assigned by NNMi.

A list of operators can be used to create an expression of attributes:

- ○ "=" (Equal)
- ○ "!=" (Not Equal)
- ○ "<" (Less than)
- ○ "<=" (Less or equal)
- ○ ">" (More)
- ○ ">=" (More or equal)
- ○ Between
- ○ In
- ○ Is not null
- ○ Is null
- ○ Like
- ○ Not between
- ○ Not in
- ○ Not like

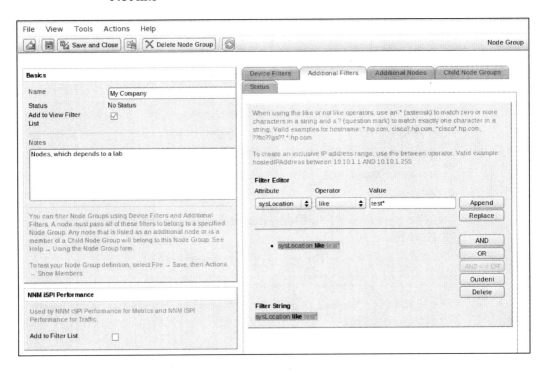

- **Additional Nodes**: This tab allows additional nodes which, in some cases, cannot fit into filters. Or administrators, for other reasons, prefer listing nodes instead of writing a filter.

> **Note**: Listing nodes is a static solution. So if new nodes are discovered, they are not covered by this tab listing.

- **Child Node Groups**: This tab allows Node Groups to be included in a group. This means that if we create a group of all Cisco devices and we have already created the "Cisco router" and "Cisco switch" group, we can add these two groups as child of the "Cisco devices" group, and "Cisco devices" will have routers and switches in this group.
- **Status**: This tab allows group nodes by their status.

If both of the **Device Filters** and **Additional Filters** tabs are configured in the **Node Group** configuration window, the logical "AND" is used to combine these settings.

Additional Nodes and **Child Node Groups** between each other work as logical "OR".

Consider the following example. If the Device Filters tab passes nodes A, B, and C, and Additional Filters tab passes nodes B, C, and D, then the node group of Device Filter and Additional Filter will consist of nodes B and C. However, if node X, Y passes the Additional Nodes tab, then the node group will consist of nodes B, C, X, and Y. If we set node Group_B, which includes nodes K and L as a child group, then our node group would consist of nodes B, C, X, Y, K, and L (see the following diagram):

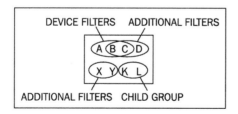

Node group configuration example

Let's take an example, which allows us to use the described filtering options. The NNMi administrator receives the following requirements:

- Create a node group to network administrators, which are in the 10.10.1.x network

- Administrators are responsible for all routers in these networks, except Cisco Firewall, which has the IP address 10.10.1.31.
- They also need to monitor each site's syslog servers, which have the following IP addresses: 10.10.1.101 and 10.10.1.102

One of the ways to create such a map is as follows:

1. Create a node group of syslog servers.
2. Create a node group of network devices in given networks, except Cisco Firewalls with specific IP addresses.
3. Add syslog server node group as a child group of the network device group.

Follow the steps given next to complete this task:

1. **Creating a node group Syslog servers**:
   i. Select **Configuration | Node Groups | New**.
   ii. Enter the name as **Syslog servers** and complete the **Notes** field in **Syslog server node group**.
   iii. Select the **Additional Nodes** tab and select the **New** icon in top left corner of window.
   iv. Enter the IP address as **10.10.1.101** and click on **Save and Close**.

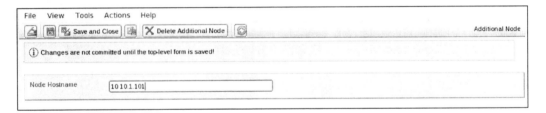

   v. Add server **10.10.2.101** in the same way.

vi. Click on **Save and Close** to close **Syslog Servers Node Group** configuration window.

2. **Creating node group of network devices with the exception of Cisco Firewall:**

    i. Select **Configuration** workspace | **Node Groups** | **New**.

    ii. Fill in the fields with the following information:

          ◦ **Name: Team A nodes**

          ◦ **Notes**: A list of nodes, which belong to team A

    iii. Select **Device Filters** | **New**.

    iv. Select **Device Category** as **Router**.

    v. Click on **Save and Close**.

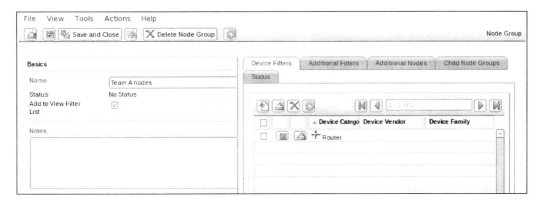

vi. Select **Additional filters** tab and enter the following information:

          ◦ **Attribute** = `hostedIPAddress`

          ◦ **Operator** = **between**

          ◦ **Value** = **10.10.1.1** and **10.10.1.254**

vii. Select **Append** and **AND**.

viii. Fill in the following values:

          ◦ **Attribute** = `hostedIPAddress`

          ◦ **Operator** = `!=`

          ◦ **Value** = **10.10.1.31**

ix. Select **Append**.

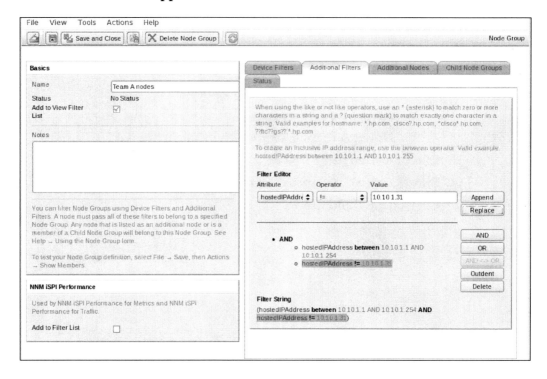

x. To make sure you filtered the correct nodes, select **Actions | Show members**.

3. **Adding syslog servers into a scope**:

   i. Open the **Team A nodes** node group (if you closed it before the previous step)

   ii. From the **Child Node Group** drop-down list, select **New**

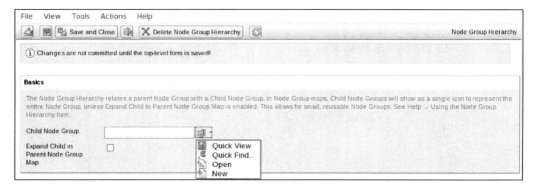

iii. Select the **Quick Find** option and select **Syslog servers** from a list of node groups.

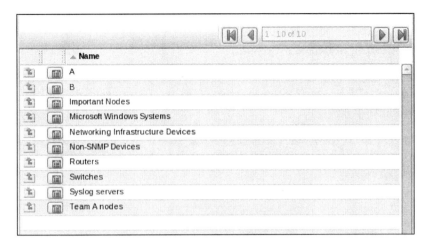

iv. Click on **Save and Close**.

4. **Ensuring node group includes nodes that we need**:

i. Select **Configuration** workspace | **Node Groups**.

ii. Open **Team A nodes** as the nodes group.

iii. Select **Actions** | **Show members**.

Congratulations! You have just created a node group by the requirements listed in this example.

Node group map configuration

Node group maps are graphical representations of nodes and node groups. Node groups can be configured with hierarchical dependencies, which help us build maps inside a map, among other things. Consider the following situation. We have a map of the world, where all node groups are located based on their geographical location, with one container per continent. Inside each container, we have nodes that depend on the continent associated to that container, with the layout based on their geographical location inside that continent. This section describes node group map configuration and provides a real life example.

What is node group map?

A node group map is a graphical representation of node groups. Any node group can be located on a map. Node group combinations can be used as a representation of some infrastructure. Such a visual representation helps us to provide a more intuitive monitoring interface for users.

As node group filtering and node group hierarchies give us a lot of flexibility, we can create practically any node group map. Here are a few examples of how we can create a node group map:

- **Geographical location**: Node and node group grouping based on geographical location, that is, this provides a geographical view for operators.

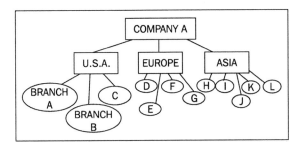

- **IP address ranges**: Node and node group grouping based on their IP address ranges/networks, that is, organized based on IP address zones.

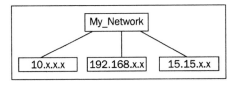

- **Vendor**: Node and node group grouping based on vendor. As an example, we can consider situation where the staff have divided their responsibility by vendors. Such maps would be organized by their responsibilities.

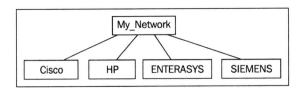

Configuring node group maps

In this section, we will provide an example of a map created for a company, which is located in Europe and has offices in France and the UK.

The NNMi administrator was asked to create a new map for Europe with the following requirements:

- A map of Europe should be presented
- Nodes of each country should be located in separate containers

The following diagram shows a graphical representation of the requirements:

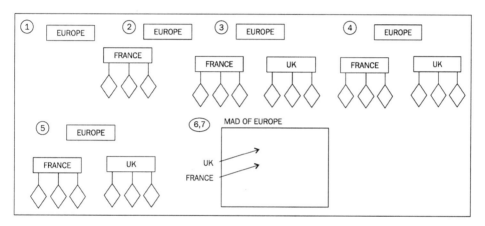

To complete this task, follow the steps provided here:

1. Create node group named Europe.
2. Create node group named France and set filters to pass only those nodes that belong to the France branch.
3. Create node group named UK and set filters to pass only those nodes that belong to the UK branch.
4. Add node groups France and UK as child groups in node group Europe.
5. Set status propagation rules for node groups France and UK.
6. Set node object layout for every node group that is used in this map.
7. Set a graphical background to node group Europe.

Note: Be careful with the use of graphical backgrounds, as they tend to use more bandwidth and can affect performance. The type of background should be considered carefully.

Layout needs to be saved to every node group, which is included in Node Group Map configuration, even if we don't need to change layout of objects.

The following are step-by-step instructions about how to complete this task:

1. Create node group named Europe.

    i.   Select **Node Groups** in the **Configuration** workspace.

    ii. Click on the **New** button.

    iii. In the newly opened window, enter **Europe** in the **Name** field. Leave the tabs on the right-hand side of the window unfilled as we don't want any nodes belonging directly to this node group.

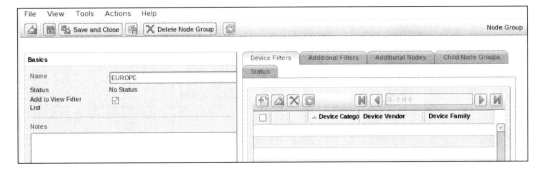

    iv. Click on the **Save and Close** button.

2. Create node group France and add filters that would be passed by nodes belonging to France.

    i.   Follow the same steps as in the previous node group creation.

    ii. Select the **Additional Filters** tab. We will use this tab because we will write a filter that will match France-related nodes.

    iii. Select **hostname** in the **Attribute** field.

    iv. Select **like** in the **Operator** field.

    v.   Enter ***.fr.company.com** in the **Value** field. Here we make an assumption that our node names follow the naming convention `<hostname>.<country_abbreviation>.<company_name>.com`.

vi. Select **Append**.

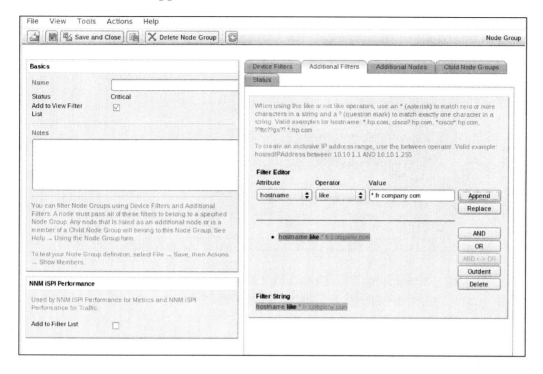

vii. Click on the **Save and Close** button.

3. The next task is to view search results for the France node group. This can be done by selecting **Actions | Show Members** in the top menu of the **Configuration** window. This step is optional.

4. Create node group UK and add filters, which would be passed by nodes belonging to UK. This can be achieved by following the same steps used for creating the France node group, with the only exception being that we have to enter a UK-related name filter in the **Value** field. (***.UK.company.com**.)

5. View results for UK node group. This step is again optional.

6. Add France and UK as child groups into Europe node group.

   i. Select **Node Groups** in **Configuration** workspace.

   ii. Open node group Europe.

   iii. Open **Child Node Group** tab.

   iv. Select **Quick Find...** in **Child Node Group** field.

v. Select Node Group France and click **Save and Close**.

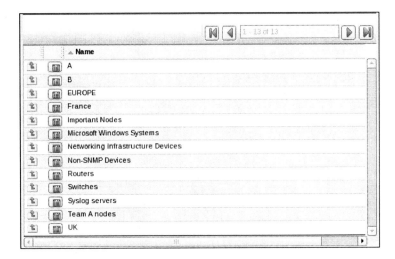

vi. Repeat steps 3 and 4 to add the UK node group into a Europe child node group list and click on **Save and Close**.

vii. Again click on **Save and Close**.

7. Set status propagation settings. This step allows to configure rules for how the status would be determined for a node group. There are two options— the most severe status of a node in a node group is used or a percentage calculation is determined. In our case, we will use the most severe status. We chose this setting because we want to represent the container's status with the most severe object inside a container.

i. Select **Status Configuration** in **Configuration** workspace.

ii. Check the **Propagate Most Severe Status** checkbox.

iii. Click on **Save and Close**.

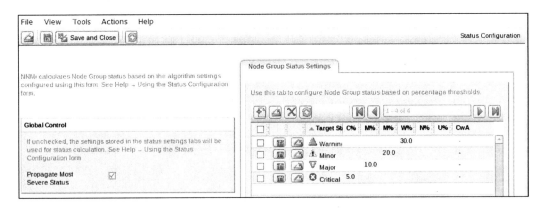

8. Save layout for every node group which is in the Node Group Map.

   Select **Configuration | Node Groups**.

   Select checkbox for node group Europe.

   Select **Actions | Node Group Map**.

   Change object layout if necessary and then save layout.

   Repeat these steps for node groups France and UK.

9. Create node group map.

   i.   Open node group from which we wish to create a map
        (**Configuration | Node Groups | Europe Map Group**).

   ii. Select **Actions** menu.

   iii. Select **Node Group Map**.

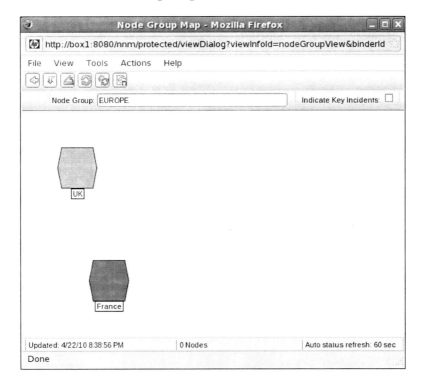

   iv. Position icons in the way we want them to appear. Remember that
       we can set a background image for any node group map too.

   v. Click on **Save Layout**.

   vi. Create node group maps for each node group we created in
       this example.

10. We can set a background image for node group map too. This is an optional step.

    i.   Select **Node Group Map Setting** in the **Configuration** workspace.

    ii. Open the Europe node group map.

    iii. Open the **Background image** tab.

    iv. Click the link provided in the window (`http://nnmi_server:port/nnmbg`).

    v.   Select a map we wish to use as the background, and right-click to select the **Copy Link Location**.

    vi. Paste link to **Background image** field.

    vii. Click on **Save and Close**.

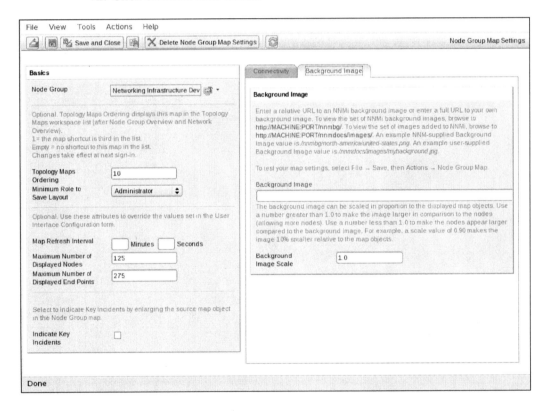

To view the results, go to Europe in the **Topology Maps** workspace and the created node group map will be opened.

If we cannot see our node group map, we can try restarting our NNMi console.

1. We can set this map as initial view when the node group map window is opened. Map priority is controlled by setting ordering number for each node group map. The lower the ordering number, the higher priority a map has.

    i. Select **Node Group Map Settings** in the **Configuration** workspace.

    ii. Enter number in **Topology Maps Ordering** field. Choose the lowest number in the **Node Group Map** list.

    iii. Click on **Save and Close**.

2. We can determine whether node group map should be shown in initial view. This, again, is an optional step.

    i. Select **User Interface Configuration** in the **Configuration** workspace.

    ii. In the **Initial view** drop-down list, select node group map—in our case **Europe**.

Creating node groups in the command line

There is a node group configuration command line tool, nnmloadnodegroups.ovpl, which may help us create node groups using the command line:

> `nnmloadnodegroups.ovpl` tool can help us achieve following:
> - Migration from NNM 6.x/7.x or a third-party monitoring tool into NNMi. (NNMi 8.13 already includes migration tools, but if for some reasons, we need a custom or limited migration, we may need this tool separately from whole migration procedure.)
> - Creation of node groups in large environments.
> - Integration of NNMi with other monitoring tools.

`nnmloadnodegroups.ovpl` tool usage:

```
nnmloadnodegroups.ovpl -? | -u <user> -p <password> -f <CSV_file> [ -r
true|false ]
```

Example:

```
        nnmloadnodegroups.ovpl -u myadminusername -p myadminpassword
-f /tmp/nnmconfig.csv
            Import the customized node group configuration in /tmp/
nnmconfig.csv file to NNM database.
        -?: print this usage statement
        -f <CSV file>: import the configuration CSV file
```

```
                -p <password>: provide password to the NNM administrator
     account
                -u <user>: provide the NNM administrator user name
                -r <true | false> : provide overwrite flag (default: false)
```

CSV file syntax:

```
NodeGroupName,Notes,AtVFL,ChNodeGroup[:ExpFlag;...],Category1:Vendor1:
Family1:Profile1[;...],Hostname[;...],HostnameWildcard[;...],hostedIPa
ddrRange[;...],managementAddrRange[;...]
```

The following is an example of the nnmloadnodegroups.ovpl resulting output:

```
Number of Node Groups processed: 1
Number of Node Groups added: 1
Number of Node Groups skipped: 0
nnmloadnodegroups.ovpl executed successfully.
```

Viewing maps

Node group maps can be viewed in the **Topology Maps** workspace, which allows us to see the following maps:

- **Node Group Overview**: A list of all node groups is presented with colored Node Group icons, where status of each group is presented
- **Network Overview**: A map of the entire network is presented
- **Networking Infrastructure Devices**: Status of networking device groups is presented (groups of routers and switches)
- **Routers**: Group of all routers with overall group status
- **Switches**: Group of all switches with overall group status
- **Custom Maps**: A list of all created node group maps is given, where the operator can select any of the custom node group maps

For more information on monitoring a network using maps, refer to *Chapter 9, Monitoring Your Network.*

Another place where part of the network can be displayed is the Troubleshooting workspace. This workspace provides the following maps, which are displayed based on discovered data:

- **Layer 2 Neighbor View**: Displays Layer 2 connections from the selected device by the custom number of hops

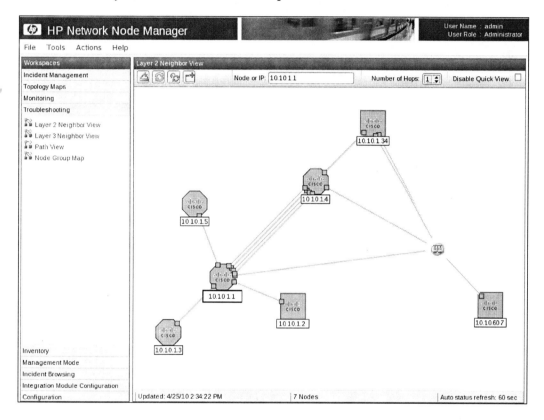

- **Layer 3 Neighbor View**: Displays Layer 3 connections from the selected device by the custom number of hops.

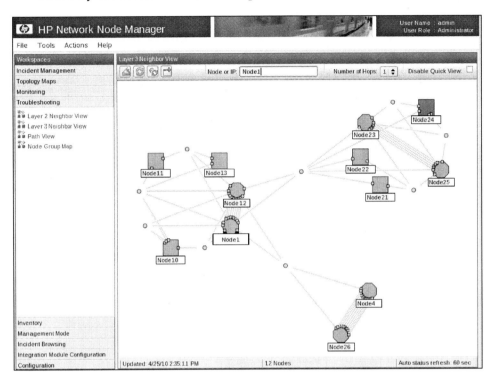

- **Path View**: Displays path view between two selected devices.

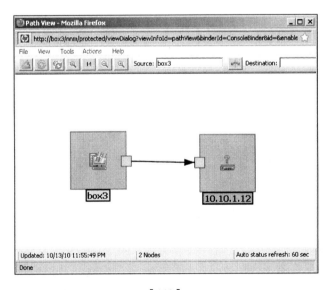

- **Node Group Map**: Displays the lowest level of node group to which the selected device belongs

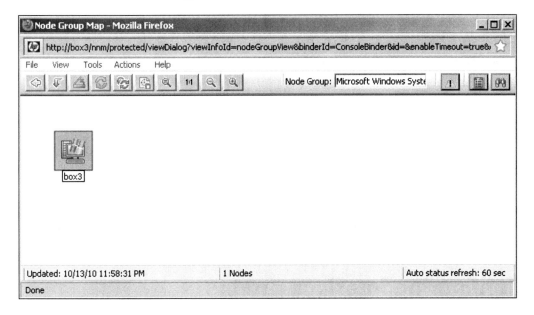

Interface groups

Interface groups are filters of interfaces by attributes (ifName, IP address, ifDescr, ifAlias, ifIndex, ifSpeed, and so on). Unlike node groups, interface groups cannot be grouped into hierarchical dependencies. Interface groups are created for filtering devices based on their hosted interfaces.

Interface groups provide filters for selective viewing of inventories and incidents, threshold monitoring, performance measurements, or defined targets for monitoring.

By default, NNMi has the following interface groups configured:

- **ISDN Interfaces**: Includes multiple interface types known to be commonly used for ISDN purposes. Interfaces that meet this criteria within the management domain are automatically included in this interface group.

- **Point to Point Interfaces**: Includes multiple interface types known to be commonly used for point-to-point purposes. Any interface within the management domain that meets the defined criteria is automatically included in this interface group.

- **Software Loopback Interfaces**: Includes any interface that is IfType 24, software loopback from the IANA ifType-MIB. Any interface within the management domain that meets this loopback address criteria is automatically included in this interface group.

- **VLAN Interfaces**: Includes interfaces of ifType l2vlan. The NNMi default Monitoring Configuration settings enables fault monitoring for these interfaces, but disable performance monitoring (collection of performance data for VLAN interfaces tends to be problematic).

- **Voice Interfaces**: Includes multiple interface types known to be commonly used for voice purposes. Any interface within the management domain that meets the defined criteria is automatically included in this interface group.

- **Link Aggregation (NNMi Advanced)**: Includes all of the Link Aggregation. Aggregator Interfaces discovered in the network. See Layer 2 Neighbor View Map Objects for more information about Aggregator Interfaces. Use the **Actions | Show Members** option to identify the Link Aggregation Aggregator Interfaces in this group.

Configuring interface groups

Interface groups can be configured by the administrator. The Interface Groups window in the Configuration workspace should be used to configure interface groups.

After we complete the main window configuration, we can use one or both of the filtering tabs:

- **Interface Type Filters**: Here we can set a filter based on the list of interface types we want to include in a filter.

- **Additional filters**: Additional filters can be created based on logical expressions of logical operators (listed in the *Configuring node groups* section) and interface attributes:
    - **ifAlias**: Interface alias, which is set on device by administrator
    - **ifDescr**: Interface description, which is set on device by administrator
    - **ifName**: Interface name, which is set on device by administrator
    - **ifIndex**: Interface index, which is set by manufacturer
    - **IP address**: IP address, which is assigned to interface

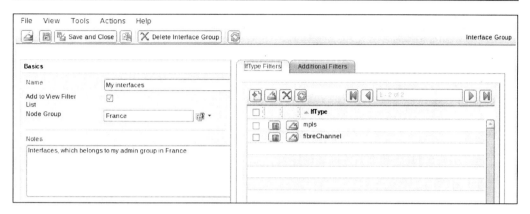

A combination of Interface Type Filters and Additional Filters works as logical AND. In order to pass a filter to an interface, it has to pass Interface Type Filters AND Additional Filters.

Consider the example where we need to create an interface group for a team located in France, who are responsible for MPLS and fiber channel interfaces. The team needs to poll these interfaces every minute, as default corporate configuration to poll interfaces every 5 minutes doesn't comply to their requirements.

An interface group needs to be created for this purpose.

Complete the following steps to create the interface group **My interfaces**:

1. Select **Interface Group** in the **Configuration** workspace.

2. Enter name for interface group—here **My interfaces**.

3. Select the **Quick Find…** option from the **Node Group** drop-down.

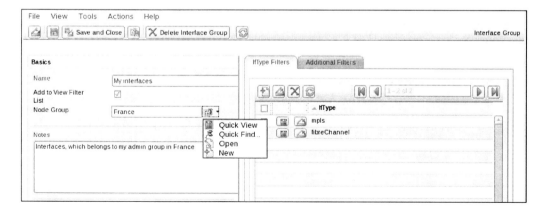

4. Select **France** in a list of **Node Groups** (assuming that this node group is already created).

5. Add notes in this field.

6. Select **IfType** filters tab.

7. Select **New**.

8. Select **Quick Find...** in **ifType** field.

9. Select **mpls** from the list.

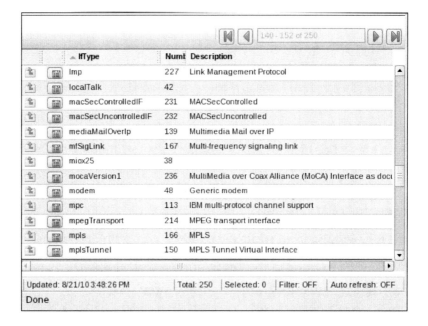

10. Click **Save and Close**.

11. Repeat steps 7 to 10 to add the fiber channel interface group.

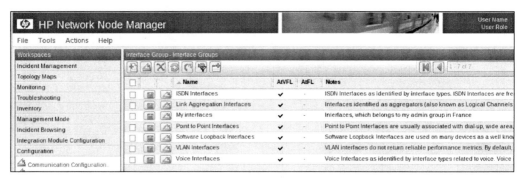

12. Click **Save and Close**.

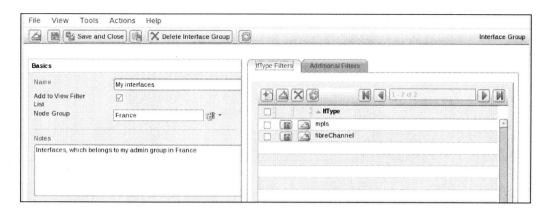

Congratulations! We have just created our interface group.

Path View map configuration

One more troubleshooting tool, which is a built-in tool for NNMi, is Path View. Path View helps identify the root cause of a problem or estimate the impact on other devices. This section provides a description of Path Views and also gives an example on how to configure it.

What is Path View?

Path View displays the path between two selected devices. Some managed networks may not be displayed using Path View if the path between the selected devices has any node that is not managed by NNMi. Such a case is common for ISP network parts, when NNMi doesn't have access to devices in the middle of the network path.

When NNMi cannot determine the path between two nodes, it uses a cloud symbol to fulfil the path between the nodes.

For such cases, NNMi wouldn't have a path between the source and the destination.

Configuring Path View

`PathConnection.xml` can be used to set the connection manually. As it is shown in the following diagram, nodes sw73 and sw70 can be added manually as part of path chain.

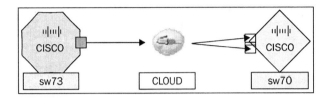

`PathConnection.xml` consists of several elements that determine the path. Some elements are mandatory, whereas some are optional. The following table lists all the elements used in the `PathConnections.xml` file:

Element	Description
`<CONNECTIONS>`	This element is used once in a file and is used to mark all connections that are configured in the `PathConnections.xml` file.
`<CONNECT>`	This element is used to define connections. It is used for every connection we define in a file. All following elements are part of every `<CONNECT>` element.
`<ID>`	This element is optional and identifies the connection.
	It is used when errors about `<CONNECTION>` are reported. If no ID is provided, NNMi sends Not Applicable in a message, otherwise the ID is sent.
`<START>`	Each path view is specified with start and end points for connections.
	This element provides specification of the path connection start and contains the following elements: • `<IP_OR_DNS>` • `<OUTBOUND_INTERFACE_IFINDEX>` • `<NEXT_HOPS>` • `<HOP>`
	No additional parameters are provided by this element.
`<IP_OR_DNS>`	This element provides IP address or DNS name of node where path starts (or ends, if it's used in `<END>` element)
`<OUTBOUND_INTERFACE_IFINDEX>`	This element provides the interface index number (`IfIndex`) of the interface where the path starts.

Element	Description
`<NEXT_HOPS>`	Each path can be described with one or more hops. This element contains `<HOP>` element or elements.
	No additional parameters are provided in this element.
`<HOP>`	This element provides every hop of the path. More than one hop can be used. Hops in Path View will be shown in the sequence we list them in this XML file .
`<END>`	This element describes the end point of Path View and it has the following elements: • `<IP_OR_DNS>` • `<INBOUND_INTERFACE_IFINDEX>`
	No additional parameters are provided with this element.
`<INBOUND_INTERFACE_IFINDEX>`	This element provides the interface index number (`IfIndex`) of the interface where the path ends.

It is important to know that PathView configuration is direction sensitive. In this example, we only set the path from node B to node E. If we want to have a path between node E and node B displayed, we need to add this configuration to the XML file too.

Depending on the OS where NNMi is installed, the `PathConnections.xml` file should be created in the following locations:

- In Unix:

  `/var/opt/OV/shared/nnm/conf/PathConnections.xml`

- In Windows:

  `<install_drive>:\Documents and Settings\All Users\Application Data\HP\HP BTO Software\shared\nnm\conf\PathConnections.xml`

> **Note:** If **RAMS (HP Route Analytics Management System)** is installed, NNMi ignores the `PathConnections.xml` file and uses data from the RAMS-discovered connection database.

Custom Path View—an example

Our initial Path View doesn't have information about the connection between device 10.10.1.1 and 192.168.1.1. We will configure the XML file to include the connection between these nodes with the following nodes between them:

- 10.10.1.254.
- 192.168.1.254.

To fulfil such requirements, the following steps need to be completed:

- `PathConnections.xml` needs to be created (if it is already created, then it needs to be modified)

- Copy file to the following locations:

  For Unix: `/var/opt/OV/shared/nnm/conf/PathConnections.xml`

  For Windows: `<install_drive>:\Documents and Settings\All Users\Application Data\HP\HP BTO Software\shared\nnm\conf\ PathConnections.xml`

Let's create an XML file based on the requirements. For the XML file, we should provide the following information:

- Start node

- Start node outbound interface

- Hostnames or IP addresses of hops we plan to add into Path View

- End node

- End node inbound interface

```xml
<?xml version="1.0" encoding="UTF-8"?>
<CONNECTIONS>
<CONNECT>
<START>
<IP_OR_DNS>10.10.1.1</IP_OR_DNS>
<OUTBOUND_INTERFACE_IFINDEX>3</OUTBOUND_INTERFACE_IFINDEX>
<NEXT_HOPS>
<HOP> 10.10.1.254</HOP>
<HOP>192.168.1.254</HOP>
</NEXT_HOPS>
</START>
<END>
<IP_OR_DNS>192.168.1.1</IP_OR_DNS>
</END>
</CONNECT>
</CONNECTIONS>
```

The two-way PathView in our example would look like the following:

```xml
<?xml version="1.0" encoding="UTF-8"?>
<CONNECTIONS>
<CONNECT>
<START>
<IP_OR_DNS>10.10.1.1</IP_OR_DNS>
<OUTBOUND_INTERFACE_IFINDEX>3</OUTBOUND_INTERFACE_IFINDEX>
```

```
<NEXT_HOPS>
<HOP>10.10.1.254</HOP>
<HOP>192.168.1.254</HOP>
</NEXT_HOPS>
</START>
<END>
<IP_OR_DNS>192.168.1.1</IP_OR_DNS>
</END>
</CONNECT>
<CONNECT>
<START>
<IP_OR_DNS>192.168.1.1</IP_OR_DNS>
<OUTBOUND_INTERFACE_IFINDEX>1</OUTBOUND_INTERFACE_IFINDEX>
<NEXT_HOPS>
<HOP>192.168.1.254</HOP>
<HOP>10.10.1.254</HOP>
</NEXT_HOPS>
</START>
<END>
<IP_OR_DNS>10.10.1.1</IP_OR_DNS>
</END>
</CONNECT>
</CONNECTIONS>
```

User interface configuration

The NNMi console already has designed user interfaces, where all workspaces and menus are prebuilt using a common layout for all windows. But there are some options for the user interface, which can be configured by the administrator:

- **Console timeout**: This parameter defines how long a session can be open if any action is performed. Default value is 18 hours. Minimum value can be set to 1 minute.

- **The map users view when they opens Topology Map:** Here the administrator can set which map should be opened by default.

- **Enable redirect:** This feature can be used with iSPI installed and single sign-on configured. It allows us to redirect URL requests to the hostname, which is used as the official FQDN.

- **Map refresh interval**: The administrator can set how frequently the map should be refreshed.

- **Maximum number of nodes displayed on map**: The administrator can limit the amount of nodes allowed to be shown on the map. This is useful when dealing with large networks. The amount of nodes directly impacts the performance of map visualization.

- **Indicate key incidents**: If this feature is enabled, NNMi enlarges an object if it is the source object for the key incident.

- **Show or hide unlicensed features**: Because NNMi is licensed by features (Advanced Edition and Starter Edition, and SPis, among others), menus, views, or workspaces that have no license installed, are dimed or marked as **Unlicensed**. The administrator can hide unlicensed features by un-checking the **Show licensed features** option. If we have already decided which licenses we will use and no additional licenses are planned to be installed in the near future, it is a good practice to hide them.

To configure these parameters, go to **Configuration | User Interface Configuration**. Depending on whether NNMi 8.x or NNMi 9.x is running, the settings may be accessed through different forms in the **User Interface Configuration** view. The following screenshot provides a view in NNMi 8.x:

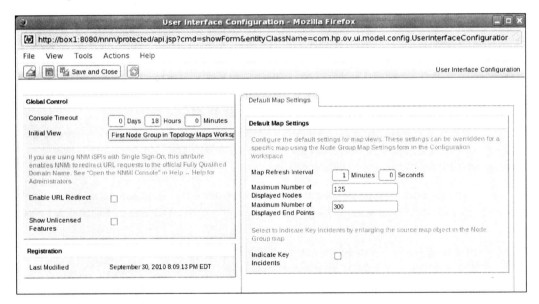

Web browser settings

NNMi console works using an internet browser. This means we don't need to install any additional software and can use NNMi tools using our web browser out of the box.

At the time of writing, NNMi supported Internet Explorer and Mozilla Firefox browsers.

However, every time we try to open a new form or window, it is opened in a new window. There are browser-specific options that allow us to configure Mozilla Firefox or Internet Explorer to open a new form or help window in new tab.

Configuring Mozilla Firefox to open a new tab

To configure Mozilla Firefox, perform the following steps:

1. Open Mozilla Firefox browser.
2. Enter **about:config** in URL line and press *Enter*.

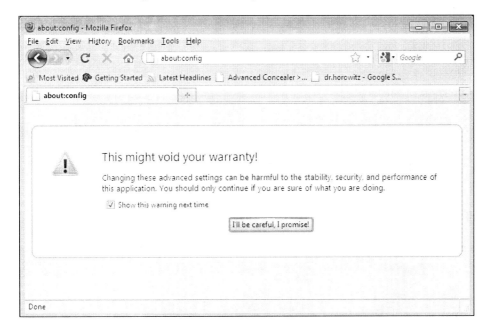

3. If we receive a notification about voiding our warranty, we should click on the **I'll be careful, I promise!** button.
4. Type **newwindow** in the **Filter** field.
5. Open `browser.link.open_newwindow` by double-clicking on link.

6. Set `browser.link.open_newwindow` to **3** and click on **OK**.

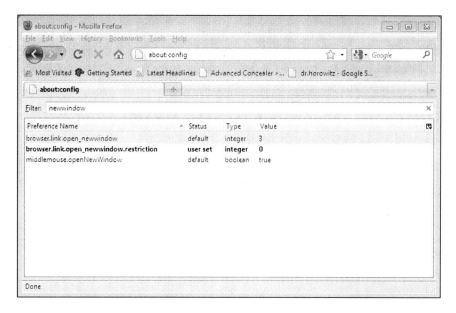

7. Open `browser.link.open_newwindow.restriction` by double-clicking on the link.

8. Set `browser.link.open_newwindow.restriction` to **0** and click **OK**.

Configuring Internet Explorer to open a new tab

To configure Internet Explorer, follow the steps given next:

1. Open Internet Explorer browser.

2. Select **Tools | Internet Options**.

3. Select **General** tab.

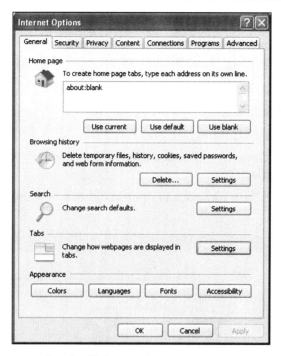

4. Click on **Settings** under the **Tabs** section.

5. Select **Always open pop-ups in a new tab** under the **When a pop-up is encountered** heading in the **Tabbed Browsing Settings** window.

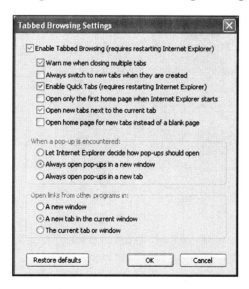

6. We have to click on the **OK** button twice.

Configuring Internet Explorer title bar

This setting allows us to select whether or not the name of the view or form should be displayed in the title bar. To configure, perform the following steps:

1. Open Internet Explorer.

2. Open the **Tools** menu.

3. Select **Internet Options**.

4. Navigate to **Security | Trusted Sites**. Click on the **Custom level...** button. Select **Miscellaneous**.

5. Disable the **Allow websites to open windows without address or status bars** setting.

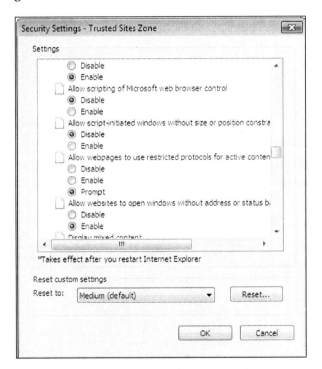

Symbols

NNMi uses map symbols to represent nodes or node groups. Node symbols are designed to represent the following information:

- **Device type**: This can be determined by symbol shape. The following table lists shapes used in NNMi:

Shapes	Description
	Computer, Server, Workstation, Unknown or NON-SNMP devices
	Gateway, Router, Switch-Router
	Switch
	IP phone
	Firewall, Wireless access point, Printer
	Child node group
	Subnet

- **Device status**: This can be determined by symbol color. The following table lists the status colors used in NNMi:

Status color	Description
	Normal
	Warning
	Minor
	Major
	Critical
	Disabled
	No status
	Unknown
	Not in database

- **Vendor and model**: The picture inside the node icon represents the node vendor and model. Vendor and model is determined by the node's system object ID (sysObjID):

Connections between nodes are presented using special symbols. The following table describes the connection icons used in NNMi:

Connection icon	Description
	This icon is used to represent Layer 2 multiple device connections. As an example, it can be a few switches connected via a hub.
	This icon is used in Layer 3 maps and represents an unidentified set of devices. As an example, it can be devices connected via ISP network.
	This icon is used in Layer 3 maps and represents subnets. Network devices which belong to the same subnet, are connected via this network icon.
	This icon is used in Path View maps and represents unknown paths.

There is a difference in map icons even between Layer 2 Neighbor maps and Layer 3 Neighbor maps.

The Layer 2 Neighbor map shows a map of the selected device and any amount of devices connected to it by the selected number of hops.

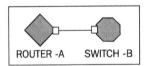

If there is an aggregated link between two nodes, NNMi shows one thick line combining all lines with one aggregated link.

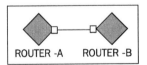

The aggregated port feature is supported by NNMi Advanced. In that case, the link status is calculated based on the status of all links, which are in the same group of a particular Aggregate Connection.

The Layer 3 Neighbor View map, just like a Layer 2 Neighbor Map, shows a map of selected device and devices connected to it by a set number of hops. The difference between Layer 2 and Layer 3 Neighbor Views is that Layer 3 Neighbor View shows router connectivity.

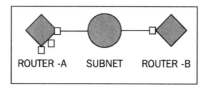

Summary

Now that we have finished this chapter, we are able to configure node groups and node group maps based on provided requirements. We have also learned principles of interface group, Path View configuration, how to set up our local web browser setup to work correctly with NNMi console, and understand the map symbols used in NNMi and what they mean. Also, as we have learned how grouping works, we are ready to design our own configuration requirements, based on our business needs.

The next chapter describes the incidents in NNMi and how we should deal with them.

4
Configuring Incidents

Just like properly configuring discovery and monitoring settings, incident configuration is another key factor that directly influences the monitoring of process efficiency. The challenge for monitoring is not about incident quantity, but it's about the incident quality. This means the more informative the incidents are, the more efficient the operator's job will be.

Incident configuration is a continuous process that never stops. This is because there are always new events that are sent to management system, new equipment with new messages, new technologies implemented, and new responsibilities for staff. New business demands may be another factor for reviewing the monitoring approach, including incidents. Successful operation centers improve their monitoring continuously. Analysts search for new solutions on how to improve monitoring and make it more efficient. There are no clear rules on how two incidents need to be configured in order to have peace of mind for NOC managers. However, based on success stories, there are a few recommendations for building the incident management process:

- It is better to have less outage or any other issues in network that cause incident. In other words, if we had issues in our network and our management tool didn't recognize these issues, here is an opportunity for us to configure monitoring, so that next time such an issue would be notified by the management tool. The best-case scenario would be if incident notification occurred before an issue. We need to review our service desk or helpdesk tickets on a regular basis for new opportunities to improve our system.

- The fewer messages in the incident browser, the better. We shouldn't try to show any possible message in incident view. Operators will be tired of reading meaningless messages and will tend to ignore even important ones. Identify the messages that are meaningful and of use, and have regular reviews of the incident list. Sometimes it's enough just to create additional comments/instructions or modify message text, and we may reduce the time it takes to repair or solve to a great extent.

Of course, the scope and details of our incident process will depend on a few circumstances, such as the environment we are working in, SLA with the customer, quality standards, and so on.

This chapter covers technical incident configuration and the business processes involved in it. The chapter covers the following topics:

- Introduction to incidents
- How incidents come into an NNMi system
- Configuring NNMi SNMP trap forwarding
- Configuring SNMP trap incidents
- Checking if NNMi is receiving SNMP traps
- Controlling the number of incoming traps
- Configuring management events
- Configuring NNM 6.x/7.x events
- Tuning incidents
- Configuring automatic actions

Introduction to incidents

Incidents are events that are important for network monitoring and carry information about changes on managed devices or connections between them. Each incident in NNMi has a level of severity. Each incident also carries information about impact priority. It is an indicator of how urgent the incident is and how fast it should be fixed.

NNMi incidents are presented as messages with several attributes, which help to group and prioritize incidents. Here is a list of incident attributes that are shown in the incident list and the incident details:

Attributes	Description	Possible values
Message	An incident description.	Text configured in incident configuration.
Severity	NNMi incident seriousness, which is calculated by NNMi or set by an administrator.	Normal, Warning, Minor, Major, Critical.
Priority	This field shows how urgent an incident is. Priority is controlled by the user.	• None [5] • Low [4] • Medium [3] • High [2] • Top [1]

Attributes	Description	Possible values
Lifecycle state	This field shows in which state of lifecycle incident currently is. Lifecycle state can be changed by user.	• Registered • In Progress • Completed • Closed
Name	The name of the rule that formats this incident.	This field is set by NNMi.
First occurrence time	This field is used when NNMi is duplicating incidents. This field shows when the incident was received for the first time.	Date and time is provided.
Last occurrence time	This field is used when NNMi is duplicating incidents. This field shows the time of the last incident for the current duplicate incident.	Date and time is provided.
Origin occurrence time	Shows time when incident was received in NNMi.	Date and time is provided.
Assigned to	Displays the user whom the incident is assigned to.	Username is displayed.
Source node	Name of the node that is associated with incident. Note: if a value of <none> is present in source node, it means that NNMi doesn't have information about the source node, that is, SNMP traps sent from NNM 6.x/7.x from nodes, which are not in the NNMi inventory.	Node name is provided.
Source object	This field shows the configuration item of the source node, which causes this incident.	Name of the object is provided.
Category	Shows the category of problem.	• Accounting • Application status • Configuration • Fault • Performance • Security • Status

Attributes	Description	Possible values
Family	Shows the family of the problem to help categorize the problem.	• Address • Aggregated Port • BGP • Board • Chassis • Component Health • Connection • Correlation • HSRP • Interface • License • Node • OSPF • RAMS • RMON • RRP • STP • Trap Analysis • VRRP
Origin	Shows the source type where the incident was generated.	• Management software • Manually created • Remotely generated • SNMP trap
Correlation nature	Shows incident's severity in root-cause calculation.	• Info • None • Root Cause • Secondary Root Cause • Service Impact • Symptom • Stream Correlation
Correlation notes	Shows notes about the incident's correlation status.	
Duplicate count	Shows the number of duplicate messages.	
Root Cause Analysis (RCA)	Shows whether or not an incident is considered as active for root cause analysis. The value is True when it is considered, it is False when it is not considered as active for root cause analysis.	• True • False

Attributes	Description	Possible values
Notes	This field is used as an additional information field to share comments or instructions. Field is limited to 255 characters.	If notes are entered, the note text is displayed.

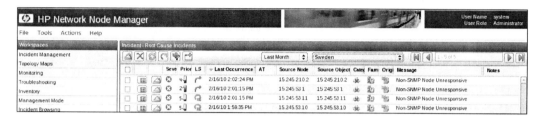

Variables can be used when configuring incidents or using automatic actions. The following tables list possible variables, parameters, and characters that can be used in incident configuration and automatic actions.

The following table describes incident form parameters:

Parameter	Description
$category, $cat	Incident category.
$count, $cnt	Incident duplication count.
$family, $fam	Incident family.
$firstOccurenceTime, $fot	Incident first occurrence time.
$lastOccurenceTime, $lot	Incident last occurrence time.
$lifecycleState, $lct	Incident lifecycle state.
$name	Incident name.
$nature, $nat	Incident nature.
$origin, $ori	Incident origin.
$originOccurenceTime, $oot	Incident origin occurrence time.
$priority, $pri	Incident priority.
$severity, $ser	Incident severity.

Parameter	Description
`$id`	Unique across whole database incident identification number.
`$ifAlias, $ifa`	Interface alias value.
`$firstOccurenceTimeMS, $fms`	Incident first occurrence time, expressed in seconds. Time counted starting from January 01, 1970, 00:00:00 GMT.
`$lastOccurenceTime, $lms`	Incident last occurrence time, expressed in seconds. Time counted starting from January 01, 1970, 00:00:00 GMT.
`$managementAddress, $mga`	SNMP management address value assigned in Node or SNMP Agent forms.
`$oid`	Incident's configuration object identifier from SNMP trap, Management Event, or Remote NNM 6.x/7.x event.
`$otherSideOfConnection, $osc`	Node and interface name of remotely connected object via Layer2 connectivity, if incident's node is part of Layer2 connection. Format: `<FQDN>[interface_name]`
`$otherSideOfConnectionIfAlias, $oia`	Interface alias of remotely connected object via Layer2 connectivity, if incident's node is part of Layer2 connection.
`$otherSideOfConnection ManagementAddress, $oma`	Management address of remotely connected object via Layer 2 connectivity, if selected interface is part of Layer 2 connectivity.
`$originOccurenceTimeMS, $oms`	Time the incident was generated, expressed in seconds. Time counted starting from January 01, 1970, 00:00:00 GMT.
`$sourceNodeUui, $snu`	Universally Unique Object Identifier source node object in incident.
`$sourceNodeName, $snn`	Node name value attribute from Node form.
`$sourceNodeLongName, $sln`	FQDN value attribute from Node form.
`$sourceObjectClass, $soc`	Object class value for the object we want to include.
`$sourceObjectName, $son`	Name of the attribute's source object value.
`$sourceObjectUuid, $sou`	Universally unique object identifier attribute value of incident's source object.
`$uuid`	Incident's universally unique object identifier attribute.

Parameter	Description
`$<position_number>`	Custom incident's attribute position number value, for example, if varbind number 3 is used in SNMP trap, enter $3.
`$<CIA_name>`	Custom incident attribute's name.
`$<CIA_oid>`	Object identifier's value for any custom incident attribute, which originated as a `varbind`.
`$*`	If this variable is used, it means that custom incident attribute values originating as varbinds will be passed to the action configuration.

Parameter	Description
`$text($<position_number>)`	`<position number>` specifies the varbind number, to be used, that is, if we plan to use varbind value in position 3, then $3 should be used.
`$text($<CIA_oid>)`	`<CIA_oid>` argument specifies the object identifier for a custom incident attribute that originated as a varbind.

Parameter	Description
`$*`	This argument returns all parsed string
`, ; &> < (space)	=`	If these special symbols are used they need to be wrapped with double quotes, that is, if we plan to use text SLA&Gold, then use argument "SLA&Gold".
`"" in Jython`	If argument is not used with $, use double quotes for argument enclosure, that is, `jythonMethod($Severity, "My message")`.

More incident descriptions and their links with ITIL can be found in *Chapter 8, Navigation Console and Learning Network Inventory*.

How incidents enter a system

NNMi has three main sources where incidents can come from:

- **Events generated by NNMi:** These incidents are provided by NNMi, where causal engine generates messages if any change or outage is recognized by analyzing the network health. It evaluates network topology and gives root cause messages.

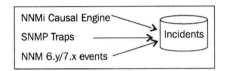

- **SNMP traps:** SNMP trap messages come from managed devices whenever an issue appears on a managed device. Trap type, which can be sent, depends on the SNMP agent capabilities and agent configuration. SNMP trap messages are also analyzed by the causal engine.

- **NNM 6.x/7.x events:** This is a group of events that can be forwarded from the NNM 6.x/7.x management tool to NNMi.

 Before being displayed, every event passes through several stages of the event pipeline. This helps to ensure that important events are not only presented as incidents, but also that all events were evaluated and processed in chronological order. However, we need to note that not all events can become incidents.

Incidents can be closed in the following ways:

- If a problem is solved, that is, the node has been back from down state to normal state, the node down incident is closed automatically.

- Pair-wise configuration includes a particular list of incidents that are received in a specific order, that is, SNMPLinkUp incident automatically closes SNMPLinkDown incident received from the same device.

- Incidents can be closed manually by the operator or administrator.

NNMi causal engine uses a set of rules to determine the root cause of the issue. It evaluates the node status, relationship, fault, and performance data.

NNMi causal engine works in the following ways:

- The causal engine generates messages about problems
- Causal engine closes outdated incidents, that is, the Node Down message is suppressed, if the **Cold Start** message is displayed in the short term interval
- Causal engine creates child incidents if they are related to one problem, that is, if a Node Down message comes, Interface Down incidents become child incidents to Node Down

The NNMi causal engine consists of the following parts:

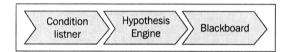

The following table provides a short description of each causal engine part:

Name	Description
Condition listener	Collects status changes and other issues from NNMi services and processes
Hypothesis engine	Analyzes collected data and provides a root cause
Blackboard	Sends messages and updates the device status based on data received from the hypothesis server

Configuring NNMi forwarding SNMP traps

SNMP trap forwarding allows us to configure which incidents should be forwarded to external tools. As an example, it can be a router and switch-related event forwarding to third-party network monitoring tools, or it can be a printer-related trap forward to one of the Help Desk monitoring tools, which takes care of the peripheral equipment. Another example could be specific trap forwarding to an expertise center.

SNMP trap forwarding configuration instructions in this section are provided for NNMi 8.x. Since version NNMi 9.x, the SNMP trap forwarding configuration window has been slightly changed. **SNMP Trap Forwarding Filters** and **SNMP Trap Forwarding Destinations** tabs, which are located in **Configuration | Incident Configuration** in NNMi version 8.x, have now been moved to a newly created view **Configuration | Trap Forwarding Configuration** in NNMi version 9.x. SNMP Trap forwarding instructions remain the same (considering that the mentioned tabs in NNM version 9.x are reachable via the other view).

We need to perform the following steps for SNMP trap forwarding configuration:

1. **Configure SNMPv3 trap forwarding settings**: This step applies only if SNMPv3 is used. User-based security model (USM) needs to be defined in NNMi so that it becomes an authoritative entity in:
   - Sending response to inform-requests (SNMPv3)
   - Forwarding SNMPv3 traps to other devices

   Follow these steps to configure the NNMi management station as an authoritative entity for SNMPv3:

   i. Select **Incident Configuration** in **Configuration** workspace.

   ii. Select **NNMi SNMPv3 Trap Forwarding Security Settings** group.

   iii. Select the NNMi SNMPv3 **Engine ID** value that is assigned to NNMi.

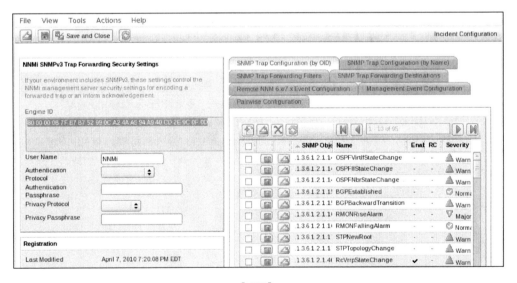

iv. Give this ID to the person who will configure the devices to send SNMPv3 traps

v. Select **Close** to close the window

2. **Configure trap forwarding filters**: SNMP trap forwarding filter is used to list patterns by SNMP OID (object ID), indicating which incidents should be forwarded. Only incidents that pass through the configured filter are forwarded.

 We need to make sure we have used the `nnmincindentcfg.ovpl` tool before we start configuration.

Follow these steps to configure SNMP trap forwarding:

i. Select **Incident Configuration** in **Configuration** workspace

ii. Select **SNMP Trap Forwarding Filters** tab

iii. Select **New** to create the SNMP Trap Forwarding Filter configuration

iv. Fill in required fields

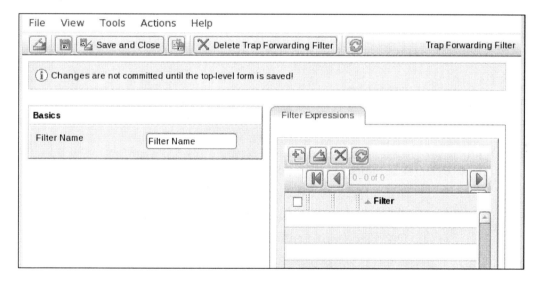

v. Click on **Save and Close** to save SNMP trap configuration form.

vi. Click on **Save and Close** to save Incident Configuration window.

3. **Configure trap forwarding destination**: SNMP trap forwarding destinations allow us to set servers, which need to receive forwarded SNMP traps described in Trap Forwarding Filters.

We need to make sure that we have used the `nnmincidentcfg.ovpl` tool before we start configuring forwarding destinations.

Follow these steps to configure the SNMP trap forwarding destinations:

    i.   Select **Incident Configuration** in **Configuration** workspace

    ii.   Select **SNMP Trap Forwarding Destinations** tab

    iii.   Select **New** to create new SNMP trap forwarding destination configuration

    iv.   Fill in required fields in **Trap Forwarding Destinations form**

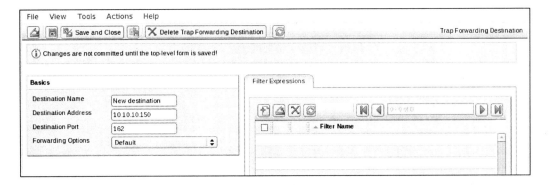

    v.   Click on **Save and Close** to save this form

    vi.   Click on **Save and Close** to save **Incident Configuration** form

4. **Configure trap forwarding filter association**: Here the link between the trap forwarding filters and forwarding destination is set. To configure the trap forwarding association, perform the following steps:

    i.   Select **Incident Configuration** in **Configuration** tab

    ii.   Select **SNMP Trap Forwarding Destination**

    iii.   Open an existing configuration

    iv.   Select **Filter Expressions** tab

    v.   Click on **New** in **Filter Expressions**

    vi.   Fill in required fields

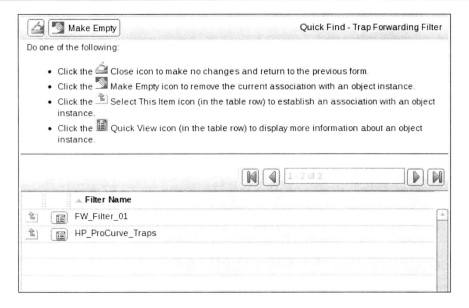

vii. Click on **Save and Close** to save to save this window.

viii.Click on **Save and Close** to save **Incident Configuration** window.

Configuring SNMP trap incidents

SNMP agents can be configured to send information messages to NNMi, providing information about some monitored parameter state changes. For example, the node's interface has been switched to state down or the SNMP agent received the SNMP request using the wrong SNMP community name, Uninterrupted Power Supply (UPS) device switched to battery mode, and UPS started to supply power from its batteries.

There are two kinds of SNMP notifications:

- **SNMP trap messages**: There are SNMPv1 or SNMPv2c traps, these messages are sent without any delivery confirmation response requirement

- **SNMP acknowledged inform messages**: There are SNMPv2c inform requests, the SNMP agent expects a reply message from the notification receiver, otherwise a repeated message is sent

So why does NNMi need SNMP notifications if it already polls network devices and checks for status updates? First of all, not all parameters are polled by network monitoring tools. Secondly, notifications are sent spontaneously when an event occurs, whereas polled messages can be shown only after the next polling cycle.

Here is a list of reasons why SNMP Inform should also be used as an additional source of information for monitoring:

- Notification message is sent spontaneously when an event occurs. No need to wait for the next polling cycle to recognize a problem.
- SNMP notification may send information that cannot be polled by polling engine, that is, UPS device switched to battery mode, SNMP authentication failure messages, environment monitoring sensor has switched state from normal to critical, which may mean smoke detection or open doors detection.

It is recommended to take advantage of SNMP inform as much as possible.

Each device has a different list of notifications that can be sent. The device configuration guide would be the first source of information to learn how to configure equipment for sending traps. Also, the manufacturer's documentation is the best place to find out which notification messages are supported.

In order to send SNMP notification, the managed node and NNMi server needs to be configured accordingly:

- The managed node needs to be configured to send notification messages. The NNMi server address should be provided as the destination address.
- NNMi needs to be configured to receive and display each SNMP notification we plan to receive. By default, NNMi has a list of most commonly used SNMP notifications.

SNMP notifications are identified by SNMP OID. Each message type has its own OID.

By default, UDP port 162 is used for SNMP traps from managed devices to management server.

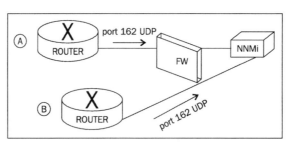

As shown in the preceding diagram, there may be cases when a firewall is connected between the NNMi server and the managed node (case A). Make sure port 162 is opened in our firewall for UDP if it is used between the management station and managed node.

When SNMP traps are received by NNMi server, they have to pass through two stages:

- **NNMi trap service**: This service is managed by nnmtrapconfig.ovpl tool and it maintains its own trap data store. nnmtrapdump.ovpl tool can be used to dump events from this data store.
- **NNMi event subsystem**: This system is controlled by user interface and all traps that pass through the previous stages are stored in the NNMi database.

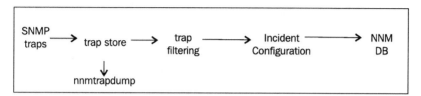

NNMi has to be configured to pass SNMP notifications and create incidents accordingly. Configuration is carried out by trap OID. To open the SNMP trap configuration window, follow these steps:

1. Select **Incident Configuration** in **Configuration** workspace.
2. Select **SNMP trap configuration** tab.
3. Review whether the particular SNMP OID is already configured, otherwise create new one by selecting the **New** icon in the top left corner of the window.

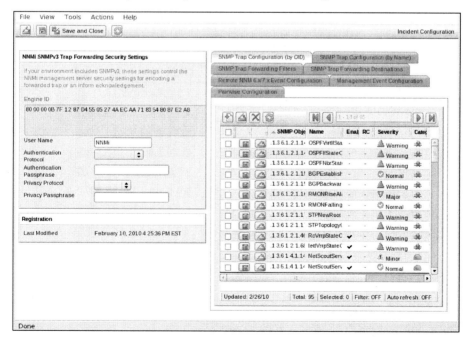

The window view between NNMi version 8.x and NNMi version 9.x may differ slightly. Most screenshots are provided based on NNMi 8.x. These features/tabs, which were introduced in NNM version 9.x, are explained in a separate section in this chapter.

The `allowedOids.conf` file keeps records of the allowed trap list. NNMi passes all the traps that have their ODIs matched with the records in this file. The following provides a list of SNMP traps, which are enabled in NNMi by default:

CiscoWarmStart	SNMPlinkUp
CiscoColdStart	RcnAggLinkUp
SNMPWarmStart	RcAggLinkUp
SNMPColdStart	RcnAggLinkDown
CiscoLinkDown	RcAggLinkDown
CiscoLinkUp	RcnSmltIstLinkUp
HSRPStateChange	RcSmltIstLinkUp
leftVrrpStateChange	RcnSmltIstLinkDown
RcVrrpStateChange	RcSmltIstLinkDown
SNMPLinkDown	

Let's take a look at how to configure some specific equipment. Consider that we have received a task to monitor a Cisco device for Cisco environment-specific messages, as listed in the following table:

Name	OID
Voltage notifications	.1.3.6.1.4.1.9.9.13.3.0.2
Temperature notifications	.1.3.6.1.4.1.9.9.13.3.0.3
Fan notifications	.1.3.6.1.4.1.9.9.13.3.0.4
Redundancy supply notifications	.1.3.6.1.4.1.9.9.13.3.0.5
Voltage status change	.1.3.6.1.4.1.9.9.13.3.0.6
Temperature status change	.1.3.6.1.4.1.9.9.13.3.0.7
Fan status change	.1.3.6.1.4.1.9.9.13.3.0.8
Supply status change	.1.3.6.1.4.1.9.9.13.3.0.9

The following diagram provides steps for what needs to be configured in order to send SNMP traps:

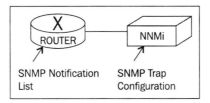

Whilst reading the vendor's documentation, we found out that besides other SNMP traps, bgp and envmon traps can be sent. The SNMP trap groups that can be configured for the Cisco router are: aaa-server, bgp, bstun, calltracker, config, dlsw, ds0-busyout, ds1-loopback, dspu, dsp, entity, envmon, frame-relay, envmon, isdn, msdp, llc2, repeater, rsrb, rsvp, rtr, sdlc, snmp, stun, syslog, tty, voice, x25, and xgcp.

So, instead of enabling all possible traps, we enable only bgp and envmon to be sent to the NNMi server. The router configuration should include the following line:

```
snmp-server host 10.1.1.1 MyCommunityName bgp envmon
```

Here:

- `<10.1.1.1>` is the IP address of NNMi server
- `<MyCommunityName>` is the SNMP trap community name
- `<bgp>` and `<envmon>` are trap groups that should be sent to the monitoring tool

Now, we need to make sure NNMi is configured to receive the following traps:

- BGP: 1.3.6.1.2.1.15.7
- Envmon: 1.3.6.1.4.1.9.9.13.3

To complete this task, perform the following steps:

1. Select **Incident Configuration** in **Configuration** workspace.
2. Select **SNMP Trap Configuration (by OID)** tab. The **SNMP Trap Configuration (by Name)** tab could be selected instead, but as we know the OID of the traps, it is more convenient to sort traps by unique ID. Trap names are assigned by administrator and they can be different than we assume.

3. Find SNMP traps in the configuration window.

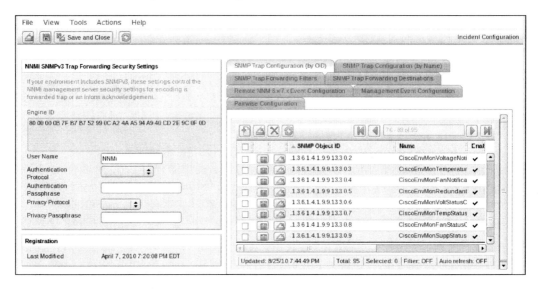

If we find these traps in the SNMP trap configuration window (refer to preceding screenshot), then we need to make sure the configuration fits our needs. Close the configuration window and we are all set. Otherwise, configure such traps to be displayed in NNMi by completing the following steps:

1. Select **Incident Configuration** in **Configuration** workspace.
2. Select the **SNMP Trap Configuration (by OID)** tab.
3. Select **New**.
4. Fill in the fields as follows to configure the voltage notification trap:
   - **Name**: CiscoEnvMonVoltageNotification
   - **SNMP Object ID**: .1.3.6.1.4.1.9.9.13.3.0.2
   - **Enable**: Select checkbox
   - **Root Cause**: Leave unchecked
   - **Category**: **Fault**
   - **Family**: **Component Health**
   - **Severity**: **Critical**
   - **Message format**: **Voltage state change on node component.$1, state $3 ($text($3))**
   - **Description**: **Enter a description for this trap type**

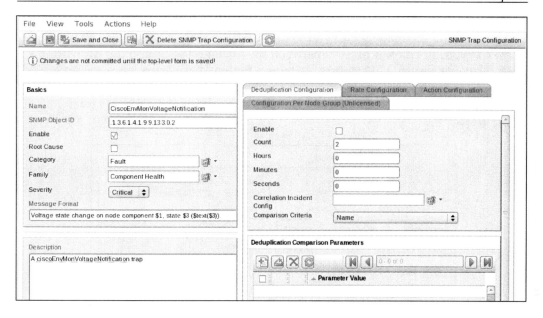

5. Click on **Save and Close**.

6. Complete steps 3 to 5 to configure other SNMP traps listed in the preceding table.

Congratulations! NNMi has been configured to receive our selected traps.

Checking whether NNMi is receiving SNMP traps

One of most common issues faced when dealing with SNMP traps is that some SNMP traps don't appear in the NNMi incident view. For fast and easy troubleshooting, we need to understand how SNMP traps come into NNMi's incident view and what the key points for troubleshooting are.

The following diagram shows a high-level path of the SNMP trap, where the SNMP trap is sent from the managed device to the NNMi management system. In some cases, we wouldn't have a firewall between the managed node and the Network Node Manager server. This picture contains a firewall between a managed node and Network Node Manager server to show a generic situation. We need to take into consideration, while designing, traffic policies or troubleshooting issues related to SNMP traps.

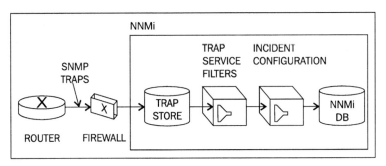

1. In the NNMi server, check if SNMP traps are entering the SNMP trap store.

   i. Run `ovstatus -v ovjboss` to check whether `NnmTrapService` is running. If it's not running, run the `ovstart -v ovjboss` command to start services.

   ii. Check the SNMP trap configuration by running the following command:

   `nnmtrapconfig.ovpl -showProp -u system -p SystemPassword`

   We should get output similar to the following:

   ```
   trapInterface        : All interfaces
   trapPort             : 162
   recvSocketBufSize    : 127 KBytes
   blockTraps           : true
   thresholdRate        : 50 traps/sec
   rearmRate            : 50 traps/sec
   overallThresholdRate : 150 traps/sec
   overallRearmRate     : 150 traps/sec
   windowSize           : 300 secs
   updateSourcesPeriod  : 30 secs
   notifySourcesPeriod  : 300 secs
   minTrapCount         : 25 traps
   numSources           : 10
   databaseQSize        : 300000 traps
   ```

```
pipelineQSize          : 50000 traps
databaseFileSize       : 100 MBytes
databaseFileCount      : 5
loopbackAddrOverride : Empty
```

    i. Check if NNMi trap service storage is increasing by listing the following files and comparing the size during a short time period (every few seconds is fine). Find traplog[0-4] in following path:

        `$NnmDataDir/shared/nnm/databases/traps`

    ii. Dump events from trap store using the following command:

```
nnmtrapdump.ovpl -u system -p SystemPassword \
-source 192.168.1.1 > /tmp/dumpedTraps.txt
```

        We should see output similar to the following:

```
Trap .1.3.6.1.4.1.11.2.17.1.0.61616161 at April 7, 2010
7:22:33 PM EDT from 15.2.115.198

Version: SNMPv1

Enterprise OID: .1.3.6.1.4.1.11.2.17.1

Agent address: 15.2.115.198

Generic trap: 6

Specific trap: 61,616,161

Timeticks: 4


.  .  .


Trap .1.3.6.1.4.1.11.2.17.1.0.61616161 at April 7, 2010
7:22:47 PM EDT from 15.2.115.198

Version: SNMPv1

Enterprise OID: .1.3.6.1.4.1.11.2.17.1

Agent address: 15.2.115.198

Generic trap: 6

Specific trap: 61,616,161

Timeticks: 4
```

[
Dump traps only from a particular device and redirect to file, to make our troubleshooting easier. Dumping traps from all sources would create too many records, so our troubleshooting would be more complicated.
]

If SNMP traps are not coming through, then we should check whether we have firewall between the managed device and NNMi server.

2. Check if SNMP traps are not filtered by **SNMP trap service filters**. This filter has two definitions: `List of allowed trap OIDs` and `List of blocked OIDs`.

   To see the configuration, we need to run the following command:

   `nnmtrapconfig.ovpl -dumpBlockList \ -u system -p SystemPassword`

   In order for the trap to be passed further to the NNMi incident list, SNMP trap OID needs to be listed in `List of allowed trap OIDs` part of the file. Also, SNMP trap needs to be loaded using the following command:

   `nnmincidentcfg.ovpl -loadTraps`

3. **Check whether traps are not filtered by** `nnmtrapd.conf` **file**: This is a configuration file where traps can be filtered by source. The `nnmtrapd.conf` file lists SNMP trap OIDs that should be blocked. Each line represents a trap, including source IP address. Wildcards ("*" symbol) and ranges ("-" symbol) can be used when defining IP addresses and OIDs. Each line can contain one or more IP addresses separated by a comma (","), and only one OID, per line. File syntax is as follows: `<IP_Address,Event_OIDs>`

   For example, to block the SNMP trap with OID .1.3.6.1.4.1.11.2.17.1.0.58915891 from all nodes, OID .1.3.6.1.4.1.11.2.17.1.0.58915892 from node 192.168.1.2, and whole 10.10.1.x network, the configuration file would look like the following:

   ```
   <*.*.*.*, .1.3.6.1.4.1.11.2.17.1.0.58915891>
   <10.10.1.*, .1.3.6.1.4.1.11.2.17.1.0.58915892>
   ```

   If a line starts with # symbol, it is considered a comment line and ignored from processing.

   To read more about `nnmtrapd.conf`, refer to the next section.

4. **Check if the SNMP trap is configured in SNMP trap configuration as an incident**: This configuration can be checked using NNMi console. Complete the following steps to check if the trap is configured:

   i. Select **Incident Configuration** in the **Configuration** workspace

   ii. Select one of the following two tabs: **SNMP Trap Configuration (by OID)** or **SNMP Trap Configuration (by Name)**

   iii. Locate trap in the listed window. If we cannot find it, it means it is not configured

5. **Check if SNMP trap incident is enabled**: If the SNMP trap OID is not enabled in the SNMP trap incident configuration window, it won't be passed to the NNMi console. It will also be listed in the `List of blocked OIDs` section of Block List in the trap configuration tool. To enable an incident, complete the following steps:

   i. Select **Incident Configuration** in the **Configuration** workspace

   ii. Select one of the following two tabs: **SNMP Trap Configuration (by OID)** or **SNMP Trap Configuration (by Name)**

   iii. Locate trap in listed window and select **Open**

6. Check **Enable** in the SNMP trap incident configuration window.

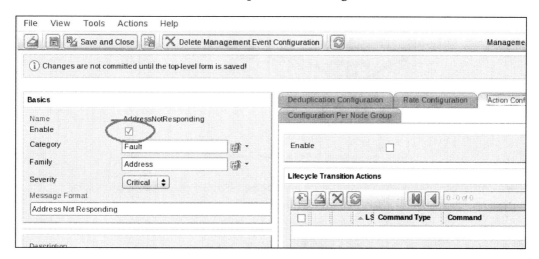

   i. Click on **Save and Close** to save current window

   ii. Click on **Save and Close** to save General Incident configuration window

The following diagram represents the SNMP trap incident troubleshooting workflow:

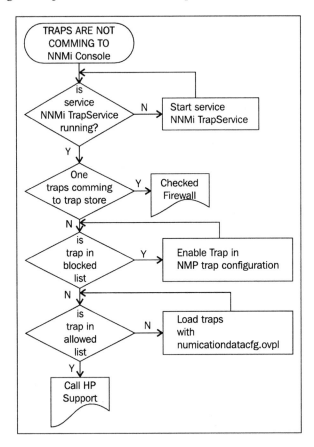

If we complete all the described steps and none of these steps help, then it is necessary to contact HP support about this issue.

Controlling the number of incoming SNMP traps

The fact that our NNMi console doesn't have too many SNMP trap incidents doesn't mean that we are doing fine with the number of SNMP trap incidents. As shown in the second diagram in the *Configuring SNMP trap incidents* section, there are two places where events are stored — the SNMP trap store and NNMi database. We should take care about both of them as:

- The NNMi database can store 100,000 traps. When this limit is reached, no more traps are stored in the NNMi database. We, as an administrator, should trim the database to make more space available for new incidents. *Chapter 6, Troubleshooting, Security, and Backup*, has instructions on how to trim the NNMi database. We should receive a notification when the database is about to fill up.

- The trap store continues storing SNMP traps even after the 100,000 figure has been reached. It stores these incidents using FIFO (First in, first out) model and deletes the oldest incidents. At the time of writing, there was no possibility to extend the number of maximum events. According to HP support, HP was working on improvements already.

As administrators, we should periodically analyze incidents that are received by NNMi. There are two ways of maintaining the incident database:

- **Periodically trimming database**: Depending on the amount of SNMP traps received, this job may need to be done every few days to every few months

- **Periodic analyzing**: Analyze SNMP traps and filter traps that don't carry any valuable information

 Note: This step doesn't prevent us from trimming the database, but can expand this period from several percents to several hundred of times.

SNMP traps can overfill our database because of several reasons, such as one or a few devices send too many traps, and one or a few traps are sent from most, if not all devices, which are meaningless for us. So, we need to analyze our SNMP traps accordingly — checking TOP nodes by the amount of traps and TOP traps sent by any device. NNMi, at the time of writing, doesn't have built-in reports for such analysis; it is recommended to export incidents to external analysis tools. One of them can be Excel from Microsoft, Spreadsheets from OpenOffice, or Numbers from Apple. To export incidents, we can use following command:

```
nnmtrimincidents.ovpl -age 1 -incr days -origin SnmpTrap \
-archiveOnly -u system -p SystemPassword
```

 We can use the Help option to see more options for this tool.

After we complete our analysis, we should have a list of SNMP traps OID and/or a list of nodes we want to block.

Note that we need to follow these steps if we cannot block incidents on the managed node side. Blocking on the managed node side would save the managed device, network, and NNMi resources. Otherwise, we would fix the real source. Blocking traps on the NNMi side is acceptable when we have no way to fix on the managed node side, that is:

- We have no access to the device that sends traps
- Traps that we want to filter are part of a group of traps, where some of them need to be sent

The nnmtrapd.conf file should be configured in order to block some traps. The file is located at the following address:

- For Unix: $NnmDataDir/shared/nnm/conf/nnmtrapd.conf
- For Windows: %data_dir%\shared\nnm\conf\nnmtrapd.conf

To block all traps from 192.168.1.1 node, use the following syntax in the file: <192.168.1.1,.*>, where ".*" is a wildcard for all SNMP traps from a particular node. To make these changes effective, force NNMi to re-read the configuration file using the following command:

```
nnmtrapconfig.ovpl -readFilter -u system -p SystemPassword
```

We need to make sure that the changes were effective and run the following command:

```
nnmtrapconfig.ovpl -dumpBlockList -u system -p SystemPassword
```

We should see changes in the **List of blocked source addresses** tab:

List of blocked source addresses

192.168.1.1

To block SNMP trap OID from all or a list of nodes, use wildcard syntax in the file. The following example line blocks the traps with OID .1.3.6.1.4.1.9.9.179.0.1 from devices with IP address range 192.168.1.1-255:

```
<192.168.1.*, .1.3.6.1.4.1.9.9.179.0.1>
```

We need to note that if we plan to block more than one OID for the same device, we should add the OID in the same line. We shouldn't use a separate line for the same node, as the first line that passes the node filter is effective and all the other records will be ignored. This means that if we want to add SNMP OID .1.3.6.1.4.1.9.9.179.0.5, we would use:

```
<192.168.1.*, .1.3.6.1.4.1.9.9.179.0.1,.1.3.6.1.4.1.9.9.179.0.5>
```

Also, if we have MIB loaded for traps, we can use the Incident Configuration window to disable the incident. It doesn't make any difference, from the performance point of view, comparing to a manual modification of the `nnmtrapd.conf` file, as the Incident Configuration window uses the same file for enabling/disabling incidents. As an administrator, changing the file directly may be more convenient, as we can use wildcards in the `nnmtrapd.conf` file.

Configuring management events

Management events from an incident configuration point of view are similar to other types of events—SNMP traps or NNM 6.x/7.x events. The only difference is the source that sends these events.

To configure Management Events, perform the following steps:

1. Select **Incident Configuration** in the **Configuration** workspace.
2. Select **Management Event Configuration** tab.
3. Select **New** to create a new incident configuration.
4. Fill in required fields in **Management Event Configuration form**.

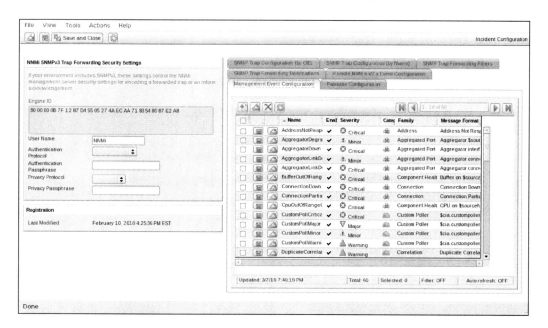

5. Click on **Save and Close** to save this window.
6. Click on **Save and Close** once again to save the incident configuration form.

Once it is saved, events are processed by NNMi's event pipeline according to the latest saved event configuration.

You can read more about incident configuration in the *Configuring SNMP trap incidents* section.

Configuring NNM 6.x/7.x events

NNM 6.x/7.x events, from an incident configuration point of view, are quite similar to SNMP trap events or management events. The only difference is the source that sends these events. It is external NNM 6.x or NNM 7.x management system. They need to be configured on NNMi as external management stations. This integration also allows access to dynamic views of forwarded events from the management station.

Also, NNMi can be configured as a management console for NNM 6.x or NNM 7.x management station users, as NNMi has the ability to create user profiles with different views. Users with filtered messages from a particular management station can be created. It also avoids the hassle of remote console installation, giving HTTP access instead.

For such NNM 6.x/7.x incident configuration, we need to perform the following steps:

- Remote NNM 6.x/7.x management stations need to be configured in NNMi
- Remote NNM 6.x/7.x events need to be configured in NNMi

To configure remote NNM 6.x/7.x management stations, complete the following steps:

1. Select **Management Stations** from the **Inventory** workspace.
2. Select **New** to configure a new remote management station.
3. Fill in the following fields in the **Management Station** form:
   - Management station IPv4 address
   - Management station **ovas** port number
   - NNM 6.x/7.x web server port number
4. Click on **Save and Close** to save this window.
5. If this is the first NNM 6.x/7.x management station in configuration, then restarting the NNMi console is needed. Restart does not apply to any additional configuration of subsequent remote management stations.

When we have completed the management station configuration, configure Management Events using the following steps:

1. Select **Incident Configuration** in the **Configuration** workspace.
2. Select **Management Event Configuration** tab.
3. Select **New** to create a new incident configuration.
4. Fill in the required fields in the **Management Event Configuration form**.

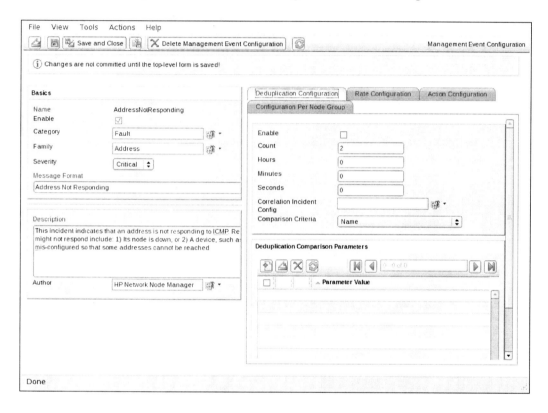

5. Click on **Save and Close** to save this window.
6. Click on **Save and Close** once again to save the incident configuration form.

Once it is saved, events are processed by NNMi's event pipeline according to the latest saved event configuration.

To read more about incident configuration, read the *Configuring SNMP trap incidents* section.

Tuning incidents

There are many cases when managed equipment starts sending us repeated events, which means the same issues. Sometimes it even causes event storms. As administrators, we need to take care that only meaningful events enter a system.

In general, we can define two major areas where alarms can potentially cause load issues:

- **Managed nodes are sending too many useless traps**: It is good practice to minimize the amount of messages that are sent from managed devices. First of all, it consumes network traffic. Also, both managed devices and the NNMi server are loaded processing these traps. Especially, it may be important if our network devices are busy enough with business critical traffic. Here the SNMP agent should be configured to send only important traps.

- **Too many incidents are on the management server**: This can be due to several reasons, such as:

  ° There is no way to filter traps on the managed device

  ° Issues happening too often on your network, that is, flapping interface

  Here, we can filter some events out or configure a correlation to minimize incidents.

The following diagram displays these two scenarios. The diagram also displays a third scenario that can make a correlation based on incoming events.

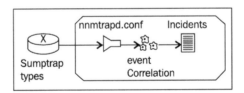

The NNMi event correlation feature provides three ways to reduce the number of events without sacrificing information efficiency. That is, if the interface from "Down" state comes into "Up" state, the "down" event is not needed anymore. Or, when a device repeatedly sends SNMP authentication failure events, such events don't have to be displayed every single time it is received; instead, only the first event could be displayed and then a number of duplicates can be shown.

NNMi provides event reduction functionality, using the following types of correlation:

- Pair wise
- Deduplication
- Rate
- Interface settings
- Node settings
- Suppression
- Enrichment
- Dampening
- Forward to Global Managers

Pairwise

Some of the incidents may be paired by logical meaning, for example, Node Down and Node Up events. Once a Node Up event has been received, there is no need to display a Node Down event and it can be suppressed by a Node Up event. These events can be paired and one can suppress the other. If an Interface Up event came after an Interface Down event appeared, there is no need to keep the Interface Down event, the last known interface status is already UpNNMi and provides a list of events that are already configured for pairwise correlation. As administrator, we can also create our own pairwise configurations.

Incidents that are suppressed are marked as child incidents, whereas incidents that initiated correlation are marked as parent incidents in incident relationship configuration. This relationship is displayed in the **Correlated children** tab.

To configure new pairwise incidents, complete the following steps:

1. Select **Incident Configuration** in the **Configuration** workspace.
2. Select **Pairwise Configuration** tab.
3. Select **New** to configure new pairwise incident and fill in required fields.

4. If our pairwise configuration is related to messages that have the same OID, then define the custom incident attributes with values that help identify correlated incidents.

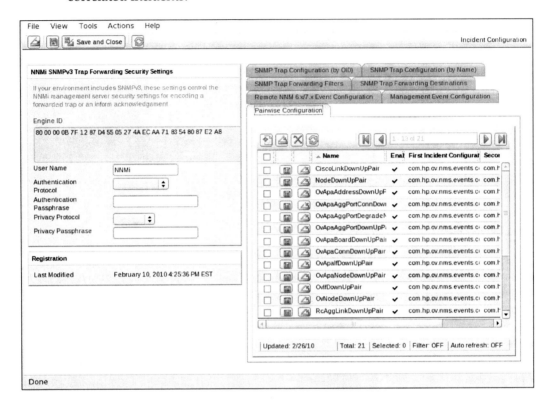

5. Click on **Save and Close** to save this form.

6. Click on **Save and Close** to save the **Incident Configuration** window.

The following table shows the pairwise incidents configuration fields.

Name	Description
Name	The name for the pairwise configuration. This must be unique.
Enable	Enables/disables configuration. Circuit is enabled if checkbox is checked.
First Incident Configuration	Provide an incident that will be the first in an arrival sequence. Use drop-down list to select an incident.
Second Incident Configuration	Provide an incident that will be the second in an arrival sequence. Use drop-down list to select an incident.
Description	Provide description for this configuration.

The next table provides a description of pair item fields used in configuration.

Name	Description
First In Pair	First incident in the pair identity, expressed as one of the following: • SNMP trap varbind ASN.1 value (OID) • SNMP trap varbind position number • Custom attribute "Name" value
Second In Pair	Second incident in the pair identity, expressed as one of the following: • SNMP trap varbind ASN.1 value (OID) • SNMP trap varbind position number • Custom attribute "Name" value

A general recommendation would be to tune the system on a regular basis (such as once a month). One of the scenarios could be to export all the incidents for all periods to Excel and make the following reports:

- **Worst event report**: Group by incident, where a list of unique incidents would be provided, along with the number of times a particular incident was found. This report gives us information on which events should be investigated more accurately. Experience shows that the first 5 to 10 events generate 40 to 70 percent of all incidents. So, if we can handle these few incidents, we have removed a big part of the incident load.

- **Worst device report**: Group nodes by the amount of incidents they have received. This may give us some clue about improving monitoring. It may indicate that a device needs replacement, configuration tuning, or other improvements. Again, experience tells us that five percent of devices generate 40 to 70 percent of all incident traffic.

Deduplication

This type of correlation suppresses incidents that have the same attributes defined in the deduplication configuration settings. An incident can be configured to match an incident for deduplication.

Deduplicated incidents are suppressed and only the following values change in the original event:

- The original event shows the number of already deduplicated incidents. Depending on the deduplicated incidents, this allows us to have an idea of how important an incident is. Operators use this field as the priority input.

- It also shows the date and time when the incident was received for the first and last time. This gives operators information on the time range when the incident was active.

The following restrictions/limitations apply:

- Duplicate Count is updated every 30 seconds. This parameter cannot be changed.

- We can have one deduplication configuration per incident. This means that no other deduplicate configurations can be created for the same incident.

- Duplicates are updated no matter what lifecycle state they are have, that is, if the deduplicate incident is in the *Closed* state, it still receives duplicates (if there are any).

- `ovjboss` process restart clears out all correlation counters. This means that all counts and parent incidents are lost after ovjboss restart.

 This chapter provides examples of deduplication configuration for NNMi version 8.x. The deduplication configuration window has been moved in NNMi version 9.x, to inside the incident configuration window. To reach this window, select **Configuration workspace | Incident Configuration**. Open a selected incident and select the **Deduplication** tab.

To configure deduplication, follow these steps:

1. Select **Incident Configuration** in the **Configuration** workspace.

2. Select incident type as **SNMP Trap Configuration, Remote NNM 6.x/7.x Event Configuration** or **Management Event Configuration**.

3. Click on **New** to create a new deduplication configuration, and click on **Open** to modify an existing deduplication configuration.

4. Select the **Deduplication** tab and fill in the required fields.

5. Click on **Save and Close** to close the **Deduplication Configuration** window.

6. Click on **Save and Close** to close the **Incident Configuration** window.

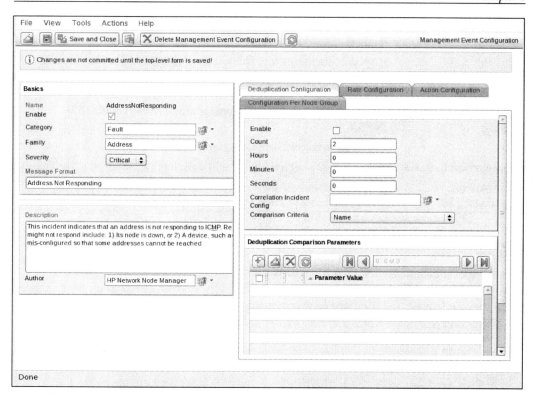

The next table lists the configuration fields and the descriptions, used in deduplication incident configuration:

Name	Description
Enable	Enables/disables configuration. Circuit is enabled if checkbox is selected.
Count	Amount of deduplicate incidents stored at one time in NNMi. For example, if five incidents are set and more than five incidences are received, NNMi releases from memory the oldest one, making space for the next incident, and so on.
Hours	Specifies how much time NNMi suppresses duplicate incidents. This means if one hour is selected, all duplicate incidents will be suppressed within one hour after the first incident is shown.
Minutes	Minute time intervals specifying how much time NNMi suppresses duplicate incidents. This means if one minute is selected, all duplicate incidents will be suppressed within one minute after first incident is shown.

Name	Description
Seconds	Time interval specifying how many seconds NNMi suppresses duplicate incidents for. This means if one second is selected, all duplicate incidents will be suppressed within one second after the first incident is shown.
Correlation Incident Config	Enables us to use deduplication configurations provided by NNMi.
	We need to select **Duplicate Correlation** as a default value.
Comparison Criteria	Select a group which NNMi will define the incident as a duplicate.
Comparison Parameter List	This is optional. At least one row in a table should be populated if the **Comparison Criteria** option is selected.

Rate

This type of incident correlation measures the incoming incident rate within a configured time range. In other words, if rate incident is configured at a rate of three within five minutes, the incident to the message browser will appear only if the NNMi received at least three incidents during the last five minute interval.

The following diagram displays an example where the rate correlation is configured at a rate of three within five minutes. Above the time line are events that are coming into NNMi, and the ones below the timeline are incidents that are generated and sent to a message browser based on the rate correlation.

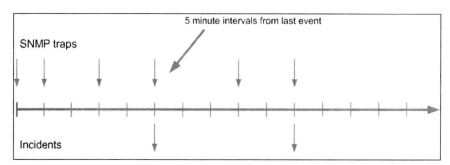

 This chapter provides examples of rate configuration for NNMi version 8.x. The rate configuration window has been moved in NNMi version 9.x to within the incident configuration window. To reach this window, select **Configuration workspace | Incident Configuration**. Open a selected incident and select the **Rate** tab.

NNMi already has some out-of-the-box rate incidents configured. As an administrator, we can always create and add our own rate incidents. To add a new rate incident, complete the following steps:

1. Select **Incident Configuration** in the **Configuration** workspace.

2. Select **SNMP Trap Configuration, Remote NNM 6.x/7.x Event Configuration** or **Management Event** configuration tab.

3. Select **New** to create a new rate incident.

4. Select the **Rate Configuration** tab and fill in the required fields for **Rate Configuration**.

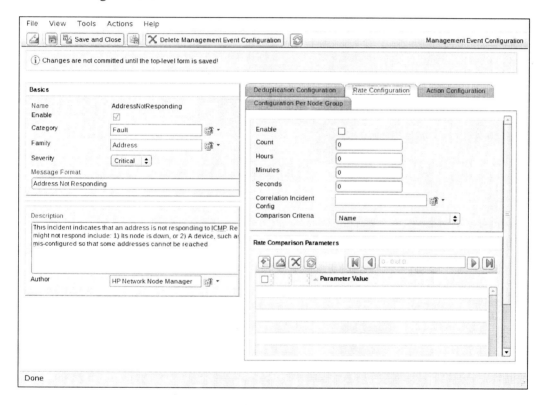

5. Click on **Save and Close** to save the existing window.

6. Click on **Save and Close** to save the **Incident Configuration** form.

The following table provides fields used in the rate configuration process:

Name	Description
Enable	Enables/disables configuration. Circuit is enabled if checkbox is checked.
Count	Number of repeated incidents required to trigger an action in Rate Configuration.
Set the time period (**hours**, **minutes**, and **seconds**)	The time period within which counts are measured.
Correlation Incident Config	The **Rate Correlation** configuration option should be selected by choosing from the drop-down list.
Comparison Criteria	The group of attributes that are compared in this circuit. Select a group from a list provided in this configuration field.
Comparison Parameter List	This is optional. At least one row in a table should be populated if the **Comparison Criteria** option is selected.

Interface settings

Interface settings for the incident configuration feature was introduced in NNMi 9.0. It allows incident suppression, enrichment, dampening, or action launching for selected interface groups.

The interface settings supersede the default settings and node settings of incident configuration. The following is how incident configuration is applied, based on interface and node settings:

1. Interface settings
2. Node settings
3. Default incident settings

For example, if the default incident configuration is configured to run an automatic action that sends an e-mail to the network operations center operator group, the node settings are configured to run an automatic action that sends an e-mail to the network operations center supervisor, and the interface group is configured to run an automatic action that sends an e-mail to the manager of the department. If an incident occurs that passes the interface, node, and default settings filter, then an e-mail would be sent to the departmental manager. Another example could be if the incident doesn't pass the interface settings filter, but passes the node settings and default settings filter, then an e-mail would be sent to the supervisor. Only if neither the node nor the interface settings filter is passed, an e-mail would be sent to the operator group.

To configure the Interface Settings, complete the following steps:

1. Select **Incident Configuration** in the **Configuration** workspace.

2. Open the incident we want to apply configuration to (SNMP traps, Remote NNM 6.x/7.x, or Management Events).

3. Select the **Interface Settings** tab.

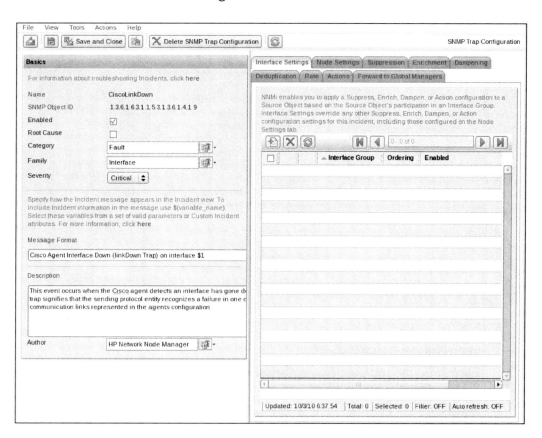

4. Click on the **New** button to create a new configuration.

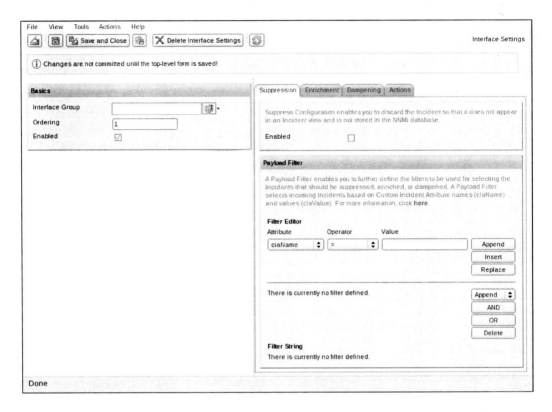

5. Select interface group in the **Interface Group** field to which we would like to apply this configuration.

6. Enter ordering number. Remember, the lower the number, the higher the priority.

7. Make sure the **Enabled** field is checked.

8. Select the **Suppression**, **Enrichment**, **Dampening**, or **Actions** tab, depending on which configuration we want to apply to these Interface Settings. Configure these tabs accordingly.

9. Configure the Payload filter using Filter Editor, if further definition of the filter is needed.

10. Click **Save and Close**.

Node settings

Node settings for the incident configuration feature were introduced in NNMi 9.0. It allows incident suppression, enrichment, dampening, or action launching to be applied for selected node groups.

Node settings supersede the default settings but are superseded by the interface settings of incident configuration. The following is how Incident Configuration is applied, based on interface and node settings:

1. Interface settings
2. Node settings
3. Default incident settings

For example, if default incident configuration is configured to run an automatic action that sends an e-mail to the network operations center operator group, then the node settings are configured to run an automatic action that sends an e-mail to the network operations center supervisor and the interface group is configured to run an automatic action that sends an e-mail to the manager of the department. If an incident occurs, which passes the interface, node, and default settings filter, an e-mail to the department manager would be sent. As an alternative example, if incident doesn't pass the interface settings filter, but passes node settings and default settings filter, then e-mail would be sent to the supervisor. And only if neither the node nor the interface settings filter is passed, an e-mail to the operators group would be sent.

To configure the node settings, complete the following steps:

1. Select **Incident Configuration** in the **Configuration** workspace.
2. Open the incident we want to configure (SNMP traps, Remote NNM 6.x/7.x, or Management Events).

3. Select the **Node Settings** tab.

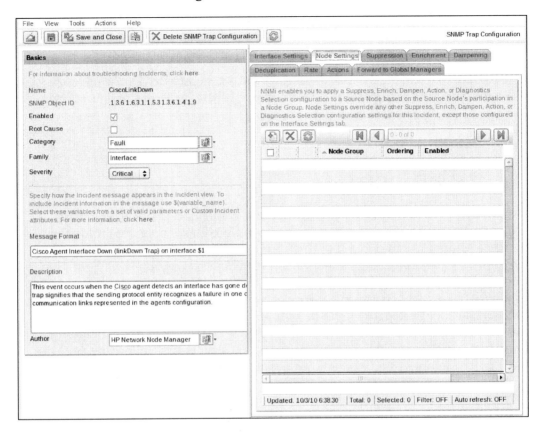

4. Click on the **New** button to create a new configuration.

5. Select the node group in the **Node Group** field to which we would like to apply the configuration.

6. Enter ordering number. Remember that the lower the number, the higher the priority.

7. Make sure the **Enabled** field is checked.

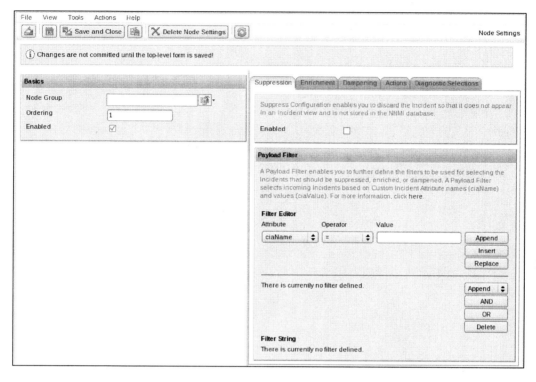

8. Select the **Suppression**, **Enrichment**, **Dampening**, or **Actions** tab, depending on which configuration we want to apply to these interface settings. Configure these tabs accordingly.

9. Configure the Payload filter using Filter Editor, if further definition of the filters is needed.

10. Click **Save and Close**.

Suppression

The suppression feature was introduced in NNMi 9.0. Using suppression, incidents can be suppressed based on interface group, node group, or default suppression can be used. Suppression is applied in the following order (the first matched suppression is applied):

1. Interface group

2. Node group

3. Enrich configuration settings without specifying an interface group or node group

For example, if an incident needs to be suppressed only if it is generated by a selected interface group, suppression should be applied to a particular suppression group. When the incident is suppressed, it does not appear in Incident View, and it is not stored in the NNMi database either.

The following is a screenshot of the **Suppression** tab:

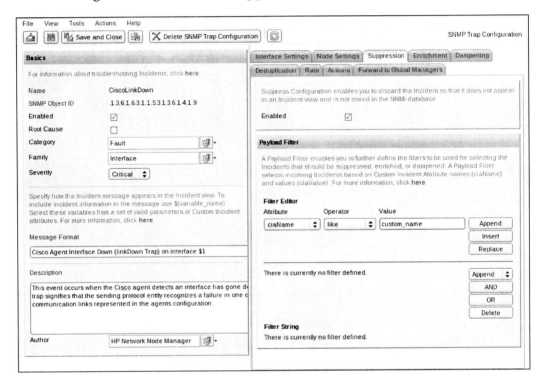

To enable suppression, the **Enabled** checkbox needs to be checked and the payload filter configured. Using Filter Editor, a combination of attributes can be applied as a filter. For example, if VIP customers has a value of "VIP" set in a custom incident attribute (cia.name), enter the value as "VIP" in cia.name attribute and such a filter would be applied to all VIP customers (which have a record in the cia.name field).

Enrichment

The enrichment feature was introduced in NNMi 9.0. Enrichment allows the incident's category, family, severity, priority, correlation nature, message format and "assigned to" values to be changed, and custom incident attributes can be added to the incident before it is stored in the NNMi database.

Enrichment settings are applied in following order:

1. Interface group
2. Node group
3. Enrich configuration settings without specifying an Interface group, or Node group

The following are screenshots from the Enrichment configuration windows:

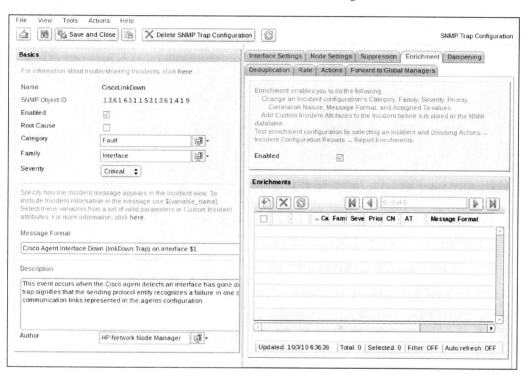

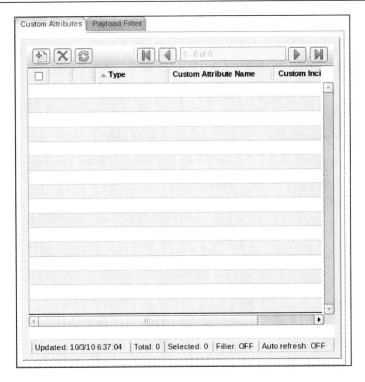

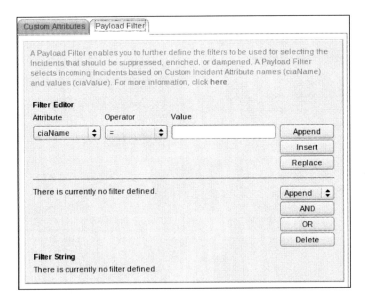

Dampening

The incident dampening feature was introduced in NNMi 9.0. It allows the following incident configuration:

- Incident to be displayed in NNMi console
- Execute automatic action assigned to incident
- Execute the Diagnostics (applied if iSPI NET is installed)

The following is the screenshot of incident Dampening configuration:

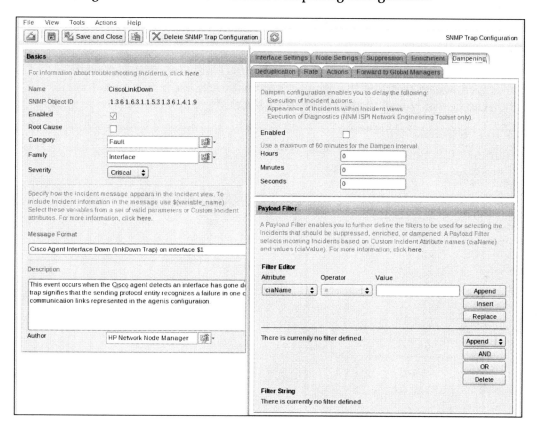

Configuring automatic actions

Additional automatic actions can be initiated based on incidents and their state in NNMi. Such actions are called automatic actions. The following incident types can have the automatic actions configured:

- NNMi management events
- SNMP traps
- NNM 6.x or NNM 7.x events

Automatic actions generate trouble tickets or e-mail messages to be sent when an incident is registered, as well as close a trouble ticket or send another e-mail when the incident is closed.

Starting from NNMi version 9.00, Interface Settings and Node Settings were introduced, which enriched the usage of automatic actions, where an automatic action can be configured to apply only for a selected group of interfaces or nodes.

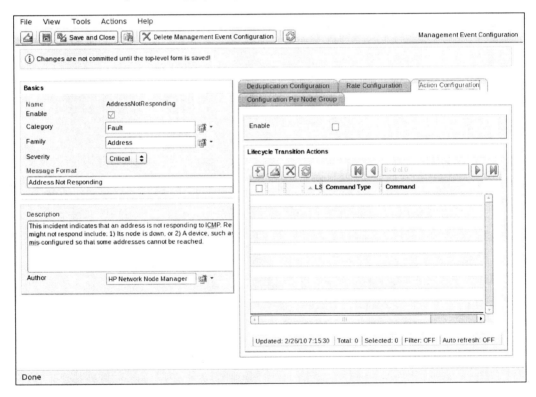

Compared to previous NNMi versions (version 7.x and earlier), the automatic action feature has expanded, as they can be launched based on incident lifecycle status. Also, multiple actions can be created for the same incident.

Automatic actions are configured in the following way:

- We need to make sure that jython files are copied into an action folder before we start configuring the automatic action
- Automatic action is assigned to the incident that meets the configured conditions

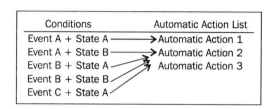

To configure the automatic action for an incident, follow this sequence:

1. Click on **Incident configuration** in the **Configuration** workspace.
2. Select one of the following tabs: **SNMP trap configuration, Remote NNM 6.x/7.x Event Configuration, Management Event Configuration**.
3. Select **New** icon.
4. Select **Action Configuration** tab.
5. Click on the **New** icon to create the action configuration.
6. Enter required information in the **Lifecycle Transition Action** form.

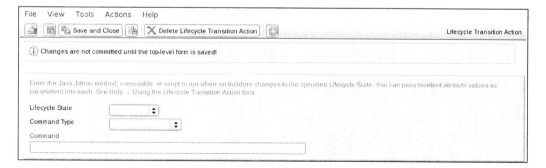

7. Click on **Save and Close**.

8. Click on **Save and Close** on the **SNMP trap, Remote 6.x/7.x Event Management**, or **Management Event Configuration** form.

9. Click on **Save and Close** on the **Incident Configuration** form.

10. Click on **Save and Close** on the main form window.

To troubleshoot issues related to automatic actions, please check following log file: `eventActions.*.*.log`.

The file is located in the following location:

- In Unix: `$NnmDataDir/log/nnm/`
- In Windows: `%NnmDataDir%\log\nnm`

A list of parameters that can be used is listed in the section *Introduction to incidents*.

Summary

This chapter has finished a major part of monitoring activities that are visible to the user and considered as a major part of the implementation. We are now ready to install the management tool, discover our network, and configure incidents to be displayed for monitoring.

The next chapter starts with the less visible part of system configuration, but it doesn't mean it's less important. I would say the first part is a must for monitoring, but the second shows the maturity level of the network operations center and/or administrator as it is about system stability, performance, and security.

5

Controlling Access to NNMi

The NNMi version was introduced with improved access control to NNMi. It allows users to be created and authenticated. Users can be assigned to user roles, which define what permissions will be given to a user. There was also the introduction of the ability to integrate user authentication into Directory Services using LDAP.

The following features were one more major step towards improving NNMi. This chapter describes how to control access to NNMi and which authentication model to choose.

The following topics will be covered in this chapter:

- Creating users in NNMi
- NNMi user roles
- NNMi authentication types
- Command line access configuration tools
- User activity audit

How access to NNMi works

Access to the NNMi console is controlled by username and role. The username, provided together with the password, is used to authenticate the connection, but the role assigned to the user determines the user's permissions to a particular functionality.

Every time one opens the NNMi console, the user is prompted for a username and password.

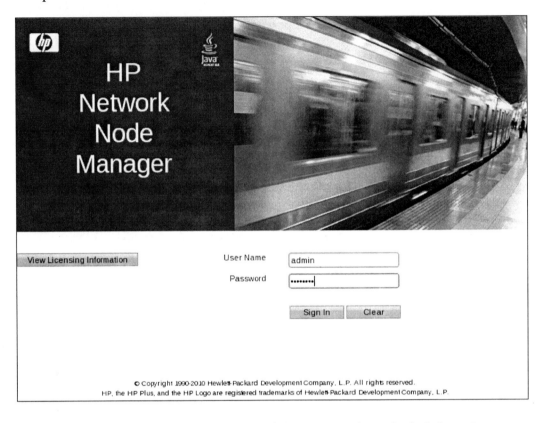

Our username is already assigned to one of the NNMi roles, which defines the permissions in NNMi we will have. The username and password need to be created by the NNMi administrator, and a role assigned to our username.

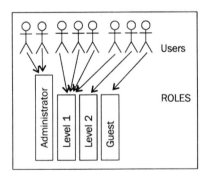

The preceding diagram shows how users are related to roles. Each user can be assigned to one role only. Each role can have an unlimited number of users assigned.

NNMi roles

NNMi has the following configured roles:

- Administrator
- Operator Level 2
- Operator Level 1
- Guest
- Client

 Note: Roles and role names cannot be changed.

Assigning a role

Username assignment to a role is configured using the following steps:

1. Select **User accounts and Roles** in the **Configuration** workspace.
2. Select the user we want to assign a role to.
3. Select **Open**.
4. In the **Role** field, select the role we want to assign to the user.

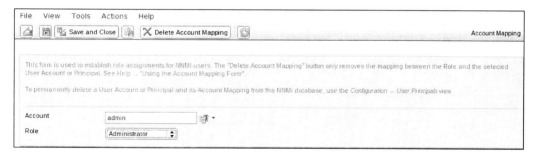

5. Click **Save and Close** to save the current window.

Before the administrator starts creating users, it is recommended to be sure about the roles that will be assigned to users. So, the administrator should understand the roles and the functionality each role has. The following four tables in the next section provide a list of features that are accessible to each role.

Permissions for each role

Different groups have different access permissions to workspaces, Action and Tools menus, as well as a URL list, which can be selected by each role.

 Note: Administrator can change the restrictions to URL actions, making them tighter.

The following table lists role permissions for workspaces:

Parameter	Guest	Level 1 Operator	Level 2 Operator	Administrator
Incident Management	✓	✓	✓	✓
Topology Maps	✓	✓	✓	✓
Monitoring	✓	✓	✓	✓
Troubleshooting	✓	✓	✓	✓
Inventory	✓	✓	✓	✓
Incident Browsing	✓	✓	✓	✓
Management Mode			✓	✓
Configuration				✓

The following table lists role permissions for Action menu items.

Parameter	Guest	Level 1 Operator	Level 2 Operator	Administrator
Ping		✓	✓	✓
Trace Route		✓	✓	✓
Monitoring Settings		✓	✓	✓
Run Diagnostics (SPI NET)		✓	✓	✓
Show Members		✓	✓	✓
Show All Incidents		✓	✓	✓
Show All Open Incidents		✓	✓	✓

Parameter	Guest	Level 1 Operator	Level 2 Operator	Administrator
6.x/7.x Neighbor View		✓	✓	✓
6.x/7.x Details		✓	✓	✓
6.x/7.x ovw		✓	✓	✓
6.x/7.x Home Base		✓	✓	✓
6.x/7.x Launcher		✓	✓	✓
SNMP Viewer		✓	✓	✓
Alarms		✓	✓	✓
Telnet			✓	✓
Configuration Poll			✓	✓
Status Poll			✓	✓
Communication Settings				✓

The following table lists role permissions for Tools menu items.

Parameter	Guest	Level 1 Operator	Level 2 Operator	Administrator
Find Node	✓	✓	✓	✓
Restore All Default View Settings	✓	✓	✓	✓
NNMi Status		✓	✓	✓
Find Attached Switch Port			✓	✓
MIB Browser			✓	✓
Status Distribution Groups			✓	✓
Visio Export (iSPI NET only)			✓	✓
Sign In/ Sign Out Audit Log				✓
Incident Actions Log				✓
Load MIB				✓
NNMi Self-Monitoring Graphs				✓
NNMi System Health Reports				✓
Signed In Users				✓
Sign In/Sign Out Audit Log				✓
Trap Analytics (iSPI NET only)				✓
Upload Local MIB File				✓

The following table lists role permissions for URL actions.

Parameter	Guest	Level 1 Operator	Level 2 Operator	Administrator
Node Group Map	✓	✓	✓	✓
Show Members		✓	✓	✓
Ping (from NNMi server)		✓	✓	✓
Traceroute (from NNMi server)		✓	✓	✓
Monitoring Settings		✓	✓	✓
Show All Incidents		✓	✓	✓
Show All Open Incidents		✓	✓	✓
Status Details		✓	✓	✓
NNMi Status			✓	✓
Browse MIB			✓	✓
Configuration Poll			✓	✓
List Supported MIBs			✓	✓
Management mode			✓	✓
Show Attached End Nodes			✓	✓
Telnet ... (from NNMi server)			✓	✓
Status Poll			✓	✓
Configuration Poll			✓	✓
Communication Settings				✓

Sign in access types

NNMi 8.x was introduced with user authentication, which allows the NNMi administrator to grant access to many users and divide them by roles. As a result, NNMi can comply with an incident management workflow, where incidents can be assigned to particular user and other users can see who is working on an incident.

By default, NNMi is installed using a built-in authentication model, where usernames and passwords for the NNMi console are stored in the NNMi database; however, two other authentication models are supported as well. The following lists all three models of authentication and briefly describes the major differences between each model.

Sign In type	Username	Password	Role mapping
1	NNMi	NNMi	NNMi
2	Both	Directory Service	NNMi
3	Directory Service	Directory Service	Directory Service

The first model, mentioned in the preceding table, is installed by default during NNMi server installation, and stores the username and password in the NNMi database. This model allows the NNMi administrator to maintain a list of users and their access levels.

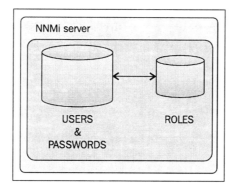

The disadvantage of this solution is that NNMi usernames are maintained separately from other usernames. So, the user has to keep in mind at least two usernames and passwords: login to the operating system and NNMi console.

To simplify authentication, it is recommended to implement the second or third solution (authentication in NNMi and Directory Service, or Directory Service only).

The second authentication, where usernames are created and stored in NNMi and the Directory Service server using LDAP, the Directory Service server stores the user's password and NNMi stores user assignment to that particular role.

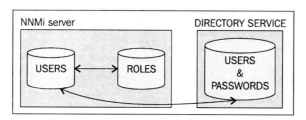

This solution is good when the NNMi administrator wants to maintain user passwords in Directory Service and user roles in NNMi. The example could be NNMi administrator and Directory Service administrator working in separate units. Usernames and passwords are maintained either way, no matter if NNMi is used in the infrastructure, but role maintenance effort is left for the NNMi administrator.

Before we start configuring this model, we, as an NNMi administrator, should retrieve information about the Directory Service configuration.

The next table lists parameters that we need to know about our Directory Services before we start implementing this model:

Parameter	Microsoft Active Directory	Other directory services
Fully Qualified Domain Name (FQDN) of Directory Service's computer	`server_name.company_name.com`	
LDAP port	389 by default for non-SSL communications	
	636 by default for SSL communications	
Is SSL required?	If yes, you need to get your company's trust store certificate file (read section "Configuring SSL to Directory Service" on page 20 for information on how to install trust certificate).	
The distinguished name for one username that is stored in Directory Service	CN=name.surname@ mycomany.com,OU=Users,O U=Accounts,DC=mycompany ,DC=com	uid=name.surname@ mycompany. com,ou=USERS-NNMi- *,ou=Groups,o=mycompany. com

The third authentication model is fully controlled by the Directory Service. This means usernames with passwords and roles are stored and maintained in Directory Service. This model is handy when the NNMi administrator has rights to the Directory Service administration.

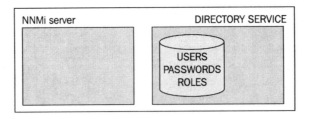

The following table, just like the previous table, lists parameters that we need to know about our Directory Services before implementing this model:

Parameter	Microsoft Active Directory	Other directory services
The distinguished name for identifying groups to which the user is assigned	`User attribute memberOf identifies groups`	<ul><li>`ou=Groups,o=mycompany.com`</li><li>`cn=USERS-NNMi-*,ou=Groups,o=mycompany.com`</li></ul>
The method that identifies user within a group	<ul><li>`CN=name.surname@mycompany.com,OU=Users,OU=Accounts,DC=mycompany,DC=com`</li><li>`CN=name.surname@mycompany.com`</li></ul>	<ul><li>`cn=name.surname@mycompany.com,ou=People,o=mycompany.com`</li><li>`cn=name.surname@mycmpany.com`</li></ul>
The group attribute that stores Directory Service user ID	member	member
Group names that Directory Service administrator has created for mapping users to roles	<ul><li>`CN=USERS-NNMi-Admin,OU=Groups,OU=Accounts,DC=mycompany,DC=com`</li><li>`CN=USERS-NNMi-Level2,OU=Groups,OU=Accounts,DC=mycompany,DC=com`</li><li>`CN=USERS-NNMi-Level1,OU=Groups,OU=Accounts,DC=mycompany,DC=com`</li><li>`CN=USERS-NNMi-Client,OU=Groups,OU=Accounts,DC=mycompany,DC=com`</li><li>`CN=USERS-NNMi-Guest,OU=Groups,OU=Accounts,DC=mycompany,DC=com`</li></ul>	<ul><li>`cn=USERS-NNMi-Admin,ou=Groups,o=mycompany.com`</li><li>`cn=USERS-NNMi-Level2,ou=Groups,o=mycompany.com`</li><li>`cn=USERS-NNMi-Level1,ou=Groups,o=mycompany.com`</li><li>`cn=USERS-NNMi-Client,ou=Groups,o=mycompany.com`</li><li>`cn=USERS-NNMi-Guest,ou=Groups,o=mycompany.com`</li></ul>
The name of the attribute that stores role	info	nnmiRole

The next sections describe how to configure each of these three mentioned models.

Control with NNMi

This section describes NNMi's embedded authentication solution and provides examples on how to manage users using this authentication method.

How it works

Controlling user authentication inside NNMi is simple to implement. No additional actions should be performed when the system is deployed. The NNMi user authentication mechanism is implemented by default. All usernames and passwords are stored in the NNMi database.

As an administrator, in terms of user authentication, we can do the following:

- Create, change, or delete usernames
- Set/change passwords
- Assign/change user role

Creating a user

This section describes steps that have to be completed in order to configure a particular feature.

To create, change, or delete a username, complete the following steps (password is assigned to the user when new user is created):

1. Select **User accounts and Roles** in the **Configuration** workspace.
2. Do any of the following:
    - Click on **New** if we want to create new user.
    - Select the user which we want to modify and select **Open**.
    - Select the user and select **Delete** if we want to delete a user (we needn't complete the next steps).
3. Fill in the **Name** field.
4. Fill in the **Password** field (if we rename a user and plan to retain the same password, we can leave the **Password** field unchanged).

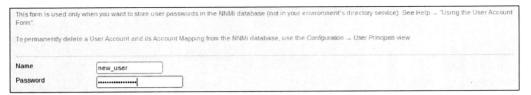

5. Click **Save and Close** to save current window.

Changing a password

To change a password, perform following steps:

1. Select **User accounts and Roles** in the **Configuration** workspace.
2. Select the **Open** button next to a user whose password you want to modify.
3. Select **Account** attribute.
4. Select **Lookup** and **Open** for the user whose password you want to modify.
5. Type new password.

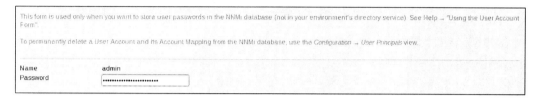

6. Click **Save** and **Close** to save current window.
7. Click **Save** and **Close** to save Account mapping form.

Changing user profile

To assign/change a role for a user, perform the following steps:

1. Select **User accounts and Roles** in the **Configuration** workspace.
2. Open the user account whose role we want to assign or change.
3. Locate the **Role** attribute and select the role we want to assign to user.
4. Click **Save and Close** to save current window.

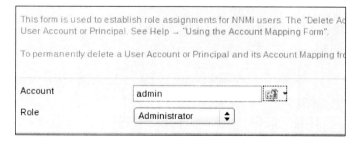

> **Note**: If we make changes to the existing user, who is currently logged in, changes will be effective when the user logs in next time.

Control with NNMi and Directory Service

This section describes the combination of two authentications models: NNMi's embedded authentication solution and Directory Service authentication. Examples on how to configure this authentication method are also provided.

How it works

Directory Services authentication is used to reduce the amount of usernames and passwords for the operator. To implement this solution, Directory Services must be running. This section describes a combined NNMi and Directory Services authentication model. It is combined because Directory Services stores usernames and passwords, but the role assignment is stored and maintained in NNMi. From the operation perspective, this solution demands additional effort due to the following reasons:

- Usernames and passwords are stored in Directory Services
- Usernames are also written in NNMi and must match the usernames stored in Directory Services
- User roles are maintained by the NNMi administrator
- The NNMi administrator maintains the `nms-ldap.properties` file, which assures that settings are correct for NNMi to communicate with Directory Services

Configuring Directory Service

To configure NNMi to access Directory Services, perform the following steps:

1. Back up NNMi user information using the following command:
    - In Unix:

      ```
      $NnmInstallDir/bin/nnmconfigexport.ovpl -c account \
      -u <user> -p <password> -f nnmi_db_accounts.xml
      ```
    - In Windows:

      ```
      %NnmInstallDir%\bin\nnmconfigexport.ovpl -c account \
      -u <user> -p <password> -f nnmi_db_accounts.xml
      ```

2. Configure SSL communication to Directory Service. This step should be carried out only if we have to configure SSL communication:

   Ask system administrator for the company's trust store certificate file.

3. Run all commands under the following folder:

   ° In Unix:

   ```
   $NnmDataDir/shared/nnm/certificates
   ```

   ° In Windows:

   ```
   %NnmDataDir%\shared\nnm\certificates
   ```

4. Import the company's trust store certificate using the following commands:

   ° In Unix:

   ```
   $NnmInstallDir/nonOV/jdk/b/bin/keytool -import \
   -alias nnmi_ldap -keystore nnm.trustore -file <Full_
     Path_To_Directory_Store_Certificate.txt>
   ```

   ° ii.   In Windows:

   ```
   %NnmInstallDir%\nonOV\jdk\b\bin\keytool -import \
   -alias nnmi_ldap -keystore nnm.trustore -file <Full_Path_
     To_Directory_Store_Certificate.txt>
   ```

5. Enter ovpass keystore password when prompted.

6. Enter Y when asked if we trust certificate.

7. Check the contents of the trust store running the following command:

   ° In Unix:

   ```
   $NnmInstallDir/nonOV/jdk/b/bin/keytool -list \
   -keystore nnm.truststore
   ```

   ° In Windows:

   ```
   %NnmInstallDir%\nonOV\jdk\b\bin\keytool -list \
   -keystore nnm.truststore
   ```

8. Enter **ovpass** when asked for a keystore password. We should see output similar to the following:

   Keystore type: jks

   Keystore provider: SUN

Your keystore contains 1 entry

nnmi_ldap, Mar 13, 2010, trustedCertEntry,

Certificate fingerprint (MD5):

57:23:A4:C2:C2:C2:87:42:87:42:57:31: 23:06:94:36

9. To restart `ovjboss`, run the following two commands:

    ```
    ovstop ovjboss
    ovstart ovjboss
    ```

10. Configure `nms-ldap.properties` file for NNMi user access from Directory Service. Depending on the Directory Service, the steps may differ. Let's now see the steps involved in Microsoft Active Directory.

    ○ **Microsoft Active Directory**: This option works with NNMi, with at least version 8.1x and Consolidated patch 3 installed.

        i.   Make a copy of the `nms-ldap.properties` file and store it in a safe location.

        ii. Write the following text into a file:

        ```
        java.naming.provider.url=ldap://<myldapserver>:389/
        bindDN=<mydomain>\\<myusername>
        bindCredential=<mypassword>
        baseCtxDN=CN=Users,DC=<myhostname>,DC=<mycompanyna
        me>,
        DC=<mysuffix>
        baseFilter=CN={0}
        defaultRole=guest
        #rolesCtxDN=CN=Users,DC=<myhostname>,DC=<mycompany
        name>,
        DC=<mysuffix>
        roleFilter=member={1}
        uidAttributeID=member
        roleAttributeIsDN=true
        roleNameAttributeID=info
        roleAttributeID=memberOf
        userRoleFilterList=admin;level2;level1
        ```

        Here all text surrounded by < > symbols should be replaced by our Directory Service settings. The following table shows a list of parameters that need to be changed in the `nms-ldap.properties` file.

Parameter	Description
`<myldapserver>`	Fully qualified name of Active Directory (AD) server
`<mydomain>`	Name of AD domain
`<myusername>`	Username and password that has rights to access AD
`<mypassword>`	
`<myhostname>`	Fully qualified hostname of Active Directory.
`<mycompanyname>`	For example, in the case of `directoryserver.company.com`, we would specify `DC=directoryserver,DC=company,DC=com`
`<mysuffix>`	

- ○ **Other Directory Service:**

    i. Make a copy of the `nms-ldap.properties` file and store it in a safe location.

    ii. Uncomment the following lines in the `nms-ldap.properties` file and replace <myldapserver> with a fully qualified hostname of the directory server.

    ```
    java.naming.provider.url=ldap://<myldapserver>:389/
    ```

 Note: If we have more than one directory server, list all servers separated by a single space character.

In the line `baseCtxDN=ou=People,o=myco.com,` replace `ou` and `o` parameter values with the name of our own Directory Service domain that stores user records.

Replace `uid` with the user name attribute from the Directory Service domain in the line `baseFilter=uid={0}`.

11. Testing our configuration:

    We need to follow the steps given next to test our configuration.

    i. For testing purposes, set `defaultRole=guest` in `nsm-ldap.properties`.

    ii. Sign in to the NNMi console with the username that is configured in Directory Services but does not exist in NNMi DB.

    iii. Make sure that the user has the guest role assigned.

    iv. If the user doesn't work, make sure we complete steps i and ii in this section.

Note: Make sure we log out from NNMi console every time we make changes in the `nsm-ldap.properties` file.

12. Remove old data to prevent unexpected access to NNMi. When our test is completed successfully and we know user authentication is working properly, we need to remove old data, which can cause unexpected behavior.

    i. We left `defaultRole` assigned to guest. Reassign it or comment it out if this setting is not desired.

    ii. The NNMi database still contains user accounts. We need to remove this data as we plan to have users only in Directory Service:

        a. Remove user access information that was stored in NNMi.

        b. Create role assignments in NNMi consoles for the users in Directory Service.

        c. All incident information has lost assignment data, so we need to reassign incidents to new users.

Control with Directory Service

This section describes the Directory Service authentication model, including examples on how to configure Directory Service for NNMi authentication.

How it works

This section describes the Directory Service authentication model, which fully takes care of user authentication and role assignment outside NNMi. This means NNMi doesn't store any users, passwords, and role assignments either.

How to configure Directory Service

The configuration of control using Directory Services is the same as previously described control using NNMi and Directory Service, only a few additional actions need to be completed, which control role mapping.

Complete steps 1 to 4 under the *Configuring Directory Service* section. Then, in addition, complete the following steps:

1. Configure NNMi role retrieval from Directory Services. The steps again vary depending on which Directory Service we opt for. Let's now look at the scenarios.

    ° **Configure Microsoft Active Directory**.

Uncomment and modify the following line in the `nsm-ldap.properties` file:

```
rolesCtxDN=CN=USERS,DC=<hostname>,DC=<company>,DX=<s
uffix>
```

Here `<hostname>`, `<company>`, and `<suffix>` are components of the Active Directory server's fully qualified domain name. For example, if our MS AD server FQDN is `adserver.mycompany.com`, then the line would look like the following:

```
rolesCtxDN=CN=USERS,DC=<adserver>,DC=<mycompany>,DX=
<com>
```

° **Configure other directory services**.

Uncomment and modify the following line in the `nsm-ldap.properties` file, accordingly:

```
rolesCtxDN=ou=Groups,o=myco.com
```

Here `ou=Groups` and `o=myco.com` are components of the Directory Service server, which stores the group records domain name. For example, consider the domain name is `nameserver.mycompany.com`, where our Directory Service server's stored group records are, the line would look like the following:

```
rolesCtxDN=ou=Groups,o=mycompany.com
```

Enter the name of the group attribute that stores the Directory Service user ID, replacing the member component in the following line:

```
roleFilter=member={1}
```

2. Test role configuration:

To test role configuration, we need to perform the following steps:

i. Sign in to NNMi using the username and password, which are configured in Directory Service and don't exist in the NNMi database.

ii. Make sure the user has a proper role assigned to it. We should see it on the title bar of the NNMi console.

 Note: If test fails, we need to make sure we complete the following configuration steps and that the role identification configuration is completed properly.

3. Now we need to configure roles for incident assignment. To complete this step, modify the `nms-ldap.properties` file accordingly:

    i. Modify the `userRoleFilterList` parameter, listing NNMi roles whose associated users can be assigned incidents in the NNMi console. Roles should be semicolon-separated, such as:

```
userRoleFilterList=admin;level2;level1
```

    ii. To make sure our configuration works, we need to sign in to the NNMi console and complete the following steps:

        a.   Select any incident and select **Actions | Assign Incident**.

        b.   Make sure we can assign incident to user from any role listed in the `userRoleFilterList` configuration.

The next table contains a full list of role names that are used in Directory Services

Role name in NNMi	String used in configuration files and directory service configuration
Administrator	admin
Operator Level 2	level2
Operator Level 1	level1
Guest	guest
Web Service Client	client

Configuring SSL to Directory Service

To use SSL in Directory Service communication, SSL protocol needs to be enabled. SSL requires a trust relationship between NNMi and the Directory Service host. The certificate needs to be installed in the NNMi trust store, which confirms the identity of the Directory Service server.

To install the certificate, perform the following steps:

1. Obtain the certificate that is used in our company. The Directory Service administrator is the person who can provide us with such a certificate.

2. Go to the following directory:

Unix: `$NnmDataDir/shared/nnm/certificates`

Windows: `%NnmDataDir%\shared\nnm\certificates`

3. Import trust store into NNMi by running the following commands:

   ° In Unix:

   ```
   $NnmInstallDir/nonOV/jdk/b/bin/keytool -import \-alias
   nnmi_ldap -keystore nnm.truststore -file <Directory_Server_
   Certificate.txt>
   ```

   ° In Windows:

   ```
   %NnmInstallDir%\nonOV\jdk\b\bin\keytool -import \
   -alias nnmi_ldap -keystore nnm.truststore -file <Directory_
   Server_Certificate.txt>
   ```

   Enter **ovpass** when prompted for keystore password and confirm the trust
   certificate by pressing the *Y* button. The following is an example of an output
   from this command:

   ```
   Owner: CN=NNMi_server.testlab.local

   Issuer: CN=NNMi_server.testlab.local

   Serial number: 123456789ab

   Valid from: Mon Aug 31 08:18:28 EST 2010 until: Thu Dec 20

   08:18:28 EDT 2110

   Certificate fingerprints:

   MD5: 45:23:AC:AC:45:45:12:00:15:D8:76:B4:78:65:65:42

   SHA1: AB:45:7E:2A:5D:7C:CC:5C:23:45:78:89:AB:AC:AD:AF:AE

   Trust this certificate? [no]: y

   Certificate was added to keystore
   ```

4. List NNMi trust store and examine records using the following commands:

   ° In Unix:

   ```
   $NnmInstallDir/nonOV/jdk/b/bin/keytool \

   -list -keystore nnm.truststore
   ```

   ° In Windows:

   ```
   %NnmInstallDir%\nonOV\jdk\b\bin\keytool \

   -list -keystore nnm.truststore
   ```

5. Restart ovjboss by running following commands:

   ```
   ovstop ovjboss

   ovstart ovjboss
   ```

Command line access configuration tools

Access to some NNMi command tools is limited by username, password, and role. System-generated usernames should be used for such command lines—for example, for loading mibs, the `nnmloadmib.ovpl` tool should be launched with the username and password provided:

```
nnmloadmib.ovpl -u username -p password -load /home/user/mib-file.
mib
```

In some environments, it may not even be safe to use command line tools with **system** username and password provided in it. An example could be if we are logged in to a server using a username, the history can be viewed by other users. It is especially not secure if these users are not in our security policy or they are not friendly to us or our departmental activity. In that case, the command line tool `nnmsetcmduserpw.ovpl` can be used. This command line tool is a replacement for username and password direct usage in the command line. `nnmsetcmduserpw.ovpl` tool creates `.nnm/nnm.properties` file in user's home directory.

System user is created during NNMi installation. It is recommended to use this username only for command line tools. It should not be used to access the NNMi console. Instead, another user with an administrator role should be created.

When using command line tools that require a system-generated username to be issued from the NNMi management server, there should at least be read-only access to the following files:

- `nnm-users.properties`
- `nnm-roles.properties`

Files are stored in the following location:

- For Unix: `/opt/OV/nonOV/jboss/nms/server/nms/conf/props/`
- For Windows: `<drive>:\Program Files (x86)\HP\HP BTO\Software\nonOV\jboss\nms\server\nms\conf\props\`

Beware of users that can assess these files for modifications. In Unix, only the root user has access to modify these files by default. In Windows, users from the administrator user group have access to modify these files.

The following table shows a list of commands where the username and password are used:

Command	Description
nnmcommconf.ovpl	Configuration settings command
nnmconfigexport.ovpl	Configuration export command
nnmconfigimport.ovpl	Configuration import command
nnmincidentcfg.ovpl	Incident configuration command
nnmloadmib.ovpl	MIB load command
nnmloadnodegroups.ovpl	Node groups load command
nnmmanagementmode.ovpl	Management mode configuration command
nnmnetdeletenodeattrs.ovpl	Node attribute deletion command
nnmnetloadnodeattrs.ovpl	Custom attribute management command
nnmnodedelete.ovpl	Node deleting command
nnmopcexport.ovpl	Exports NNM policies for OpenView Operations
nnmseeddelete.ovpl	Seed deletion command
nnmstatuspoll.ovpl	Status poll command
nnmtopodump.ovpl	Topology dump command
nnmtrapconfig.ovpl	SNMP trap configuration command
nnmtrapdload.ovpl	SNMP trap loading command
nnmtrimincidents.ovpl	Incident trim command

The command line tool description can be found in the reference pages (**Help | Document Library**).

An example—creating nnm.properties file

Let's launch /opt/OV/bin/nnmsetcmduserpw.ovpl (path for Windows OS is %NnmInstallDir%\bin\) and create the nnm.properties file for NNMi user admin. This user is logged in to OS as user1. The following is how a prompt looks when the tool is launched:

WARNING: This change will affect the credentials to be used in place

of the -u/-p command line options whenever this user executes

a script requiring these. Please ensure you are logged in as

the desired user before executing this script.

Executing this script will create/edit the .nnm/nnm.properties

file in the users home directory.

Would you like to continue? [n] Y

y

Thank you!

Please provide a username: admin

Please enter your password:

Please enter your password again:

User/Password values stored successfully in /home/user1/.nnm/nnm.properties

If we open an nnm.properties file, we can see user admin credentials saved in this file.

```
#Sat Mar 13 13:37:50 EST 2010
nnm.password=SAY9enxr6s5L6us8OJoD9QiG4Mxgt3Tz
nnm.username=admin
```

 Note: Password in the nnm.properties file is encrypted.

Now this user can ignore the username and password options in command line tools, as they will be retrieved from the nnm.properties file.

User activity audit

This section describes how the user activity audit is organized in NNMi.

What is user activity

NNMi tracks user activity in the application and includes the following activity parts:

- Sign in/sign out activity
- User activity audit information

The next sections describe each of these activity types in greater detail.

Sign in/sign out activity

The `signin.0.0.log` file stores users' sign in/ sign out activity information. This log includes the date, time, when the user signed in or signed out, username, role assigned to user, hostname where user has logged in and port number. File is stored in the following location:

- In Unix: `/var/opt/OV/log/nnm`
- In Windows: `<drive>:\Documents and Settings\All Users\ Application Data\HP\HP BTO Software\log\nnm\`

Filename changes every time NNMi server restarts and number in a filename increases after every restart, accordingly. The following is how the logging information is provided:

Mar 8, 2010 1:06:34.996 PM [ThreadID:123] INFO: com.hp.ov.ui.util. SignInOutAuditLog logSignIn: Successful Sign In

User:	**admin**
Role:	**Administrator (admin)**
Remote Host:	**192.168.1.1**
Remote Port:	**35092**
Locale:	**en_US**

Sign In/Out Audit Since 2/18/10 2:16 PM

=======================================

Currently Signed In:

    #1:   **admin**   **127.0.0.1**   **3/8/10 1:06 PM (last access 3/8/10 1:06 PM)**

Previously Signed Out:

    #1:   **user-1**   **192.168.1.1**   **3/8/10 1:06 PM -> 3/8/10 1:06 PM**

This part of the log file shows that on **March 08, 2010**, at **1:06:34**, the user **admin** has signed in. User belongs to Administrator group and connected from the local machine (IP address 127.0.0.1). The audit has been running since **February 18, 2010** in this file. As can be observed, the user named **user-1** has been signed in from IP address **192.168.1.1** on **March 8, 2010** at **1:06 PM**.

User activity auditing

This file contains records about other user activity and stores it in the
nnmui.0.0.log file. The file is stored in the following location:

- In Unix: /var/opt/OV/log/nnm
- In Windows: <drive>:\Documents and Settings\All Users\
  Application Data\HP\HP BTO Software\log\nnm\

The filename changes every time the NNMi server restarts, increasing the number
in the filename after every restart, accordingly. The following is how the logging
information is provided:

Feb 23, 2010 12:56:31.161 PM [ThreadID:143] INFO: com.hp.ov.ui.map.
UIMapServiceManager getMapView: Created map with layout: Circular, 0 graph
nodes, 0 ports, and 0 edges

Feb 23, 2010 1:05:54.102 PM [ThreadID:143] INFO: com.hp.ov.ui.util.
SignInOutAuditLog logSignOut: Successful Sign Out

User:	admin
Role:	**Administrator (admin)**
Remote Host:	127.0.0.1
Remote Port:	58239
Locale:	en_US

Sign In/Out Audit Since 2/18/10 2:16 PM

=======================================

No users currently signed in.

Previously Signed Out:

     #1:   admin 127.0.0.1   2/23/10 12:44 PM -> 2/23/10 1:05 PM

Feb 23, 2010 1:05:54.102 PM [ThreadID:143] INFO: com.hp.ov.wcf.ui.console.
ConsoleBean dispose: Unregistering 24 views and 1 binders

Feb 24, 2010 11:38:20.602 AM [ThreadID:123] INFO: com.hp.ov.ui.util.
SignInOutAuditLog logSignIn: Successful Sign In

> User: admin
>
> Role: Administrator (admin)
>
> Remote Host: 127.0.0.1
>
> Remote Port: 39036
>
> Locale: en_US

Sign In/Out Audit Since 2/18/10 2:16 PM

=======================================

Currently Signed In:

> #1:   admin 127.0.0.1   2/24/10 11:38 AM (last access 2/24/10 11:38

AM)

No users currently signed out.

Feb 24, 2010 11:38:20.609 AM [ThreadID:123] CONFIG: com.hp.ov.
wcf.ui.api.common.Utils getConsoleOnLoad: Using starting view of
"networkOverviewView" as configured by User Interface Settings

Feb 24, 2010 11:38:20.624 AM [ThreadID:123] CONFIG: com.hp.ov.wcf.ui.action.
ActionManager loadActionInfosFromDatastore: loaded UrlActionInfo Ping
(from server)

To configure logging behavior, the `logging.properties` file should be modified.
The file is stored in the following location:

- In Unix: `/var/opt/OV/shared/nnm/conf/ovjboss/logging.properties`
- In Windows: `<drive>:\Documents and Settings\All Users\`
  `Application Data\HP\HP BTO Software\shared\nnm\conf\ovjboss\`
  `logging.properties`

The following table provides the `logging.properties` file configuration options.

Parameter	Options	Description
`SignInOutAuditLog.level`	`CONFIG` | `OFF`	To enable sign in and sign out user information in `signin.0.0.log` file, use following:
		`com.hp.ov.ui.util.SignInOutAuditLog.level = CONFIG`
		To disable sign in and sign out user information in `signin.0.0.log` file, use following:
		`com.hp.ov.ui.util.SignInOutAuditLog.level = OFF`
`SignInOutAuditLog.useParentHandlers`	`TRUE` | `FALSE`	To enable sign in and sign out user information in `nnmui.0.0.log` file, use following:
		`com.hp.ov.ui.util.SignInOuAuditLog.useParentHandlers = true`
		To disable sign in and sign out user information in `nnmui.0.0.log` file, use following:
		`com.hp.ov.ui.util.SignInOuAuditLog.useParentHandlers = false`
`SignInFileHandler.count`	`<number>`	Each time the jboss process is restarted, a new file is created and the number in the filename is increased by 1. This parameter controls the number of files to be created.

Summary

After completion of this chapter, we are now able to make a decision as to which authentication model is the best for our organization. We are also able to implement any of the selected authentication model in our NNMi monitoring environment. Additional troubleshooting tools, described in this chapter, will help us enable user activity audits and investigate user activity-related issues.

The next chapter of this book describes troubleshooting tools and techniques used while maintaining NNMi, how to organize NNMi backup, and restore solutions so that our management system would be able to have a fast recovery after any outage or disaster.

6

Troubleshooting, Security, and Backup

A large proportion of our daily activity is usually based around system administration, tuning, improving system performance and security, troubleshooting different issues, and assuring continuity. This chapter describes the processes and services that run on the NNMi system and explains how to deal with them. There are topics on system backup and recovery, and improving system continuity (which is very important to understand backup and recovery strategies). This chapter should give an understanding of what approach for system continuity improvement can be taken and how to deal with it. It will also cover technical realization. We will find examples, with commands and options provided. We will also find interesting troubleshooting tools listed in one of following chapter topics.

To summarize, the chapter covers:

- Describing NNMi processes
- Describing NNMi services
- Using NNMi logging processes
- Ports used by NNMi
- Troubleshooting tools
- Environment variables
- Command security issues
- Backing up NNMi
- Restoring NNMi
- Backup and restore strategies
- Configuration migration

Describing NNMi processes

This section describes a list of processes that are responsible for NMMi functionality. All these processes need to be running in order for NNMi to work properly. The following table lists all NNMi processes:

Process name	Description
OVsPMD	This is the control process, which manages all other NNMi processes.
pmd	<ul><li>Event post master daemon (pmd) ensures routing between event producers to event consumers.</li><li>Producers are NNMi processes and NNM 6.x/7.x management stations.</li><li>Consumers are event pipeline and third-party applications.</li></ul>
ovjboss	The ovjboss process controls the ovjboss application server, where all NNMi services are located.
nmsdbmgr	NMS Data Manager controls the embedded database and the connectivity to it. It also performs connectivity tests on a regular basis.

As an administrator, we can start, stop, or check the status of all or any of our processes from a command line using ovstart, ovstop, and ovstatus commands:

- ovstart -c: Starts all processes
- ovstop -c: Stops all processes
- ovstatus -c: Lists the status of all processes

To start, stop, or check the status of one process, the following syntax should be used:

- ovstart <process name>, that is, ovstart ovjboss
- ovstop <process name>, that is, ovstop ovjboss
- ovstatus <process name>, that is, ovstatus ovjboss

If we want to check the status of the NNMi processes, we would run the ovstatus -c command. Then the list indicating the status of all processes will be displayed.

```
# /opt/OV/bin/ovstatus -c
Name                    PID  State         Last Message(s)
OVsPMD                  3654 RUNNING       -
pmd                     -    NOT_RUNNING   -
nmsdbmgr                3655 RUNNING       Database available.
ovjboss                 3669 RUNNING       Initialization complete.
```

If the system is healthy, we should get a response with RUNNING as the state of all processes. The preceding example shows that the pmd process is not running. We can try to start the pmd process with following command:

```
ovstart -c pmd
```

If it's still in the NOT_RUNNING state, check the log files for possible issues. We can also run the command that starts all processes:

```
ovstart -c
```

We should get the following response:

Name	PID	State	Last Message(s)
OVsPMD	3654	RUNNING	-
nmsdbmgr	3655	RUNNING	Database available.
ovjboss	3669	RUNNING	Initialization complete.

ovspmd: Attempt to start HP OpenView services is complete.

To stop all processes, we would run the following command:

```
ovstop -c
```

We should get the following response:

Name	PID	State	Last Message(s)
pmd	-	DONE	-
ovjboss	3669	DONE	Exiting due to user request.
nmsdbmgr	3655	DONE	Exited due to user request
OVsPMD	3654	DONE	-

ovspmd: No HP OpenView services are running.

Describing NNMi services

Under the `ovjboss` process there are a number of services running. The following table lists all the services that belong to NNMi.

Process name	Description
	Monitors internal statistics for measuring SNMP and ICMP configuration performance.
IslandSpotterService	This service performs Island Node Groups auto-discovery using topology Layer 2 connectivity information.
ManagedNodeLicenseManager	This service tracks the number of managed nodes in NNMi topology and ensures that the number of nodes doesn't exceed the managed node license number.
ModelChangeNotificationAdapter	This service monitors certain models and notifies about their changes. Models are as follows: Global Settings, Spiral Discovery Configuration, Discovery Seeds, Management Node.
MonitoringSettingsService	This service makes calculations for monitoring each device based on the Monitoring Configuration Settings.
NamedPoll	This service is used by the Causal Engine to trigger immediate state polls of a monitored object during neighbor analysis and interface up/down investigations.
NmsApa	The NMS Active Problem Analyzer (APA) service determines the root cause of network problems and reports to the NMS Event Service.
NmsDisco	This service discovers and adds new devices to the database and periodically polls existing devices and keeps an up to date configuration of them. This data is used by NNMi to maintain current device configuration information.
	As the Causal Engine for calculations uses device configuration information, this service also depends on the `NmsDisco` service.

Process name	Description
NmsEvents	This service is responsible for information displayed in the incident table.
NmsEventsConfiguration	This service is responsible for handling changes in the incident configuration.
NmsModel	This service enables communication between NNMi services and the NNMi database.
SpmdjbossStart	This service interacts with the OVsPMD process during the ovstart, ovstop, and ovstatus -v ovjboss processes.
StagedIcmp	This service is used by the State Poller to ping IP addresses. It is also used by auto-discovery, if Ping Sweep is enabled.
StagedSnmp	This service is used by the State Poller to make SNMP queries.
StatePoller	This service assesses the state of discovered devices based on collected information.
	As input it uses data from NmsDisco service results.

There are two ways to check the status of NNMi services:

- Using NNMi console menu: **Tools | NNMi Status**.
- Using the ovstatus -c ovjboss command in a command line.

We should get an output similar to the following:

```
# /opt/OV/bin/ovstatus -v ovjboss
 object manager name: ovjboss
 state:              RUNNING
 PID:                3617
 last message:       Initialization complete.
 exit status:        -
 additional info:
          SERVICE                                STATUS
          CPListener                             Service is started
          CommunicationModelService              Service is started
          CommunicationParametersStatsService    Service is started
```

CustomPoller	Service is started
EventsCustomExportService	Service is started
ExtensionDeployer	Service is started
InstanceDiscoveryService	Service is started
IslandSpotterService	Service is started
KeyManager	Service is started
ManagedNodeLicenseManager	Service is started
ModelChangeNotificationAdapter	Service is started
MonitoringSettingsService	Service is started
NMSLogManager	Service is started
NamedPoll	Service is started
NetworkApplication	Service is started
NmsApa	Service is started
NmsDisco	Service is started
NmsEvents	Service is started
NmsEventsConfiguration	Service is started
NmsExtensionNotificationService	Service is started
NmsModel	Service is started
NmsWorkManager	Service is started
NnmTrapService	Service is started
PolicySynchronizer	Service is started
RbaConfig	Service is started
RbaManager	Service is started
SpmdjbossStart	Service is started
StagedIcmp	Service is started
StagedSnmp	Service is started
StatePoller	Service is started
TrustManager	Service is started

Use the following commands to start or stop NNMi services:

- `ovstart -c ovjboss`
- `ovstop -c ovjboss`

The `ovjboss` process writes data into the following log files:

- `ovjboss.log` and `ovjboss.log.old`: This log file creates a new file after every restart and the existing file is copied to the `ovjboss.log.old` file.
- `jbossServer.log` and `jbossServer.<date>.old`: This log file is created every day as a new one and the existing log file is copied with a date stamp added into the filename.

Each service has its own log file. The log files are located in the following folders:

- In Unix: `/var/opt/OV/log/nnm/`
- In Windows: `<drive>:\Documents and Settings\All Users\ Application Data\HP\HP BTO Software\log\nnm\`

Log files comply to the following naming convention: `<name>.%g.%u.log`.

- `%g=0` (equals zero): If log file is active. Otherwise, it amounts to the number of previous restarts or the fact that the log file size limit has been reached (which causes a new file to be created and the existing file to be moved, increasing the number in the filename), whichever condition is first met.
- `%u=0` (equals zero): If log file is active. Increased number is added if parent process, `ovjboss`, fails. In order to protect against write conflicts, a lock file (`<service_name>.0.0.log.lck`) is created while log information is written. If another service wants to write while the lock file is created, another lock file `<name>.0.1.log.lck` is created and information is written to the `<name>.0.1.log` file.

The following table lists the log file names of all NNMi services:

Process name	Log file
`CommunicationParametersStatusService`	`snmp.%g.%u.log`
`ManagedNodeLicenseManager`	`nmslic.%g.%u.log`
`ModelChangeNotificationAdapter`	`nmsmodel.%g.%u.log`
`MonitoringSettingsService`	`mon-config.%g.%u.log`
`NMSLogManager`	`admin.%g.%u.log`
`NamedPoll`	`statepoller.%g.%u.log`
`NmsApa`	`apa.%g.%u.log`
`NmsDisco`	`disco.%g.%u.log`
`NmsEvents`	`events.%g.%u.log`
`NmsEventsConfiguration`	`events.%g.%u.log`
`NmsModel`	`nmsmodel.%g.%u.log`
`NmsNotification`	`nmsmodel.%g.%u.log`
`NmsNotificationDestinationManager`	`nmsmodel.%g.%u.log`
`SpmdjbossStart`	`admin.%g.%u.log`
`StagedIcmp`	`snmp.%g.%u.log`
`StagedSnmp`	`snmp.%g.%u.log`
`StatePoller`	`statepoller.%g.%u.log`

Using NNMi logging processes

To investigate NNM performance or to observe how NNM processes and services behave, we can view log files that show the history of the process and service activity. We can find these files at the following locations:

- Windows: `%NNM_LOG%\nnm\`
- Unix: `$NNM_LOG/nnm`

NNM stores these log files in the form of `service.%g.%u.log`.

The portion of the filename that is termed `service` refers to the name of the NNM component that is logged in the log file. The `%g` portion of the filename relates to the archived log files. When the `%g` portion of a log file name is set to a zero, it means that the subsystem is actively logging to the `service.0.%u.log` file. To verify this, we should also see a `service.0.%u.log.lck` file.

The `%u` portion of the log file will normally have a zero value, unless the process/ service crashed during a logging session. For more information about log files, see *Verify that NNM Services Are Running* in the NNM help menu.

There are two ways for a log file to become an archived log file:

- The process or service is restarted.
- The size of the log file for a subsystem exceeds the limit value.

After a process or service is restarted or a log file size exceeds the limit value, the last active log file is archived. For example, the contents of file `subsystem.0.0.log` is archived as the `subsystem.1.0.log` file. The process or service begins logging to a newly created `subsystem.0.0.log` file.

We can control the size of the log file for each service by adjusting the `.limit` property for the NNM service in the `logging.properties` file. We can also control the number of archived files by adjusting the `.count` property for the NNM component in the `logging.properties` file.

We can find the `logging.properties` file in the following directory:

- Windows: `%NNM_DATA%\shared\nnm\conf\ovjboss`
- Unix: `$NNM_DATA/shared/nnm/conf/ovjboss`

NNMi logging levels

There are various levels of logging, as explained in the following list:

- **SEVERE**: This is the most concise logging and consumes the fewest system resources. The output describes events that relate to normal NNM behavior and are of considerable importance to NNM administrators.

- **WARNING**: This level of logging includes more details than SEVERE. The output describes events of interest to end users or system managers, or events which indicate potential problems.

- **INFO**: This level of logging includes more details than WARNING. The output includes messages written to the NNM console or its equivalent. The INFO logging level logs messages that will make sense to end users and system administrators. INFO logging messages might be the result of a user event or a significant transaction such as starting a backup, a user-initiated action, or a scheduled action. Another example of an INFO logging message is the result of an operation that failed due to incorrect user input, assuming that a corresponding message is written to the NNM console.

- **CONFIG**: This level of logging includes more details than INFO. The output includes messages intended to provide a variety of static configuration information and assist system administrators in debugging problems that may be associated with particular configurations.

- **FINE**: This level of logging includes more details than CONFIG. The last three logging levels, FINE, FINER, and FINEST, are the most detailed. When we use the FINE logging level, NNM logs the most important and fewest number of messages among these three logging levels. Examples of a FINE logging level message might include a recoverable failure or a potential performance problem.

- **FINER**: This level of logging includes more details than FINE. The output includes a higher number of messages than the FINE logging level, and includes information related to program calls for entering, returning, or throwing exceptions.

- **FINEST**: This level of logging includes more details than FINER. The output includes a higher number of messages than the FINER logging level, and includes the most verbose level of logging. We can refer to the `logging.properties` reference page (or the Unix manpage) for additional information about logging.

If we use the FINE, FINER, or FINEST logging levels, it can noticeably affect NNMi application performance. Only use the FINEST logging level to find problems that can be duplicated, as the system performance could slow down when using this logging level.

Adjusting logging parameters

To view or modify the current logging level, we can use the `nnmgetLoggingLevel.ovpl` or `nnmsetLoggingLevel.ovpl` Perl scripts. Files are located in the following directory:

- In Unix: `$NNM_SUPPORT`
- In Windows: `%NNM_SUPPORT%`

To get usage information about these commands, we need to type `nnmgetLoggingLevel.ovpl -help` or `nnmsetLoggingLevel.ovpl -help`.

Temporarily changing logging levels

To view the current logging level, we can use the `nnmgetLoggingLevel.ovpl` Perl script. We can make temporary modifications to NNM using the `nnmsetLoggingLevel.ovpl` Perl script.

Permanently changing logging levels

If we make modifications to NNM using the `nnmsetLoggingLevel.ovpl` Perl script, we will lose our modifications once we restart NNM. To make permanent changes to the logging level, we need to make changes to the `logging.properties` file and run the `nnmrereadlogging.ovpl` Perl script.

For example, to make permanent changes, we can edit the `logging.properties` file, make changes to the `.limit`, `.count`, and/or `.level` parameters of the process, then run the `nnmsetLoggingLevel.ovpl` Perl script to implement the changes to make them permanent.

Changing the logging level configuration

Occasionally, we may need to view a larger quantity of logged information to investigate slow NNM performance. We can configure NNM to log more information by adjusting the following logging parameters: `.count` and `.limit`.

Suppose you want to increase the number of log files and the amount of logged information for the discovery process. To do this, use the following procedure:

1. Open the `logging.properties` file in an ASCII editor.

2. Increase the number of log files for the discovery process to 10. This can be achieved by changing the following line:

   ```
   com.hp.ov.nms.admin.log.DiscoFileHandler.count = 5
   ```

   to read:

   ```
   com.hp.ov.nms.admin.log.DiscoFileHandler.count = 10
   ```

3. Increase the amount of logged information for the discovery process. Again, this can be achieved by changing the following line:

   ```
   com.hp.ov.nms.admin.log.DiscoFileHandler.limit = 10000000
   ```

   to read:

   ```
   com.hp.ov.nms.admin.log.DiscoFileHandler.limit = 50000000
   ```

4. Run the `nmmrereadlogging.ovpl` command (from the support directory).

Log file management

We should regularly monitor the log files contained in `%NNM_LOG%\nnm` (Windows OS) or `$NNM_LOG/nnm` (Unix OS) as they will continue to grow in size when a high level of logging is set. If we leave permanent or temporary logging at a high level, this can affect performance.

We need to remove any archived files that are using up too much of our disk space. If we modify the logging levels to FINE, FINER, or FINEST, we need to make sure we change them back to normal levels once we complete our diagnostics. If we have an intermittent problem, using the FINEST level may be aggressive and the log files will roll in seconds.

Ports used by NNMi

This section lists ports that are used by NNMi for internal communication and communication between the NNMi server and other systems.

The next table lists ports that NNMi uses on the management server for listening. The `Description` field provides a configuration file name that should be modified in case an other application is listening on a particular port and the NNMi default port needs to be changed.

Port	Protocol	Name	Description
80	TCP	`jboss.http.port`	HTTP port that is used for Web console UI and web services. If we need to change it, modify the `nms-local.properties` file.
162	UDP	`trapPort`	Port for SNMP traps. If we need to change it, modify the `nnmtrapconfig.ovpl` script.
443	TCP	`jboss.https.port`	HTTPS port (SSL), which is used for web console UI and web services. If we need to change it, modify the `nms-local.properties` file.
1098	TCP	`jboss.rmi.port`	Port for RMI naming service. If we need to change it, modify the `nms-local.properties` file.
1099	TCP	`jboss.jnp.port`	Port for bootstrap JNP service. If we need to change it, modify the `nms-local.properties` file.
3873	TCP	`jboss.ejb3.port`	Port for EJB3 remote connections. If we need to change it, modify `nms-local.properties` file.
4444	TCP	`jboss.jrmp.port`	RMI object port (JRMP invoker). If we wish to change it, modify the `nms-local.properties` file.
4445	TCP	`jboss.pooled.port`	RMI pooled invoker port. If we need to change it, modify the `nms-local.properties` file.
4446	TCP	`jboss.socked.port`	Port for RMI remote server connector. If we need to change it, modify the `nms-local.properties` file.
4457	TCP	`jboss.bisocked.port`	Message bi-socket connector. If we need to change it, modify the `nms-local.properties` file.
4458	TCP	`jboss.jmsControl.port`	JMS control port for global network management communication. If we need to change it, modify the `nms-local.properties` file.
4459	TCP	`jboss.sslbisocket.port`	Messaging bi-socket connector for secure global network management. If we need to change it, modify the `nms-local.properties` file.
4460	TCP	`jboss.ssljmsControl.port`	JMS control port for secure global network management. If you need to change it, modify the `nms-local.properties` file.
5432	TCP		Port for Postgres. Port is not configurable.

Port	Protocol	Name	Description
7800-7810	TCP		JGroups multicast ports, which are used for multi-subnet application failover. If we need to change it, modify the `nms-cluster.properties` file.
8083	TCP	`jboss.ws.port`	jboss Web Service port. If we need to change it, modify the `nms-local.properties` file.
8886	TCP	`OVsPMD_MGMT`	NNMi ovspmd management port. If we need to change it, modify the `/etc/services` file.
8887	TCP	`OVsPMD_REQ`	NNMi ovspmd request port. If we need to change it, modify the `/etc/services` file.
45588	UDP	`jgroups.udp.mcast_port`	JGroups multicast port, which is used for LAN application failover. If we need to change it, modify the `nms-cluster.properties` file.

The following table provides a list of default ports that NNMi uses to communicate to other systems. In case a firewall is used between the NNMi server and external application, ports listed in this table for a particular service should be opened.

Port	Protocol	Description	Client/Server
80	TCP	HTTP port for NNMi for Web UI and Web Services.	Server
80	TCP	HTTP port for NNMi to connect to other applications.	Client
161	UDP	Port for SNMP requests.	Client
162	UDP	Port for SNMP traps sent to NNMi.	Server
162	UDP	Port for SNMP traps forwarded from NNMi.	Client
389	TCP	LDAP port.	Client
395	UDP	SNMP port for nGenius Probe.	Client
443	TCP	Secure NNMi port that is used for connecting to other applications.	Server
443	TCP	HTTPS port that is used for WebUI and Web Services.	Client
636	TCP	Secure (SSL) LDAP protocol.	Client
1741	TCP	Web Services port for Cisco Works LMS.	Client
4457	TCP	Bi-socket messaging connector used for global network management communication — from global manager towards regional manager.	Client/Server

Port	Protocol	Description	Client/Server
4458	TCP	JMS control port used for global network management communication—from global manager towards regional manager.	Client/Server
4459	TCP	Bi-socket messaging connector used for secure global network management communication—from global manager towards regional manager.	Client/Server
4460	TCP	JMS control port used for secure global network management communication—from global manager towards regional manager.	Client/Server
7800-7810	TCP	JGroups Multicast port for multi-subnet application failover.	Client/Server
8004	TCP	NNMi port if port 80 is already taken by another web server.	Server
8080	TCP	Used to connect to Network Automation, if it is installed on the same system as NNMi.	Client
8443 or 8444	TCP	Port used to connect to HP Operations Manager for Unix.	Client
9300	TCP	Port used to connect to iSPI for Performance.	Client
45588	UDP	JGroups Multicast port for LAN application failover.	Client/Server
50000	TCP	HTTPS port used for connecting to **HP System Insight Manager (HP SIM)**.	Client

Troubleshooting tools

This section describes troubleshooting tools, which are most often used while administering NNMi.

System information

Starting from NNMi version 9.0, additional NNMi state information was delivered to system administrators over the console menu (**Help | System menu**) for the following areas:

- Discovery state check
- Health
- Server
- Database

- State poller
- Custom poller
- Extensions
- Component versions

Each piece of information is very useful while troubleshooting issues related to NNMi server. Also, it is recommended that the system administrator checks this information on a regular basis. How often such information should be checked depends on the environment that is being monitored:

- If a large number of devices are monitored (over 1000 devices), and the environment is dynamic and constantly growing, good practice would be to check the status on a daily basis.

- If a small or medium number of devices are monitored, the environment is stable, and the new equipment growth number is low, the status can be checked on a weekly basis.

The information is delivered in an easy to understand output window, where each of the mentioned information areas are presented as separate tabs.

Discovery state check

Probably the most often used troubleshooting activity is the discovery state check, which includes:

- Finding how many objects have been discovered
- Checking if the number of discovered objects hasn't exceeded the number of installed licenses
- Monitoring if the network is dynamic (number of devices in network changes) and the dynamic discovery rules are configured

By doing this we are trying to eliminate the risk that too many devices would be discovered and the license limit will be exceeded. Even if we have an unlimited license, we may still care about the amount of managed objects, as the amount of monitored objects directly influences our system performance.

The fastest and easiest way to do so is by using the application menu: **Help | About HP Network Node Manager I | Licensing Information**, which pops up a report window with discovered nodes and the installed license.

The following screenshot shows how licensing information is displayed.

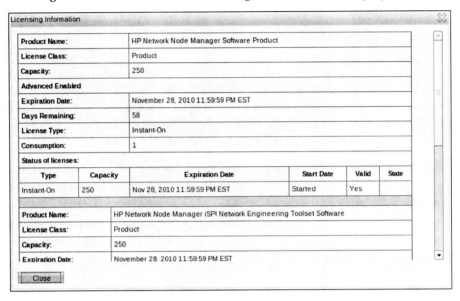

Health

The general system health is displayed in the **Health** tab, where the general health status is provided, if the status is not **Normal** the reasons are listed and should be fixed by the system administrator. To get a clearer picture, look at the following screenshot that shows the buffer configuration issue sent by the network socket:

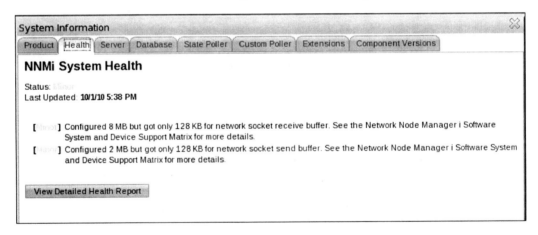

This information window was introduced in the version 9.0 of NNMi.

Server

General information about the server is provided in the Server tab, which provides very generic information about the server where NNMi is installed. The information provided includes:

- Hostname
- IP address
- IPv6 management
- Server's FQDN
- Single sign on configuration information
- Server's operating system
- Installation directory, where NNMi is installed
- Data directory
- The number of allocated processors for NNMi
- The number of free and allocated memory for NNMi
- NNMi's Maximum Attemptable Memory size

This information window was introduced in the version 9.0 of NNMi.

Database

The general information such as the number of objects in a database is provided in the **Database** tab. The information provided includes:

- Objects
- SNMP agents
- Interfaces
- IP addresses
- Incidents
- Node components

Information in this tab gives a rough idea about the monitored environment, as the monitored environment size in NNMi is described not only by the number of nodes but also by other objects, which are listed in this tab.

The server performance and capacity sizing shouldn't be made only based on information provided in this tab. **State Poller** and **Custom Poller** tab information should be also taken for a full system performance and capacity sizing or judging.

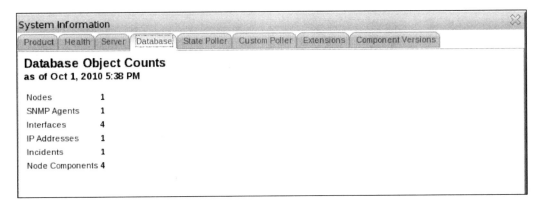

This information window was introduced in the version 9.0 of NNMi.

State Poller

The **State Poller** tab presents data about the NNMi system monitoring state and capacity. Based on these numbers we can tell how busy the system is. Information provided by this tab is also used for system tuning and sizing estimations.

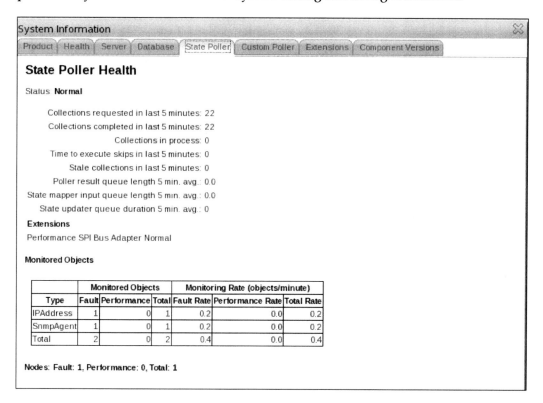

This information window was introduced in the version 9.0 of NNMi.

Custom Poller

The **Custom Poller** tab provides information about the state and performance of the custom poller. Based on these numbers we can tell how busy the custom poller is. Information provided by this tab is also used for system tuning and sizing estimations.

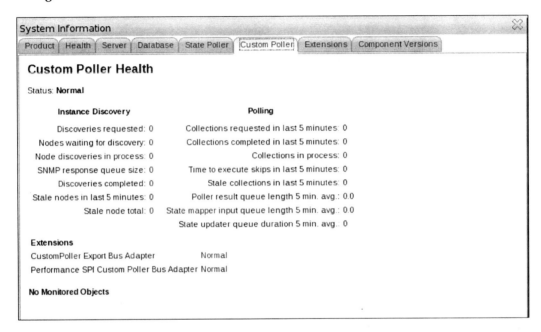

This information window was introduced in the version 9.0 of NNMi.

Extensions

This tab provides information about the extensions and the version that is installed on the NNMi server. This information is useful while searching for system patches or investigating issues related to system bugs.

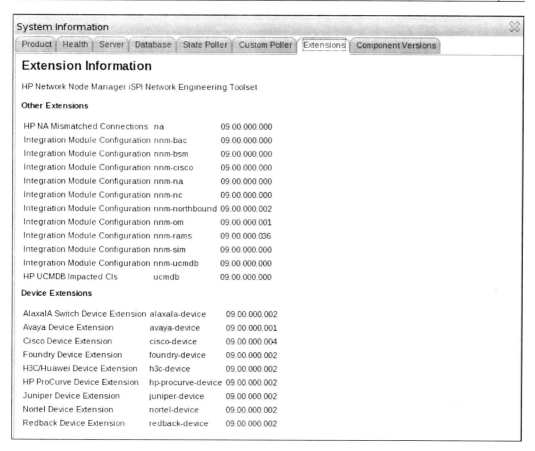

This information window was introduced in the version 9.0 of NNMi.

Loading MIBs

If we need to configure SNMP traps in NNMi, we have two options:

- Configuring each SNMP trap in Incident Configuration
- Loading SNMP MIB files

We need to check if we have or can download an MIB file before we decide to configure SNMP traps manually. Good sources for searches are:

- Manufacturer's website.
- Manufacturer's technical representatives.
- MIB depot website: `http://www.oidview.com/mibs`. This website contains a long list of MIB files from many vendors.
- Web search.

If we already have an MIB file, we can load it into NNMi using the nnmmibload.ovpl tool, which loads MIBs into NNMi and makes the SNMP trap configuration. So, if we are troubleshooting trap issues, we may find it interesting to check the MIBs already in the NNMi system. We can use the `nnmloadmibs.ovpl -list` that gives us a list of loaded MIBs.

Trimming incidents

All incidents are stored in our Postgres database and we may find some troubleshooting activities interesting, including:

- Trimming old incidents if want to create some space in our database.
- Exporting our incidents to third-party applications, such as Microsoft Excel, a Data Warehouse, and so on, for long term storage, archiving, or incident analysis.

We need to use the nnmtrimincidents.ovpl tool, which has a wide list of options to choose for trimming or exporting. Listed here is the usage of the nnmtrimincidents. ovpl tool:

```
Usage: nnmtrimincidents.ovpl -age <age> [-incr <incr>] | -date <date>
[-nature <nature>] [-lifecycle <lifecycleState>] [-family <family>]
[-origin <origin>] [-name <name>] [-sysobjectid <sysobjectid>] [-path
<path>] [-archiveOnly] [-trimOnly] [-batch <batchSize>] [-quiet] -u
<username> -p <password>

  -age <age>: specify the age of incidents to trim, in conjunction
with -i <incr>
        Must be greater than 0 if specified.
  -archiveOnly: Creates an archive file. Does not trim incidents.
  -batch <batch>: optionally specify the batch size when deleting
incidents. Default: 1000.
        Must be greater than 0 if specified. Maximum is 1000.
  -date <date>: specify an exact date from which older incidents are
trimmed
```

date is specified in ISO 8601 standard format: yyyy-mm-ddThh:mm:ss[+ or -]hhmm

-family <family>: optionally specify the family of incidents matching age | date to trim

Example families include:

Address

Interface

Node

HSRP

-incr <incr>: optionally specify the increment for age

Supported increments include: hours, days, weeks, months. Default: days

-jndiHost <hostname>: The server jndi host; default is localhost

-jndiPort <port>: The server jndi port; default is 1099

-lifecycle <lifecycle>: optionally specify the lifecycle state of incidents matching age | date to trim

Example lifecycle states include:

Registered

InProgress

Completed

Closed

-name <name>: optionally specify the name of incidents matching age | date to trim

-nature <nature>: optionally specify the nature of incidents matching age | date to trim

Example natures include:

RootCause

SecondaryRootCause

Symptom

ServiceImpact

StreamCorrelation

None

-origin <origin>: optionally specify the origin of incidents matching age | date to trim

Example origins include:

ManagementSoftware

ManuallyCreated

RemotelyGenerated

SnmpTrap

Syslog

Other

-p <password>: The password of the user

-path <path>: Archive file name with complete path.

-quiet <quiet>: optionally specify non-prompt mode.

-sysobjectid <sysobjectid>: optionally specify the device system

```
object id of incidents matching age | date to trim
  -trimOnly: Trim incidents without archiving off deleted incidents.
  -u <username>: The username to run this command
```

Here are a few examples using this tool:

- **Example 1**:

  Trim and export all incidents that have a Closed lifecycle state and are older than one month. We would use a tool with the following parameters:

  ```
  # /opt/OV/bin/nnmtrimincidents.ovpl -u username -p password -age 1
  -incr months -lifecycle Closed
  ```

  After we initiate the command, the tool makes estimations and prompts us to confirm our selection:

  ```
  Number of incidents selected for operation: 2.
  ```

  ```
  Reference date from which older incidents will be selected for
  operation: 2/24/10 8:12 PM.
  ```

  ```
  Percentage of the database selected for operation: 25.00%.
  ```

  ```
  Do you wish to continue (y/n)?
  ```

  If we select y as confirmation of our command, the incident trim and archiving starts and we will see a response similar to the following:

  ```
  Archiving selected incidents...
  ```

  ```
  Number of incidents archived: 2. Archive file: /var/opt/OV/tmp/
  incidentArchive.2010-03-24.1269475946585.txt.gz.
  ```

  ```
  Number of incidents successfully trimmed: 2.
  ```

  ```
  Done
  ```

  Archive file in the `/var/opt/OV/tmp` folder, which will have following naming convention: `incidentArchive.yyyy-mm-dd.unix_time_in_sec-onds.txt.gz`.

- **Example 2**:

  Export all incidents older than six days into archive and do not trim them from the database. We would run the tool with the following arguments:

  ```
  # /opt/OV/bin/nnmtrimincidents.ovpl -archiveOnly -age 6 -incr days
  ```

- **Example 3**:

  Trim only those SNMP traps that are older than March 20, 2010. We would run the tool with the following arguments:

  ```
  # /opt/OV/bin/nnmtrimincidents.ovpl -trimOnly -date 2010-03-
  20+02:00 -origin snmpTrap
  ```

- **Example 4**:

  Export incidents with lifecycle state as "Closed", without leaving them in the database, which are older than March 25, 2010. We would run the tool with the following arguments:

  ```
  # /opt/OV/bin/nnmtrimincidents.ovpl -date 2010-03-25+02:00 -
  lifecycle Closed
  ```

> Please note that if we trim incidents from the database, it will free up more space in the Postgres database, but the database file itself won't decrease in size. The database file grows with the size of data in the database, and it can be trimmed using external tools only.

Trimming Postgres database

Our Postgres database file grows when the amount of data increases in our database. If we delete some data (that is trim incidents), the size of the Postgres database file will remain the same. Incident trimming or deleting other data from Postgres does not reduce the database file size. We need to use external tools to trim database files. The `vacuumdb` tool is provided in NNMi for trimming the database.

This tool is not documented by HP at the time of writing. As long as we don't have issues with disk space, in most cases, we don't have to use this tool. If we need to use it, we should use it carefully.

Vacuum tool has two modes—offline and online.

- **Offline**: This mode helps free database space. Offline vacuum takes a long time and requires NNMi processes to be stopped, except the `nmsdbmgr` process. Owing to long downtime, it is not recommended to use this mode too often in production environments. We need to follow these steps while using the tool in this mode:

  i. Stop NNMi processes using the `ovstop -c` command.

  ii. Start only `nmsdbmgr` process using the `ovstart -c nmsdbmgr` command.

  iii. Run vacuum command with the following options: `vacuumdb -d nmm -U postgres -z -f`. Note that if we have any SPIs (Smart Plugins) installed on our NNMi, we should use following command: `vacuumdb -a -U postgres -z -f`. It will ask you for a password. Use `postgres` as the password.

  iv. Start NNMi processes using the `ovstop -c` command.

- **Online**: This mode does not free up our database space, but it ensures that our database doesn't keep on growing. This mode doesn't require any processes to be stopped. It is recommended to run this command on a regular basis, as it ensures that any space after an incident trim can be reused. An online database trim should be run using the following command:

```
vacuumdb -d nnm -U postgres -z -v
```

Connecting to Postgres database

NNMi doesn't provide native tools for connecting to the Postgres database and browsing through its tables and data.

Postgres offers the pgAdmin III tool that has a graphical user interface and allows us to browse through the entire database. We can download this tool from the Postgres website (`http://www.pgAdmin.org/download/`).

The following screenshot provides pgAdmin GUI for Linux:

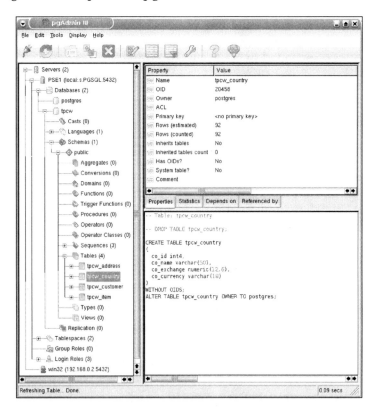

The website `pgAdmin.org` has pgAdmin III downloads for other OSes as well.

By default, Postgres denies connections from external hosts. To make a connection available, we need to configure our NNMi Postgres DB for external connections. Complete the following steps to make Postgres DB accessible from external machines:

1. Add the following line to `postgresql.conf` file:

    ```
    listen_address = '*'
    ```

    This will make the Postgres database listen to incoming remote TCP connections.

2. Reconfigure the Postgres database to allow external connections in the `pg_hba.conf` file:

    ```
    host    all    all    0.0.0.0/0    md5
    ```

    This will allow a connection from any address. If we want to be more specific about the address, we can replace `0.0.0.0/0` with a specific IP address and subnet mask.

3. To apply changes, restart Postgres DB:

    ```
    ovstop -c nmsdbmgr
    ovstart -c nmsdbmgr
    ```

Recreating Postgres database

There may be cases when we need to recreate our Postgres database. As an example, sometimes NNMi 8.03 and NNMi 8.10 installations on Windows have issues creating the Postgres database during installation. Another example could be a corrupted Postgres database during operations.

To recreate the Postgres DB, complete the following steps:

1. Stop NNMi processes using the `ovstop -c` command.

2. Delete present files from the Postgres database directory.

3. Initialize the Postgres database. Open console to run as `nmsdbmgr`:

    ```
    cd %NnmInstallDir%\nonOV\Postgres\bin

    runas /user:nmsdbmgr cmd

    %NnmInstallDir%\nonOV\Postgres\bin\initdb.exe -E UTF8 -D "D:\
    Application Data\HP\HP BTO Software\shared\nnm\databases\Postgres"
    -U postgres --pwfile="D:\Application Data\HP\HP BTO Software\
    shared\nnm\conf\embeddedDb\postgrespw.txt"
    ```

4. Copy `%NnmInstallDir%\newconfig\HPOvNnmGen\Postgres\postgresql. conf` into `D:\Application Data\HP\HP BTO Software\shared\nnm\ databases\Postgres`.

5. Restart `nmsdbmgr` process using the `ovstart -c nmsdbmgr` command.

6. Create the NNMi database using:

```
cd %NnmInstallDir%\nonOV\Postgres\bin
```

7. Run the following command to create the NNMi database:

```
nmscreatedb.vbs
```

8. To make sure that the database has been properly created, run the following command:

```
psql -U postgres -d nnm
```

Enter \q to exit the psql client.

9. Restart NNMi processes using the `ovstart -c` command.

Environment variables

To make access faster to the folder that is most commonly used, HP Software NNMi uses environment variables. This helps administrators save time typing paths and also makes system paths more consistent, that is, two NNMi servers may be installed on different paths. In that case, the administrator should remember the full path for both systems. What if the administrator maintains more than two systems—disaster! Also, imagine scripts for automatic actions or other scripts used to interact with NNMi; each script would have to have the full path to the file it tries to reach. To make the path easier, environment variables are used, that is, the path to log files is called using `$NNM_LOG` (if it's Unix/Linux OS) or `%NNM_LOG%` (if it's Windows OS).

Unix-based operating system environment variables

NNMi installation on Unix or Linux-based operating systems does not create environment variables. They need to be created manually. The following are the variables provided for default installation:

```
$NnmInstallDir:   /opt/OV
$NnmDataDir:      /var/opt/OV
```

Note: Path may be different, if paths other than default were selected during installation.

An extended list of environment variables may be used. The following script configures all extended variables for the NNMi system:

`/opt/OV/bin/nnm.envvars.sh`

The following table lists all extended variables that are configured when the script is launched:

Variable	Path
$NNM_BIN	/opt/OV/bin
$NNM_CONF	/var/opt/OV/conf
$NNM_DATA	/var/opt/OV
$NNM_DB	/var/opt/OV/databases
$NNM_JAVA	/opt/OV/nonOV/jdk/b/bin/java
$NNM_JAVA_DIR	/opt/OV/java
$NNM_JAVA_PATH_SEP	:
$NNM_JBOSS	$NNM_JBOSS
$NNM_JBOSS_DEPLOY	/opt/OV/nonOV/jboss/nms/server/nms/deploy
$NNM_JBOSS_LOG	/opt/OV/nonOV/jboss/nms/server/nms/log
$NNM_JBOSS_ROOT	/opt/OV/nonOV/jboss/nms
$NNM_JBOSS_SERVERCONF	/opt/OV/nonOV/jboss/nms/server/nms
$NNM_JRE	/opt/OV/nonOV/jdk/b
$NNM_LOG	/var/opt/OV/log
$NNM_LRF	/var/opt/OV/shared/nnm/lrf
$NNM_PRIV_LOG	/var/opt/OV/log
$NNM_SHARED_CONF *	/var/opt/OV/shared/nnm/conf
$NNM_SHARE_LOG	/var/opt/OV/log
$NNM_SNMP_MIBS	/var/opt/OV/share/snmp_mibs
$NNM_SUPPORT	/opt/OV/support
$NNM_TMP	/var/opt/OV/tmp
$NNM_USER_SNMP_MIBS *	/var/opt/OV/shared/nnm/user-snmp-mibs
$NNM_WWW	/opt/OV/www

* - variable was introduced in NNMi version 9.0 and is not in NNMi version 8.x.

Windows OS environment variables

If we install NNMi 8.01 or later, then the following environment variables for Windows-based NNMi installation are configured during the installation process:

- **Windows 2003**:

  ```
  %NnmInstallDir%:      <drive>\Program Files\HP\HP BTO Software
  %NnmDataDir%:         <drive>\Documents and Settings\All Users\
  Application Data\HP\HP BTO Software
  ```

- **Windows 2008**:

  ```
  %NnmInstallDir%:      <drive>\Program Files\HP\HP BTO Software
  %NnmDataDir%:         <drive>\ProgramData\HP\HP BTO Software
  ```

An extended list of environment variables may be used. The following script configures all extended variables for the NNMi system:

```
C:\Program Files\HP\HP BTO Software\bin\nnm.envvars.bat
```

The following table lists all extended variables that are configured when script is launched.

 Note: If NNMi 8.00 is running or was upgraded from this version, then the next table should be checked.

Variable	Path
%NNM_BIN%	C:\Program Files\HP\HP BTO Software\bin
%NNM_CONF%	• Windows 2003: C:\Documents and Settings\All Users\Application Data\HP\HP BTO Software\conf • Windows 2008: C:\ProgramData\HP\HP BTO Software\conf
%NNM_DATA%	• Windows 2003: C:\Documents and Settings\All Users\Application Data\HP\HP BTO Software • Windows 2008: C:\ProgramData\HP\HP BTO Software
%NNM_DB%	• Windows 2003: C:\Documents and Settings\All Users\Application Data\HP\HP BTO Software\databases • Windows 2008: C:\ProgramData\HP\HP BTO Software\databases

Variable	Path
%NNM_JAVA%	C:\Program Files\HP\HP BTO Software\nonOV\jdk\b\bin\java.exe
%NNM_JAVA_DIR%	C:\Program Files\HP\HP BTO Software\java
%NNM_JAVA_PATH_SEP%	;
%NNM_JBOSS%	C:\Program Files\HP\HP BTO Software\nonOV\jboss\nms
%NNM_JBOSS_DEPLOY%	C:\Program Files\HP\HP BTO Software\nonOV\jboss\nms\server\nms\deploy
%NNM_JBOSS_LOG%	C:\Program Files\HP\HP BTO Software\nonOV\jboss\nms\server\nms\log
%NNM_JBOSS_ROOT%	C:\Program Files\HP\HP BTO Software\nonOV\jboss\nms
%NNM_JBOSS_SERVERCONF%	C:\Program Files\HP\HP BTO Software\nonOV\jboss\nms\server\nms
%NNM_JRE%	C:\Program Files\HP\HP BTO Software\nonOV\jdk\b
%NNM_LOG%	<ul><li>Windows 2003: C:\Documents and Settings\All Users\Application Data\HP\HP BTO Software\log</li><li>Windows 2008: C:\ProgramData\HP\HP BTO Software\log</li></ul>
%NNM_LRF%	<ul><li>Windows 2003: C:\Documents and Settings\All Users\Application Data\HP\HPBTO Software\shared\nnm\lrf</li><li>Windows 2008: C:\ProgramData\HP\HP BTO Software\lrf</li></ul>
%NNM_PRIV_LOG%	<ul><li>Windows 2003: C:\Documents and Settings\All Users\Application Data\HP\HP BTO Software\log</li><li>Windows 2008: C:\ProgramData\HP\HP BTO Software\log</li></ul>
%NNM_PROPS% *	<ul><li>Windows 2003: C:\Documents and Settings\All Users\Application Data\HP\HP BTO Software\shared\nnm\props</li><li>Windows 2008: C:\ProgramData\HP\HP BTO Software\shared\nnm\props</li></ul>

Variable	Path

%NNM_SHARED_CONF% *	• Windows 2003:
	`C:\Documents and Settings\All Users\`
	`Application Data\HP\HP BTO Software\shared\`
	`nnm\conf`
	• Windows 2008:
	`C:\ProgramData\HP\HP BTO Software\shared\`
	`nnm\props`

%NNM_SHARE_LOG%	• Windows 2003:
	`C:\Documents and Settings\All Users\`
	`Application Data\HP\HP BTO Software\log`
	• Windows 2008:
	`C:\ProgramData\HP\HP BTO Software\log`

%NNM_SNMP_MIBS% *	`C:\Documents and Settings\All Users\Application`
	`Data\HP\`
	
	`HP BTO Software\share\snmp_mibs`

%NNM_SUPPORT%	`C:\Program Files\HP\HP BTO Software\support`

%NNM_TMP%	• Windows 2003:
	`C:\Documents and Settings\All Users\`
	`Application Data\HP\HP BTO Software\tmp`
	• Windows 2008:
	`C:\ProgramData\HP\HP BTO Software\tmp`

%NNM_USER_SNMP_MIBS% *	• Windows 2003:
	`C:\Documents and Settings\All Users\`
	`Application Data\HP\HP BTO Software\shared\`
	`nnm\user-snmp-mibs`
	• Windows 2008:
	`C:\ProgramData\HP\HP BTO Software\shared\`
	`nnm\user-snmp-mibs`

%NNM_WWW%	`C:\Program Files\HP\HP BTO Software\www`

* - variable was introduced in NNMi version 9.0 and is not in NNMi version 8.x.

If we have installed NNMi 8.00 version, or have upgraded from this version, we should see the following table for an extended list of environment variables. This table is also valid for later NNMi versions, if they were upgraded from NNMi 8.00. The following variables are created automatically during installation:

```
%NnmInstallDir%:        <drive>\Program Files (x86)\HP OpenView
%NnmDataDir%:           <drive>\Program Files (x86)\HP OpenView\data
```

Environment variables can be set up by running the following script:

```
C:\Program Files(x86)\HP OpenView\bin\nnm.envvars.bat
```

The next table lists the environment variables for NNMi 8.00:

Variable	Path
%NNM_BIN%	C:\Program Files (x86)\HP OpenView\bin
%NNM_CONF%	C:\Program Files (x86)\HP OpenView\data\conf
%NNM_DATA%	C:\Program Files (x86)\HP OpenView\data
%NNM_DB%	C:\Program Files (x86)\HP OpenView\data\ databases
%NNM_JAVA%	C:\Program Files (x86)\HP OpenView\nonOV\ jdk\b\bin\java.exe
%NNM_JAVA_DIR%	C:\Program Files (x86)\HP OpenView\java
%NNM_JAVA_PATH_SEP%	;
%NNM_JBOSS%	C:\Program Files (x86)\HP OpenView\nonOV\ jboss\nms
%NNM_JBOSS_DEPLOY%	C:\Program Files (x86)\HP OpenView\ nonOV\ jboss\nmsserver\nms\deploy
%NNM_JBOSS_LOG%	C:\Program Files (x86)\HP OpenView\ nonOV\ jboss\nms\server\nms\log
%NNM_JBOSS_ROOT%	C:\Program Files (x86)\HP OpenView\ nonOV\ jboss\nms
%NNM_JBOSS_SERVERCONF%	C:\Program Files (x86)\HP OpenView\ nonOV\ jboss\nms\server\nms
%NNM_JRE%	C:\Program Files (x86)\HP OpenView\nonOV\ jdk\b
%NNM_LOG%	C:\Program Files (x86)\HP OpenView\data\log
%NNM_LRF% *	C:\Program Files (x86)\HP OpenView\data\ shared\nnm\lrf
%NNM_PRIV_LOG%	C:\Program Files (x86)\HP OpenView\data\log
%NNM_PROPS% *	C:\Program Files (x86)\HP OpenView\data\ shared\nnm\conf\props
%NNM_SHARE_LOG%	C:\Program Files (x86)\HP OpenView\data\log
%NNM_SHARED_CONF% *	C:\Program Files (x86)\HP OpenView\data\ shared\nnm\conf
%NNM_SNMP_MIBS%	C:\Program Files (x86)\HP OpenView\ data\ share\snmp_mibs
%NNM_SUPPORT%	C:\Program Files (x86)\HP OpenView\suport
%NNM_TMP%	C:\Program Files (x86)\HP OpenView\data\tmp
%NNM_USER_SNMP_MIBS% *	C:\Program Files (x86)\HP OpenView\data\ shared\nnm\user-snmp-mibs
%NNM_WWW%	C:\Program Files (x86)\HP OpenView\www

* - variable was introduced in NNMi version 9.0 and is not in NNMi version 8.x.

Command security issues

Many NNMi command line tools require a system or administrator-level username and password in order to complete commands. Such a solution was implemented because, in the previous NNM versions (version 6.x/7.x), command line tools were secured relying only on file system security. So, if a user has executed permission access to the command line tool file, it can be launched. On the other hand, a username and password in a plain text command line is not secure enough, especially in a Unix-based OS, as some user history can be viewed (and usernames and passwords).

Some improvements were introduced, which avoids entering a username and password in the command line if the user has created an `nnm.properties` file that keeps the username and encrypted password. Since NNMi version 8.13, this feature was widened in the sense that `nnm.properties` files could be created for all users (while previous versions allowed this only for users with a system or administrator profile). The following commands are accessible for all users without entering a username and password:

Tool	Description
nnmmanagementmode.ovpl	Management mode configuration command line tool.
nnmcommconf.ovpl	Communication mode configuration command line tool.
nnmcommload.ovpl	Communication settings load command line tool. For example, loading SNMP settings to NNMi.
nnmsnmpbulk.ovpl	snmpbulk command line tool provided by NNMi.
nnmsnmpget.ovpl	snmpget command line tool provided by NNMi.
nnmsnmpnext.ovpl	snmpnext command line tool provided by NNMi.
nnmsnmpset.ovpl	snmpset command line tool provided by NNMi.
nnmsnmpwalk.ovpl	snmpwalk command line tool provided by NNMi.
nnmincidentcfg.ovpl	Incident configuration command line tool.
nnmtrimincidents.ovpl	Incident trimming command line tool.
nnmtrapconfig.ovpl	SNMP trap configuration in NNMi command line tool.
nnmconfigexport.ovpl	NNMi configuration export command line tool.
nnmconfigimport.ovpl	NNMi configuration import command line tool.
nnmstatuspoll.ovpl	NNMi status poll configuration command line tool.
nnmloadnodegroups.ovpl	NNMi node group loading command line tool.
nnmsnmpnotify.ovpl	Snmpnotify command line tool provided by NNMi.
nnmtopodelete.ovpl	Topology data deletion command line tool.
nnmtopodump.ovpl	Topology dump command line tool.
nnmtrapdump.ovpl	SNMP trap dumping from NNMi database, command line tool.

An exception for the `nnmloadmib.ovpl` file has been left (at least until NNMi 8.13, at the time of writing).

It is good practice to use the `nnm.properties` file for all users who run tools in a command line. This improves system security.

Backing up NNMi

A well-planned and maintained backup plan can save a lot of effort and avoid data losses. I'm sure no one wants their system to crash so that it needs to be deployed from scratch. What about incidents? If we are re-deploying the system, they would be lost forever. Well-planned backup and recovery activities may also be part of our system's disaster recovery plan. We should not be surprised if managers from the business unit start asking whether we have such a plan and, most important, if it is working. Here is an area in which business people are interested. Imagine that our system has crashed and we lost alarms for the last month. Our company has SLAs with customers or our unit has SLAs with other departments within a company, where one of our company's (department's) obligations is to deliver availability reports on a regular basis. And, of course, we have lost that data. Here is the moment when the fun ends. So, every system administrator knows how boring backups are, but by doing so we can avoid the situation described above. I'm sure that most of the system administrators understand the importance of system backups.

NNMi has two types of data that needs to be backed up:

- Files in a file system
- Data in database—either embedded or external (like Oracle)

NNMi backup copies files from the file system and some, or all, tables in a Postgres database to the defined backup location. It can also archive to a tar file during backup.

 Note: NNMi backup does not copy external database. Backup of external databases has to be done with native tools of the external databases.

Also, NNMi backup may not include some of the SPI data. Read online help documents for each Smart Plugin (iSPI), as the backup procedure for each iSPI may differ. Manuals in PDF version can be downloaded from the HP Software product manual website (`http://support.openview.hp.com/selfsolve/manuals/`).

The following tools are used for system backup:

- `nnmbackup.ovpl`: This tool creates a backup of all necessary file system data and data stored in the NNMi embedded database.

- `nnmbackupembdb.ovpl`: This tool creates a complete backup of the NNMi embedded database.

Backup types

NNMi has the ability to create backups in two ways:

- **Online backup**: This type of backup can be created without stopping any services, and operators can continue working during online backup. Online backup ensures that data in the database are synchronized in the backed up data. We can use the scope option to define our backup scope, which can be either all NNMi data or only part of it. If backup of an embedded database is performed, the `nnmdbmgr` service must be running.

- **Offline backup**: This type of backup is created when all NNMi services are completely stopped. Offline backup applies to file system files only. All files of the embedded database are copied regardless of the scope. If an external database is used, offline backup performs a backup of file system data only.

The following table lists main differences between online and offline backups:

Data	Online	Offline
Ability to work with open consoles	✓	
Define backup scope	✓	
`nmsdbmgr` process must be running	✓	
All processes must be stopped		✓

We probably will find online backup more convenient, as we don't have to stop NNM processes. We can also create a cron job or scheduled action, so the backup will be created automatically. The only thing we have to take care is to make sure we have enough disk space for backups, our backups are running without errors, and that the backup we are overwriting on a regular basis is not the only one we have. If the system fails to make a backup and it crashes, we are left without any backup files.

Backup scope

When running the `nnmbackup.ovpl` tool, there is an option to set a scope for backup, which allows a backup to be created only for some parts of the NNMi database. This option makes sense only during online backup, as offline backup copies all Postgres database files without analyzing data inside these files.

The following table lists all scopes used in the nnmbackup.ovpl tool.

Scope	Description
Configuration	This scope covers what is included in the Configuration workspace. Usage: `nnmbackup.ovpl -scope configuration`
Topology	This scope covers what is included in the Inventory workspace and configuration scope, as topology is related to data that is stored in configuration scope. Usage: `nnmbackup.ovpl -scope topology`
Event	This scope covers what is included in Incident Browsing workspace, configuration, and topology scopes as well, because incident information is related to topology and configuration scope. Usage: `nnmbackup.ovpl -scope event`
All scope	This scope covers all important NNMi files and the complete embedded database. Usage: `nnmbackup.ovpl -scope all`

The following diagram shows the area that covers each scope option:

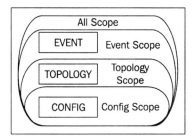

During either backup type (online or offline) and backup scope, the configuration scope directories listed in the following table are backed up.

[**Note**: Custom poller database tables are included in complete backup only.]

Data	Default location
(Windows only)	Configuration information.
`%NnmInstallDir%\conf`	
`$NnmInstall/misc/nnm`	Miscellaneous configuration information.
`%NnmInstallDir%\misc\nnm`	
`$NnmInstall/misc/nms/lic`	License information.
`%NnmInstallDir%\misc\nms\lic`	
`$NnmInstall/newconfig`	Installation configuration staging area.
`%NnmInstallDir%\newconfig`	
`$NnmInstall/nonOV/jboss/nms/serves/nms/conf`	jboss configuration information.
`%NnmInstallDir%\nonOV\jboss\nms\serves\nms\conf`	
`$NnmInstall/nonOV/jboss/nms/serves/nms/deploy`	jboss deployment directory.
`%NnmInstallDir%\nonOV\jboss\nms\serves\nms\deploy`	
`$NnmDataDir/share/snmp_mibs` `%NnmInstallDir%\snmp_mibs`	SNMP MIB information.
`$NnmDataDir/conf`	Configuration information (This folder may be used by other HP Software (HP OpenView) products as well.)
`%NnmDataDir%\conf`	
`$NnmDataDir/HPOvLIC/LicFile.txt`	NNMi license file.
`%NnmDataDir%\HPOvLIC\LicFile.txt`	
`$NnmDataDir/NNMVersionInfo`	NNMi version information file
`%NnmDataDir%\NNMVersionInfo`	
`$NnmDataDir/shared/nnm/certificates`	Shared NNMi SSL certificates.
`%NnmDataDir%\shared\nnm\certificates`	
`$NnmDataDir/shared/nnm/conf`	Shared NNMi configuration information.
`%NnmDataDir%\shared\nnm\conf`	

Data	Default location
`$NnmDataDir/shared/nnm/conf/` `licensing`	Shared NNMi license configuration information.
`%NnmDataDir%\shared\nnm\conf\` `licensing`	
`$NnmDataDir/shared/nnm/lrf`	Shared NNMi component registration files.
`%NnmDataDir%\shared\nnm\lrf`	

Data	Default location
`$NnmDataDir/log/nnm/` `signin.0.0.log`	NNMi console sign-in log.
`%NnmDataDir%\log\nnm\` `signin.0.0.log`	

Backups are made using `nnmbackup.ovpl` tool. The following are the tool usage options provided:

`nnmbackup.ovpl [-?|-h|-help] [-type (online|offline)] [-scope (config |topology|events|all)] [-force] [-archive] -target <directory>`

- `-?|-h|-help`: Display usage
- `-type`: Backup type to perform
- `-scope`: Scope of the backup operation
- `-force`: Stop NNM if it is running
- `-archive`: Archive output to a tar file
- `-target`: Target directory

If we need to back up only the embedded database without backing up the NNMi filesystem data while NNMi is running, we can use the `nnmbackupembedded.ovpl` tool. Tool usage options are provided here:

`nnmbackupembdb.ovpl [-?|-h|-help] [-force] -target <directory>`

- `-?|-h|-help`: Display usage
- `-force`: Start NNM if not already running
- `-target`: Target directory

 Note: We should run NNMi processes manually after backup is complete, if we use the `-force` option.

- **Example 1**:

    Let's take an example where we want to create an online backup of all NNMi scope and store the archive in the /tmp folder. The command would be:

    ```
    # /opt/OV/bin/nnmbackup.ovpl -force -type online -scope all -
    archive -target /tmp/
    ```

    We will get many output lines running, which will tell us which special file placement key it found, list different scopes of what it attempts to backup, what blocks are moving, and so on. The line **NNM backup operation completed successfully!** will tell us that online backup is complete. The following is an example of possible output:

    ```
    Skipping empty property definition: topology.fs in file /var/opt/
    OV/shared/nnm/backup.properties.


    Found special file placement key embdb.dir=<OV_DATA>/shared/nnm/
    databases/Postgres


    Found special file placement key hostspecific.files=<OV_DATA>/
    shared/nnm/conf/fqdn.properties,<NON_OV>/jboss/nms/server/nms/
    conf/lwssofmconf.xml


    . . .


    Attempting to backup /opt/OV/misc/nms/lic to /tmp/nnm-bak-
    20100324201007/misc/nms/lic


    . . .


    Moving /tmp/nnm-bak-20100324201007/data/shared/nnm/certificates/
    nnm.keystore to /tmp/nnm-bak-20100324201007/special_files/cert_
    merge/data/shared/nnm/certificates/nnm.keystore for certification
    merge during restore


    . . .


    pg_dump: [archiver] WARNING: requested compression not
    available in this installation -- archive will be uncompressed


    NNM backup operation completed successfully!
    ```

Note: Lines with "..." symbols show cut output areas that were repeating the same type of message.

- **Example 2:**

  Let's say we want online backup for configuration scope, without archiving a backup, which should be stored in the `/home/user/nnmi_backups folder`.

  The command would look like:

  nnmbackupembdb.ovpl -force -type online -scope configuration \

  -target /home/user/nnmi_backups

  To make the very same backup but without forcing it to stop NNMi processes, we need to run the following command:

  nnmbackupembdb.ovpl -type online -scope configuration \

  -target /home/user/nnmi_backups

Restoring NNMi

Now we know how to make a backup, let's take a look how to restore NNMi. When restore is launched, it places all backed up data into the NNMi management server. Depending on which type of backup is restored (online or offline), a different approach is taken. In either case, system files are replaced from the backup.

- **Online backup:** During restore from online backup, NNMi overwrites the content of database tables:
  - ○ If new objects have been created since the last backup, they are deleted.
  - ○ If some objects have been deleted since the last backup, they are created.
  - ○ If some objects have been modified since the last backup, they are overwritten.

  Service nnmdbmgr must be running if embedded database is restored.

  If an external database is used, no processes should be running during this restore.

- **Offline backup:** During restore from offline backup, NNMi overwrites Postgres files on the file system.

Note: As the NNMi database structure may be changed during version changes, data restores cannot be made on other version of NNMi.

 Note: To check which version and patch level your NNMi is running, we need to select following: **Help | About NNMi**.

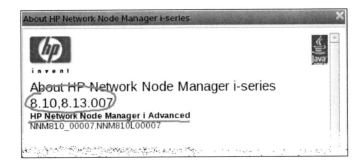

If the backup is compressed as a tar file, NNMi extracts this file during restore to the temporary folder of the current working directory.

We need to make sure we have enough space in our working directory before running a restore.

A system restore can be applied on the same NNMi server, or it can be applied to a different NNMi server for transfer purposes. Some criteria must be met for each of these restore scenarios.

Same system restore

The following information must be identical between the backed up and restored systems:

- **Operating system version and type**: For example, a restore wouldn't work if NNMi has been backed up on Windows 2003, and the restored system is running on Windows 2008.

- **NNMi version and patching level**: For example, a restore wouldn't work if the patch level was installed after the last backup was made. Consider making a new backup after every patch installation.

- **Character set**: Character settings (language) must be the same.

- **Hostname**: NNMi server hostname must be the same. Consider making a backup if the server name has been changed.

- **Domain**: Server domain name must be the same as it was during a backup. Consider making a backup if the server name has been changed.

 Note: NNMi doesn't pay attention to the system IP address.

```
nnmrestore.ovpl [-?|-h|-help] [-force] [-lic] [-partial] -source
<directory>
```

- `-?|-h|-help:` Display usage
- `-force:` Stop/start NNM as required
- `-lic:` Restore licensing if a same system restore is detected
- `-partial:` Do not restore the database and SSL certificates
- `-source:` The source directory or tar file

Different system restore

The following information must be identical between backed up and restored systems:

- Operating system version and type
- NNMi version and patching level
- Character set

Backup and restore embedded database only

When you test an NNMi configuration, you may want to make a backup of the full embedded database without backing up system files, so you could restore only the database. The following tools are provided for managing the embedded database:

- nnmbackupembdb.ovpl
- nnmrestoreembdb.ovpl

These commands create only online backups, so at least the service `nmsdbmgr` must be running.

`nnmbackupembdb.ovpl [-?|-h|-help] [-force] -target <directory>`

- `-?|-h|-help`: Display usage
- `-force`: Start NNM if not already running
- `-target`: Target directory

It is recommended to reset the database before you restore it. This ensures that no errors have been left on the database. The following command should be used to reset the database:

`nnmrestoreembdb.ovpl [-?|-h|-help] [-force] -source <file>`

- `-?|-h|-help`: Display usage
- `-force`: Stop/start NNM as required
- `-source`: Source file

Restore system files only

If you need to restore system files only, without restoring the database, run the following command:

`nnmrestore.ovpl -partial \`

`-source nnmi_backups/offline/latest_backup_version`

As an example this can be the NNMi system with the Oracle database. In that case, you need to restore the database using Oracle native management tools.

Backup and restore strategies

Most NNMi implementations are made in dynamic environments, where network monitoring demand or amount of monitored network equipment is constantly changing, and so are our NNMi changes. We wish we were guaranteed that any change we made in NNMi wouldn't affect our expectations negatively. We wish our system never crashed either. But Murphy's Law comes when we least expect such things: *Anything that can go wrong, will go wrong.*

Some crash or misconfiguration scenarios we cannot predict, but we can be prepared to minimize losses. The more scenarios we list and prepare for, the safer we will be, and we can assure better system operation continuity.

The following topics describe backup strategies, which may be met most frequently.

Back up NNMi before making configuration changes

Before we make configuration changes, we can create a configuration backup. This type of backup backs up only NNMi configuration changes. In case our changes were not successful or, for some other reason, we decided to revert to the previous version, we will restore by running the configuration restore tool.

Here are example commands for making a configuration backup:

```
nnmbackup.ovpl -type online \
-scope config -target nnmi_backups/config
```

To restore from backup, stop NNMi processes and run the following command:

```
nnmrestore.ovpl -force \
-source nnmi_backups/config/latest_backup_version
```

We need to make sure we start the service again.

Back up NNMi before upgrading

HP recommends making a complete backup of the system before applying any patch or making an upgrade. For this purpose, create an offline backup:

```
nnmbackup.ovpl -type offline \
-scope all -target nnmi_backups/offline
```

To restore the system from the following backup on the same server, run the following command:

```
nnmrestore.ovpl -lic \
-source nnmi_backups/offline/latest_backup_version
```

 Note: If we perform the restore on different servers, the license information is not restored. We need to provide license information for our new system.

Back up all data on a regular basis

No matter how often we make changes to our system configuration, it is wise to create backups on a regular basis. We can schedule this task to initiate automatically using cron (Linux, Unix OS) or scheduled action (Windows OS). The command for such a backup would look like following:

```
nnmbackup.ovpl -force -type online \
-scope all -archive -target nnmi_backups/automatic
```

To recover a system from the following backup we would:

- Install NNMi to the same version and very same patch level.
- Restore the NNMi data. If we restore the system to the same server, we should also include restore license information. The command would look like the following:

```
nnmrestore.ovpl -force -lic \
-source nnmi_backups/automatic
```

  Otherwise, if we restore our system on a different server, we need to run the restore without the license recovery option. The command should look like following:

```
nnmrestore.ovpl -force \
-source nnmi_backups/automatic
```

Real life story: A trainer asked students to raise their hands who performed system backups. All students raised their hands. Then the trainer asked those students to raise their hands to see who performed restores on a regular basis. Only 30 percent of the class raised their hands. Those who didn't raise their hands on the recovery question had many examples when they needed to restore but the restore of the backup didn't work. It was because of old or damaged tape, wrongly configured or failed backup, among other reasons; but nobody cared to check the log files. The lesson of this story is to exercise disaster recovery on a regular basis, just to make sure we have the right backups and the backup system is working properly.

Configuration migration

Configuration changes in NNMi are a part of daily operations. Examples of such actions could be: a user being created, discovery scope being changed, new communication settings added, new maps being created, and so on.

NNMi provides a tool that enables configuration export and import. This allows us to make configuration copies for backup purposes or make a configuration transfer from one NNMi system to another, which includes:

- Configuration migration from test to production environment
- Configuration migration to another NNMi system

The following two tools are used for configuration export and import: nnmconfigexport.ovpl and nnmconfigimport.ovpl.

The following is the usage of these tools:

```
Usage: nnmconfigexport.ovpl -? | -u <user> -p <password> -c <configuratio
n>[,configuration...]
                              [ -a <author_key> ] [ -f <xml file or
directory> ] [-x <file prefix>] [ -jndiHost <hostname> ] [ -jndiPort
<port> ]
Valid configurations:
        account     - export user/role
        author      - export author
        comm        - export communication
        custpoll    - export custom poller configuration (depends on
nodegroup)
        device      - export device profile (depends on author)
        disco       - export discovery
        discoseed   - export discovery seeds
        ifgroup     - export interface group (depends on nodegroup and
iftype)
        iftype      - export interface type
        incident    - export incident (depends on author)
        monitoring - export monitoring (depends on nodegroup, ifgroup,
device, iftype, author)
        nodegroup   - export node group (depends on device, author)
        ngmap       - export node group map (depends on nodegroup)
        rams        - export route analytics management server(s)
configuration
        station     - export management station
        status      - export Status settings
        urlaction   - export URL action (depends on author)
        ui          - export User Interface settings
        all         - export all configuration areas (requires -f)
```

Examples:

        nnmconfigexport.ovpl -u adminuser -p adminpassword -c comm
                export the communication configuration to stdout

        nnmconfigexport.ovpl -u adminuser -p adminpassword -c comm,disco
-f /tmp
                export the communication and discovery configurations to the
files /tmp/comm.xml and /tmp/disco.xml

        nnmconfigexport.ovpl -u adminuser -p adminpassword -c urlaction
-a com.hp.nas.nnm.author -f /tmp/urlactionconfig.xml
                export the urlaction configuration created by author with key
com.hp.nas.nnm.author to the file /tmp/urlactionconfig.xml

        -?: print this usage statement

        -c <configuration>: export XML schema for the specified
configuration.
                (comma separated for multiple configurations, requires
output directory)

        -a <author_key>: export for incremental import, filtered by
author with specified key
                (only for author, device, incident, or urlaction)

        -f <xml file or directory>: save the output of the exported XML
schema to a file or directory

        -x <file prefix>: prefix for file names if output specified for
-f is a directory

        -jndiHost <hostname>: the server jndi host; default is localhost

        -jndiPort <port>: the server jndi port; default is 1099

        -p <password>: provide password to the NNM administrator account

        -u <user>: provide the NNM administrator user name

Usage: nnmconfigimport.ovpl -? | -u <user> -p <password> -f <xml file or
directory> [-x <file prefix>] [-jndiHost <hostname>] [-jndiPort <port>
]

  Example:
        nnmconfigimport -u myadminusername -p myadminpassword -f /tmp/
nnmconfig.xml
                Import the customized configuration in /tmp/nnmconfig.xml
file to NNM database.

```
        -?: print this usage statement
        -f <xml file or directory>: import the configuration xml file or
directory contents
        -x <file prefix>: prefix for file names if input specified for -f
is a directory
        -jndiHost <hostname>: the server jndi host; default is localhost
        -jndiPort <port>: the server jndi port; default is 1099
        -p <password>: provide password to the NNM administrator account
        -u <user>: provide the NNM administrator user name
```

No matter whether configuration is transferred to a new host or imported back to the original host, the export/import sequence is the same:

1. If we export a part of the configuration, we need to check whether the configuration parts we export have any dependencies before we start the export. Some additional configuration parts may be required.

2. Run export command with necessary dependencies and options.

3. Make sure locale of NNMi server, where configuration is imported, matches with locale of NNMi from which configuration has been exported.

4. Now we need to import configuration into target server.

Import/export behavior and dependencies

Some configuration dependencies may exist during configuration import. This is because some configuration parts may be dependent on the data located on other configuration parts. We need to make sure we know dependencies before we make an export and have exported all the required configuration parts.

The next to next table provides dependencies of every configuration part.

Another thing that we should understand about import is how imported data behaves. There are the following import behavior types:

- Replace all
- Incremental
- Incremental subset

The next table describes each of behavior types:

Behavior	Description
Replace all	When using this option, NNMi import does the following: • NNMi replaces all object instances that have matching key identifiers • If import has object instances with key identifiers that don't exist in database, they are added • If import does not have object instances that are in database, NNMi deletes such object instances from database
Incremental	Export files with this behavior include configuration changes that were made by one author. When using this option, NNMi import does the following: • NNMi replaces all object instances that have matching key identifiers • If import has object instances with key identifiers that don't exist in database, they are added • If import does not have object instances that are in database, NNMi does not delete them
Incremental subset	When using this option, NNMi import does the following: • NNMi replaces all object instances that have matching key identifiers • If import has object instances with key identifiers that don't exist in database, they are added • If import does not have object instances that are in database, NNMi does not delete them

The following table lists the behavior type within each of the configuration part:

View name of configuration workspace	Export option	Behavior	Dependencies
Author*	`-c author`	Incremental	No dependencies. Import requires one export file (`author.xml`).
	`-c author -a <author>`	Incremental subset	No dependencies. Import requires one export file (`author.xml`).

View name of configuration workspace	Export option	Behavior	Dependencies
Communication	`-c comm`	Replaces all	No dependencies. Import requires one export file (`comm.xml`). Please note that SNMPv3 credentials are not imported.
Custom Poller	`-c custpoll`	Incremental	Import requires the following Export files, which must be imported in order: • `author.xml` • `device.xml` • `nodegroup.xml` • `custpoll.xml` (Active state attribute is set to Suspended for all imported policies, when Custom Poller configurations are imported.)
Device Profiles	`-c device`	Incremental	Import requires the following Export files, which must be imported in order: • `author.xml` • `device.xml`
	`-c device -a author`	Incremental subset	No dependencies. Import requires one export file (`device.xml`) and required author information is already embedded in the export file.
Discovery	`-c disco`	Replaces all	Import requires the following export files, which must be imported in the following order: • `comm.xml` • `discoseed.xml` • `disco.xml`

View name of configuration workspace	Export option	Behavior	Dependencies
Discovery Seeds	`-c discoseed`	Incremental	Import requires the following export files, which must be imported in order: • `comm.xml` • `discoseed.xml`
Incident	`-c incident`	Replaces all	Import requires following export files, which must be imported in order: • `author.xml` • `incident.xml`
	`-c incident` `-a <author>`	Incremental subset	No dependencies. Import requires one export file (`incident.xml`) and required author information is already embedded in export file.
Interface Groups	`-c ifgroup`	Incremental	Import requires following Export files, which must be imported in the following order: • `iftype.xml` • `author.xml` • `device.xml` • `nodegroup.xml` • `ifgroup.xml`
IfTypes	`-c iftype`	Incremental	No dependencies. Import requires one export file (`iftype.xml`).
Management Stations (6.x/7.x)	`-c station`	Incremental	No dependencies. Import requires one export file (`station.xml`).

View name of configuration workspace	Export option	Behavior	Dependencies
Monitoring	`-c monitoring`	Replaces all	Import requires the following Export files, which must be imported in order: • `author.xml` • `device.xml` • `nodegroup.xml` • `iftype.xml` • `ifgroup.xml` • `monitoring.xml`
Node Groups	`-c nodegroup`	Incremental	Import requires the following Export files, which must be imported in order: • `author.xml` • `device.xml` • `nodegroup.xml` (Island Nodes Groups are not exported.)
Node Group Map Settings	`-c ngmap`	Incremental	Import requires the following Export files, which must be imported in order: • `author.xml` • `device.xml` • `nodegroup.xml` • `ngmap.xml`
RAMS Servers	`-c rams`	Incremental	No dependencies. Import requires one export file (`rams.xml`).
Status	`-c status`	Replaces all	No dependencies. Import requires one export file (`status.xml`).

View name of configuration workspace	Export option	Behavior	Dependencies
URL actions	`-c urlaction`	Incremental	Import requires the following Export files, which must be imported in order: • `author.xml` • `urlaction.xml`
		Incremental subset	No dependencies.
	`-c urlaction` `-a <author>`		Import requires one export file (`urlaction.xml`). (Author information is embedded in the Export file.)
User Accounts and Roles User Principals	`-c account`	Incremental	No dependencies. Import requires one export file (`account.xml`).
User Interface	`-c ui`	Incremental	No dependencies. Import requires one export file (`ui.xml`).

Some additional options can be set during configuration import, which allow timeout or memory limits to be set.

Option	Default value	Description
`-timeout <seconds>`	1800 seconds	Minimum value: 1800 seconds
`-memory <megabytes>`	512 megabytes	

Let's see a few examples:

- **Example 1**:

  Export and import all configurations. Let's say we need to export all configurations and, after some time, to import it back into the same system. In that case, we would run the export command to export all configurations into the /tmp folder:

  ```
  # /opt/OV/bin/nnmconfigexport.ovpl -u system -p password -c all
  -f /tmp
  ```

  After we run this command, we should see the following output, which lists export files. Each file name represents an export area:

  ```
  Successfully exported /tmp/status.xml.
  Successfully exported /tmp/incident.xml.
  Successfully exported /tmp/comm.xml.
  Successfully exported /tmp/custpoll.xml.
  Successfully exported /tmp/ifgroup.xml.
  Successfully exported /tmp/monitoring.xml.
  Successfully exported /tmp/nodegroup.xml.
  Successfully exported /tmp/urlaction.xml.
  Successfully exported /tmp/ngmap.xml.
  Successfully exported /tmp/ui.xml.
  Successfully exported /tmp/station.xml.
  Successfully exported /tmp/device.xml.
  Successfully exported /tmp/rams.xml.
  Successfully exported /tmp/account.xml.
  Successfully exported /tmp/disco.xml.
  Successfully exported /tmp/discoseed.xml.
  Successfully exported /tmp/iftype.xml.
  Successfully exported /tmp/author.xml.
  ```

  In order to import data into the system, we run the following command:

  ```
  # /opt/OV/bin/nnmconfigimport.ovpl -u system -p password -f /
  tmp\
  ```

  This command imports all configuration from files, found in the /tmp directory.

  Note that in this example we have assumed that the password for the user system is password.

- **Example 2**:

  We plan to export and import only the monitoring area. So, we export the monitoring area using the following command:

  ```
  # /opt/OV/bin/nnmconfigexport.ovpl -u system -p password -c
  monitoring -f /tmp -x testlabserver
  ```

  We should receive the following output as a result of a successful export:

  ```
  Successfully exported /tmp/testlabserver-monitoring.xml.
  ```

  The XML file contains the monitoring configuration in XML format. The following example displays part of the configuration file:

  ```xml
  <?xml version="1.0" encoding="UTF-8"?>
  <ex:exchange
      xmlns:ns2="http://openview.hp.com/xmlns/nnm/export?type=com.
  hp.ov.nms.monitoring.config.model.MonitoredAttribute"
      xmlns:ns5="http://openview.hp.com/xmlns/nnm/export?type=com.
  hp.ov.nms.monitoring.config.model.ThresholdSetting"
      xmlns:ns4="http://openview.hp.com/xmlns/nnm/export?type=com.
  hp.ov.nms.monitoring.config.model.NodeSettings"
      xmlns:ns1="http://openview.hp.com/xmlns/nnm/export?type=com.
  hp.ov.nms.monitoring.config.model.InterfaceSettings"
      xmlns:ns3="http://openview.hp.com/xmlns/nnm/export?type=com.
  hp.ov.nms.monitoring.config.model.MonitoringConfiguration" xmlns:
  ex="http://openview.hp.com/x
  mlns/nnm/configExchange/1">
      <ex:header>
          <ex:date>2010-09-06T21:06:21.543Z</ex:date>
      </ex:header>
      <ex:area>monitoring</ex:area>
      <ex:items>
          <ns1:interfaceSettings>
              <ns1:interfaceGroup>
                  <ex:ref>
                      <ex:key>f58dd68d-ad16-4722-ab40-877f6ea7eb77</
  ex:key>
                      <ex:type>com.hp.ov.nms.monitoring.groups.
  model.InterfaceGroup</ex:type>


  . . .
  </ex:items>
  </ex:exchange>
  ```

When we need to import monitoring a area configuration, we would run the following command:

```
# /opt/OV/bin/nnmconfigimport.ovpl -u system -p password -f /
tmp/monitoring.xml
```

As a result of a successful import, we should receive the following output:

```
Successfully imported monitoring.xml
```

> **Note**: For import, we can use configuration files from the export of a wider configuration area. In general, the only thing that must be met is that the export files have to have configuration areas needed for import. The table in the *Import/Export behavior and dependencies* section lists all dependencies and requirements. For example, for monitoring configuration import we can use the export that was done for all configurations. But we cannot do this in reverse to import configuration areas that do not have all the required import areas.

Summary

This chapter has finished the single management server deployment and administration section. We should now be able to make the most of administrator activity, including single server design and implementation. The next topic moves us forward to more complex solutions with high availability systems.

7
Application Failover and High Availability Solutions

For many organizations, network monitoring is a business-critical activity and for such environments network monitoring tools play a very important role. However, no system is protected against crashes or service disruptions caused by system maintenance. Standalone NNMi management servers are not enough for such environments, and more reliable solutions should be designed. There are two main options for improving system performance and availability: designing **Application Failover (AF)** or **High Availability (HA)** solutions.

Both of them are designed for improving system availability; but at the same time, which one of these to choose depends on performance requirements and system load forecasts.

The AF solution recovers the failed server by automatically switching to a standby server. Here, one server works as active, and another as standby, and the application is operational for use only on an active node.

The HA solution has two or more servers, which work at the same time and not only switches over when primary server fails, but also performs load balancing for application load.

This chapter will describe the following topics in more details:

- AF in NNMi
- NNMi in HA Server

Application Failover in NNMi

NNMi is designed to support AF configuration, which allows us to improve NNMi availability in case of server failovers, or during maintenance windows when one of the management server needs to be switched off or disconnected for maintenance purposes.

This section describes how Application Failover works on NNMi and how it is configured. The following topics are covered in this section:

- Application Failover overview
- Configuring Application Failover
- Disabling Application Failover
- Application Failover administration
- Applying patches to NNMi with Application Failover
- Recovery from previous database in Application Failover
- Application Failover in multi-subnet environments
- iSPI and Application Failover

Application Failover overview

When NNMi AF is configured, NNMi can work without interruption even when one of the Application Failover servers goes down. AF is configured so that one of the servers acts as the primary server and the second one as a standby and is ready to take over all work if the primary server goes out of service.

 NNMi 8.x supports Application Failover only if embedded database is installed. NNMi 9.x already supports Application Failover in both cases: with embedded or Oracle database installed.

For Application Failover to work, the following requirements must be met:

- Both servers must run on the same operating system
- Both servers must have the very same version of NNMi installed, including patch level
- *System* password must be the same on both servers
- Both servers must have identical licensing attributes installed
- Wait while NNMi is in advanced stage of initial discovery before enabling Application Failover

- If your NNMi servers are located in different subnets, make sure you configure TCP communication in `jgroupsconfig.xml` configuration file, which is located in following directory:

  Unix: `$NnmDataDir/shared/NNM/conf/nnmcluster/jgroupsconfig.xml`

  Windows: `%NnmDataDir%\shared\NNM\conf\nnmcluster\jgroupsconfig.xml`

The following are possible scenarios which can cause Application Failover:

- System administrator shuts down or reboots an active server.
- Failure of active NNMi management server.
- System administrator shuts down the cluster.
- Lost network connection between the active and standby servers. In this case, both servers will work as primary until the network connection between servers is restored and auto-negotiation decides which server should work as primary.

Power failure would also cause a loss of one or both members of the cluster. Redundant power would help to avoid this situation.

When both application servers are started, the standby node detects the active node, keeps NNMi services stopped, and requests database backup of the active node.

 If the file already exists on standby node and NNMi detects that this is already synchronized, the file is not transferred.

The active node sends transaction logs to the standby node on a regular basis, as long as both servers are running (as shown in the diagram in the section entitled *Configuring Application Failover*). The frequency of the transaction log transfer can be configured in the `ov.conf` file modifying `NNMCLUSTER_DB_ARCHIVE_TIMEOUT` parameter (the `ov.conf` file example is displayed in the next section).

Full database backup is placed into the standby server's database as soon as it is received, and a `recovery.conf` file is created, which informs the database that all transaction logs should be consumed and to start over services after that.

When the active node fails, the standby node synchronizes all data and transaction logs. When synchronization is finished, network discovery and object polling is started.

The node is now active until the failed node is fixed.

Configuring Application Failover

Before you start configuring NNMi for Application Failover, assume that you have NNMi installed on two servers and meet all the requirements listed in previous section.

Description of Application Failover configuration will be provided based on the following figures:

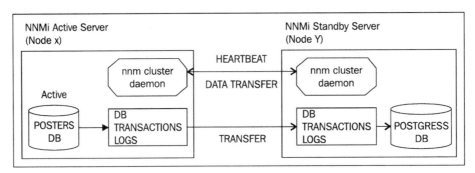

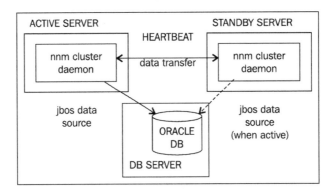

Complete the following steps to configure NNMi for Application Failover:

1. Obtain and install non-production license on the standby server (node Y) with the same features and capacity as the active server (node X).

2. Stop all NNMi processes on both servers by running the `ovstop` command.

3. (For NNMi 8.x only) Set the Application Failover configuration on the `ov.conf` files, based on the instructions provided inside a file on both servers. The file is located in:

   Unix:`$NnmDataDir/shared/nnm/conf/ov.conf`

   Windows:`%NnmDataDir%\shared\nnm\conf\ov.conf`

i. Set a unique name for the NNMi cluster:

```
NNMCLUSTER_NAME=LabCluster
```

ii. Define the NNMCLUSTER_* parameters in ov.conf file (this is optional):

```
NNMCLUSTER_COMM_TIMEOUT
NNMCLUSTER_STARTUP_TIMEOUT
NNMCLUSTER_DB_ARCHIVE_DIR
NNMCLUSTER_DB_ARCHIVE_TIMEOUT
NNMCLUSTER_DB_BASE_BACKUP
NNMCLUSTER_DB_ARCHIVE_RETENTION
NNMCLUSTER_DIR_SCAN_INTERVAL
NNMCLUSTER_SEND_ALL_INTERVAL
```

```
See ov.conf file example:
########################################################
################
# BEGIN: NNM Application Failover Clustering
# Uncomment the lines in this block to enable and
configure the NNM
# Clustering for application-failover.
########################################################
#################
# Declare a unique name for the NNM Cluster.  NNM nodes
on the same
# LAN with the same cluster name will discover each
other.  To have two
# different NNM clusters on the same network, choose
different cluster names
# for each.
# Status: REQUIRED - You must declare some name for the
cluster.
NNMCLUSTER_NAME=MyCluster

# The timeout, in seconds, for network communications
between cluster nodes.
# Increase this value for high-latency networks.
# Status: OPTIONAL - Default value if not specified: 5
seconds.
#NNMCLUSTER_COMM_TIMEOUT=5

. . .

#NNMCLUSTER_STARTUP_TIMEOUT=60

. . .

#NNMCLUSTER_DB_ARCHIVE_DIR="${NnmDataDir}/shared/nnm/
databases/Postgres_standby"

. . .
```

```
#NNMCLUSTER_DB_ARCHIVE_TIMEOUT=15

.  .  .

#NNMCLUSTER_DB_BASE_BACKUP=24

.  .  .

#NNMCLUSTER_DB_ARCHIVE_RETENTION=2

.  .  .

#NNMCLUSTER_DIR_SCAN_INTERVAL=5

.  .  .

#NNMCLUSTER_SEND_ALL_INTERVAL=15


###########################################################
##############
# END: NNM Application Failover Clustering
###########################################################
#######
```

4. (For NNMi 9.x only) Set the Application Failover configuration on the
    `nms-cluster.properties` file based on instructions provided inside a
    file on both servers. The file is located in:

    Unix: `$NnmDataDir/shared/nnm/conf/props/nns-cluster.properties`

    Windows:`%NnmDataDir%\shared\nnm\conf\props\nns-cluster.properties`

    i.   Set a unique name for the NNMi cluster:

         `com.hp.ov.nms.cluster=LabCluster`

    ii. In case the active and standby servers reside on different subnets,
         two additional parameters have to be set in the `nms-cluster.prop-erties` file:

         ```
         com.hp.ov.nms.cluster.protocol = TCP
         com.hp.ov.nms.cluster.member.hostnames = active_server_fqdn,
         standby_server_fqdn
         ```

    iii. (Optional) Define the `com.hp.ov.nms.cluster*` parameters in
         `nms-cluster.properties` file (see `nms-cluster.properties`).

5. Copy the `nnm.keystore` and `cluster.keystore` files from the active node to
    the standby node (from server X to server Y). File path is:

    Unix:`$NnmDataDir/shared/nnm/certificates/nnm.keystore`

    `$NnmDataDir/shared/nnm/conf/nnmcluster/cluster.keystore`

    Windows:`%NnmDataDir%\shared\nnm\certificates\nnm.keystore`

    `%NnmDataDir%\shared\nnm\conf\nnmcluster\cluster.keystore`

Important: If a node is a Unix node, change the permissions of both copied files (on server Y) to 400:

```
chmod 400 $NnmDataDir/shared/nnm/certificates/nnm.keystore
chmod 400 $NnmDataDir/shared/nnm/conf/nnmcluster/cluster.keystore
```

6. If NNMi is on Windows, complete the following:

   i. Set HP OpenView Process Manager service to start manually and HP NNM Cluster Manager service to start automatically:

      a. Open the Services menu. Right-click on **My Computer | Manage | Services and Application | Services**.

      b. Locate the **HP OpenView Process Manager** service and change it to **Manual**. Right-click on the service and select **Manual** from the drop-down menu on **Startup Type**.

      c. Locate the **HP NNM Cluster Manager** service and change it to **Automatic**.

   ii. Prevent the HP OpenView Process Manager service from terminating after the administrator logs off by modifying the nnmcluster.jvm. properties file:

   Insert the following line anywhere in the file:

   To make administration easier, insert it at the very bottom of the file, including comments with # symbol at beginning of each comment line.

   ```
   Xrs
   # This file defines additional properties for the NNM
   cluster.
   #
   # The following properties are pre-defined:
   #        ${NnmInstallDir} - location of the NNM
   installation directory
   #        ${NnmDataDir} - location of the NNM data
   directory
   #
   # For any pathnames defined as properties within this
   file, always use Unix-style forward slash,
   # even on Windows (e.g. use "-Dmy.prop=C:/a/b/c" instead
   of "-Dmy.prop=C:\a\b\c")
   #
   # The location (full pathname) of the cluster keystore
   file used for encryption of communications.
   ```

```
-Dcom.hp.ov.nnmcluster.keystore=${NnmDataDir}/shared/
nnm/conf/nnmcluster/cluster.keystore
# The address used for NNM Cluster multicast UDP
#-Djgroups.udp.mcast_addr=228.10.10.10
# The multicast UDP port
#-Djgroups.udp.mcast_port=45588
# The TTL for multicast UDP packets
#-Dhgroups.udp.ip_ttl=2
# Added by NNMi administrator
# Date: Jan 1, 2010
-Xrs
```

7. Start the NNMi cluster manager on the primary server (node X):

    `nnmcluster -daemon`

8. Wait for a few minutes while node X becomes an active server in a cluster. To make sure that node became active, run the following command:

    `nnmcluster - display`

    Search for results something like ACTIVE, ACTIVE_NNM_STARTING, or ACTIVE_ <some_text>

    The example of a failed process startup:

```
# /opt/OV/bin/nnmcluster -display
========================= Current cluster state ===================
=======
 State ID: 000000003000000010
 Cluster name: MyCluster
 Automatic failover: Enabled
 NNM configured ACTIVE node is: NO_ACTIVE
 NNM current ACTIVE node is: NO_ACTIVE
 Cluster members are:
  Local?    NodeType  State                      OvStatus
Hostname/Address
  ------    --------  -----                      --------      -----
----------------------
  (SELF)    CLI       n/a                        n/a           box1.
testlab.local/10.10.1.11:38691
* LOCAL     DAEMON    QUERY_CONTROLLER           NOT_RUNNING   box1.
testlab.local/10.10.1.11:57637
==================================================================
=======
Example of successful process startup:
# /opt/OV/bin/nnmcluster -display
```

```
================== Current cluster state =========================
======
  State ID: 000000005000000022
  Cluster name: MyCluster
  Automatic failover: Enabled
  NNM configured ACTIVE node is: 10.10.1.11:57637
  NNM current ACTIVE node is: 10.10.1.11:57637
  Cluster members are:
   Local?    NodeType  State                    OvStatus
  Hostname/Address
   ------    --------  -----                    --------    -----
  ----------------------
   (SELF)    CLI       n/a                      n/a         box1.
  testlab.local/10.10.1.11:56314
  * LOCAL    DAEMON    ACTIVE_NNM_RUNNING       RUNNING     box1.
  testlab.local/10.10.1.11:57637
  ===============================================================
  =======
```

 Do not go to the next step until you make sure that the node is active.

9. Start cluster manager on the secondary node by running the following command:

nnmcluster -daemon

The following output sequence should be displayed:

- ○ STANDBY_INITIALIZING: This shows that active server is detected.

- ○ STANDBY_RECV_DBZIP: This shows that new database backup is proceeded from primary node to standby.

- ○ STANDBY_RECV_TXLOGS: This shows that standby server has received a minimum set of transaction logs.

- ○ STANDBY_READY: This shows that the standby node has switched into a standby mode. It receives heartbeat signals and transaction logs from primary node.

10. Network devices should be configured to send traps to both nodes (active and passive).

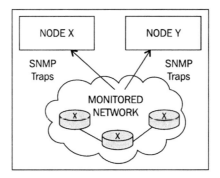

11. As two servers are in use, notify users to bookmark both servers (node X and node Y) connecting to NNMi. If node X is active, a link to node X should be opened on web browsers. If node Y is active, a link to node Y should be opened.

Once Application Failover is configured, cluster manager is used to check the cluster status, which has three modes:

- **Daemon mode**: `ovstop` and `ovstart` commands are used to run and stop NNMi services. Cluster manager process is running in the background.
- **Interactive mode**: This mode runs in an interactive session, where the administrator can manage cluster attributes, that is, shutdown process, and enable/disable Application Failover.
- **Command line mode**: This mode allows you to change cluster attributes at the command prompt.

`ovstop` command options: When Application Failover is configured, additional options for `ovstop` command apply.

- `ovstop-failover`: This is the same as running the `nnmcluster-enable-shutdown` command. It stops the local daemon mode cluster process and forces a switch to the standby NNMi management server. If failover mode was disabled, it re-enables it.
- `ovstop-nofailover`: This is same as running the `nnmcluster-disable-shutdown` command. It disables failover mode and stops the local daemon mode cluster process. No failover is using this command.
- `ovstop-cluster`: This is the same as running the `nnmcluster-halt` command. It stops active and standby nodes, and both of them are removed from the cluster.

When Application Failover is configured and running, and the ovstop and ovstart commands are started, NNMi runs the following commands:

ovstart: nnmcluster-daemon

ovstop: nnmcluster-disable-shutdown

Application Failover generates the following alarms:

- NnmClusterStartup: This incident indicates that the NNMi cluster was started and no active node was present. Therefore, the node was started and it is in the active state.

- NnmClusterFailover: This incident indicates that the NNMi cluster detected a failure of the active node and the standby node became active. All NNMi services on the new active node were started.

Disabling Application Failover

If you decide to disable Application Failover, that is, decided to go back to single server monitoring, complete the following steps to completely disable Application Failover on NNMi nodes. (Assume that node X is the active server and node Y is the standby server)

1. Run the following commands on the active node:

   nnmcluster -enable

   nnmcluster -shutdown

   Wait few minutes for the node Y to become an active server.

2. Make sure that the standby node has become active:

   Run the following command:

   nnmcluster-display

   Repeat this step until you see ACTIVE_NNM_RUNNING.

3. Shutdown the daemon on standby node by running the command:

   nnmcluster-shutdown

   Make sure that the DAEMON process is not running anymore (run the nnmcluster -display command until you don't see DAEMON process).

4. Change the configuration on both servers (node X and Y), unconfiguring cluster. NNMi 8.x only: comment out `NNMCLUSTER_NAME` line in file:

Unix:`$NnmDataDir/shared/nnm/conf/ov.conf`

Windows:`%NnmDataDir%\shared\nnm\conf\ov.conf`

NNMi 9.x only: comment out `com.hp.ov.nms.cluster.name` line in file:

Unix:`$NnmDataDir/shared/nnm/conf/nms-cluster.properties`

Windows:`%NnmDataDir%\sahred\nnm\conf\nms-cluster.properties`

5. Remove the postgres database configuration for Application Failover archiving, removing `archive_command`, and `archive_timeout` in the following file of both servers:

Unix:`$NnmDataDir/shared/nnm/databases/Postgres/postgresql.conf`

Windows:`%NnmDataDir%\shared\nnm\databases\Postgres\postgresql.conf`

6. If it is NNMi on Windows, change services startup configuration by setting following:

   ◦ **HP NNM Cluster Manager** service set to **Disabled**.
   ◦ **HP OpenView Process Manager** service set to **Automatic**.

7. Start node X by running `ovstart`.

8. Don't start node Y until you install a standalone license. It had a secondary license when you were running Application Failover.

9. When you make sure that both servers start successfully, remove the `Postgres_standby` and `Postgres.OLD` directories from both servers:

Unix:`$NnmDataDir/shared/nnm/databases/Postgres_standby`

`$NnmDataDir/shared/nnm/databases/Postgres.OLD`

Windows:`%NnmDataDir%\shared\nnm\databases\Postgres_standby`

`%NnmDataDir%\shared\nnm\databases\Postgres.OLD`

Application Failover administration

This section describes the main administration tasks related to the Application Failover configuration administration. The following topics are covered in this section:

- Restarting servers in Application Failover
- Applying patches to NNMi with Application Failover
- Recovery from a previous database in Application Failover

Restarting servers in Application Failover

If you plan to restart the active and standby servers, please follow the following instructions provided:

 You don't need to follow any special instructions if you plan to restart only the standby server.

Complete following steps for restarting a server (either active or standby):

1. Disable the Application Failover by running the following command on the NNMi server:

   `nnmcluster-disable`

2. Restart the NNMi server by running the following commands:

   `ovstop`

   `ovstart`

3. Enable the Application Failover feature by running the following command:

   `nnmcluster-enable`

Applying patches to NNMi with Application Failover

Complete the following steps if you plan to apply patches on NNMi with configured Application Failover:

1. Export configuration on both active and standby NNMi servers by running the following command:

   `nnmconfigexport.xml`

2. Back up your data on both the active, standby, and NNMi servers.

3. Synchronize the database of NNMi servers before you start applying patches by running the following command on the active node:

   `nnmcluster`

   Enter `syncdb` when you are prompted and make sure you receive the following messages:

   `ACTIVE_DB_BACKUP`

   `ACTIVE_NNM_RUNNING`

   `STANDBY_READY`

   `STANDBY_RECV_DBZIP`

   `STANDBY_READY`

4. (NNMi 8.x only) Stop the standby management server by running the `ovstop` command.

5. (NNMi 8.x only) Stop the active management server by running the `ovstop` command.

6. (NNMi 9.x only) Run `nnmcluster-halt` command on active server.

7. (NNMi 9.x only) Make sure no nnmcluster node is running on the active and standby servers by completing following:

    Run the `nnmcluster` command and make sure there are no nnmcluster nodes, except the node marked by (SELF).

8. Run the `quit` or `exit` command to stop the interactive nnmcluster process. Apply patch to the active management server and start a server by running `ovstart` command. Patches can be downloaded from the HP Patch website `http://support.openview.hp.com`. Depending on the OS where NNM is installed, in general, patch installation is as follows:

    °   Back up the system.

    °   Copy the patch file (files) into a temporary directory.

    °   Launch installation (for Linux OS, run the `rpm -i` command with the path to installation file provided; for Windows OS, run the `msi` file). Read both patch installation instructions, as each patch may have individual instructions.

9. Make sure that the patch is installed correctly by checking the NNMi help window (**Help | About Network Node Manager i-series**).

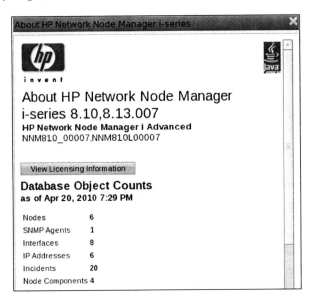

10. Create a new backup by running the `nnmcluster-syncdb` command.

11. Apply the patch to the standby management server and start a server by running the `ovstart` command.

 If you are running NNM iSPI for Performance, NNM iSPI Performance for Metrics, or NNM iSPI Performance for Traffic, you should also run NNM iSPI enablement script for each NNM iSPI on both Application Failover servers (active and standby), which is provided with the patch.

The following diagram shows a graphical workflow of how to apply patches on the NNMi Application Failover servers:

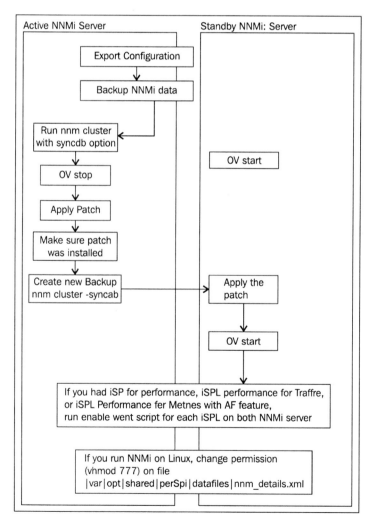

Recovery from a previous database in Application Failover (embedded database only)

As a database in NNMi with Application Failover is always copied to the standby server, database recovery it is enough to recover only the active node and leave database to synchronize with the standby server.

Complete the following steps to make a recovery from a previous database:

1. (NNMi 8.x only) Stop the standby NNMi server and then the active NNMi server by running the `ovstop` command.

    It is very important you stop the standby server first and only then stop active server.

2. (NNMi 9.x only) Run `nnmcluster - halt` command on the active server.

3. Delete or relocate the following directory from both servers:

   Unix:`$NnmDataDir/shared/nnm/database/Postgres_standby`

   Windows:`%NnmDataDir%\shared\nnm\database\Postgres_standby`

4. Restore the database on the active management server by completing the following steps:

   i. Comment out the cluster name in the cluster configuration file:

   NNMi 8.x only:

   Unix:`$NnmDataDir/shared/nnm/conf/ov.conf`

   Windows:`%NnmDataDir%\shared\nnm\ov.conf`

   NNMi 9.x only:

   Unix:`$NnmDataDir/shared/nnm/conf/nms-cluster.properties`

   Windows:`%NnmDataDir%\shared\nnm\ nms-cluster.properties`

   ii. Restore the database. Use the regular NNMi database restore the procedure.

   iii. Stop an active management server by running the `ovstop` command.

   iv. Uncomment the cluster name in the cluster configuration file:

   NNMi 8.x only:

   Unix:`$NnmDataDir/shared/nnm/conf/ov.conf`

   Windows:`%NnmDataDir%\shared\nnm\ov.conf`

NNMi 9.x only:

Unix:`$NnmDataDir/shared/nnm/conf/nms-cluster.properties`

Windows:`%NnmDataDir%\shared\nnm\ nms-cluster.properties`

5. Start an active management server by running the `ovstart` command.

6. Wait for a few minutes until the active management server generates a new backup. To verify when it is completed, run the following command:

   `nnmcluster -display`

   Look for `ACTIVE_NNM_RUNNING` message.

7. Start the standby management server by running `ovstart` command. The standby server starts to copy and extract the new backup. To verify it is completed, run the following command:

   `nnmcluster -display`

   Message `STANDBY_READY` indicates that the task is completed.

The graphical workflow picture of data restore is provided as follows:

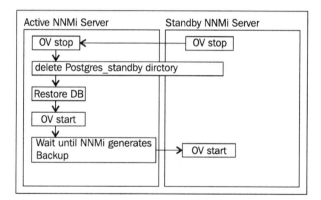

Application Failover in multi-subnets (NNMi 8.x only)

This section covers Application Failover configuration in environments where Application Failover member servers are installed on separate subnets. This section also describes why Application Failover in multi-subnet environments should be taken into consideration.

Following topics are covered:

- Why multi-subnets are an issue
- Configuring Application Failover in a multi-subnet environment
- Network bandwidth and latency requirements

Why multi-subnets are an issue

The Application Failover feature was introduced in the NNMi 8.11 version and by default it was configured to use UDP multicast messages on a single subnet.

In this configuration, Application Failover couldn't work if the active and standby NNMi servers are on different subnets. It means that packets are not transferred to the other subnet.

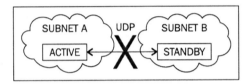

Manual configuration needs to be done for failover server communication using TCP.

Before you configure in a multi-subnet environment

Make sure you have completed the requirements for Application Failover configuration described in the previous sections:

- NNMi is installed on both servers with the very same version and patch-level
- Identical licenses are installed
- The `cluster.keystore`, `nnm.keystore` and `nnm.truststore` files are copied from the active server to the standby server
- The `ov.conf` file is configured with NNMi Application Failover clustering enabled

Configuring Application Failover for multi-subnets

To configure Application Failover for TCP communication, you need to complete a few additional steps after you configure Application Failover:

1. If you have a firewall between failover servers, you need to open ports for TCP communication on port 7800–7809. Ports are provided, followed by the example in the next step where the `jgroupsconfig.xml` file has configured 10 ports, starting from 7800.

2. Change the `jgroupsconfig.xml` file providing information for TCP communication.

   To modify the `jgroupsconfig.xml` file, complete the following steps:

   i. Back up the existing `jgroupsconfig.xml` file. That is, `cp /var/opt/ OV/shared/nnm/conf/nnmcluster/jgroupsconfig.xml \ /var/ opt/OV/shared/nnm/conf/nnmcluster/jgroupsconfig.xml.bak`.

   ii. Edit the `jgroupsconfig.xml` file, listing the active and standby servers with the FQDN or IP Address and port number 7800 in `<TCPPING...` line's `initial hosts` section:

   ```
   <TCPPING timeout="3000" initial_hosts="box1.testlab.
   local[7800],box2.testlab.local[7800]" port_range="10"
   num_initial_members="2"/>
   ```

    If you have iSPI for Performance, NNM iSPI Performance for Metrics or NNM iSPI Performance for Traffic installed on the third node, declare this server as we did in the same list.

   ```
   <TCPPING timeout="3000" initial_hosts="box1.testlab.
   local[7800],box2.testlab.local[7800] \ box3.testlab.local[7800]"
   port_range="10" num_initial_members="3"/>
   ```

3. Copy the configured file to the standby server, so that it has the same configuration.

   Copy the modified `jgroupsconfig.xml` file to the initial standby server `$NnmDataDir/shared/nnm/conf/nnmcluster` directory.

4. Startup Application Failover services.

   Now, when you have configuration ready for Application Failover TCP communication, you are ready to start nodes. Follow these steps to start Application Failover servers:

   i. Run `nnmcluster` on the initial active node and wait until this node completes the transition to `ACTIVE_RUNNING`.

ii. Run nnmcluster on the initial standby node. Make sure that the display shows both ADMIN processes in the cluster. If you don't see both ADMIN processes, it means that the nodes don't see each other. Check the jgroupsconfig.xml file configuration.

iii. Run nnmcluster -daemon on the initial active node.

iv. Wait for a few minutes until you see the DAEMON nodes join the cluster and the states become ACTIVE_RUNNING.

v. When you see ACTIVE_RUNNING on the initial active running node, run nnmcluster –daemon on initial standby mode. It will connect to a cluster and become standby.

vi. Run quit to exit the two sessions described in step (i) and step (ii).

Congratulations!!! Your servers are now configured for NNMi Application Failover using TCP communications and are ready to communicate across the subnets.

Network bandwidth and latency requirements

Network bandwidth and latency issues should be one of your major considerations when Application Failover is designed.

If your active and standby failover servers are in the same subnet, you should be fine. Challenges come when your primary and secondary servers are in separate subnets, and it is even more challenging when they are connected via WAN connections.

Application Failover works by exchanging heartbeats, and that's how they decide which server should be active and which server should be passive. Long packet delays may cause fraud failover.

Also, in the embedded database case, the database files, transaction logs, or configuration files are transferred via the same connections. NNMi database size can be one GB or even larger. Also, hundreds, or even thousands of transaction logs may be needed to transfer. Transaction log file size can be up to 16 MB. Failing to transfer such amounts of data may cause failures of node switching during failover and data loss as well.

If Oracle database is used, it uses approximately 1% of all traffic compared to an embedded database. This is because there are no database replications using Oracle as an external database.

So when you make the AF design, please make sure that bandwidth is good enough to transfer the designed amount of data on time and that your network latencies are low. Otherwise your AF may turn into your carrier's failover, and your good aims turn into your nightmares.

iSPI and Application Failover

iSPIs can work with NNMi Application Failover if they meet the following requirements:

- The NNM iSPI runs on the NNMi server
- The NNM iSPI uses the same Postgres instance as NNMi
- It is not iSPI for Performance, iSPI Performance for Metrics, or iSPI Performance for Traffic

The end of this section provides a description how to deal with these iSPIs.

To install NNM iSPI on NNMi with Application Failover configured, complete the following steps:

1. Export configuration on both the active and standby NNMi servers by running:

   nnmconfigexport.xml

2. Back up your data on both the active and standby NNMi servers.

3. Synchronize the database of NNMi servers before you start applying patches by running the following command on the active node:

   nnmcluster -syncdb

4. Stop the cluster on the standby node by running the following command:

   nnmcluster -shutdown

5. Comment out the NNMCLUSTER_NAME line in file:

   Unix: $NnmDataDir/shared/nnm/conf/ov.conf

   Windows: %NnmDataDir%/shared/nnm/conf/ov.conf

   Part of the ov.conf file is as follows:

   ```
   ################################################################
   ###
   # Declare a unique name for the NNM Cluster. NNM nodes on the same
   # LAN with the same cluster name will discover each other. To have
   two
   # different NNM clusters on the same network, choose different
   cluster names
   # for each.
   # Status: REQUIRED - You must declare some name for the cluster.
   #NNMCLUSTER_NAME=MyCluster
   ```

6. Install iSPI on the active NNMi server.

7. Run the following command on the active NNMi management server:

   ```
   nnmcluster -halt
   ```

8. Uncomment the NNMCLUSTER_NAME line in the ov.conf file on both active and standby NNMi management servers. Part of the configuration file is as follows:

   ```
   ################################################################
   ########
   # Declare a unique name for the NNM Cluster.   NNM nodes on the
   same
   # LAN with the same cluster name will discover each other.   To
   have two
   # different NNM clusters on the same network, choose different
   cluster names
   # for each.
   # Status: REQUIRED - You must declare some name for the cluster.
   NNMCLUSTER_NAME=MyCluster
   ```

9. Start the active NNMi management server by running the ovstart command.

10. Wait for a few minutes while one of the nodes becomes an active server in a cluster. To make sure that the node became active, run the following command:

    ```
    nnmcluster - display
    ```

    Search for results, something like ACTIVE, ACTIVE_NNM_STARTING, or: ACTIVE_<some_text>

     Do not go to the next step until you make sure that the node is active.

11. Start the standby server by running the ovstart command.

If you use iSPI for Performance, iSPI Performance for Traffic, or iSPI Performance for Metrics, to make them work as part of Application Failover, you need to install these iSPIs on separate servers. The iSPI enabled script needs to be launched to enable these iSPIs for Application Failover.

iSPIs automatically connect to the active NNMi server.

NNMi in High Availability (HA) Server

HA clusters are computer clusters that are implemented for the purpose of providing High Availability of services. This solution helps to avoid service outages if one of the NNMi servers is down.

Starting from NNMi 8.0x, NNMi supports HA solutions and from version 8.13, many iSPIs are also supported under HA configuration. The following table provides a list of iSPIs that are supported under HA in NNMi.

Module	NNMi 8.0x	NNMi 8.13
NNMi	✓	✓
iSPI for MPLS		✓
iSPI for Multicast		✓
iSPI for Telephony		✓
iSPI for Performance		✓
iSPI Performance for Traffic		
iSPI Performance for Metrics		
iSPI for NET Diagnostics		

NNMi HA solution should be implemented in NOCs, where NNMi is a business critical application, and tolerance for application failures is very low.

NNMi configuration for HA depends on the HA products, and this chapter provides a high-level description about NNMi and HA. Detailed step-by-step instructions are not provided in this chapter.

The NNMi HA section covers the following topics:

- HA concepts
- Supported HA products
- Licensing in NNMi for HA solution
- Configuring and un-configuring HA
- Upgrading NNMi in HA from 8.0x to 8.13
- Maintaining the HA configuration
- Troubleshooting the HA configuration

HA concepts

Nodes in a cluster are configured so that they work as one entity. Nodes are connected to each other in a private internal network for transmitting data between cluster nodes. Each cluster node is also connected to an external network (public network), where users are connecting from.

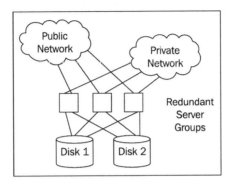

The following figure shows a typical HA Resource group layout. The HA resource group represents an application running in a cluster. Some HA products may use a different name to represent a previously described HA resource group. For example, HP Service Guard uses *Package*, Veritas Cluster Server uses *Service Group*, and Microsoft Cluster Services uses *Resource Group*.

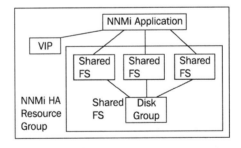

There might be several scenarios configuring the NNMi HA Cluster. It depends on whether the third party database and iSPIs will be used. The scenarios can be as follows:

- NNMi only
- NNMi with Oracle database
- NNMi with iSPI
- NNMi with Oracle database and iSPI

NNMi-only cluster

In this scenario, nodes A and B have fully installed NNMi and iSPI on the same system. The shared disk is accessed by the active cluster node for runtime data.

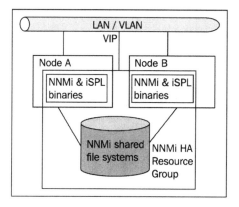

If the cluster contains more than two NNMi nodes, additional nodes are configured as node B in the next figure.

NNMi with Oracle database cluster

If your NNMi contains Oracle database, then for performance reasons Oracle should be installed on a separate server. Two resource groups should be configured within the NNMi HA cluster:

- NNMi resource group which includes the NNMi nodes and shared disk for NNMi data that is not stored in the Oracle database.

- Oracle HA resource group which contains Oracle database server and the database disk.

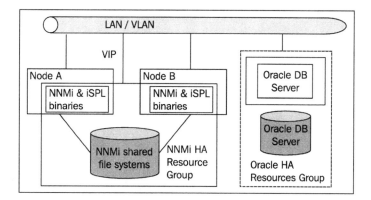

NNMi with iSPI cluster

If you are running iSPI on a dedicated server, you should configure this iSPI to run as a separate HA resource group within the NNMi HA cluster:

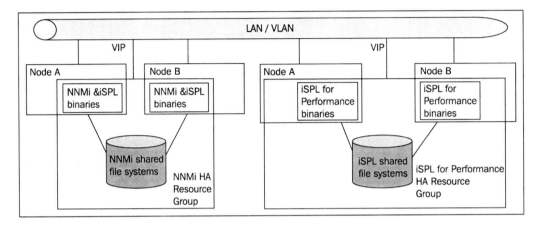

NNMi with Oracle database and iSPI cluster

If you run NNMi with Oracle database and run iSPI for Performance on a dedicated server, you can configure three HA resource groups within the NNMi HA cluster:

- NNMi HA resource group
- iSPI HA resource group
- Oracle HA resource group

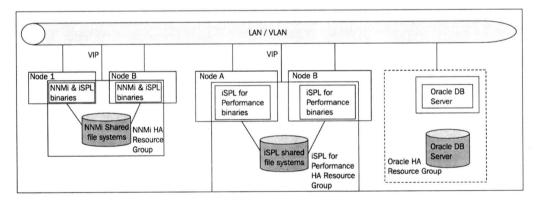

Supported HA products

NNMi is supported to work on the following HA products:

- Windows: Microsoft Cluster Services for Windows 2003
- HP-UX/Linux: HP Service Guard version 11.18 or later
- Solaris: Veritas Cluster Server version 5.0

NNMi cluster may work on other products as well, but HP doesn't support any other HA product than those listed earlier.

Licensing NNMi in HA cluster

NNMi HA cluster requires one NNMi license and it is tied to the **Virtual IP (VIP)** address of the cluster.

To install an NNMi license on a HA cluster, complete the following tasks on the active NNMi cluster node:

1. Open the license management window by running:

   Unix:$NnmInstallDir/bin/nnmlicense.ovpl NNM -g

   Windows:%NnmInstallDir%\bin\nnmlicense.ovpl NNM -g

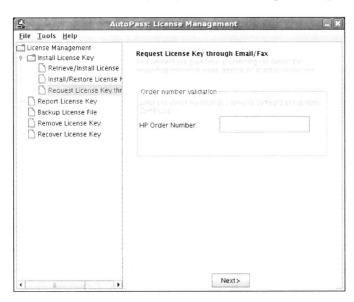

2. Select **Request license**, as shown in the preceding screenshot.
3. Obtain the permanent license passed for the VIP address of the HA cluster.

4. Update your system by running:

Unix:`$NnmInstallDir/bin/nnmlicense.ovpl NNM -f <license_file>`

Windows:`%NnmInstallDir%\bin\nnmlicense.ovpl NNM -f <license_file>`

5. Update the license information from the active disk to the NNM directory on the shared disk:

Unix: from `/var/opt/OV/HPOvLIC/LicFile.txt` to `/nnmount/NNM/licenses.txt`

Windows: from `%AUTOPASS_HOME%\data\LicFile.txt` to `S:\NNM\licenses.txt`

 If a file already exists, append the new license keys in a shared disk.

Configuring HA

This section describes high-level configuration steps for HA. Because of specific instructions in different environments, you should check manufacturer's documents for detailed configuration instructions.

The following topics are covered in this section:

- Configuring certificates on HA
- Prerequisites to configuring NNMi for HA
- Configuring NNMi for HA
- Configuring NNM iSPI for HA
- Configuring NNMi for HA in an Oracle environment

Prerequisites to configuring NNMi for HA

If you plan to configure NNMi for HA, you must meet the following requirements:

- Hardware meets all requirements for the particular HA product installation.
- Hardware meets the NNMi installation requirements listed in this *Chapter 2, Discovering and Monitoring Your Network* of this book.
- Supports virtual IP address and shared disk.

- If it is Windows, it has following patch installed:

  Microsoft hotfix for Connecting to SMB share on a Windows 2000-based computer or a Windows Server 2003-based computer may not work with an alias name. The patch is available at following link: `http://support.microsoft.com/?id=281308`.

The following items should be included in the HA cluster configuration:

- Virtual IP address for the HA cluster that is resolved by DNS (IP address has hostname described in DNS server).
- Virtual hostname for the HA cluster that is resolved by DNS.
- For Unix only: ssh and remsh.

NNMi certificate configuration for HA

If you plan to use default certificates for HA configuration, you don't have to take any additional actions, as the NNMi installation process configures a self-signed certificate for communication between the NNMi database and console.

Configuring NNMi for HA

For HA configuration on NNMi, the following steps need to be completed:

1. Copy the NNMi data files to the shared disk on the primary node.
2. Complete HA configuration on all NNMi servers: first configure a primary node and then configure all other nodes, which are in HA configuration.

Configuration sequence has to be followed. NNMi doesn't support HA configuration simultaneously.

The following diagram represents the NNMi for HA configuration high-level workflow:

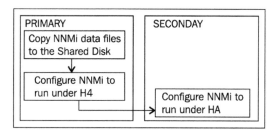

From the user perspective, the console won't respond during failover and the user has to log in to NNMi again after the failover completes.

The following table lists all the information which needs to be configured by the administrator during HA configuration.

HA configuration item	Description
HA resource group	HA cluster resource group name, given by administrator. For example, nnmresourcegroup
Virtual host short name	Short name, which is mapped to the virtual IP address of NNMi's HA resource group. This parameter is very critical for HA and HA configuration may be unstable if name is not resolved.
	Both name and IP address must be resolvable by the `nslookup` command. It is recommended to include these names into a hosts file as an alternative solution in case the DNS fails.
	The Hosts file is located in the following directory:
	Unix: `/etc/hosts`
	Windows: `%System_Root%\system32\drivers/etc/hosts`
Virtual host netmask	Subnet mask of IPv4 network where virtual host IP address is used.
Virtual host network interface	Name of network interface where virtual host IP address is configured. For example:
	Linux: `eth0`
	HP-UX: `lan0`
	Windows: Local Area Network
Shared file system type	Shared disk type configuration:
	disk — this option is used when the physically attached disk is attached to the shared disk with standard file system type.
	none — this option is used when anything other than a *disk* option is chosen . For example, SAN or NFS.
File system type	Shared disk file system type: It is used when *disk* option is configured in shared file system type. At the moment the book was written, the following shared disk formats were supported:
	VXFS on HP-UX.
	LVM2 on Linux.
	VXFS on Solaris.
	Basic on Windows OS.

HA configuration item	Description
Disk group	Only if HA is configured on Unix.
	NNMi shared file system's disk group name. Name is configured based on HA resource group name.
	For example, nnmresourcegoup-dg
Volume group	Only if HA is configured on Unix.
	NNMi shared file system's volume group name. Name is configured based on HA resource group.
	For example, nnmresourcegroup-vol
Mount point	NNMi shared disk directory mount location. For example:
	Unix: /nnmmount
	Windows: U:\

The following figure provides a high-level HA configuration workflow:

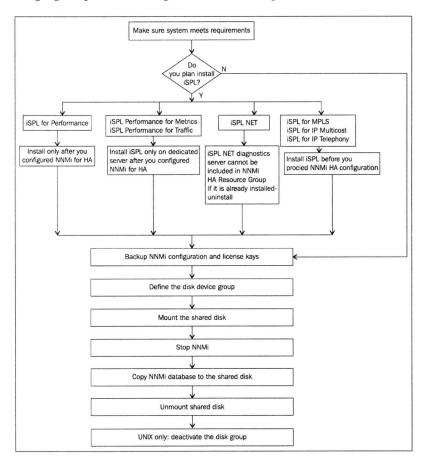

To configure NNMi on the Primary Cluster Node, where the embedded database is installed, complete the following steps:

1. Make sure the system meets all the requirements mentioned at the beginning of this section.

2. Install NNMi and check if you have the latest consolidated patches. If you plan to install any iSPI, please read the section about installing iSPIs on HA in this chapter.

3. Back up all NNMi data. For example: `nnmbackup.ovpl -type offline -scope all -target nnmi_backups`

4. Make a copy of the NNMi license key by copying the following file to a more safe location:

   Unix:`/var/opt/OV/HPOvLIC/LicFile.txt`

   Windows:`%AUTOPASS_HOME%\data\LicFile.txt`

5. Define the disk device group. For example:

   - **Service Guard**: To initialize the disk and create volume group and the logical volume. Use LVM commands, that is, `pvcreate`, `vgcreate`, and `lvcreate`.

   - **VCS**: Symantec Veritas Storage Foundation should be used for the these actions: `vxdiskadm` for adding and initializing the disk and `vxassist` for allocating disks by space.

     `mkfs -F vxfs /dev/vx/dsk/<disk_group>/<logical_volume_group>`

   - **MSCS or MSFC**: Disk Management should be used for disk mount point configuration and disk formatting.

6. Create a directory as a mounting point for the shared disk. For example:

   Unix: /nnmmount

   Windows: u:\

7. Mount the shared disk. For example:

   Unix: `mount /dev/<disk_group>/<logical_volume> /nnmmount`

   Linux or Solaris (VCS):

   VXFS: `mount /dev/vx/dsk/<disk_group>/<volume_group> /nnmmount`

   Windows: Use disk management for mounting the shared disk.

8. Stop NNMi by running the following command:

    `ovstop -c`

9. Copy the NNMi database to the shared disk:

    Unix: from `$NnmInstallDir/misc/nnm/ha/nnmhadisk.ovpl` NNM \ to `<HA_mount_point>`

    Windows: from `%NnmInstallDir%\misc\nnm\ha\nnmhadisk.ovpl` NNM \ to `<HA_mount_point>`

    Database corruptions may appear if more than one command is launched.

10. Un-mount the shared disk:

    Unix: un-mount `<HA_mount_point>`

    Windows: Use Windows Explorer and Disk Manager to un-mount the shared disk.

11. For Unix only: deactivate the disk group: `vgchange -a n <disk_group>`

12. Make sure that NNMi is not running by running the following command:

    `ovstop -c`

13. Configure the NNMi HA resource group:

    Unix:`$NnmInstallDir/misc/nnm/ha/nnmhaconfigure.ovpl NNM`

    Windows:`%NnmInstallDir%\misc\nnm\ha\nnmhaconfigure.ovpl NNM`

14. For Unix only: change the NNMi locale by running the following command:

    `$NnmInstallDir/misc/nnm/ha/nnmhaclusterinfo.ovpl \`

    `-config NNM -set HA_LOCALE <locale>`

15. If *none* was selected as the shared file system type in step 13, shared disk should be configured:

    ° Service Guard:

      ° HP-UX: `/etc/cmcluster/<resource_group>/<resource_group>.cntl`

      ° Linux:`/usr/local/cmsluster/conf/<resource_group>/<resource_group>.cntl`

    ° VCS: use the following command to add disk entries and links:

      `/opt/VRTSvcs/bin/hares`

    ° MSCS or MSFS: for adding resources to the resource group, use one of the following commands:

      `cluadmin.exe`
      `cluster.exe`

16. Start the NNMi resource group:

    Unix: `$NnmInstallDir/misc/nnm/ha/nnmhastartrg.ovpl NNM \ <re-source_group>`

    Windows: `%NnmInstallDir%\misc\nnm\ha\nnmhastartrg.ovpl NNM \ <resource_group>`

    The following diagram represents the Primary node configuration for HA workflow, where the main steps are:

    i.   Stop NNMi services.

    ii. Configure the NNMi HA resource groups.

         If *disk* option has been chosen, then proceed to the step 5.

         If *none* option was chosen, then configure shared disk.

    iii. Start NNMi HA resource group.

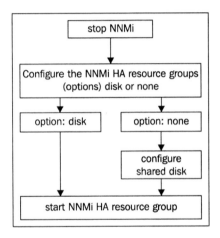

To configure NNMi with an embedded database on the secondary cluster nodes, complete the following steps:

1. Make sure you have configured NNMi on the primary cluster node.

2. Make sure the system meets all the requirements mentioned at the beginning of this section.

3. Make sure NNMi is already installed on the secondary cluster node, including the latest consolidated patch (if any).

4. If you have installed any iSPIs on the primary cluster node, please install same iSPIs on the secondary cluster nodes as well.

5. Stop NNMi by running the `ovstop -c` command.

6. Create a mount shared disk point with the very same name as it is on the primary cluster node.

7. Configure the NNMi HA resource group by running:

   Unix:$NnmInstallDir/misc/nnm/ha/nnmhaconfigure.ovpl NNM

   Windows:%NnmInstallDir%\misc\nnm\ha\nnmhaconfigure.ovpl NNM

8. Verify the configuration by running:

   Unix:$NnmInstallDir/misc/nnm/ha/nnmhaclusterinfo.ovpl \ -group <resource_group> -nodes

   Windows:%NnmInstallDir%\misc\nnm\ha\nnmhaclusterinfo.ovpl \ -group <resource_group> -nodes

The following diagram represents the secondary node configuration for HA workflow, where the main steps are:

1. Make sure the node has NNMi installed and all planned iSPIs are installed on the primary node.

2. Create the same mount point as for the primary node.

3. Configure the NNMi HA resource group.

4. Verify configuration.

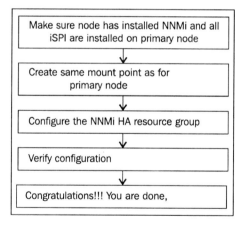

Configuring NNMi for HA in an Oracle environment

This section shortly describes NNMi with an Oracle database configuration under HA. NNMi and an Oracle database has to be installed on separate resource groups when they run under HA.

The following figure shows a high-level configuration workflow for an NNMi with an Oracle database under HA:

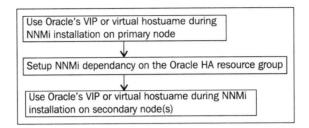

Configuring NNM iSPIs for HA

If you plan to use any iSPI in NNMi on the HA infrastructure, you need to follow special instructions in order to install iSPI properly. Depending on the iSPI, there may be a different procedure for installation.

NNM iSPI for MPLS, iSPI for Multicast, and iSPI for IP Telephony

The following iSPI can be installed only on the NNMi server (no standalone configuration is supported):

- NNM iSPI for MPLS
- NNM iSPI for Multicast
- NNM iSPI for IP telephony

These iSPIs should be installed on NNMi before configuring for HA. No other special instructions are for installations described in the section entitled *NNM iSPI Network Engineering Toolset on NNMi running under HA*.

NNM iSPI for Performance: Metrics, Traffic, or QA

The following iSPIs can be installed on the NNMi server and on the standalone server as well:

- NNM iSPI Performance for Metrics
- NNM iSPI Performance for Traffic
- NNM iSPI for QA

Depending which method is chosen (on the NNMi management server or standalone installation), follow these recommendations:

- If the listed iSPIs are installed on the NNMi management server, then install iSPI on the NNMi management server before HA configuration.

- If the listed iSPIs are installed on a dedicated server, then install iSPI after NNMi for HA is configured. Also, provide a NNMi resource group virtual hostname as the NNMi server name during installation.

NNM iSPI Network Engineering Toolset on NNMi running under HA

As NNM iSPI NET Software SNMP trap analytics and MS Visio export functionality are installed on NNMi by default installation, there are no additional actions needed for running these tools under HA, but the NNM iSPI NET diagnostics server cannot be installed on NNMi HA configuration. The diagnostic server has to be configured outside the NNMi HA resource group by the following steps:

1. Configure the NNMi HA resource group.

2. Install the NNM iSPI NET diagnostic server on a system, which is outside the NNMi HA resource group. The NNMi resource group virtual hostname as the NNM Server Hostname should be provided during iSPI NET diagnostic server installation.

Upgrading NNMi in HA from 8.0x to 8.13

If you are running NNMi 8.0x under HA and plan to upgrade to NNMi 8.13, you should first un-configure NNMi 8.0x from HA, install NNMi 8.13 and then reconfigure NNMi 8.13 for HA.

The following figure represents a workflow picture of such upgrade:

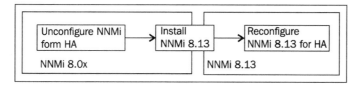

Complete the following steps to upgrade your NNMi under HA:

1. Verify NNMi 8.01 configuration consistency across all HA nodes:

   Unix: `$NnmInstallDir/misc/nnm/ha/nnmdatareplicator.ovpl NNM`

   Windows: `%NnmInstallDir%\misc\nnm\ha\nnmdatareplicator.ovpl NNM`

2. Determine which node in NNMi HA is active:

   Unix: `$NnmInstallDir/misc/nnm/ha/nnmhaclusterinfo.ovpl -group <resource_group> -state`

   Windows: `%NnmInstallDir%\misc\nnm\ha\nnmhaclusterinfo.ovpl -group <resource_group> -state`

3. Un-configure NNMi 8.0x HA on each passive node:

   Unix: `$NnmInstallDir/misc/nnm/ha/nnmhaunconfigure.ovpl <resource_group>`

   `rm -rf $NnmDataDir/hacluster/<resource_group>/*`

   Linux: `rm -rf /usr/local/cmcluster/conf/<resource_group>/*`

   HP-UX: `rm -rf /etc/cmcluster/<resource_group>/*`

   Solaris: you don't have to delete anything else in addition

   Windows: `%NnmInstallDir%\misc\nnm\ha\nnmhaunconfigure.ovpl <resource_group>`

4. Delete the following folder: `%NnmDataDir%\hacluster\<resource_group>\`

5. Un-configure NNMi 8.0x HA on the active node by completing the following steps:

   i. Create the following file in order to disable HA resource group monitoring:

      Unix:`$NnmDataDir/hacluster/<resource_group>/maint_NNM`

      Windows:`%NnmDataDir%\hacluster\maint_NNM`

   ii. Stop NNMi by running `ovstop -c`.

   iii. Back up the NNMi database on a shared disk by running:

      `nnmbackup.ovpl -type offline -target <backup_directory>`

   iv. Copy the NNM files from the shared disk to the node:

      Unix: `$NnmInstallDir/misc/nnm/ha/nnmhadisk.ovpl -from <ha_mount_point>`

      Windows: `%NnmInstallDir%\misc\nnm\ha\nnmhadisk.ovpl -from <ha_mount_point>`

v.   Remove all NNMi files and directories which are on a shared disk:

Unix: `rm -rf $HA_MOUNT_POINT`

Windows: delete all files under folder `%HA_MOUNT_POINT%`

vi.   Stop the NNMi HA resource group:

Unix: `$NnmInstallDir/misc/nnm/ha/nnmhastoprg.ovpl NNM <re-source_group>`

Windows: `%NnmInstallDir%\misc\nnm\ha\nnmhastoprg.ovpl NNM <resource_group>`

vii. Un-configure NNMi from the HA cluster:

Unix: `$NnmInstallDir/misc/nnm/ha/nnmhaconfigure.ovpl <re-source_group>`

Windows: `%NnmInstallDir%\misc\nnm\ha\nnmhaconfigure.ovpl <resource_group>`

viii. Remove the resource group specific files:

HP-UX: `rm -rf $NnmDataDir/hacluster/<resource_group>/*`

`rm -rf /etc/cmcluster/<resource_group>/*`

Linux: `rm -rf $NnmDataDir/hacluster/<resource_group>/*`

`rm -rf /usr/local/cmcluster/conf/<resource_group>/*`

Windows: delete files using Windows Explorer from following directory:

`%NnmDataDir%\hacluster\<resource_group>\`

ix.   Delete the maintenance file:

Unix: `$NnmDataDir/hacluster/<resource_group>/maint_NNM`

Windows: `%NnmDataDir%\hacluster\maint_NNM`

6. Upgrade to NNMi 8.13 on each node:

i.   For a node which was active before un-configuring NNMi 8.0x from HA, do the following:

a.   Upgrade to NNMi 8.13 and install the latest consolidated patch (if any).

b.   Configure NNMi on the primary cluster node as described in the *Configuring HA* section.

You don't need to define a disk device group and logical volume, neither do you have to create a mount point for the shared disk and configure the shared disk.

ii. For the node(s) which was/were passive before un-configuring NNMi 8.0x from HA, do the following:

a. Upgrade to NNMi 8.13 and install the latest consolidated patch (if any).

b. Configure NNMi on the secondary cluster node as it is described in the *Configuring HA* section.

 A Mount point for the shared disk is not needed.

Configuration reference

This section provides a reference for HA configuration and troubleshooting, and provides data for NNMi and iSPI for Performance such as:

- Configuration files
- Configuration scripts
- Configuration log files

NNMi HA configuration files

NNMi HA configuration uses configuration files `ov.conf` and `nnmdatareplicator. conf`, which also applies to add-on NNM iSPIs. These files are located in:

- Unix: `$NnmDataDir/shared/nnm/conf`
- Windows: `%NnmDataDir%\shared\nnm\conf`

The `ov.conf` file provides configuration for NNMi HA implementation and is read by the NNMi processes to determine the HA configuration. This file is updated by the `nnmclusterinfo.ovpl` command.

The `nnmdatareplicator.conf` file is used by the `nnmdatareplicator.ovpl` command and it determines which NNMi folders and files are included in data replication.

NNM iSPI for performance HA configuration files

If you use NNM iSPI for performance on the same server as NNMi, then the `ov.conf` file is used for configuring HA:

- Unix: `$NnmDataDir/shared/perSpi/conf/perfspi.conf`
- Windows: `%NnmDataDir%\shared\perSpi\conf\perfspi.conf`

NNMi HA provided configuration scripts

For HA configuration, NNMi provided scripts that can be used rather than commands, and which are located in following location:

- Unix: `$NnmInstallDir/misc/nnm/ha`
- Windows: `%NnmInstallDir%\misc\nnm\ha`

The following table provides a list of NNMi HA scripts provided by NNMi:

Script name	Description
`nnmhastart.ovpl`	Starts NNMi in an HA cluster.
`nnmhastop.ovpl`	Stops NNMi in HA cluster.
`nnmhaconfigure.ovpl`	Configures NNMi or an NNM iSPI for an HA cluster. This command should be run on all nodes in a cluster.
`nnmhaunconfigure.ovpl`	Un-configures NNMi or an NNM iSPI for an HA cluster. This command can be run on one or more nodes in a cluster.
`nnmhamonitor.ovpl`	Monitors processes in HA cluster.
`nnmhaclusterinfo.ovpl`	Displays information about the NNMi cluster. This script can be run on any cluster node.
`nnmhadisk.ovpl`	Copies data files of NNMi and NNM iSPI to and from the shared disk. Follow the script instructions on script usage.
`nnmdatareplicator.ovpl`	Checks the configuration file `nnmdatareplicator.conf` for changes, and copies files to remote systems.
`nnmharg.ovpl`	Starts, stops, and monitors NNMi in an HA cluster.
`nnmhastartrg.ovpl`	Starts NNMi in an HA cluster.
`nnmhargconfigure.ovpl`	Configures HA resources and resource groups.
`nnmhamscs.ovpl`	This is template script for starting, stopping, and monitoring NNMi processes in an MS Cluster Services HA cluster.

NNMi HA configuration log files

NNMi HA configuration, including add-on NNM iSPIs on the management server, provides a list of runtime and configuration log files, which help troubleshooting HA issues.

Configuration log files:

- Unix: `$NnmDataDir/tmp/HA_nnmhaserver.log`

  $NnmDataDir/log/haconfigure.log

- Windows: `%NnmDataDir%\tmp\HA_nnmhaserver.log`

  %NnmDataDir%\log\haconfigure.log

Runtime log files:

- HP-UX: `/var/adm/syslog/syslog.log`

  `/var/adm/syslog/OLDsyslog.log`

  `$HA_MOUNT_POINT/NNM/dataDir/log/nnm/ovspmd.log`

  `$HA_MOUNT_POINT/NNM/dataDir/log/nnm/public/postgres.log`

  `$HA_MOUNT_POINT/NNM/dataDir/log/nnm/public/nmsdbmgr.log`

  `$HA_MOUNT_POINT/NNM/dataDir/log/nnm/jbossServer.log`

  `$HA_MOUNT_POINT/NNM/dataDir/log/nnm/ovet*.log`

  `/etc/cmcluster/<resource_group>/`
  `    <resource_group>.cntl.log`

- Linux:`/usr/local/cmcluster/conf/<resource_group>/<resource_group>.cntl.log`

  `/var/log/cmcluster`

  `/var/log/messages*`

  `$HA_MOUNT_POINT/NNM/dataDir/log/nnm/ovspmd.log`

  `$HA_MOUNT_POINT/NNM/dataDir/log/nnm/public/postgres.log`

  `$HA_MOUNT_POINT/NNM/dataDir/log/nnm/public/nmsdbmgr.log`

  `$HA_MOUNT_POINT/NNM/dataDir/log/nnm/jbossServer.log`

  `$HA_MOUNT_POINT/NNM/dataDir/log/nnm/ovet*.log`

- Solaris: `$HA_MOUNT_POINT/NNM/dataDir/log/nnm/ovspmd.log`

    `$HA_MOUNT_POINT/NNM/dataDir/log/nnm/public/postgres.log`

    `$HA_MOUNT_POINT/NNM/dataDir/log/nnm/public/nmsdbmgr.log`

    `$HA_MOUNT_POINT/NNM/dataDir/log/nnm/jbossServer.log`

    `$HA_MOUNT_POINT/NNM/dataDir/log/nnm/ovet*.log`

    `/var/VRTSvcs/log/Application_A.log`

    `/var/VRTSvcs/log/DiskGroup_A.log`

    `/var/VRTSvcs/log/Volume_A.log`

    `/var/VRTSvcs/log/Mount_A.log`

    `/var/VRTSvcs/log/IP_A.log`

    `/var/adm/messages*`

- Windows: Windows Event Viewer log

    `%HA_MOUNT_POINT%\NNM\dataDir\log\nnm\ovspmd.log`

    `%HA_MOUNT_POINT%\NNM\dataDir\log\nnm\public\postgres.log`

    `%HA_MOUNT_POINT%\NNM\dataDir\log\nnm\nmsdbmgr.log`

    `%HA_MOUNT_POINT%\NNM\dataDir\log\nnm\jbossServer.log`

    `%HA_MOUNT_POINT%\NNM\dataDir\log\nnm\ovet*.log`

    `%SystemRoot%\Cluster\cluster.log`

NNM iSPI for Performance HA log files

Besides many of the log files listed in the NNMi HA configuration files mentioned earlier, NNM iSPI for Performance on HA maintains few additional log files, which are listed as follows:

- Configuration log files:

    Unix: `$NnmDataDir/NNMPerformanceSPI/logs/prspiHA.log`

    Windows: `%NnmDataDir%\NNMPerformanceSPI\logs\prspiHA.log`

- Runtime log files:

    Unix: `$HA_MOUNT_POINT/NNMPerformanceSPI/dataDir/ \NNMPerformanc-eSPI\logs/*.log`

    Windows: `%HA_MOUNT_POINT%\NNMPerformanceSPI\dataDir \ \NNMPer-formanceSPI\logs\*.log`

Summary

Congratulations! You have completed probably the most complicated and most advanced topic in administration of the Network Node Manager monitoring tool. Now you are able to describe what Application Failover and High Availability solutions are, and the difference between them. You are also able to make design decisions, if you need more reliable or even better performing management tools.

The next chapter describes topics for NNMi management tool users. It describes management console features and how to use the console for learning your network inventory.

8

Navigating Console and Learning Network Inventory

This chapter starts a new section of the book and is dedicated to NNMi console users, such as operators or network administrators. It explains the main features of console and discusses how NNMi console is divided. We have a key to successful monitoring if we know how the console works and how to retrieve the desired information quickly and efficiently. This chapter also tells us how to retrieve network inventory information from NNMi, based on discovered data and how to retrieve additional custom data using SNMP MIBs and MIB expressions. The following topics will be covered in this chapter:

- Navigating console
- Workspaces
- Tools menu
- Navigating network inventory and accessing details
- Working with MIBs
- MIB expressions

After completing this chapter, one will have a good understanding of the NNMi features and how to use network inventory information. We will also be able to determine network topology and understand what network services are running in our network or as part of our network.

Navigating console

NNMi has web-based GUI, which can be launched in an Internet Explorer or Mozilla web browser. NNMi completed the one web-based console philosophy, which has now been implemented in NNM 7.x. Originally, version NNM 7.x had a native ovw console (left-hand side screenshot of the screens shown on next page), which required installation on every workstation and had limited usage flexibility (because of client installation requirement and no user authentication at that time). Version 7.x has introduced the Home Base console, which was a good start for using NNM over a web browser (right-hand side screen in the following screenshot), but this wasn't a complete solution because of a lack of some features such as poor user authentication, graphical map representation limitations, among others that ovw had. There was also confusion about functionality between different types of consoles.

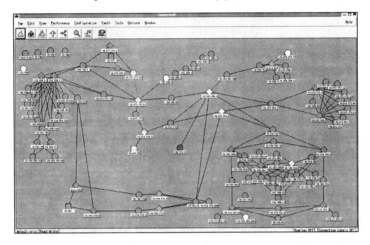

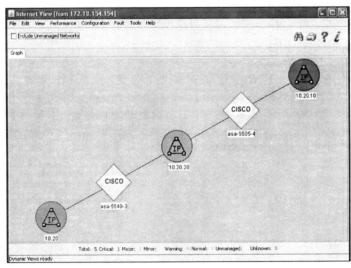

At the time of writing, NNMi is supported on the following web browsers:

- **On remote clients** (connecting to NNMi console from desktop computer):
    - Internet Explorer 7.0.5730.11 or higher with cumulative patch released not earlier than October 2007.
    - Internet Explorer 8.
    - Mozilla Firefox version 3.6 or newer. It is recommended to use a new window instead of new tabs in the Firefox browser.

- **On local management server**:
    - All browsers as listed above.
    - Mozilla Firefox 3.0.10.00 or newer for HP-UX or IPF server.
    - Mozilla Firefox 3.6 or newer for Solaris SPARC 10.

> **Note**: Web browsers such as IE6, Apple Safari (all versions), Opera (all versions), and Google Chrome (all versions) are not supported.

So, unlike previous NNM versions (NNM 6.x/7.x), NNMi can be accessible anywhere within a network. The default path for NNMi console is:

`http://<nnmi_server_name_or_ip_address>:<port_number>/nnm.`

> **Note**: Port number is chosen during installation and it can be changed afterwards.

Access to NNMi is authenticated by username and password. Depending on which user group we are assigned to, we may have some feature limitations (*Chapter 5, Controlling Access to NNMi*, provides a more detailed description about permissions for every user group), but the main console parts and principles are the same for all users.

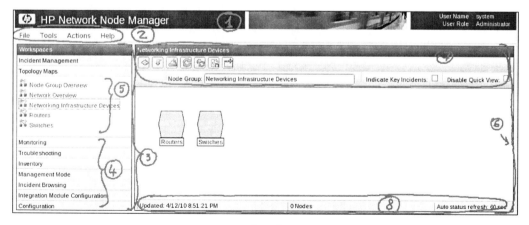

The preceding screenshot shows the NNMi console, when the user is already logged in. Console consists of the following main areas:

Name	Description
Title bar	This area is an application header and it shows which application we are running. The top right corner shows User Name, which is used to connect to console and the user role to which the user is assigned.
Main menu bar	This area lists all commands that are available to the console user. Default NNMi installation has the following command groups: • File • Tools • Actions • Help The screenshot under the *Tools* section describes the main menu bar actions.
Workspace navigation panel	This area helps navigate between workspaces and views.
Workspaces	This area is part of the workspace navigation panel. Each workspace groups some views, where grouping is made by functionality. The *Workspaces* section describes all workspaces and views used in default NNMi installation.
View	This area shows views that are available in each workspace. Each view lists some specific data about managed network objects. Views are described in the *Workspaces* section within every workspace description.
View panel	This is the workspace results area. The results of the selected workspace will be shown here.
View toolbar	This area is designed to filter data in the view panel of the selected workspace. Here we can the narrow results or manipulate with columns.
Status bar	This area is used to show summary data of the presented view. Data fields may vary depending on whether table or map view is selected. It may include information such as the total number of items displayed, how many items are selected, filter, and auto-refresh data.

Note: Depending on our license and what iSPIs are installed, we may see a slightly different list of menu items, panels, or views.

To be more generic, depending on functionality, console can be divided into three major areas:

- **Inventory**: Lists all network inventories NNMi knows about. This includes nodes, interfaces, topology maps, and other attributes related to them.

- **State monitoring**: This includes the state of the inventory items NNMi is aware of. In other words, NNMi has discovered and has been enabled to monitor the state using either ICMP or SNMP polls.

- **Actions and tools**: This includes all additional activities NNMi has or can be configured to have. This makes NNMi a more interactive management tool and allows proactive actions to be initiated.

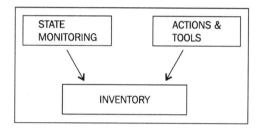

At first glance look, NNMi console may look a little bit complicated because of many frames inside a console window, menus, workspaces, toolbars, views, and so on. The following description should make NNMi console a relatively simple and intuitive console.

First of all, we should forget about all windows, buttons, tables, and other things in the console. We should think about NNMi console as a regular File Explorer window where we have files as main attributes, folders as an instrument to sort files into categories or groups, and a tool menu that includes all actions we can make with a selected item.

NNMi is organized in the same way. The files are our results in the view panel. All possible actions that we can perform with a particular view are listed in the menu. Toolbars, views, and workspaces are created to make it easier to navigate. The following diagram represents NNMi from a File Explorer architecture point of view:

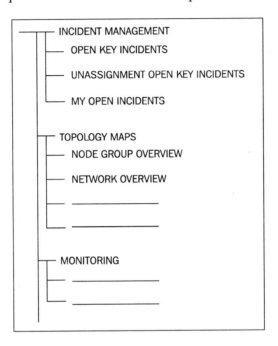

 Note: The second screenshot in *Navigating console* section represents the View toolbar as part of the View panel. But from functionality architecture, we may get a different view, depending on the selections/filters we choose in View toolbars.

Mainly all results we are interested in are presented in View panel or in a newly opened pop-up window. The next section lists all of the workspaces used in NNMi and describes the View toolbars and views within each of these workspaces.

Workspaces

All views in NNMi console are categorized into nine workspaces. In the previous section, we listed the three main areas NNMi covers. All workspaces can be grouped into these three areas as follows:

Area name	Workspaces
Inventory area	• Topology Maps • Inventory
Monitoring area	• Incident Management • Monitoring • Incident Browsing
Tools and actions area	• Troubleshooting • Management Mode • Integration Module Configuration • Configuration

This section describes all workspaces that are used within NNMi console, including a description of the toolbars and views of each workspace.

Incident Management

The **Incident Management** workspace is one of two workspaces where the operator deals with incidents. The second workspace is the **Incident Browsing** workspace. The Incident Management workspace includes the following views (refer the next screenshot):

- **Open Key Incidents**: All incidents that have **Life cycle** state as **Registered, In Progress**, or **Completed**, and **Correlation Nature** set to **None, Root Cause, Service Impact**, or **Stream Correlation** are listed here.

- **Unassigned Open Key Incidents**: Here we have listed all **Key Incidents** that have **Lifecycle State** as **Registered, In Progress**, or **Completed** and are unassigned.

- **My Open Incidents**: This view lists all incidents that have **Lifecycle State** as **Registered, In Progress**, or **Completed**, and are assigned to current user.

The following screenshot represents the Incident Management workspace views in NNMi console:

If we don't find the incident we are looking for, we should go to the **Incident Browsing** workspace.

Topology Maps

The **Topology Maps** workspace holds all maps that are used in NNMi. By default, there are the following configured views for Topology Maps:

- **Node Group Overview**: It gives a view of all top level node groups created in NNMi.

- **Network Overview**: This is a map of in the Layer 3 network most highly connected nodes in the Layer 3 network.

- **Networking Infrastructure Devices**: This is a map of routers and switches.

- **Routers**: This is a Router node group map, which shows Layer 3 connectivity. If the number of node groups is larger than the number of maximum allowed map objects, then the map will be filtered to show only routers that have interfaces with an address in the largest number of overall subnets in the network.

- **Switches**: This is a Switch Node group map, which shows Layer 2 connectivity. If number of node groups is larger than number of maximum allowed map objects, then map will be filtered to show only those switches that have interfaces with address in the largest number of overall subnets in the network.

The following screenshot shows a screenshot of the views in the **Topology Maps** workspace:

The system administrator can also create maps, including maps with background pictures, saved custom layout, and so on. This allows maps to be created that are most suitable for an NOC operator or group of operators.

 Note: The same node can be in more than one map, which gives flexibility when creating custom maps.

As an example, let's take a network that consists of three branches with 50 nodes in each branch. We may want to create one map that has all network devices and the other three maps with each branch network device only. In that case, the same device would be in two maps. Creating custom maps is described in *Chapter 3, Configuring and Viewing Maps*.

Monitoring

The **Monitoring** workspace provides views related to monitored items. The main difference between the Monitoring and Inventory workspaces is the fact that Monitoring workspace provides a list of components based on its status. The following screenshot shows the **Monitoring** workspace:

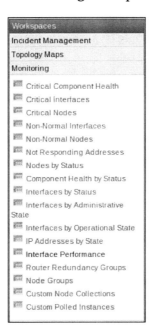

Here is a list of views provided in the Monitoring workspace:

- **Critical Component Health**: Lists all components that have component health in a **critical** status.

- **Critical Interfaces**: Lists interfaces that have a **Critical** status.

- **Critical Nodes**: Lists nodes that have a **Critical** status.

- **Non-Normal Interfaces**: Lists interfaces that are in a state other than **Normal**.

- **Non-Normal Nodes**: Lists nodes that are in a state other than **Normal**.

- **Not Responding Addresses**: Lists addresses that don't respond to ICMP requests and have a status of **Not Responding**.

- **Nodes by Status**: Lists nodes filtered by status. Operator can select a filter for desired status.

- **Component Health by Status**: Lists components filtered by status. Operator can select a filter for desired status.

- **Interfaces by Status**: Lists interfaces filtered by status. Operator can select a filter for desired status.

- **Interfaces by Administrative State**: Lists interfaces filtered by administrative state. Operator can select a filter for desired state.

- **Interfaces by Operational State**: Lists interfaces filtered by operational state. Operator can select a filter for desired state.

- **IP Addresses by State**: Lists IP addresses filtered by state. Operator can select a filter for desired state.

- **Interface Performance**: Identifies underused and overused interfaces. This feature requires NNMi iSPI Performance for Metrics to be installed.

- **Router Redundancy Groups**: Lists all router redundancy groups.

- **Node Groups**: Lists all node groups created within NNMi.

- **Custom Node Collections**: Lists node collections configured using custom polling.

- **Custom Polled Instances**: Lists instances configured by custom polling.

Here are a few examples on how these views can be used.

- **Example1**:

  Problem: Network administrator starts working day and wants to see all issues that need the most urgent attention. The administrator wants to see a list of nodes that are not normal and a list of interfaces that are critical.

  Solution: Administrator will have to use two views: **Non-Normal Nodes** and **Critical Interfaces**.

- **Example2**:

  Problem: Network administrator wants to review network switches and check how many ports are available.

  Solution: Assuming that the network administrator maintained the network, every unused port is set to administrative down state. So, launching **Interfaces by Administrative State** view would give a clear answer.

- **Example3**:

  Problem: Network administrator wants to know a list of interfaces, which have status as *Operational Down*.

  Solution: **Interfaces by Operational State** view provides a list of interfaces sorted by operational status.

Troubleshooting

The **Troubleshooting** workspace provides an ability to open maps that are displayed from the selected node's point of view. The following screenshot shows views provided in the **Troubleshooting** workspace:

- **Layer 2 Neighbor View**: Gives a Layer 2 Neighbor View from selected device by the set number of hops (maximum number of hops is 9).

- **Layer 3 Neighbor View**: Gives a Layer 3 Neighbor View from selected device by the set number of hops (maximum number of hops is 9).

- **Path View**: Provides a path view between two selected nodes.

- **Node Group Map**: Provides a map of Layer 2 and Layer 3 devices in our infrastructure, including all top-level Node Group Maps as well.

This workspace is useful when impacted nodes need to be determined or other topology-specific issues are to be solved.

Inventory

The **Inventory** workspace provides information about the inventory that is on the NNMi database, no matter what state it is. The following screenshot lists views provided in the **Inventory** workspace:

This workspace is good to use when the operator wants to see the whole inventory. Provided views help to list the inventory in different perspectives:

- **Nodes**: Lists all discovered nodes.

- **Interfaces**: Lists all discovered interfaces.

- **IP Addresses**: Lists all discovered IP addresses.

- **IP Subnets**: Lists all subnets and their statuses.

- **VLANs**: Lists all discovered VLANs. This view is very useful as VLAN is a logical entity and several VLANs can be assigned to a node or port.

- **Layer 2 Connections**: Lists all layer 2 connections.

- **Nodes by Device Category**: Lists all nodes filtered by device category. Category filter is provided as a drop-down menu in the toolbar area.

- **Interfaces by IfType**: Lists all interfaces filtered by interface type. Type filter is provided as a drop-down menu in the toolbar area.

- **Custom Nodes**: Lists all nodes with their attributes.

- **Custom Interfaces**: Lists all interfaces with their attributes.

- **Custom IP Addresses**: Lists all IP addresses with IP address attributes.

- **Router Redundancy Groups**: Lists all Router Redundancy Groups discovered in network. NNMi Advanced discovers router redundancy groups and their virtual IP addresses, which are configured using the following protocols: **HSRP (Hot Standby Router Protocol), VRRP (Virtual Router Redundancy Protocol), FDVRRP (Foundry Virtual Router Redundancy Protocol), HPVRRP (HP Virtual Router Redundancy Protocol), RCVRRP (Nortel Rapid City Virtual Router Redundancy Protocol)**.

- **Node Groups**: Lists all node groups and their corresponding statuses.

- **Interface Groups**: Lists all interface groups and their corresponding statuses.

- **Management Stations**: Lists all NNM 6.x/7.x management stations that are configured to forward messages to NNMi.

Management Mode

The **Management Mode** workspace is similar to the **Inventory** workspace as it provides information about the NNMi inventory. It has views that list objects by management mode, while the **Inventory** workspace lists the whole inventory. The following screenshot provides the views in the **Management Mode** workspace:

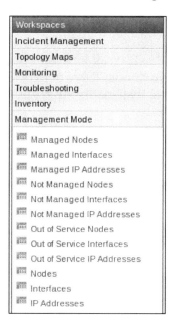

The Management Mode workspace has the following views:

- **Managed Nodes**: Lists all nodes that are discovered by NNMi and are not in **Not Managed** mode.

- **Managed Interfaces**: Lists all interfaces that are discovered by NNMi and are not in **Not Managed** mode.

- **Managed IP Addresses**: Lists all IP addresses that are discovered by NNMi and are not in **Not Managed** mode.

- **Not Managed Nodes**: Lists all nodes that are discovered by NNMi and are in **Not Managed** mode. These objects are excluded from the monitored object list and their status is not updated until they are switched back to **Managed Mode** with value as **Managed**.

- **Not Managed Interfaces**: Lists all interfaces that are discovered by NNMi and are in **Not Managed** mode. These objects are excluded from the monitored object list and their status is not updated until their **Management Mode** is switched back to **Managed** mode.

- **Not Managed IP Addresses**: Lists all IP addresses that are discovered by NNMi and are in **Not Managed** mode. These objects are excluded from the monitored object list and their status is not updated until they are switched back to **Managed** mode.

- **Out of Service Nodes**: Lists all nodes that are discovered by NNMi and are in **Out of Service** mode. These objects are excluded from the monitored object list and their status is not updated until they are switched back to **Managed** mode.

- **Out of Service Interfaces**: Lists all interfaces that are discovered by NNMi and are in **Out of Service** mode. These objects are excluded from the monitored object list and their status is not updated until they are switched back to **Managed** mode.

- **Out of Service IP Addresses**: Lists all IP addresses that are discovered by NNMi and are in **Out of Service** mode. These objects are excluded from monitored the object list and their status is not updated until they are switched back to **Managed** mode.

- **Nodes**: Lists all nodes discovered by NNMi, sorted by their management mode.

- **Interfaces**: Lists all interfaces with management mode of interface and node associated to interface.

- **IP Addresses**: Lists all IP addresses with management mode of IP addresses and interfaces associated to it.

Incident Browsing

The **Incident Browsing** workspace allows all incidents to be browsed in NNMi. The following screenshot shows views of the **Incident Browsing** workspace:

Unlike the **Incident Management** workspace, we can list all incidents by criteria that are not limited to the logged-in user or a particular state, as is the case with **Incident Management**.

The **Incident Browsing** workspace includes the following views, where key incidents are sorted by state:

- **Open Key Incidents by Severity**: Lists open incidents that can be filtered by severity.

- **Open Key Incidents by Priority**: Lists open incidents that can be filtered by priority.

- **Open Key Incidents by Category**: Lists open incidents that can be filtered by category.
- **Open Key Incidents by Family**: Lists open incidents that can be filtered by family.
- **Closed Key Incidents**: Lists closed incidents and allows making of reports or analysis of closed issues.
- **Key Incidents by Lifecycle State**: Lists key incidents filtered by Lifecycle state.
- **Root Cause Incidents**: Lists all root cause incidents.
- **Open Root Cause Incidents**: Lists root cause incidents that have not been solved and their state is **Not Solved**.
- **Service Impact Incidents**: Lists incidents that have a relationship with other incidents, which in turn can impact network services.
- **Stream Correlation Incidents**: Lists incidents that are recognized as correlation patterns in the event pipeline.
- **Incidents by Family**: Lists incidents by a specified family.
- **Incidents by Correlation Nature**: Lists incidents that are filtered by correlation nature.
- **All Incidents**: Lists all incidents.
- **Custom Incidents**: This view helps customize our own view of incidents.
- **NNM 6.x/7.x Events**: Lists events sent from NNM 6.x/7.x management stations to NNMi.
- **NNM 6.x/7.x Events by Category**: Lists events sent from NNM 6.x/7.x management stations to NNMi and allows them to be filtered by category.
- **SNMP Traps**: Lists incidents that came to NNMi as SNMP traps.
- **SNMP Traps by Family**: Lists incidents that came to NNMi as SNMP traps and allows them to be filtered by family.

Integration Module Configuration

The **Integration Module Configuration** workspace is dedicated to NNMi integration with third-party tools. The following screenshot displays views provided by **Integration Module Configuration.** Version NNMi 8.13 has the following integration configuration views:

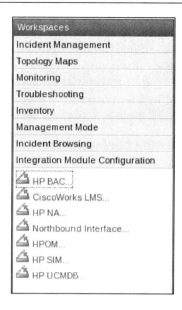

- **HP BAC...**: Provides a configuration window for integration with HP Software Business Availability Center.

- **CiscoWorks LMS...**: Provides a configuration window for integration with CiscoWorks LAN Management Solution.

- **HP NA...**: Provides a configuration window for integration with HP Software Network Automation.

- **Northbound Interface...**: Provides a configuration window for integration with HP Northbound Interface.

- **HPOM...**: Provides a configuration window for integration with HP Software Operations Manager.

- **HP SIM...**: Provides a configuration window for integration with HP System Insight Manager.

- **HP UCMDB...**: Provides a configuration window for integration with HP Software Universal Configuration Management Database.

Chapter 11, Integrating NNMi with Other Management Tools, describes in more detail, the integration of NNMi with other management tools.

Configuration

The **Configuration** workspace contains the main NNMi configuration tasks. Here, users who belong to the administrator group can make configuration changes such as discovery scope, the SNMP communities that NNMi should use for particular devices or device groups, what incidents and how they will be displayed, which actions can be launched, what third-party tools will be integrated, and so on.

The following screenshot shows the **Configuration** workspace views:

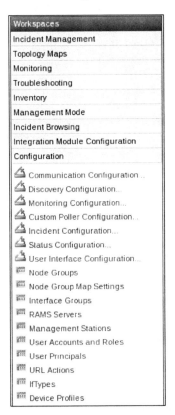

- **Communication configuration...**: This view allows us to configure a communication settings that NNMi should use for accessing polled nodes. This includes SNMP community names, login credentials for accessing managed nodes, ports used for polling, and so on.

- **Discovery Configuration...**: This view is used for setting discovery boundaries. Using a combination of the provided tabs (auto discovery rules, excluded IP addresses, seeds, subnet connection rules), we can set our discovered network boundaries in a flexible way. We can make dynamic rules static as well.

- **Monitoring Configuration...**: This view is used to monitor policy configuration. This includes configuration of which protocols should be used for status poll (ICMP, SNMP), polling intervals, component health or redundancy groups monitoring, and so on. Monitoring configuration is pretty flexible, as we can configure using an interface, node, or default settings. *Chapter 2, Discovering and Monitoring Your Network*, describes in more detail the monitoring configuration approach and provides some monitoring use cases.

- **Custom Poller Configuration...**: Custom Poller custom monitoring policies to be set up for selected SNMP object. This means our UPS device also has external triggers that can tell if the light in a room is on or off. This configuration is stored in some SNMP OID and UPS device doesn't send any SNMP traps on this event. We can configure NNMi Custom Poller to monitor the light switch SNMP OID and generate an incident every time the light is turned off.

- **Incident Configuration...**: This view configures all incidents that are in NNMi or can be in NNMi. If we need to configure a new incident, then we need to use this view. A more detailed description, with examples on how to configure incidents, is provided in *Chapter 4, Configuring Incidents*.

- **Status Configuration...**: Using this view, we can configure rules that help NNMi determine the object status (Warning, Minor, Major, or Critical).

- **User Interface Configuration...**: This view allows us to configure user interface-specific parameters such as console timeout, initial view during startup, the maximum number of displayed nodes or endpoints, and so on.

- **Node Groups**: This view provides node group configuration. We should use this view if we need to create a new or modify an existing node group.

- **Node Group Map Settings**: This view allows us to configure map-specific parameters. Maps are created using already preconfigured node groups in Node Group View. This view is used to set map-specific parameters such as map background, connectivity-specific parameters, access role, maximum number of allowed nodes or endpoints, and so on.

- **Interface Groups**: This view is used for creating and configuring Interface Groups.

- **RAMS servers**: This view is used to configure NNMi integration with HP Software Route Analytics Management Software (HP RAMS).

- **Management Stations**: If our solution uses any management stations, they are configured in this view. We can list more than one management station.

- **User Accounts and Roles**: This view is used for creating new or modifying existing users and their password, and also assigning them to one of NNMi's user groups. *Chapter 5* describes user management in more detail.

- **User Principals**: This view lists all users that exist in NNMi. Every time we create a user using the User Accounts and Roles view, the username is listed in this view as well. Usernames are also listed if we use authentication mode combined with directory services. If we use only directory service authentication, then User Principals view may remain empty.

- **URL actions**: We should use this view if we need to create new or modify existing URL actions. If we create a new action, it will appear in the **Actions** menu item list. In other words, this view helps customize NNMi according to our specific needs, providing operators with all actions that they can initiate from one menu toolbar.

- **IfTypes**: This view allows us to create our own interface types, which can be used for interface group determination.

- **Device Profiles**: This view provides information about existing assigned device profiles and allows us to change the model and vendor assigned to the device.

 Note: Only users who are assigned to the administrator group have access to this workspace.

Tools menu

The **Tools menu** is located at the top of the NNMi console and is accessible from any view. The default NNMi installation has the following menus:

- File
- Tools
- Actions
- Help

The NNMi system administrator can create new menu items such as URL actions and they would be located within the Actions menu. This chapter describes all menu items used in Tools menu.

File

The **File** menu has only one item, **Sign Out**, which signs one out of the current NNMi session.

Tools

The **Tools** menu holds tools that are generic for all NNMi systems and are not sensitive to the selected context, which means that we will be able to launch all **Tools** menu items no matter what workspace we are in or what objects we have selected.

The following screenshot provides a view of the **Tools** menu items:

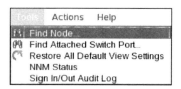

The following table lists all **Tools** menu items and provides brief description for each of them.

Name	Description
Find Node...	This menu item allows us to search for a node in the NNMi inventory database. We can search by using the following values:
	• Hostname: FQDN or IP address can be used, depending which is shown in the device Node form
	• IP address for any interface
	• System name: It is a name, which is found in the device system name field (using SNMP)
	• Name: A name can be used, which appears in the Node form Name field
Find Attached Switch Port...	Finds a switch port to which the node is plugged in.
	Note that the information about the node we provide doesn't have to be discovered by NNMi. We may enter one of these values as a search keyword:
	• Hostname
	• IP address for any interface
	• MAC address
Restore All Default View Settings	This menu item removes all view customizations that were made and all views are reset to their default settings.

Name	Description
NNM Status	Shows the status of NNM processes and services. Note that this is the same output we would get when we run the following commands in a command line: • `ovstatus -c` • `ovstatus -v ovjboss`
Sign In/Out Audit Log	Displays the output of the signin.0.0.log file.

The **Find Node** tool is provided as an external tool, which is opened in a new window. The following is a screenshot of the Find Node window (**Tools | Find Node**):

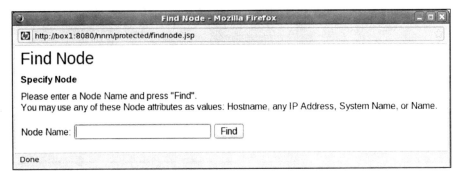

The **Find Attached Switch Port** feature queries switch configuration for information about connected nodes. We have to enter a node search keyword and it doesn't have to be a node from the NNMi topology. Available search keywords are listed in the preceding table.

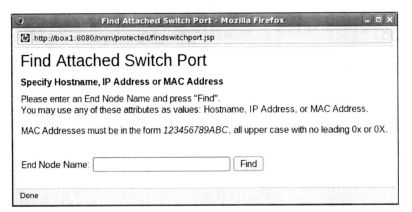

The Find Attached Switch Port feature is useful in troubleshooting issues when network administrators need to know which switch is connected to which port node.

To reduce command line tool usage, the NNMi status tool was introduced in NNMi. Previous NNM versions (6.x/7.x) only had a command line tool. The following is a screenshot of the **NNM Status** result window:

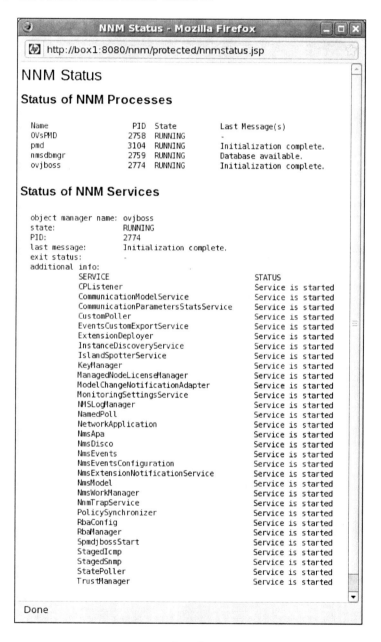

A User activity tracking tool is introduced in NNMi, which provides output of signin.0.0.log file. The following is a screenshot of the **Sign In/Sign Out Audit Log** tool:

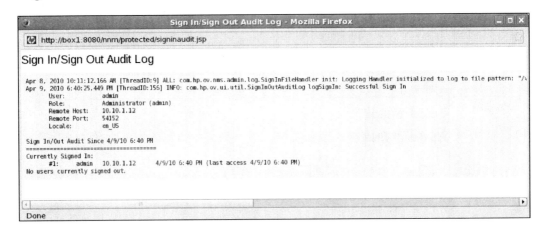

Actions

The **Actions** menu contains items that can be launched as action-based tools on a selected object. Because it is an object selection-sensitive tool, depending what type of object is selected, different kinds of actions may be listed.

The following is a screenshot of the **Actions** menu items:

The next table lists general actions that can be launched on any object:

Name	Description
Layer 2 Neighbor View	This view shows Layer 2 connections with a selected node within a specified number of hops. Results are presented as map view. Layer 2 connector devices are switches and bridges.
	The hop number can be 1 to 9.
Layer 3 Neighbor View	This view shows the Layer 3 map that shows displayed subnets and they are in which selected node participates. Layer 3 connector devices can be routers or switch/routers.
Path View	The path view between two selected devices can be drawn. When the view is requested, it calculates the active flow of data between devices. If we have HP Software RAMS integrated with NNMi, RAMS routing information is used to provide more accurate views.
	Note: If we don't see some paths as we expect and have missing data, we need to ask the administrator to configure the path manually. NNMi has a `PathConnections.xml` file that can be configured to be forced to draw connections. This may happen if NNMi doesn't have access to some devices inside a path.
Ping (from server)	Initiates ICMP pings from NNMi server to selected node.
Trace Route (from server)	Initiates trace route from NNMi server to selected node.
Telnet... (from client)	Initiates telnet command from console, where NNMi is launched to selected device.
Communication Settings	Displays communication configuration settings such as timeouts, retries, port, among others for selected device (ICMP and SNMP settings).
Monitoring Settings	Displays the configured monitoring settings for a selected object.
Status Poll	This menu item launches a status poll of the selected device and updates status information based on the poll results.
Configuration Poll	This menu item launches a configuration poll for the selected device and updates the configuration data information based on the poll results.
Delete	Deletes selected object and all objects that are contained within that object. This means that if we delete a node, all interfaces that are associated with this node will be deleted as well.
	Note: Some roles may not be allowed to run this menu.

Name	Description
Manage	Sets selected object to **Managed** mode. For any contained interface and address **Direct Management Mode** is left.
Manage (Reset All)	Sets selected object to **Managed** mode. For any contained interface and address, the management mode is changed from **Direct Management Mode** to **Inherited**.
Unmanage	Sets selected object to **Unmanaged** mode.
Out of Service	Sets selected object to **Out of Service** state.
Run Diagnostics	This menu item opens the **Diagnostics** tab in the Node Form and shows the history of all the reports that have been run for this node using NNMi iSPI NET Diagnostic.
Show Attached End Nodes	This menu item shows a list of nodes that are connected to a selected switch. The following information is presented as a result: • Hostname • MAC address • IP address

The following table lists node group-specific actions that can be launched only in node group related views. This means when we select the **Inventory** workspace, go to the **Node Groups** view, select any object and go to the **Actions** menu; we will see a list of actions that are described in the next table.

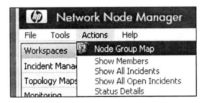

The following table provides a description of the menu items:

Name	Description
Node Group Map	This is for node groups only. Shows the status and connectivity of predefined members of a node group, including map layout and background image.
Show Members	Shows all members of selected node or interface group.
Show All Incidents	Shows all incidents for selected node group only.
Show All Open Incidents	Shows all incidents for selected node group that have as Open status.
Status Details	Provides summary report of every status of a selected node group. This includes the number and percentage of nodes that have a particular status.

Help

The **Help** menu provides basic information about how to use NNMi. It provides help information for operators and administrators. The following screenshot shows the **Help** menu items:

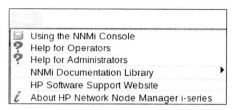

The following table lists all **Help** menu items:

Name	Description
Using the NNMi Console	Launches web help pages with the **Using the NNMi Console** section opened.
Help for Operators	Launches web help pages with the **Help for Operators** section opened.
Help for Administrators	Launches web help pages with the **Help for Administrators** section opened.
NNMi Documentation Library	Gives an option to open one of the following documents: • Reference pages • URL Launch Reference • Deployment and Migration Guide • Installation Guide • Release Notes
HP Software Support Website	Launches the HP Software Support website using the default web browser.
About HP Network Node Manager i-series	Opens the **About...** window that shows the current situation in NNMi, including the NNMi version, patch level, discovered nodes, managed nodes, installed licenses, server configuration, and so on.

Most of documentation is provided as web help pages that allow navigation through different manuals, searches within each manual using keywords, and so on. It also has indexes to make navigation faster within a document.

The following is a screenshot of one of the manuals within the **Help** menu items:

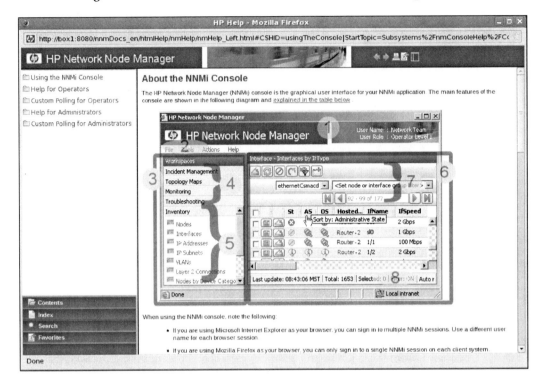

Navigating network inventory and accessing details

As already mentioned in the *Navigating console* section, the network inventory is one of three major areas of NNMi. It is the foundation for two other areas (Monitoring and Tools/Applications).

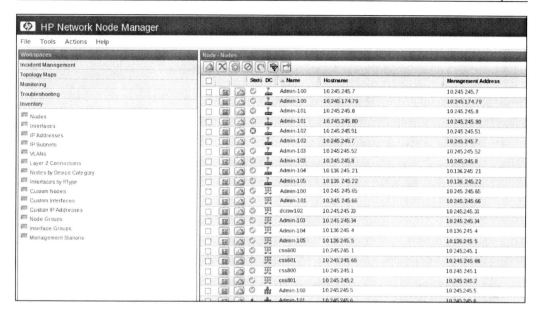

First, a detailed and accurate network inventory is needed for accurate network status presentation, display, and calculation of impacted services. As an example, let's take a case where one of 24 interface cards of a switch is broken. If we can locate the card, we can tell which physical interfaces are impacted. But network is not only about physical equipment. For instance, how about VLANs? If the management tool hasn't calculated this, it would be hard to determine it and we don't always have the possibility to connect to switch command line configuration and take a look at a configuration file. So, without having this information in an up-to-date inventory database, it would be harder to determine the impact and troubleshoot issues.

Another example is two routers that are configured as members of the same VRRP group. In such a configuration, if one router goes down, another router takes over all tasks and there are no service interruptions from the user's point of view. This means this event is not critical enough for the single device without redundancy to go down. If the management tool wouldn't know that, it would display message **Router 1 down**, and the network administrator should either remember all the VRRP groups or spend way more time for troubleshooting.

One more good reason for an accurate inventory is network documentation and planning. The management tool is an excellent source for the most recent inventory information.

It is important for NNMi users to know how to use this tool in order to find out about the network inventory as quickly as possible.

Before we go on to a NNMi description about how to use this tool to navigate inventory data, let's take a look at what we may need to know about our network. Picture yourself as a fresh team member of the network administrators or operators who need to know what the network is and what it contains.

As an example, let's consider Internet Service Provider's (ISP) network, which has a few thousand network devices. The first few questions we would probably ask are:

- What is network topology?
- What nodes are used in the network?
- What IP addresses are assigned to nodes?
- Do you have any redundancy groups, VPNs, VLANs, and so on?

This section gives a description about which views we should use for each of the mentioned issues, which helps us to understand our network inventory.

The network inventory includes data such as a list of nodes, node types and models, IP addresses, a list of interfaces (Layer 2 and Layer 3), membership of VLAN or redundancy group (HSRP, VRRP, and so on.), among others.

For inventory presentation, NNMi console has the following workspaces:

- Topology maps
- Node inventory

Topology maps

Topology maps give us a visual picture of our network. We can view layer 2 and layer 3 networks, where each of them is different but both give a good understanding of how our network looks.

Node group overview

The **Node Group Overview** option gives us a brief overview of each node group status. By default, NNMi provides four node groups: important nodes, Microsoft Windows Systems, Networking infrastructure, and Non-SNMP Devices.

We can create our own node groups, grouping our devices by the activity that is most suitable for us. Node Group Overview would list all our node groups in this view.

The next screenshot provides a view of the Node Group Overview:

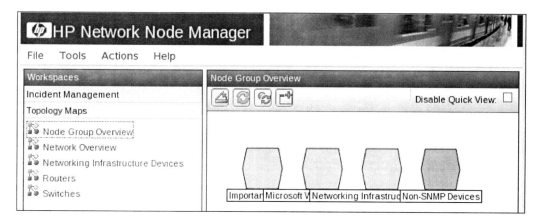

Network overview

The **Network Overview** view presents a layer 3 topology map of highly connected nodes, including connections between nodes and the most recent status. If the status of a device changes, the map is updated automatically.

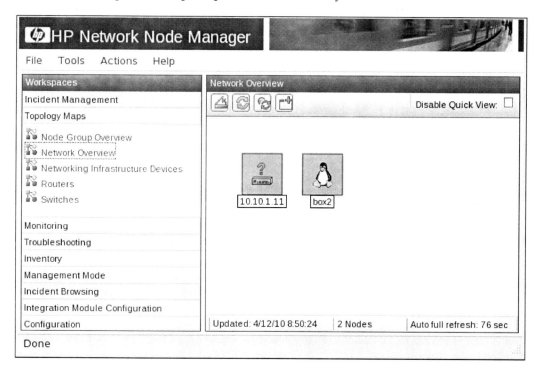

The map refresh cycle is dynamic, the more frequently the network changes, the more frequently the map refreshes.

 Note: We cannot save a custom network layout in this view. If we need custom map layouts, we should create our own map. *Chapter 3* describes, in more detail, how to create maps by providing examples.

In most cases, we will find this view and our custom map views most useful, as these maps provide the overall information. Topology maps allow us to identify issues and estimate impact very quickly.

Networking infrastructure devices

This view lists networking device groups and their corresponding status. Such groups are routers, switches, and also may include firewalls, voice gateways, and chassis. The following is a screenshot of the **Networking Infrastructure Devices** view:

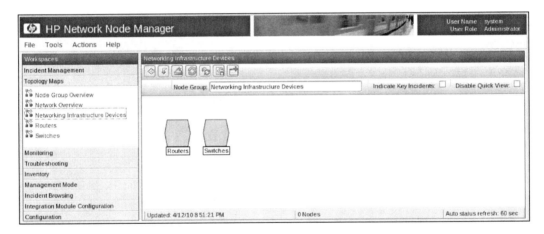

Routers

This view displays the map of the Router Node Group and layer 3 connectivity. If the number of displayed nodes exceeds the maximum allowed number in the display, then the node display will be filtered, allowing only those nodes that have interface addresses in largest number of subnets.

The NNMi administrator can configure the maximum allowed number of nodes that can be displayed.

Switches

This view displays the map of the Switch Node Group and layer 2 connectivity. If the number of displayed nodes exceeds the maximum allowed number in the display, then the node display will be filtered, allowing only nodes that are mostly connected.

The NNMi administrator can configure the maximum allowed number of nodes that can be displayed.

Node inventory

After NNMi completes node discovery, using NNMi console, we can check node information such as:

- List of nodes discovered
- Interfaces
- IP addresses
- IP subnets
- VLANs
- Router redundancy groups

All this information (and more) can be accessed via the **Inventory** workspace. Let's take a look at each of these areas.

List of nodes

The **Nodes** view (**Inventory | Nodes**) gives a list of all discovered nodes, including the following information:

- **Status**: Node status.
- **Device category**: Icon of category to which device is assigned.
- **Name**: Name is provided from DNS, SNMP sysName field, or IP address, depending on how the name resolving sequence is configured by the NNMi administrator.
- **Hostname**: Fully qualified domain name of device. If the device has no hostname, then assigned name is queried using SNMP. If SNMP doesn't have any name assigned, then the IP address is used. If the device has more than one name assigned, it picks a name using the following rules:
    - Takes loopback address. Note that NNMi filters loop back addresses that belong to 127.*.*.*. Network also ignores virtual addresses (HSRP/VRRP) or an Anycast Rendezvous Point IP Addresses.

  ° If the device has more than one loopback address, NNMi takes the address with lowest number.

- **Management Address**: The address that is used to communicate with the node's SNMP agent.

- **System Location**: Shows the system location records stored in the device's MIB.

- **Device Profile**: Shows which device the profile node is assigned to. Device profile determines the node's shape, icon, and how the node will be managed.

- **Status Last Modified**: Date and time when object was last modified.

- **Notes**: Operators can provide their own notes.

The following is a screenshot of the **Node** view window:

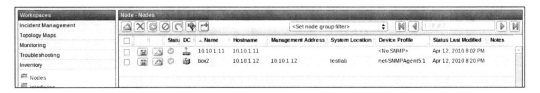

To find out more about each node, we can open each node's details, where we will find more detailed information related to the selected device.

- **General**: The general information retrieved from the node: system name, system contact, system location, system object ID, and system description.

- **IP Addresses**: Lists IP addresses found on the device, including their status, state to which interface it is assigned to, subnet, and notes.

- **Interfaces**: Lists all interfaces that are discovered on node, including additional information such as status, administrative and operational status, name, type, speed, alias of interface, and layer 2 connections.

- **VLAN Ports**: Lists VLANs discovered on node, including additional information such as port and VLAN names, member node count, and member node.

- **Ports**: Lists all ports on this node.

- **Capabilities**: Lists node capabilities, discovered on node.

- **Custom Attributes**: Lists all custom attributes assigned to this node.

- **Node Groups**: Lists all node groups to which the node is assigned.

- **Component Health**: Lists health status of each component discovered on a node, for example, CPU, memory, swap space, or fan state.

- **Diagnostics**: This tab lists diagnostic activities related to a selected node. Tab is active only when iSPI NET license is purchased.

- **Incidents**: Lists all incidents related to the selected node.

- **Status**: Lists node status history.

- **Conclusions**: Lists outstanding status conclusions, related to the assigned node.

- **Registration**: Lists registration information such as when the node was created or the last time it was modified in NNMi.

- **Custom Polled Instances**: Lists custom polled instances for selected node.

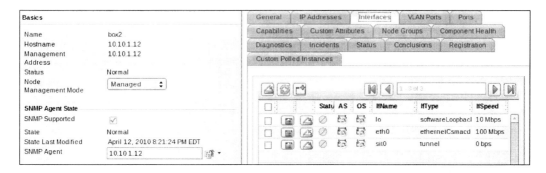

Interfaces

The **Interfaces** view lists discovered interfaces. This view differs from the Interfaces tab view in Node view. This is because here all interfaces from all nodes are displayed, unlike in the Node view's Interfaces tab where only interfaces from the selected node are displayed.

The following is a screenshot of the **Interfaces** view:

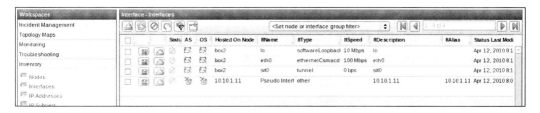

Interface view provides the following fields:

- **Status**: Provides current interface status.

- **Administrative State (AS)**: Provides current administrative state.

- **Operational State (OS)**: Provides current operational state.

- **Hosted on Node**: Shows on which node the interface is hosted.
- **IfName**: Provides interface name queried from the device `IfName` registry.
- **IfType**: Provides interface type queried from the device `IfType` registry.
- **IfSpeed**: Provides interface speed queried from the device `IfSpeed` registry.
- **IfDescription**: Provides interface description queried from the device's `IfDescr` registry.
- **IfAlias**: Provides interface alias name queried from device `IfAlias` registry.
- **Status Last Modified**: Provides date and time when interface status was last modified.
- **Notes**: Displays additional notes.

If we select an interface and open an interface detail window, we will find additional information related to the selected interface. The following screenshot shows the interface details:

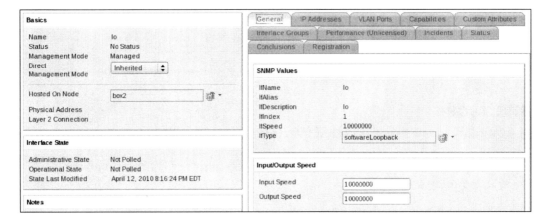

The **interface details** window has the following tabs:

- **General**: The general information retrieved from the node regarding the selected interface: **IfName, IfAlias, IfDescription, IfIndex, IfSpeed, IfType, Input Speed**, and **Output Speed**.
- **IP Addresses**: Lists IP addresses assigned to interface and their status.
- **VLAN Ports**: Lists VLAN ports configured on selected interface.
- **Capabilities**: Lists interface capabilities.
- **Custom Attributes**: Lists custom attributes assigned to selected interface.
- **Interface Groups**: Lists interface groups to which the interface is assigned.
- **Incidents**: Lists incidents related to the selected interface.

- **Status**: Lists status history of selected interface.

- **Conclusions**: Lists conclusions related to selected interface.

- **Registration**: Lists registration information related to interface, such as the date and time when the interface was created and last modified.

IP addresses

The **IP Addresses** view lists IP addresses that are discovered. As NNMi uses SNMP queries to gather configuration information from devices, this view may contain IP addresses that are not reachable from NNMi. This means that here we will find all addresses that are configured on our network devices and we don't have to worry whether a particular IP subnet is reachable from NNMi.

IP Addresses view provides the following information regarding IP addresses:

- **Status**: Shows status of IP address

- **State**: Shows state of IP address

- **Address**: Displays IP address

- **In interface**: Displays interface to which the address is assigned to

- **Hosted On Node**: Displays node on which the interface is configured

- **In Subnet**: Displays subnet where IP address is configured to

- **PL (Prefix Length)**: Displays IP address prefix length

- **Status Last Modified**: Displays date and time when the status was last modified

- **Notes**: Shows notes assigned to selected IP address

The following screenshot provides the **IP Addresses** view:

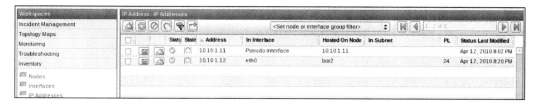

When we open any IP address record, NNMi provides more detailed information regarding the selected IP address.

- **Incidents**: Lists incidents related to IP address.

- **Capabilities**: Lists capabilities assigned to this address.

- **Status**: Lists the status history related to selected IP address.

- **Conclusions**: Displays conclusions related to selected IP address.

- **Registration**: Displays registration information, such as date and time when IP address was created and last modified.

The following is a screenshot of the **IP Address** view details:

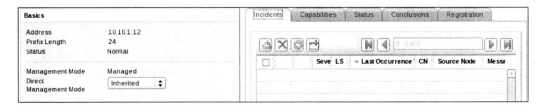

IP subnets

This view provides a list of discovered subnets. The view window provides the following information about each IP subnet:

- **Name**. Name of the subnet.

- **Prefix**: Subnet address, that is, if subnet ranges from 192.168.1.0 to 192.168.1.255, with subnet mask of 255.255.255.0 (with prefix length of 24), then prefix for such subnet would be 192.168.1.

- **Prefix Length**: Subnet mask length in bits, that is, subnet mask of 255.255.0.0 is 16 bits, mask of 255.255.255.0 is 24 bits, and so on.

- **Notes**: Description text with respect to each subnet.

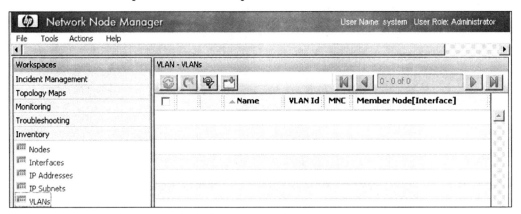

VLANs

VLANs view lists information about all discovered VLANs.

If we open a selected VLAN window, we will be provided with the following tabs for each VLAN:

- **VLAN ID**: VLAN ID number, which is assigned to the VLAN on the device when it is configured.

- **Name**: VLAN name.

- **Member Node [Interface]**: What is the member node and interface.

- **MNC (Member Node Count)**: The number of nodes that are members of selected VLAN.

- **Port Name**: Port name where selected VLAN is assigned.

- **Node Name**: Name of the node where the port assigned to a selected VLAN is hosted.

- **Associated Interface Name**: The name of associated interface assigned to a selected VLAN.

The following screenshot shows the **VLAN details** window:

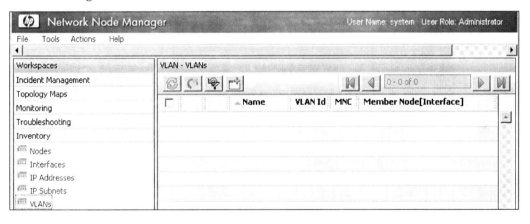

Working with MIBs

The collection of data objects using SNMP is described by a hierarchical structure, so the same parameter on any device can be retrieved by the same object ID, with the very same syntax. Such definition is provided by SNMP MIB (Management Information Base) files. NNMi deals with monitored parameters using SNMP MIB files as well. Also, each device type or model can provide information about different parameters, which means other MIBs should be used while dealing with it. For example, the interface incoming byte rate (ifInOctets) is retrieved using .1.3.6.1.2.1.2.2.1.10 object ID from any device (if the device can support such information). Another example is specific information such as mail queues can be provided by mail server, and room temperature can be retrieved from environment monitored devices only. However, a router wouldn't provide any such parameters. So management servers need to know what information, or which OIDs, can be used for one or the other parameter retrieval. An SNMP MIB file, when loaded into the management server, provides that **knowledge base**.

Dealing with SNMP MIBs in NNMi includes the following activities:

- Loading MIB into the NNMi server. This enables MIB expression, creation and gives flexibility to custom polling configuration.
- Checking a list of supported MIBs on managed devices. This allows admin to know which additional parameters can be monitored, other than the ones monitored by NNMi.
- Checking MIB values on monitored devices. This helps us find parameters and their type while creating MIB expressions and custom polling policies.

The following section describes these activities in more details.

Checking supported MIBs

NNMi 9.x allows us to check which MIBs are supported by the node. NNMi uses SNMP queries to capture a list of supported MIBs from the selected device. There are at least two ways to list supported MIBs:

- **By selecting a node from Inventory or incident from Incident View**: Complete the following steps to see a list of supported MIBs using this method:
    i. Select a node from Inventory View, or select an incident from Incident View.
    ii. Select **Actions | List Supported MIBs**.

- **By using MIB browser**: Complete the following steps to see a list of supported MIBs using this method:

    i. Select **Tools | MIB browser**.

    ii. Complete required fields. The fields include Node name or IP Address of a node, which MIBs we plan to see, and SNMP community name. If the SNMP community name is not provided, then the default configured name for that device from **Communication Settings** will be applied.

    iii. Select **Tools | List Supported MIBs**.

NNMi will list all MIBs that are supported by the node. It will also include MIBs that are supported but not loaded.

List MIBs Supported by box2

The following MIBs (and interesting child MIB variables) are supported by 10.10.1.12.

1. EtherLike-MIB
   - dot3StatsTable
2. HOST-RESOURCES-MIB
   - hrStorageTable
   - hrDeviceTable
   - hrProcessorTable
   - hrNetworkTable
   - hrDiskStorageTable
   - hrPartitionTable
   - hrFSTable
   - hrSWRunTable
   - hrSWRunPerfTable
   - hrSWInstalledTable
3. IF-MIB
   - ifTable
   - ifXTable
4. IP-FORWARD-MIB
   - ipCidrRouteTable
   - inetCidrRouteTable
5. IP-MIB
   - ipAddrTable
   - ipv4InterfaceTable
   - ipv6InterfaceTable
   - ipSystemStatsTable
   - ipIfStatsTable
   - ipAddressPrefixTable
   - ipAddressTable
   - ipNetToPhysicalTable
   - ipv6ScopeZoneIndexTable
   - ipDefaultRouterTable
   - icmpStatsTable
   - icmpMsgStatsTable
6. IPV6-MIB
   - ipv6IfTable
7. RFC1213-MIB
   - atTable
   - ipRouteTable
   - ipNetToMediaTable
   - tcpConnTable
   - udpTable
8. RMON-MIB
   - etherStatsTable
9. SNMPv2-MIB
   - SNMPv2-SMI
   - sysORTable
   - RAPID-CITY
10. Unloaded MIBs (Click to Load or Upload MIB files)
    - .iso.org.dod.internet.mgmt.mib-2.28.1.1.1.1 (.1.3.6.1.2.1.28.1.1.1.1)
    - .iso.org.dod.internet.mgmt.mib-2.88.1.1.1.0 (.1.3.6.1.2.1.88.1.1.1.0)
    - .iso.org.dod.internet.mgmt.mib-2.92.1.1.1.0 (.1.3.6.1.2.1.92.1.1.1.0)
    - .1.3.6.1.4.1.2021.4.1.0
    - .1.3.6.1.4.1.8072.1.2.1.1.4.0.1.0.0
    - .1.3.6.1.6.3.11.2.1.1.0
    - .1.3.6.1.6.3.12.1.1.0

Checking loaded MIBs

There are two methods to check which MIBs are loaded into NNMi management server:

- Using **Loaded MIBs** view
- Using nnmloadmib.ovpl command line tool

The following section shows instructions on how to list loaded MIBs using each of these methods.

Loaded MIBs view

To see loaded MIBs in the NNMi management server, complete the following steps:

1. Open the **Configuration** workspace in NNMi console.
2. Select **Loaded MIBs**.

NNMi lists all loaded MIBs in a newly opened window.

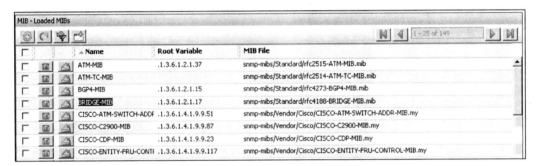

Listing loaded MIBs using nnmloadmib.ovpl tool

To list loaded MIBs using the command line, the following tool should be used: nmloadmib.ovpl –list.

The list of loaded MIBs will be provided in the command line.

```
The following MIBs are loaded:

ATM-MIB (snmp-mibs/Standard/rfc2515-ATM-MIB.mib)

ATM-TC-MIB (snmp-mibs/Standard/rfc2514-ATM-TC-MIB.mib)

BGP4-MIB (snmp-mibs/Standard/rfc4273-BGP4-MIB.mib)

BRIDGE-MIB (snmp-mibs/Standard/rfc4188-BRIDGE-MIB.mib)

CISCO-ATM-SWITCH-ADDR-MIB (snmp-mibs/Vendor/Cisco/CISCO-ATM-SWITCH-ADDR-
MIB.my)
```

```
CISCO-C2900-MIB (snmp-mibs/Vendor/Cisco/CISCO-C2900-MIB.my)

CISCO-CDP-MIB (snmp-mibs/Vendor/Cisco/CISCO-CDP-MIB.my)


. . .


VMWARE-ROOT-MIB (snmp-mibs/Vendor/VMware/VMWARE-ROOT-MIB.mib)

VMWARE-SYSTEM-MIB (snmp-mibs/Vendor/VMware/VMWARE-SYSTEM-MIB.mib)

VMWARE-VMINFO-MIB (snmp-mibs/Vendor/VMware/VMWARE-VMINFO-MIB.mib)

VRRP-MIB (snmp-mibs/Standard/rfc2787-VRRP-MIB.mib)

WINS-MIB (snmp-mibs/Vendor/Microsoft/wins.mib)

X-DDI-MIB (snmp-mibs/Vendor/Nortel/x-ddi-adapter-mib)
```

Loading MIBs

To load MIB files to NNMi, two steps should be performed:

1. Copy the MIB file to the server. This step covers only copying the file to a server as any other regular file would be copied.

2. Load copied MIB file to NNMi management server by loading from the console, completing the following steps:

   i. Select **Tools | Upload Local MIB File**.

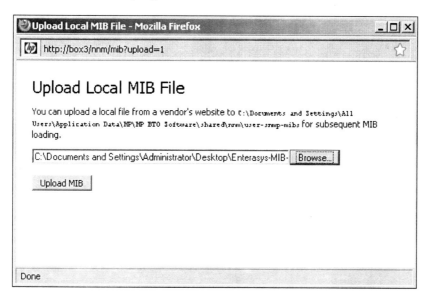

ii. Select **Browse…** in the Upload Local MIB File window.

iii. Select MIB file.

iv. Click on the **Open** button.

v. Click **Upload MIB**.

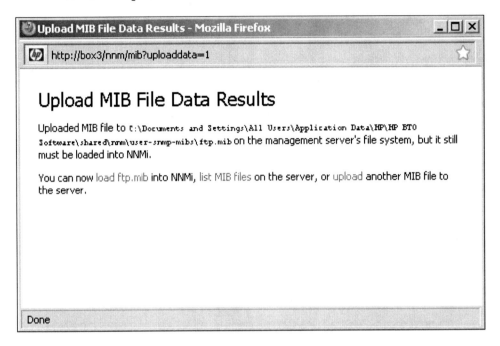

vi. When **Upload MIB File Data Results** window opens, select the `load <mib_file_name.mib>` link, where `<mib_file_name.mib>` is the MIB file name of the file uploaded in the previous step.

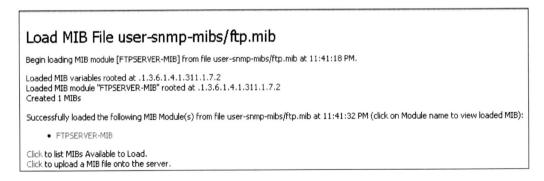

vii. Result window will now be opened. We can review results and close the window.

We have just finished loading the MIB file to the NNMi management server!

If one prefers to use the command line instead, note where the MIB file is located and run the following command in a command line console (assuming that the MIB filename is `ftp.mib` and the MIB file is copied to `/tmp` directory):

`nnmloadmib.ovpl -u <nnmi_admin_username> \`

`-p <nnmi_admin_password>  -load /tmp/ftp.mib`

MIB files can be retrieved from the following sources:

- The manufacturer usually provides MIB files with equipment, or allows them to be downloaded from a website. If we cannot find MIB files on the manufacturer's site, we need to contact our manufacturer directly.

- Some MIB warehouses on the Internet can be used to download MIB files. For example, `http://www.oidview.com/mibs`.

- If none of these sources have the MIB file, try posting in forums such as `http://itrc.hp.com`, or simply Google the file we are searching for.

Checking MIB variables supported by node

To see what MIB variables are supported by node, an MIB browser should be used. We need to perform the following steps:

1. Select **Tools | MIB Browser**.

2. Complete required fields:

    i. Enter node name or IP address in the **Name** field.

    ii. Enter SNMP community name. If SNMP community name is provided, SNMP v1 queries will be applied. Otherwise, NNMi will take SNMP community names from Communication configuration and the corresponding SNMP version will be used for queries. This step is optional.

iii. Enter SNMP OID, if it is known (it should always start with a dot ".").

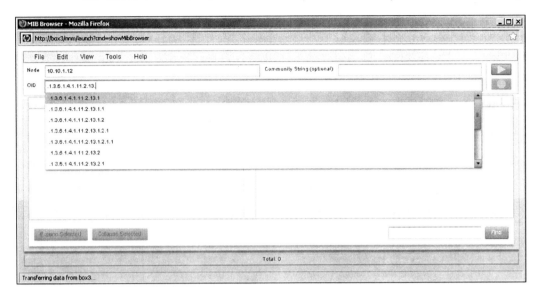

iv. Also, the SNMP OID name can be entered in the OID field. SNMP OID names can be checked in the OID Alias table (by selecting **Tools | OID Aliases in MIB Browser**).

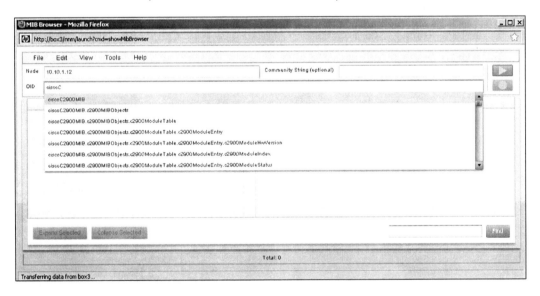

3. Press *Enter* key or select green **Play** button on the right-hand side of the SNMP MIB browser.

We can navigate through a result window by expanding/collapsing the tree structure results in an SNMP MIB browser window.

Displaying MIB content

If, for some reason, the MIB file content needs to be displayed, NNMi provides a *Display MIB file* feature. The reason for checking an MIB file can be to see the file structure, find supported OIDs for MIB expression, OIDs listed in an MIB file, or even modification of the MIB file (before it is uploaded to the NNMi management server). It is not recommended to modify the MIB file, unless we are sure of what we are doing.

To display the MIB file content, perform the following steps:

1. Select **Loaded MIBs** in the **Configuration** workspace.

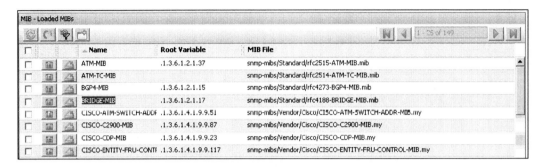

2. Select **Actions | Display MIB File**.

MIB file content will be displayed in a new window.

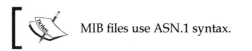 MIB files use ASN.1 syntax.

MIB expressions

SNMP MIB monitoring empowers monitoring by the capability to monitor almost any SNMP OID. However, in real life, there are many examples when a single OID doesn't provide much information and an expression of several SNMP OIDs needs to be monitored. Here are a few examples:

- **Interface utilization**: SNMP MIBs provide information about each interface's incoming and outgoing traffic. They also provide information on an interface's speed. But, in order to get utilization, expression of these objects needs to be made, where interface utilization is equal to the summarized incoming and outgoing traffic, divided by the interface speed and multiplied by 100.

- **Memory utilization**: SNMP MIBs provide information such as the total configured memory on object and used memory. In order to get utilization, expressed as a percentage of the memory capacity, calculations need to be made based on the following MIB expression: used memory, divided by total capacity, and multiplied by 100.

NNM 7.x and older versions had the MIB expression feature, which was based on configuring the `mibExpr.conf` file. Starting from NNMi version 9.x, the SNMP MIB expression feature was implemented in the management console.

MIB expressions are used by SNMP Graphs and Custom Poller.

Listing MIB expressions

To see what MIB expressions have already been configured, complete the following steps:

1. Select **MIB expressions** from the **Configuration** workspace. A list of configured MIB expressions is displayed.

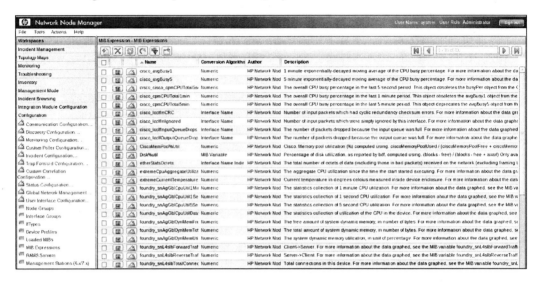

2. To view the configuration of each MIB expression, click on the **Open** button for the MIB expression we want to open.

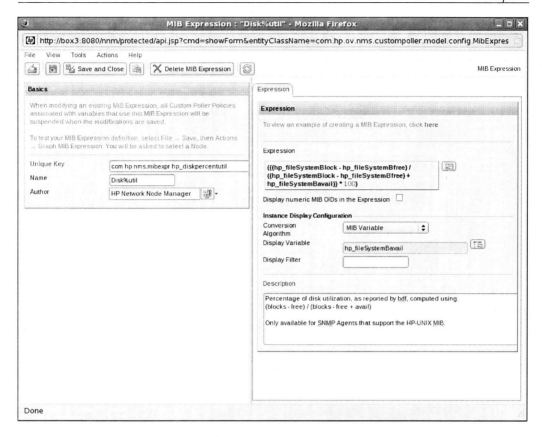

As it is shown in the preceding screenshot, disk utilization is calculated as **(blocks–free)/(blocks–free+avail)**.

Configuring MIB expression

This section describes how to create a new MIB expression. As an example, let's create an MIB expression to monitor error rate, expressed in percent, where error rate is equal to `(((((ifInErrors + ifOutErrors)*8)/ifSpeed)*100)/sysUpTime)`.

`sysUpTime` is needed when evaluating MIB variables with type counter (`Counter`, `Counter32`, `Counter64`, `time_ticks`), where `sysUpTime` is used by NNMi to detect a system reboot. When a system reboot is detected, NNMi cannot display the first polled value after reboot. This is because to display the counter type value, two pollings need to be completed, where the calculation is made with the help of an error rate calculated over the time.

Because errors are provided as bytes, we transfer bytes into bits by multiplying with 8.

To create an MIB expression, complete the following steps:

1. Select **MIB Expressions** in the **Configuration** workspace.

2. Click the **New** button on top left corner of the MIB **Expression** listing window.

3. Click the MIB expression editor button on the top right-hand side of the **Expression** tab.

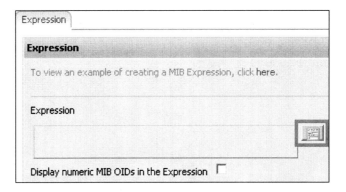

4. When the new window opens, click the following sequence of operators to build an expression:

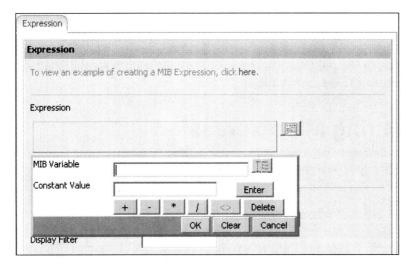

- ° Click / (divide)
- ° Click * (multiply)

- ° Select ***** sign in **Expression** window, so **(*)** would be marked
- ° Click **/** (divide)
- ° Select **/** symbol on left-hand side, so inner **(/)** would be marked.
- ° Click ***** (multiply).
- ° Select ***** symbol on left-hand side, so inner **(*)** would be marked.
- ° Click **+** (add).

The following sequence should be displayed in the **Expression** window:

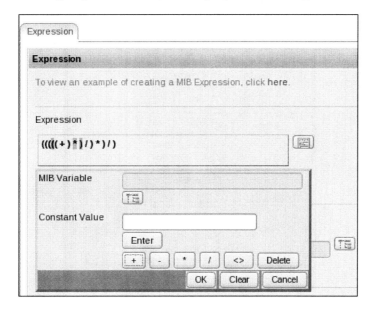

5. Select **+** symbol, so **(+)** would be marked.
6. Click the browse button close to the **MIB variable** window to select a SNMP OID for the expression.

7. From an MIB browser, select `ifInErrors`, which is under the `.org.`
`internet.mgmt.mib-2.interfaces.ifTable.ifEntry` branch.

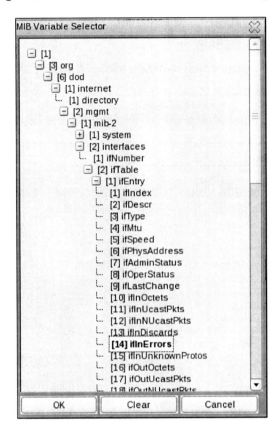

8. Click **OK**.

9. Click the browse button close to the **MIB variable** window to select an SNMP OID for expression and select `ifOutErrors` in the same way as described in previous step.

10. Select * on left-hand side.

11. Enter **8** in the **Constant value** field and press *Enter*.

12. In the **Expression** window, select / next to **8** (most left / of / symbols).

13. As described in previous steps, select `ifSpeed`.

14. Select * on right-hand side of `ifSpeed` in the **Expression** window.

15. Enter **100** in the **Constant Value** field and press *Enter*.

16. Select / symbol on a right-hand side of / symbol.

17. Select `sysUpTime` from the `.org.internet.mgmt.mib-2.system` branch.

18. Click **OK** and we should see the following window:

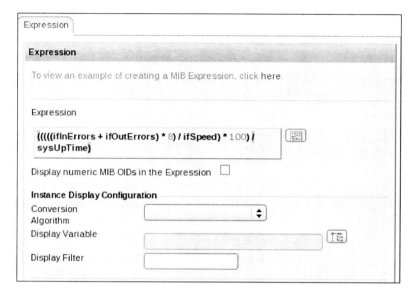

19. Enter com.hp.nms.mibexpr.ifErrorRate in the **Unique Key** field.

20. Enter ifErrorRate in the **Name** field.

21. Make sure **Author** field doesn't contain HP Network Node Manager name. If HP Network Node Manager is entered, configuration may be lost during the next patch installation.

22. Click **Save and Close**.

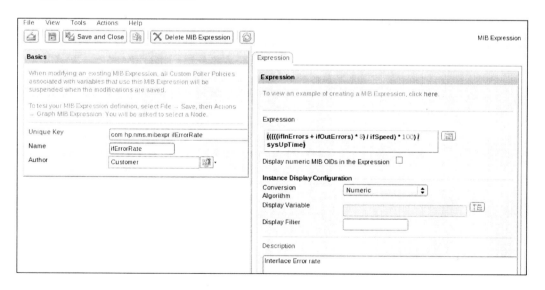

The following table provides a description of fields used in MIB expression configuration.

Parameter	Description
Unique key	This field must be unique. It is recommended to use the Java name space convention: `com.<company_name>.nnm.mibexp.<mib_expression_name>`
	The example is `com.hp.nnm.mibexp.ErrorRate`.
	This unique key name can be changed at any time later on (unlike the other object Unique Key attributes). The length of the name is limited to 80 characters.
Name	The name that will be used for MIB information being polled.
	Name cannot contain spaces and special characters such as (~, !, @, #, $, %, ^, &, *, (), _, and +).
Author	The author or editor of MIB expression.
	If **HP Network Node Manager** is selected, there is a risk of configuration being overwritten in the future, for example by applying patches.
Expression	The field where expression is written. Read the next section that describes the basic rules of expressions.
Display numeric MIB OIDs in the Expression	If the option is checked, numeric values for SNMP OID values are displayed instead of MIB names. For example, `ifSpeed` would be displayed by its SNMP OID value, which is `.1.3.6.1.2.1.2.2.1.5`.
Conversion algorithm	Determines the format of how `<instance_string>` appears in the line label of the Line Graph legend.
	The following format of line labels in Line Graph is used: `<node_name><line_label><instance_string>`
	A list of possible conversion algorithms is: • **Numeric**: This option should be used to display the instance number as the `<instance_string>` value. • **MIB variable**: This option should be used to display the SNMP MIB value stored in the instance as `<instance_string>` value. • **Alphabetic**: This option should be used with legacy Cisco Arrow Point load balancers only. • **Interface name**: This option should be used to display the interface name as the `<instance_string>` in the Line Graph legend. • **Interface name indirect**: This option should be used to display the interface name, which is obtained from an indirect reference in the MIB table. For example, the interface name value resides in the RMON MIB table.

Parameter	Description
Display variable	MIB variable can be selected to display `<instance_string>` value in the Line Graph legend line label.
Display filter	Java regular expression can be used to determine the value to be displayed in the `<instance_string>` value of each line.
Description	The description field for MIB expression. We need to remember the following: • A maximum of 2,000 symbols are allowed • Alphanumeric and special characters (~, !, @, #, $, %, ^, &, *, (,), _, and +) are not allowed in this field

Using MIB expression editor

MIB expression editor is used to create custom MIB expressions. Editor is launched from the **MIB Expression** configuration window, by clicking the following MIB Expression Editor symbol:

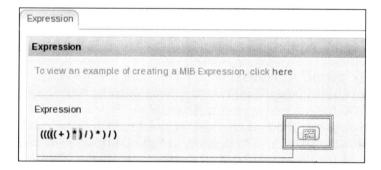

The editor can create expressions based on the following values:

- SNMP OID, which is selected during configuration
- Constant value, which can be entered during configuration

The editor can create expressions based on the following arithmetic operators:

- Plus (+)
- Minus (-)
- Multiply (*)
- Divide (/)

For example, to calculate the interface error rate, the following expression should be used:

```
(((((ifInErrors + ifOutErrors)*8)/ifSpeed)*100)/sysUpTime)
```

In this expression,

- `ifInErrors`, `ifOutErrors`, `ifSpeed`, and `sysUpTime` are SNMP OID values

- 8 and 100 are constant numbers

The Custom Collection polling configuration example, provided in previous section, gives detailed instructions on how to configure such expressions using MIB expression editor. Here are basic rules, based on which MIB Expression Editor is used:

- MIB expression should be written by listing arithmetic operators. Once the arithmetic operators are listed, then the value configuration should be proceeded with.

- Arithmetic operators should be entered, listing from right to left. For example, if the interface error rate expression is being written from the previous example, the following sequence of operators should be entered: **/, *, /, *, +**.

- After the second operator is entered, the editor needs to know where the next operator should be applied. The additional operator will be applied to the left part of the selected operator. For example, after we entered **/** and *****, we see **((*)/)** expression. The next operator we want to include is **/**, which should be applied to the left side of ***** operator, so ***** should be selected before inserting **/** again. When ***** is selected and **/** is inserted, we get the following expression: **(((/)*)/)**

- When we are done with arithmetic operators, we can insert values in the expressions. Values are applied from left to right of the selected operator. For example, when we have completed the operator part of the expression, we have the following sequence: **(((((+)*)/)*)/)**. If **+** is selected, then the first entered value goes to the left side of **+** operator (in our example `ifInErrors`), and the second one to the right side (`ifOutErrors`). Then, next operator should be selected, going from the left to the right side (in our example, most left *****). This operator already has the left side filled in (in our case **(ifInErrors+ifOutErrors)**), so next entered value will go to the right side of this operator. After completing all steps, we finally get our expression: **(((((ifInErrors + ifOutErrors)*8)/ifSpeed)*100)/sysUpTime)**.

- Use the **<>** symbol to replace an operator by selecting the operator that needs to be replaced and clicking the **<>** button.

- In order to replace a value, the value should be selected and a new value can be entered or selected from an MIB browser.

- For constants, use the **Constant value** field, where the constant value can be entered and **Enter** button clicked.

Summary

After acquiring a good understanding of the NNMi console and our network's inventory, we are now ready to learn the status of our network, find issues, and prioritize troubleshooting tasks. The next chapter is dedicated to network monitoring tasks, such as understanding the status of the network, locating issues, and working with incidents to be able to have quick and accurate information to facilitate our primary job of fixing issues.

9

Monitoring Your Network

This chapter is dedicated to the description of key activities in NNMi—monitoring a network. It describes how monitoring can be organized using NNMi and explains the main views, which help us efficiently monitor our network.

After completion of this chapter, you will have a good understanding of the following topics:

- Monitoring with NNMi
- Monitoring devices for problems
- Monitoring incidents for problems
- Investigating problems
- Configuring MIB expressions
- Configuring Custom Polling

Each topic provides practical examples with a description of how this can be adopted in real-life scenarios.

Monitoring with NNMi

This section describes basic definitions for monitoring. To increase our knowledge, a few examples are provided.

Monitoring definition

According to the official definition, monitoring is a close observation of a certain situation. Monitoring an IP network is more complicated than just the devices and cables between them. The **Open Systems Interconnection (OSI)** model describes communication systems as seven layer systems (physical, data link, network, transport, session, presentation, and, application layers), and based on this model, NNMi covers up to OSI Layer 3 networks. So, NNMi monitors OSI Layer 2 and Layer 3 networks where, except physical, logical networks and subnets exist and each of these layers need to be observed.

Monitoring in NNMi

NNMi monitors Layer 2 and Layer 3 networks, including features such as devices and their configuration automatic discovery, network topology presentation based on discovered data, and network device polling on a regular basis to present an up-to-date network status. NNMi presents this data in a few ways:

- Maps
- Tables
- Incident views

Each of these views carries its own specific information, a combination of these views used in monitoring provides a clearer picture of the entire network situation and improves the quality of information needed for monitoring.

The following figure shows the triangle where a combination of these views gives the full picture of the network status:

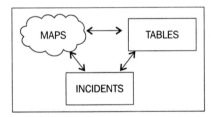

There is no such thing as the right way to monitor your network. In many cases, a combination of two or three monitoring methods would be used. The following table lists all three views and describes the advantages and disadvantages of each:

View	Advantages	Disadvantages
Maps	The bigger picture of the situation can be seen. Easier to determine root cause of problem or impacted nodes.	Node status color cannot tell us exactly what happened, how many and what messages were received.
Tables	Easy to sort by selected field. More details can be viewed than using a map.	Node status color cannot tell us exactly what happened, how many and what messages were received.
Incidents	Details about each incident can be viewed. Incidents can be sorted by attributes.	Hard to prioritize messages. Even if they come with a severity status, without seeing the bigger picture it can still be hard to determine priorities.

These views are used to fulfill different monitoring approaches:

- Monitoring devices for problems
- Monitoring incidents for problems

Activities, which can be done in each of these views, are described in the next section of this chapter.

The following table provides a list of status colors used in NNMi:

Status color	Description
	Unknown
	Normal
	Warning
	Minor
	Major
	Critical
	Disabled
	No status

Case studies

Let's take a few cases and see, how monitoring could be organized using these views, in order to understand clearly where each view is useful and how it can help our monitoring.

Example: when map is initial source for monitoring

Map view is used as the initial monitoring view. Whenever a node changes in color (for example, from green (normal) to red (critical)), incident view is opened by the operator for more details. Table views are used if needed.

In map view, we can see that this is a node which has a duplicate node in case if it goes down. After a short time troubleshooting, we can make the conclusion that an alternative node's has taken the first node responsibilities and no impact to the service is made. All traffic is routed, neighbor routers are accessible and no traffic interruptions are recognized. But we don't know exactly what happened to that node.

Incident view would give us more detailed information as to what exactly happened. We can find incident/incidents related to that node and start our investigation.

Example: when incident view is initial source for monitoring

Consider, that incident view is opened. When a new incident occurs, in most cases, the map view is checked first to view what impact the incident may have had through out the network. The map would show what devices are connected to the impacted device. By switching to table views we would get more detailed information, so a more accurate assessment can be made.

In this case, the incident tells us exactly what has happened on a particular device. But, without seeing the whole network picture, it is hard to determine what impact has been made on the network or that particular incident.

Monitoring devices for problems

Devices can be monitored for problems in two ways: map and table views. The user can reach one view type from another in both directions the user can reach maps from table views and table views from maps.

Map view

NNMi has three map types:

- **Layer 2 Neighbor View**: Displays selected node and Layer 2 connections with that node by specified number of hops. Layer 2 devices are switches and bridges.

- **Layer 3 Neighbor View**: Displays selected node and subnets to which connected node belongs to by specified number of hops.

- **Path View**: Displays the connectivity path between the selected two nodes.

Maps can be reached by opening the **Topology Maps** workspace.

Device monitoring using maps is mainly done by monitoring the device status, where the status of each device is expressed in colors, representing the severity of each device. The table, provided in the *Monitoring in NNMi* section, lists all node colors and their descriptions.

The following is a list of actions which can be achieved from a device using a map:

- Test problem node
- Access node details
- Access related incidents

Testing problem node actions

This is a list of possible actions in NNMi to test a problem node:

- **Ping node from NNMi server**: This action initiates ICMP pings to selected node from the NNMi management server. Please bear in mind that some devices may be restricted for ICMP pings, but have ports for SNMP communication opened on a network by firewall. This action is useless since even if the devices are up and running, any replies would be received. Status poll should be used instead, which uses SNMP queries for status polling..

- **Trace Route from NNMi server**: This action runs the trace route command from the NNMi server to the selected device.

- **Telnet to node from NNMi server**: This actions telnets to the selected node. Remember, that telnet login credentials need to be configured in the Communication Settings. Out of the box, NNMi doesn't provide an action menu with SSH connections to a node. Refer to *Chapter 10, Extending NNMi* for custom menu actions to create your own menu for ssh'ing to a node.

- **Initiate status poll**: This action runs a SNMP query and checks the status of each interface, which is configured to monitor. It is more accurate than the **Ping node** action because of the following reasons:

    ○ Status poll provides the status of all interfaces on a device, while ICMP ping gives a response only for the interface which was pinged. Some interfaces on a device may be unreachable because of no routing to them. Status poll uses SNMP, which queries the status of all interfaces on a device via one interface, which is reachable from NNMi. The following figure provides an example, where router is monitored via interface A. Interfaces C and D are not reachable as there is no route to these interfaces. Using SNMP poll, NNMi queries the device for the interface status via interface A using a SNMP query.

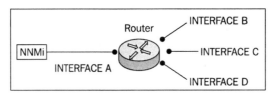

    ○ Status poll provides two statuses: administrative and operational, while ICMP gives just a result of ping success. The administrative status shows if the interface is enabled in the configuration by the administrator, and the operational status shows how the object operates (for example, if the cable of the configured and enabled interface is unplugged, the operational status would be *down*, while the administrative status would be *up*) .

- **Initiate configuration poll**: This action runs a SNMP query for configuration information from the selected device. Device information in NNMi is updated with the most current configuration information. For example, you open a node in NNMi and do not see the interface which you think is on a device. One of the reasons could be that the interface was configured after NNMi initiated its last configuration scan (scan cycles can be set in the **Configuration** workspace). Configuration poll, as with status poll, requires SNMP communication to be configured between the NNMi server and managed node. Also, for accuracy, device specific MIBs need to be loaded in NNMi. By default, NNMi ships with a list of already preloaded MIBs. See the latest product release notes for a specific list of nodes that have MIBs loaded in NNMi already. MIBs are provided by the equipment manufacturer, or can be downloaded from the manufacturer's website.

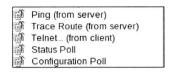

These actions can be launched by selecting a node and selecting the **Action** menu
from the main menu at the top of the window.

Accessing node details

Node details in a map can be accessed by the following methods:

1. Double-click on a node.
2. Select the node and click the **Open** icon in the top left corner of the window.

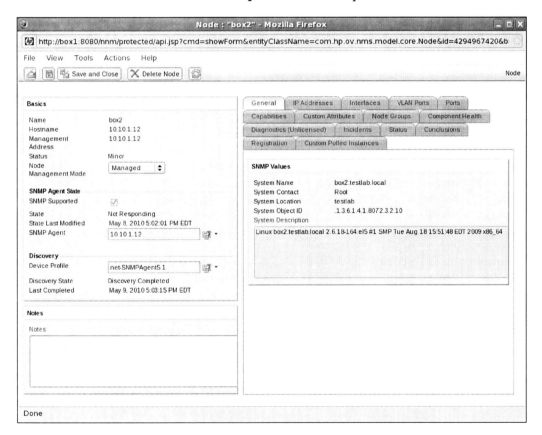

Accessing related incidents

To see incidents related to a node, follow these steps:

1. Open **Node Detail** window (double-click on the node in a map).
2. Select the **Incidents** tab.

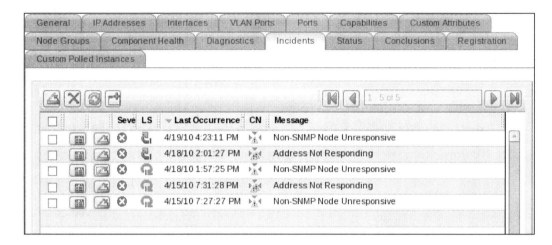

Table views

Table views provide detailed information for monitoring, thus allowing for filtering and sorting monitored nodes or interfaces by selected criteria. For example, the operator, who wants to list nodes which have a critical status or list interfaces, which have any status except normal. NNMi has dedicated views for such a monitoring approach, which can be accessed by opening the **Monitoring** workspace.

Depending on the NNMi version (version 8.x or 9.x), the following views, which help to achieve such approach, can be accessed in NNMi:

- NNMi 8.x views:
    - **Critical Component Health**: Nodes with critical status due to problems with node component.
    - **Critical Interfaces**: Interfaces with status *critical*.
    - **Critical Nodes**: Nodes with status *critical*.
    - **Non-Normal Interfaces**: Interfaces with status other than *normal*.
    - **Non-Normal Nodes**: Nodes with status other than *normal*.
    - **Not Responding Addresses**: A list of IP addresses that don't respond to ICMP pings.

- ○ **Nodes by Status**: Nodes, listed by status.

- ○ **Component Health by status**: Components listed by status.

- ○ **Interface by Status**: Interfaces listed by status.

- ○ **Interfaces by Administrative State**: Interfaces listed by administrative state.

- ○ **Interfaces by Operational State**: Interfaces listed by operational state

- ○ **IP Addresses by State**: IP addresses listed by state.

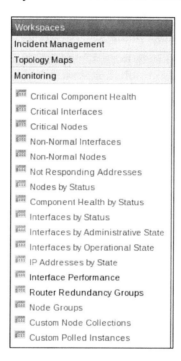

- • NNMi 9.x views:

  - ○ **Non-Normal Node Components**: Nodes which may need operator attention due to component health of the node.

  - ○ **Non-Normal Cards**: Cards which may need operator attention.

  - ○ **Non-Normal Interfaces**: Interfaces which may need operator attention.

  - ○ **Non-Normal Nodes**: Nodes which may need operator attention.

  - ○ **Not Responding Addresses**: Lists IP addresses which do not respond to ICMP ping.

- ○ **Interface Performance**: Enabled only if iSPI Performance for Metrics is installed and lists interfaces which are over or under used.

- ○ **Card Redundancy Groups**: Lists discovered card redundancy groups.

- ○ **Router Redundancy Groups**: Lists discovered router redundancy groups.

- ○ **Node Groups**: Lists node groups, which are created by the NNMi administrator.

- ○ **Custom Node Collections**: Lists custom node collections which are created by custom polling.

- ○ **Custom Polled Instances**: Lists custom poll instances, which were created by custom polled instances.

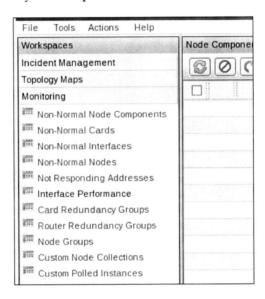

Views from both, NNMi version 8.x and 9.x are described in the following sections.

Critical Component Health

Critical Component Health view displays a list of nodes, which have a critical status due to a problem with the node component. This includes memory, fan, and temperature.

It is useful to see a list of nodes, which are critical because of component failures.

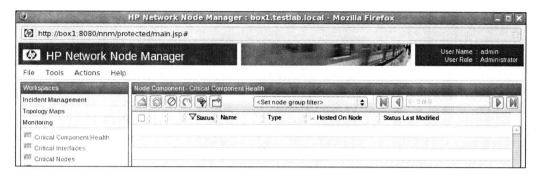

In addition, NNMi provides additional information about listed components, such as: status, name, type, name of hosted node, and the date and time of when the last status was modified.

Critical Interfaces View

Critical Interfaces View lists all interfaces, which have critical status.

The following screenshot represents the **Critical Interface View** window:

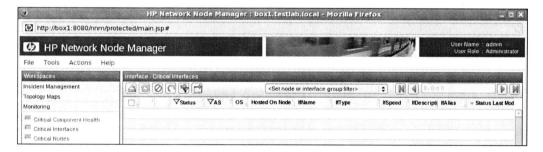

In addition, NNMi provides additional information about the listed interfaces, such as: status, **Administrative State (AS)**, **Operational State (OS)**, on which the node interface is hosted, name, type, speed, description and alias of interface, date and time of when the last status was modified, Layer 2 connections and notes.

Critical Nodes View

Critical Nodes View lists all nodes, which have a critical status.

The following screenshot represents the **Critical Nodes View** window:

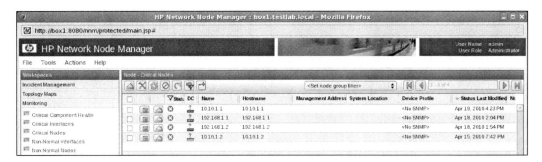

In addition, NNMi provides additional information about listed nodes, such as: name or IP address of node, hostname, management address, system location, device profile, date, and time of when the last status was modified, and notes.

Non-Normal Interfaces View

Non-normal Interfaces View lists all interfaces, which have Administrative state Up and the following status:

- Warning
- Major
- Minor
- Critical

In other words, any interface which does not have a normal status and is not disabled by the administrator.

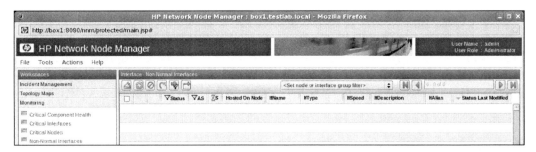

In addition, NNMi provides additional information about listed interfaces, such as: status, AS, OS, Hosted On Node (on which node interface is hosted), interface name, type, speed, description and alias, date and time of when the last status was modified, Layer 2 connections, and notes.

Non-Normal Nodes View

Non-normal Nodes View lists all nodes which have following status:

- Warning
- Minor
- Major
- Critical

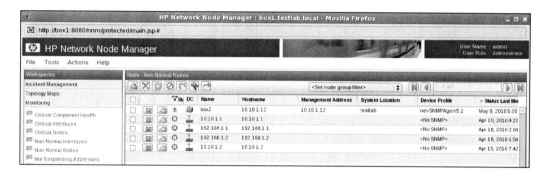

In addition, NNMi provides additional information about listed nodes, such as: status, device category, name or IP address of node, hostname, management address, system location, device profile, date and time of when the last status was modified, and notes.

Not Responding Address View

Not Responding Address View lists all IP addresses which don't respond to ICMP pings. Such interfaces have the status **Not responding**.

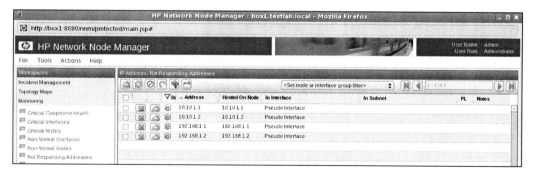

In addition, NNMi provides additional information about listed IP addresses, such as: status, IP address, hostname of device where address is hosted, interface type it is assigned to, subnet, prefix length, and notes.

Nodes by Status

The **Nodes by Status** window lists nodes by selected status. Selected status values can be:

- No Status
- Disabled
- Unknown
- Normal
- Warning
- Minor
- Major
- Critical

 Note: Node group filter can also be used along with status filter.

		Statu	DC	Name	Hostname	Management Address	System Location	Device Profile	Status Last Mor
☐			⊘		10.10.1.11	10.10.1.11			<No SNMP>	Apr 12, 2010 8:02

In addition, NNMi provides additional information about listed nodes, such as: status, device category, name or IP address, hostname, management address, system location, device profile, date and time of when the last status was modified, and notes.

Component Health by Status

Component Health by Status lists all components filtered by status. Selected status values can be:

- No Status
- Normal
- Disabled
- Unknown
- Warning
- Minor
- Major
- Critical

Note: Node group filter can also be used in combination of status filter.

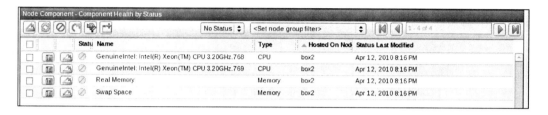

In addition, NNMi provides additional information about listed components, such as: status, name, type, name of hosted node, and date and time of when the last status was modified.

Listing Interfaces by Status

The **Interfaces by Status** window lists interfaces filtered by their status. Selected status values can be:

- **No Status**: When NNMi cannot determine the status of the object *No status* status is displayed

- **Normal**

- **Disabled**: Interface is set to *Disabled* mode on NNMi management server

- **Unknown**

- **Warning**

- **Minor**

- **Major**

- **Critical**

 Note: Node group or interface group filter can also be used in combination with status filter.

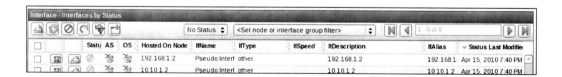

In addition, NNMi provides additional information about listed interfaces, such as: status, administrative state, operational state, on which node interface is hosted, interface name, type, speed, description and alias, date and time of when the last status was modified, and notes.

Interfaces by Administrative State

Interfaces by Administrative State view lists interfaces filtered by their administrative status. Selected status values can be:

- **Up**: Interface responded, **ifAdminsStatus** is *Up*.
- **Down**: Interface responded, **ifAdminsStatus** is *Down*.
- **Testing**: The state when the interface is set to testing mode (interface is looped for testing).
- **Other**: Device SNMP agent responded to **ifAdminStatus** value as not recognized.
- **Unset**: This state is not used in NNMi yet.
- **Unavailable**: NNMi was unable to determine the state. Null value provided, or value outside the range of possible values.
- **Not Polled**: Interface has intentionally not been polled.
- **Agent Error**: NNMi cannot communicate with device SNMP agent.
- **No Polling Policy**: There is no polling policy set for the particular object in monitoring settings.

[**Note**: Node group or interface group filter can also be used in combination with status filter.]

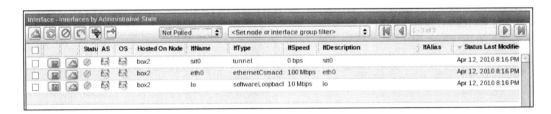

In addition, NNMi provides additional information about listed interfaces, such as: status, administrative state, operational state, on which node interface is hosted, interface name, type, speed, description and alias, date and time when last status was modified, and notes.

Interfaces by Operational State

Interfaces by Operational State lists interfaces filtered by their operational status. Selected status values can be following:

- **Up**: Device responded, ifOperStatus of interface is *up*.

- **Down**: Device responded, ifOperStatus of interface is *down*.

- **Testing**: Device responded, ifOperStatus of interface is in test mode.

- **Other**: Device responded, with unrecognized ifOperStatus value of interface.

- **Unset**: This state is not used in NNMi yet.

- **Unknown**: Device responded, ifOperStatus of interface is *unknown*.

- **Dormant**: Device responded, ifOperStatus of interface is in pending state and waiting for an external event.

- **Not Present**: This state indicates that an interface is missing a hardware component.

- **Lower Layer Down**: Device responded, ifOperStatus of interface is down because of lower layer interface status.

- **Minor Fault**: Device responded, ifOperStatus of interface is in minor fault state, interface is still operational, but close attention is needed.

- **Unavailable**: NNMi was unable to determine the state. Null value provided, or value outside the range of possible values.

- **Agent Error**: NNMi has received an error while querying an agent.

- **No Polling Policy**: There is a no polling policy set for a particular object in monitoring settings.

- **Not Polled**: Interface has intentionally not been polled.

 Note: Node group or interface group filter can also be used in combination with status filter.

The following screenshot represents the **Operational State** window:

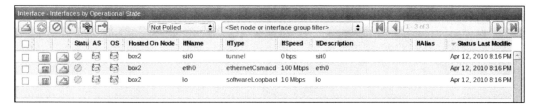

In addition, NNMi provides additional information about listed interfaces, such as: status, administrative state, operational state, on which node interface is hosted, interface name, type, speed, description and alias, date and time when last status was modified, and notes.

IP addresses by State

IP Addresses by State lists IP addresses filtered by state. Selected status values can be following:

- **Responding**: Indicates that IP address has been polled and responded to ICMP ping.

- **Not Responding**: Indicates, that IP address has been polled but didn't respond to ICMP ping.

- **Unset**: This state is not used in NNMi yet.

- **Not Polled**: Indicates that IP address intentionally hasn't been polled, based on monitoring settings policy.

- **No Polling Policy**: Indicates, that no polling policy exists for this IP address.

- **Unavailable**: NNMi was unable to determine the state. For example, response was null or outside the accepted value range.

 Note: Node group or interface group filter can also be used in combination with status filter.

The following screenshot represents the **State** window:

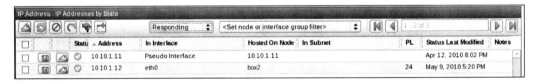

In addition, NNMi provides additional information about listed IP addresses, such as: status, IP address, interface name to which IP address is assigned, hostname of device where address is hosted, subnet, prefix length, date and time when last time status was modified, and notes.

Node Groups

Node Groups lists all node groups with their status.

The following screenshot represents the **Node Groups** window:

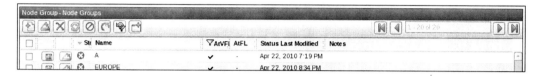

In addition, NNMi provides additional information about listed node groups, such as: status, group name, whether it was added to view filter list and filter list, date and time when last status was modified, and notes.

Custom Node Collections

Custom Node Collections lists the status of all configured custom policies.

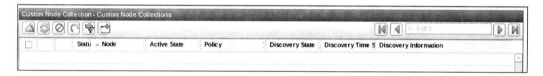

In addition, NNMi provides additional information about listed node collections, such as: status, node name, active state, policy name, discovery state, discovery time, and discovery information.

Custom Polled Instances

Custom Polled Instances lists the status of all configured instances. This view is useful to check the status of configured polled instances. Depending on sorting, the user can check activities such as:

- What is the status of polled MIB instances on particular node/nodes?
- What is the status of a particular polled MIB instance on each configured node?
- What polled MIB instances are in a particular state?

More questions may be answered using this view, only major ones were listed previously.

In addition, NNMi provides additional information about listed custom polled instances, such as: state, last state change, MIB instance, node name, variable, active state, and date and time when last state was modified.

Non-Normal Node Components

Non-Normal Node Components lists nodes that have components with the following statuses:

- Warning
- Minor
- Major
- Critical

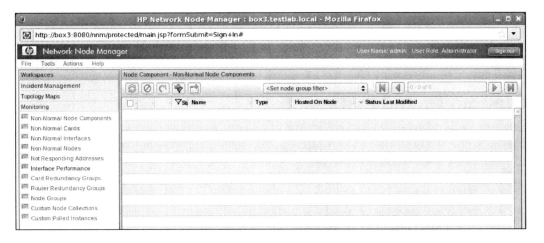

Non-Normal Cards

Non-Normal Cards lists cards with the following status:

- Warning

- Minor

- Major

- Critical

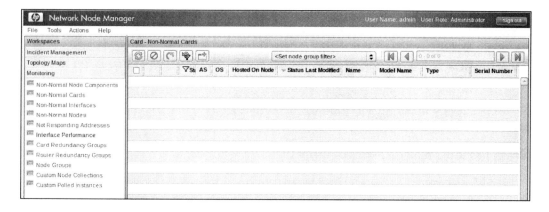

In addition, NNMi lists the administrative and operational state of listed cards, the node name where cards are hosted, date and time when the status was last modified, model name, type, serial number, firmware, hardware, software, redundant group, and so on.

Card Redundancy Groups

Card Redundancy Groups lists discovered card redundancy groups, with the status of each group.

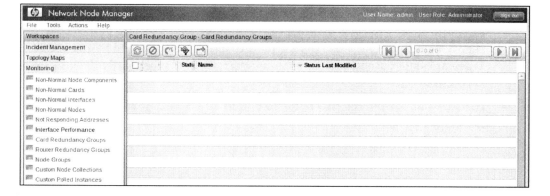

Monitoring an incident for problems

This section describes how to monitor incidents for problems in NNMi. This section also provides information about views used for incident monitoring.

What is an incident?

HP Software NNMi follows ITIL recommendations, which are one of IT infrastructure management methodologies. According to ITIL, an incident is an unplanned interruption to an IT service or a reduction in the quality of an IT service. Failure of a Configuration Item that has not yet impacted service is also an incident, for example, failure one of the **VRRP (Virtual Router Redundancy Protocol)** group routers, where when one router fails, the other one takes over operations. Service is not interrupted but the device has failed and needs to be fixed.

NNMi is a tool which helps to monitor network services, one of NNMi's functions is to deliver incidents for operators to the incident browser for the monitored network.

NNMi has three major sources of incidents:

- **Management software**: Incidents generated by NNMi server.
- **SNMP traps**: Incidents received as SNMP traps from managed devices.
- **NNM 6.x/7.x events**: Incidents created based on events received from the NNM 6.x/7.x management server.

NNMi incidents carry mandatory data, such as message text, the incident source and date, but also include additional information to help comply with ITIL as much as possible. Incidents hold data such as:

- **Severity**: Severity is assigned by NNMi, based on incident configuration settings and can be changed by the user.
- **Priority**: Priority is assigned by NNMi, based on incident configuration settings and can be changed by user.
- **Lifecycle state**: Lifecycle state is assigned by NNMi (*registered* and *closed* states), based on what state the incident is and can be changed by the user. There are state values, such *in progress* and *completed* where only the user can set these states.
- **Assigned to**: Displays a username to whom an incident is assigned. This field is changed by the NNMi user.

- **Category**: Displays the incident category. This field is assigned by NNMi based on the incident configuration settings. This field can also be changed by the NNMi user.

- **Family**: Displays incident family. This field is assigned by NNMi based on the incident configuration settings.

- **Origin**: Displays the source of the incident. This field is set by NNMi.

- **Correlation nature**: Displays incident's nature of correlation. This field is set by NNMi.

The next section describes each of these fields in more details.

Incident details in NNMi

This section describes the incident details used in NNMi. Listing incidents in different views, the user sees the main information regarding the incident. The following screenshot displays an Incident list window:

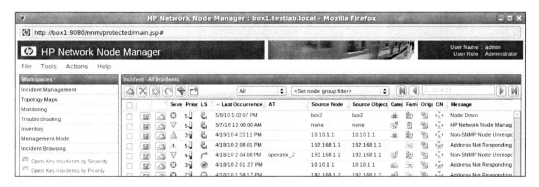

More details about every incident are located in the incident tabs. To access detailed incident information, each incident needs to be opened. From the Incident window (like the previous screenshot) any incident can be opened by:

- Selecting the **Open** button for each incident.

- Selecting an incident with the help of the checkbox and clicking the **Open** button in the top left corner of the window.

This section describes each attribute of the incident and lists all the values.

Severity

Severity shows how serious the incident is. The following table lists all the values of incident severity:

Severity	Description
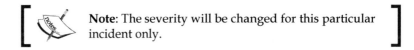	Normal
	Warning
	Minor
	Major
	Critical

Incident severity can be changed in two ways:

- **Change severity for one particular existing incident**: This change can be done by any user. Open an incident and change the severity value from the drop-down list.

> **Note**: The severity will be changed for this particular incident only.

- **Change severity for all incoming incidents of this type**: This change can be done by the administrator. Severity for all new incidents, of a selected type, can be changed in the **Configuration** workspace using the **Incident Configuration** view. For example, if we want all **Interface down** incidents to have the severity **Warning**, we should use this type of configuration.

Priority

The priority tells us how urgent an incident is. The priority value is set manually for every incident. Priorities are numbered from one to five. The lower number is given higher priority. For example, priority number one is **Top** priority and priority number four is **Low**. The following table lists all priorities used in NNMi:

Priority	Description
5	None
4	Low
3	Medium
2	High
1	Top

By default, priority is always set to **None**.

Lifecycle state

The lifecycle state shows where the incident is in its lifecycle. This value is controlled by the user (except in cases when NNMi automatically sets the state to **Registered** or **Closed**). NNMi automatically sets all new incidents to **Registered** and sets incidents to the **Closed** state to confirm when the problem listed by the incident is solved.

The list of incident lifecycle states is provided in the following table:

Lifecycle state	Description
	Registered
	In progress
	Completed
	Closed

NNMi can set an incident to **Closed** when NNMi confirms that the problem reported by incident is solved. An example of this is:

- Node Down incident is automatically set to **Closed** when Node Up incident is received
- Interface Down incident is automatically set to **Closed** when Interface Up incident is received

Assigned to

The **Assigned to** field indicates the user who is assigned to a particular incident. All new incidents have no user assigned by default. The user is selected from a list of users that are configured in NNMi. For example, to assign an incident to user **operator 1**, complete the following steps:

1. Open an incident.
2. Select drop-down menu close to **Assigned to…** field.
3. Select **Quick Find…**.
4. Select the user **operator 1** (you can select any other user you have on your configured system).
5. Click **Save and Close** to save your changes.

The incident is assigned to user **operator 1** (or any other you selected in the previous step).

To make sure you assigned the incident, go to the incident list and view the **Assigned to** field. It should display **operator 1** in this field (or any other you selected during configuration).

Category

The **Category** is generated by NNMi to indicate the problem category. The following table lists all category values used by NNMi:

Category	Description
	Accounting
	Application Status
	Configuration

Category	Description
	Fault
	Performance
	Security
	Status

The user can change the category for a selected incident by opening an incident and selecting another category from the drop-down list.

The administrator can also change the category for all incoming incidents using **Incident Configuration** in the **Configuration** workspace. For example, Interface Down incidents would have the status **Accounting** instead.

Family

Family is used to categorize the types of incidents further. The following table lists all family values used by NNMi. Family values cannot be changed by the user once the incident is generated.

Family	Description
	Address
	Aggregated port
BGP	BGP
Board	Board
	Chassis
	Component Health
	Connection
	Correlation

Family	Description
	HSRP
	Interface
	License
	Node
	OSPF
	RAMS
RMON	RMON
	RRP
STP	STP
Trap Analysis	Trap Analysis
	VRRP

Origin

The **Origin** field displays the source type for how the incident was generated. The following table lists all origin values used by NNMi:

Origin	Description
	Management Software
	Manually Created
	Remotely Generated
	SNMP Trap

Correlation nature

This field is used for root cause calculations. The following table lists all correlation nature values used in NNMi:

Correlation Nature	Description
(i)	Info
?₂	None
▶△◀	Root Cause
▶△◀	Secondary Root Cause
Ⴑ	Symptom
▶▶	Stream Correlation
▶☖◀	Service Impact

Incident form

This section describes incident form tabs that are used to provide more detailed information about incidents.

By navigating through the incident form tabs, the user can gain access to the more detailed information needed for troubleshooting issues. The incident form can be reached in the following ways:

- Selecting incident by marking a checkbox and clicking **Open** in the top left corner of the window.
- Selecting the **Open** icon close to the incident you want to open.

The next section describes each incident tab.

General tab

The **General** tab provides general information about the incident. This tab provides the most information about the incident compared to other incident tabs. In real life this is probably used the most for incident details.

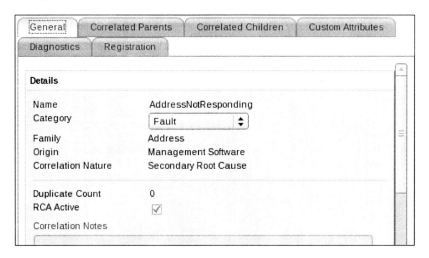

Correlated Parents tab

When the root cause of a problem is detected, a parent incident is created. In that case, they would be listed in **Correlated Parents**. For example, a Node Down incident is a parent to an Interface Down incident, so Node Down might be listed in the Interface Down **Correlated Parents** tab.

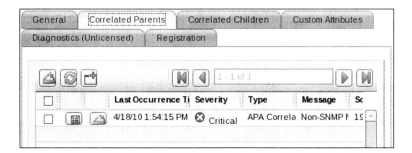

Correlated Children tab

The **Correlated Children** tab lists all correlated children incidents that may occur if an incident is a correlated parent. For example, an Interface Down incident would appear in the Node Down **Correlated Children** tab.

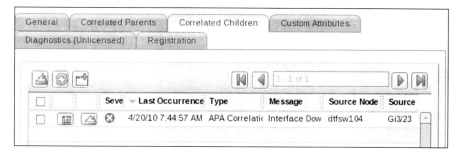

Custom Attributes tab

Custom Attributes can be used for incidents to provide some additional information. As an example, SNMP trap varbind values can be used as custom attributes to provide more information about an incident. **CIA (Custom Incident Attribute)** includes the name, type, and value group.

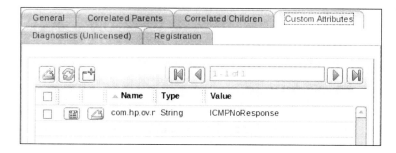

Diagnostics tab

This tab is used in NNM iSPI NET. It lists a history of all iSPI NET diagnostic reports that have been run on the incident's source node. If you don't have the iSPI NET license installed, this tab will be empty.

Registration tab

This tab provides the date and time when this object was created and modified.

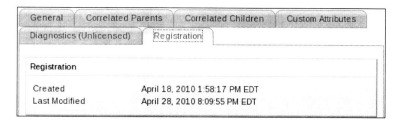

Working with incidents

NNMi is designed to work with incidents during its lifecycle—starting from generating an incident, to fixing and closing a problem. NNMi allows incidents to be assigned to a particular person during the incident management process. So, in real life, when an incident occurs, you not only want basic information such as the severity, priority, source, and issue description, but also some additional information which helps to manage the whole incident management process as well.

Let's take an example. An incident about fan failure on a router is displayed in incident view. The operator in charge wants to assign the incident to a specialist, so later on any other operator can see who is working on this issue and what stage it is at. When the issue is fixed, the operator wants to see the information about the incident details, whether the incident is solved or even closed.

This section describes how to work with incidents using the following fields:

- Assignment
- Lifecycle
- Displaying a map

Changing assignment

The **Assignment** field for an incident indicates who is assigned to a particular incident. Only users who are configured on NNMi can be assigned to an incident. Also, the assigned person can see all incidents assigned to them.

The Assignment field ensures that the incident is assigned to somebody and that the person knows about it. So it improves the incident management process and confusion about who is or should be working on the incident can be avoided.

There are at least three ways to assign an incident to a user:

- Select an incident you want to assign to a person, select **Actions** in Menu and chose an action you want to initiate:
    - **Assign incident…**: When the window opens, select a user who you want to assign the incident to
    - **Own incident**: Incident will be assigned to the user you are logged-in as
    - **Unassign incident**: Removes incident from assigned user

 Note: Using this way of assignment, you can also assign more than one incident to the selected user at a time.

- Open an incident, select **Assign to**, select **Quick Find…**, choose a user from the **User** window. Then click **Save and close** to save your new assignment.

- Open an incident by selecting **Actions** and chose an action you want to initiate:

    ○ **Assign Incident**: Select user from **User** window and click **Save and close** to save your new assignment.

    ○ **Own incident**: Incident will be assigned to the user you are logged-in as.

    ○ **Unassign incident**: Removes incident from assigned user.

Maintaining up-to-date lifecycle

The **Lifecycle** field ensures that the stages of the incident are known to involved users and these stages are managed. There are five incident lifecycle stages in NNMi:

- **Dampened**: This lifecycle state is used by NNMi internally and means that the incident is in the holding state and is waiting for correlation with some other incident/incidents.

- **Registered**: Newly created incidents are set as *Registered*. The user can also set the incident to this state.

- **In progress**: This state means that the incident has been assigned to an NNMi user for investigation. The state is changed by NNMi users.

- **Solved (completed)**: This state is set by NNMi users and indicates that the assigned user has finished investigating/troubleshooting. The full meaning of this state depends on internal agreement within the support team. For example, it may mean that a solution is ready for deployment, or the problem is fixed, and so on.

- **Closed**: This state is set by NNMi, but, NNMi users can also set the incident to this state. *Closed* means that problem is solved.

The section *Lifecycle state* describes every step of the incident lifecycle. There are at least two ways to change the incident lifecycle:

- Select an incident, select **Actions**, and then select one of the following lifecycle states: **In Progress, Completed,** or **Closed**.

- Open an incident, select **Actions**, and then select one of the following lifecycle states: **In Progress, Completed,** or **Closed**.

Displaying a map

When you are working with incidents, there are many cases when you would like, or even need, to see a map so you could make faster or more accurate decisions when troubleshooting or fixing issues.

NNMi provides the ability to reach a map from selected incidents. The following are two ways to show how a map can be shown for the involved incident:

- Select incident, select **Actions**, and then select one of the map types you want to open:
    - **Layer 2 Neighbor View**
    - **Layer 2 Neighbor View**
    - **Node Group Map**
    - **Path View**

 Note: Only one incident must be selected.

- Open an incident, select **Actions**, and then select one of map types you want to open:
    - **Layer 2 Neighbor View**
    - **Layer 2 Neighbor View**
    - **Node Group Map**
    - **Path View**

Investigating problems

When issues in a network occur, system administrators or operators starts investigating and troubleshooting. This activity is called **problem investigation**, although the definition of problem investigation in NNMi and ITIL don't really match or mean the same.

To investigate a problem, NNMi has a list of tools, which are needed in most cases while investigating:

- **To get more details about problem device**: This covers information about what NNMi has discovered about the device, how NNMi is configured to monitor a particular device, and see the current status of the selected device.

- **Find object if needed**: There may be cases when we need to find objects using NNMi. This includes finding a node, attached to a switch port or a list of nodes attached to a switch.

- **Carry out tests**: This can include tests from simple ICMP ping, trace route or telnet to a device from NNMi console.

This section describes each of these tools or features.

Verifying device configuration details

NNMi checks for device configuration changes on a regular basis and ensures that any changes to device configuration a discovered. For example, if we install new card with additional interfaces to a switch, NNMi will recognize this after the next configuration poll. By default, configuration poll runs every 24 hours. The administrator can change the polling value by completing the following steps:

1. Select **Discovery configuration** in the **Configuration** workspace.

2. Enter new value in **Rediscovery Interval**.

3. Click **Save and close** to save your changes.

   When diagnosing problems, the user can check the current configuration status of the device by forcing NNMi to make a configuration poll of selected devices:

   i.   Select device you want to force configuration poll.

 Note: You can use any map view, table or workspace to select a node. If you select a node from incident view, the node associated with the incident will be polled.

   ii. Select **Actions | Configuration Poll**.

   The window showing configuration poll results will be opened. If more than one node was selected, the according number of windows will be opened.

Verifying current status of device

NNMi updates the status of devices in real time based on received incidents and also completes status polling on a regular basis using the configured schedule in **Monitoring Configuration**.

The user can force a check on a selected device status by running **Status Poll**. To run **Status Poll** the following needs to be done:

1. Select one or more devices that you want to force.

 Note: Up to 10 devices can be selected. If you select incidents, nodes associated to the incident will be polled.

2. Select **Actions | Status Poll**.

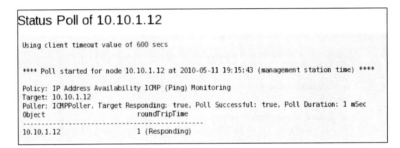

```
Status Poll of 10.10.1.12

Using client timeout value of 600 secs


**** Poll started for node 10.10.1.12 at 2010-05-11 19:15:43 (management station time) ****

Policy: IP Address Availability ICMP (Ping) Monitoring
Target: 10.10.1.12
Poller: ICMPPoller, Target Responding: true, Poll Successful: true, Poll Duration: 1 mSec
Object                          roundTripTime
-------------------------------------------------------
10.10.1.12                      1 (Responding)
```

A window showing polling results will be opened. If more than one node was selected, the according number of windows will be opened.

Viewing monitoring configuration

NNMi allows you to configure monitoring settings for a specific node, interface, or group of nodes or interfaces. To view monitoring configuration in NNMi see **Monitoring Configuration** in the **Configuration** workspace.

Also, NNMi allows monitoring settings to be checked for a selected node, interface, IP address, or redundancy group. To check these settings for a selected object, complete the following steps:

1. Select an object:

    i. To select a node, interface or IP address, navigate to **View** to display the object and select an object.

    ii. To select a router redundancy group member, navigate to a **Router Redundancy Group** view (**Inventory | Router Redundancy Group**).

    iii. To select a **Node Component**, navigate to **Node** view (**Inventory | Nodes | Open**) to open a node.

2. Select **Actions | Monitoring Settings**.

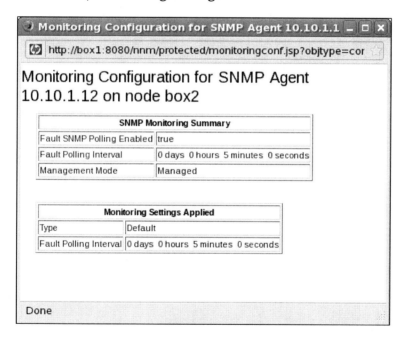

A configuration result window will open. If more than one object was selected, the according number of windows will be opened.

Finding a node

To search for a node in NNMi inventory, you can use the **Find** action, by selecting **Tools | Find ....**

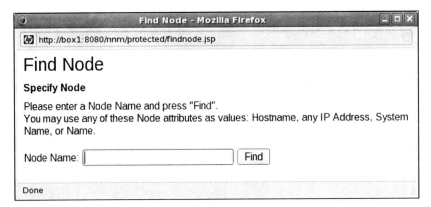

In the search field you can enter one of the following:

- IP address of any interface
- Fully qualified domain name
- DNS name
- System name, which is recorded in the sysName field in SNMP

Finding an attached switch port

If you need to find a switch port to which an investigated node is connected to, NNMi provides the tool **Find Attached Switch Port**. Let's say you need to find a switch and the port where the problem node is connected.

This feature works only if communication between NNMi and the switch is configured properly.

To search, enter one of the following:

- MAC address of node you are searching
- IP address of node you are searching
- DNS name of node

 Note: DNS name must all be lowercase.

To search for an attached switch port, complete the following:

1. Select **Tools | Find Attached Switch Port**.
2. Specify MAC address, IP address, or hostname of node in **End Node Name**.
3. Select **Finish**.

As a result, NNM lists the node name, the node's interface, and port number.

 Note: If more than one attached switch is found, NNMi shows the first matching switch it finds.

Displaying end nodes attached to a switch

Another nice troubleshooting tool is for listing all nodes that are connected to a particular switch. This tool lists all nodes connected to the selected switch. For example, you need to turn off a switch for maintenance and need to know what nodes are connected to it so you could prepare for outages.

To launch this tool, complete the following:

1. Select a switch from any form, table or map (For example, **Monitoring | Node Groups | Switches |** select switch you are interested in).
2. Select **Actions | Show Attached End Nodes**.

Testing node access with ICMP ping

While investigating problems, you can check if the device is reachable from the NNMi server by running ICMP pings.

To run ICMP pings from the NNMi server, complete the following:

1. Select one or two objects you want to ping.
2. Select **Actions | Ping (from server)**.

The results will be displayed in new window. If two objects were selected, a separate window for each object will be opened.

 Note: A maximum of two selected objects are allowed. If you select more than two objects, an error message will be displayed.

Tracing the route

While investigating problems, you can check the path from the NNMi management server to the selected device.

To run a trace route from the NNMi server, complete the following:

1. Select one or more objects you want to check the route of.

2. Select **Actions | Trace Route (from server)**.

The results will be displayed in a new window. If more objects were selected, a separate window for each object will be opened.

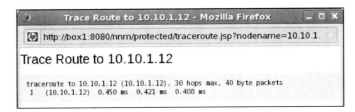

Note: The maximum of 10 selected objects are allowed. If you select more than the allowed number of maximum objects, an error message will be displayed.

Telnet to a device

While investigating problems, you may want to telnet to a device to check the device configuration:

1. Check if your `FEATURE_DISABLE_TELNET_PROTOCOL` registry settings are configured properly for an IE browser:
2. Set `iexplorer.exe=dword:00000000` value to registry key: `[HKEY_LOCAL_MACHINE\SOFTWARE\Microsoft\Internet Explorer\Main\FeatureControl\FEATURE_DISABLE_TELNET_PROTOCOL]`

For more details check article MS537169 on the MSDN library (`http://msdn2.microsoft.com/en-us/library/ms537169.aspx`).

To telnet to a device from a client console, complete the following:

1. Select one object you want to telnet to.
2. Select **Actions | Telnet... (from client)**.

Results will be displayed in a new window.

 Note: Only one telnet session is allowed. If you select more than one object, an error message will be displayed.

For security reasons, in many cases, network administrators use SSH to connect to network devices instead of telnet. NNMi doesn't provide a menu tool to SSH to selected nodes, NNMi administrator can create their own menu item. Read *Chapter 10* for more details on how to create custom tools on NNMi.

Configuring Custom Polling

Custom poller allows us to monitor custom MIB expression objects on monitored devices. For example, when a five minute CPU load average on backbone network routers exceeds 50% for more than 10 minutes, the network administrator wants network operations center staff to be notified by sending an incident with a **Major** state.

Starting from NNMi version 9.0 the Custom Poller feature was introduced, which was missing in NNMi version 8.x and 7.x. Earlier versions used the **Data Collection and Thresholding** feature.

To start monitoring a MIB expression by Custom Poller, the following steps need to be completed:

1. Enabling **Custom Poller**.
2. Configuring **Custom Poller Collection**.
3. Configuring **Policy**.

In other words, to complete Custom Polling configuration, all three steps need to be completed.

The way Custom Poller works is, once it is enabled, it starts polling all objects defined in policies. Each policy defines the polling intervals and the node group to which the collection should be applied. Each object has a MIB expression configured and how to consider the status of the collected MIB expression values. The graphical representation of Custom Poller configuration is displayed in the following figure:

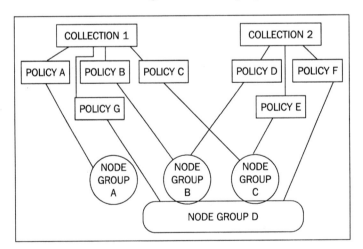

As a result, we will configure custom polling configuration to monitor an object using the following requirements: a five minute CPU load average needs to be polled on all routers in a network every five minutes, and if the CPU load exceeds 60% by three polling cycles in a row, send an incident and consider that router as Major status. The status is not critical if the CPU load drops below a 50% load. If the router CPU load drops below 5% for at least three polling cycle in a row, operators needs to be notified by generating an incident and status Warning should be set, until the CPU load increases above 10% limit. The following figure provides a graphical example of thresholds and rearm configuration in NNMi:

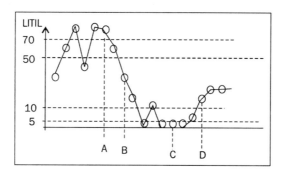

In the preceding diagram:

- **A** represents a high value threshold limit, which has been exceeded by a trigger count of two. A high value threshold incident would be generated.

- **B** represents high value rearm, which is triggered because the measured object has dropped below the high value rearm limit. A rearm incident would be generated.

- **C** represents a low value threshold limit, which has been exceeded by a trigger count of two. A low value threshold incident would be generated.

- **D** represents a low value rearm, which is triggered because the measured object has dropped below the low value rearm limit. A rearm incident would be generated.

This topic can be explained using a five minute CPU load collection example given previously.

Enabling or disabling Custom Polling

Custom Poller needs to be enabled in order to use this feature. By default, it is disabled. To enable Custom Poller, complete the following steps:

1. Select **Custom Poller Configuration** in the **Configuration** workspace.

2. Select a checkbox on **Enable Custom Poller** to enable Custom Poller (uncheck this checkbox if you want to disable **Custom Poller**).

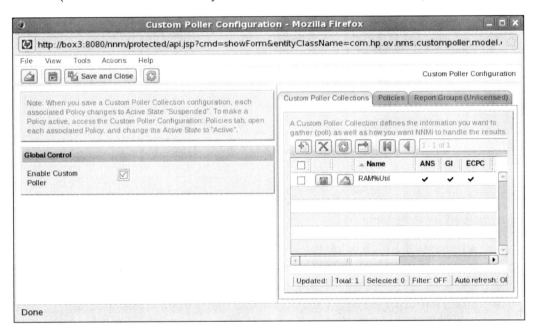

3. Click **Save and Close** to save your changes.

Once you have enabled Custom Poller, your configured collections have started to be monitored. By default, there are no custom collections configured to poll. To create new collections, proceed to the next section.

Custom Poller Collections

Custom Poller Collection defines the MIB expression that needs to be polled, and also defines how one or the other collection value will impact on monitoring: what values are accepted monitored value limits (thresholds and rearms), when is a limit considered to be exceeded (count number when considered as limit exceeded), and whether incident should be generated.

Each collection can have one or more policies, which define the polling intervals and boundaries (which node groups should be polled).

To configure a collection, complete the following steps (steps will be provided based on five minute CPU load example listed above):

 Note: Example assumes that Custom Poller is enabled already, as described in the previous section.

1. Select **Custom Poller Configuration** in the **Configuration** workspace.
2. Select **Custom Poller Collections** tab.
3. Select **New** button.
4. Complete or select following fields:
    ○   In the **Name** field, enter 5min CPU load (or any name you find it meaningful).
    ○   Select checkbox for **Affect Node Status**.
    ○   Select checkbox for **Generate Incident**.

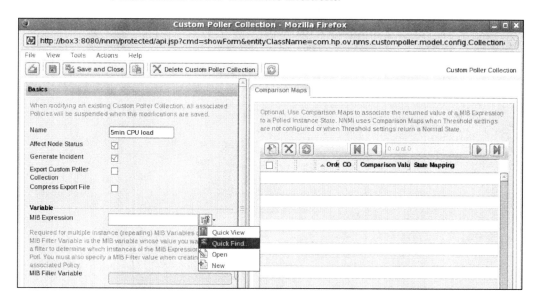

5. Select **Quick Find...** by clicking the button to the right-hand side of the **MIB Expression** field.

6. Select **cisco_avgBusy5** from the MIB expression list.

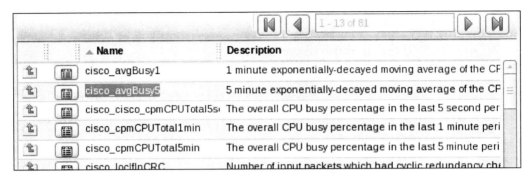

7. Configure threshold settings by completing or selecting the following fields:

    i.   In the **High State** field, choose **Major** from the drop-down menu.

    ii.   Enter 70 in **High Value** field.

    iii.   Enter 50 in **High Value Rearm** field.

    iv.   Enter 2 in **High Trigger count** field.

    v.   In the **Low State** field, choose **Warning** from the drop down menu.

    vi.   Enter 5 in **Low Value** field.

    vii.   Enter 10 in **Low Value Rearm** field.

    viii.   Enter 2 in **Low Trigger Count** field.

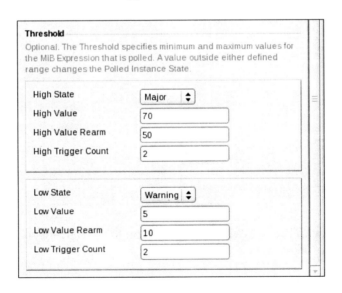

8. Click **Save and Close**.

Congratulations! You have successfully configured your collection. Now, you are ready to configure more collections and proceed to policy configuration.

The following table gives a description of fields used in the **Collection** configuration window:

Parameter	Description
Name	The name for the collection. This name also appears on all incidents generated by this collection.
	Name can be up to 255 symbols in length and no special symbols should (#, &, <, >, ", ', \) be used.
	Name can be changed at any time. In case if the name is changed, NNMi removes all the historical data for that Custom Poller Collection that is exported.
Affect Node Status	If checkbox is selected, polled instance affects associated Node's status.
Generate Incident	If checkbox is selected, incident is generated every time a threshold is reached or exceeded.
Export Custom Poller Collection	If checkbox is enabled, Custom Poller Collection is exported to a CSV file. The export is made to the following directory:
	Unix: `$NnmDataDir/shared/nnm/database/custompoller/export/final`
	Windows: `%NnmDataDir%\shared\nnm\database\custompoller\export\final`
Compress Export File	If checkbox is enabled, NNMi archives a file adding `.gz` at the end of `.csv` suffix.
MIB Expression	MIB expression can be chosen or created from this field. The following values can be chosen from the drop-down menu:
	• **Quick View**
	• **Quick Find...**
	• **Open**
	• **New**
MIB Filter Variable	Required for multiple instance MIB variables only. The MIB Filter Variable is the MIB variable whose value you want to use as a filter, to determine the instances of the MIB Expression to Custom Poll.
	MIB Filter value must be also set when associated policy is created.
High State	The state which should be set if the high threshold has been exceeded.
High Value	Threshold value for a high state.
High Value Rearm	The value when the high threshold is being reset.

Parameter	Description
High Trigger Count	The number of counts when high threshold should be triggered.
Low State	The state which should be set if the low threshold has been exceeded.
Low Value	Threshold value for a low state.
Low Value Rearm	The value when the low threshold is being reset.
Low Trigger Count	The number of counts when low threshold should be triggered.

When export to CSV is selected, the following data is included in exports:

- Node UUID
- IP address
- Node name
- The MIB expression or numeric OID
- Timestamp (milliseconds)
- Poll interval (milliseconds)
- MIB instance (number, which is used to identify row in a table)
- Metric value

Custom poller writes data to a disk and monitors space consumed by these exports. By default, if a directory reaches a GB of data, NNMi removes the oldest files and writes the new ones. If HA configuration is implemented, the exported data is stored to a shared disk. If application failover is implemented, NNMi replicates these files to the failover system.

Configuring Comparison Maps

Parameter	Description
Ordering	The ordering number of Comparison Map. The lower the number, the higher the priority.
Comparison Operator	The operator which is used to compare the Comparison value, so it could determine the state.
Comparison Value	When value is returned from MIB expression, it is compared against this value, using Comparison Operator. There are following values of Comparison Operators: • < (Less than) • <= (Less than or equal to) • = (Equal to) • != (Not equal to) • > (Greater than) • >= (Greater than or equal to) • Is null (value is null or is not available) • Is not null (the result contains a value) • Default (When no matches are found, it sets the State using the other Comparison Operators) *Default* should be ordered the least.
State Mapping	The state, which is assigned if MIB expression value, matches the comparison expressions. There are the following possible values: • Normal • Warning • Minor • Major • Critical For example, every time a returned value is equal to zero, you can set NNMi to set the polled instance state to *Critical*.

Policies

Policy is a part of the custom poller configuration, which defines the schedule and boundaries of the assigned collection. For example, a five minute CPU load collection is assigned to a policy, which defines that the collection needs to be applied to all routers (node group definition) and should be polled every five minutes.

Some collection can have multiple policies assigned. For example, the same five minute CPU load collection can be assigned to a policy, which is configured to poll all VIP customer routers every minute.

Based on the preceding examples, at the beginning of the *Configuring Custom Polling* section, the following is an example of how to configure a policy:

 Note: Example assumes that Custom Poller is already enabled, and Custom Poller Collection is configured, as described in the previous section. Also node group to which the policy will be assigned to, is configured already.

1. Select **Custom Poller Configuration** in the **Configuration** workspace.
2. Select the **Policies** tab.

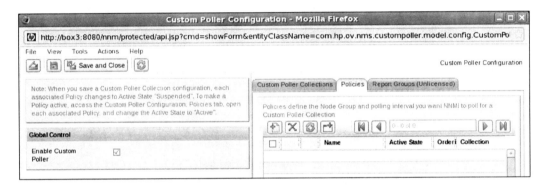

3. Select **New** to create a new policy.
4. When the new form is opened, complete the following fields:
    i. Enter Routers in the **Name** field.
    ii. Enter 10 in the **Ordering** field (The lower the number, the higher the priority is. **10** is chosen to leave space in case policies with a higher priority will need to be created in the future).
    iii. Select **Quick Find...** from the drop-down menu on the right-hand side of the **Collection** field.
    iv. Select **5min CPU load** from the list of collections (this collection was created in a previous section).

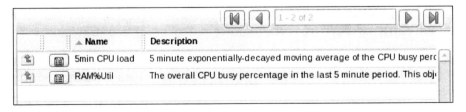

v. Select **Active** from the **Active State** field's drop-down menu to make this collection active.

vi. From the drop-down menu on the right-hand side of the **Node Group** field, select **Quick Find...** and select a node group **Routers** from the list of node groups.

vii. In the **Polling Interval** window, set 5 minute polling time interval.

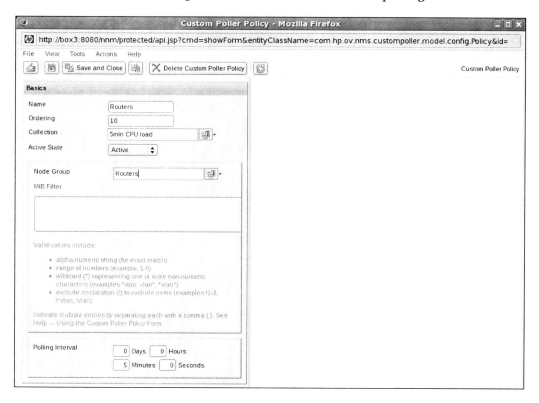

5. Click **Save and close** to save and close this form.

Congratulations! You have successfully configured a collection described in the preceding example. Now you are ready to create more policies for this collection, and new collections with new policies as well.

Summary

Now you have completed this chapter, you will have a good understanding of what role NNMi plays in network monitoring and how it helps to improve the incident management process.

We have all that we need right in front of us for excellent monitoring when NNMi has discovered the network with the required granularity. It's just about using the tools in the right way.

This chapter has described how to monitor a network for problems taking two different approaches: monitoring devices and monitoring incidents. Browsing between views (maps, tables, and incidents) fulfills all incident management processes and allows us to accurately evaluate the situation.

Troubleshooting tools are very handy when detecting a problem and troubleshooting the issue. We have learned the main tools used within NNMi for network troubleshooting as well.

The next chapter is dedicated to describing how NNMi can be extended to cover more features and adopt more specific infrastructures and requirements.

10
Extending NNMi

There are situations when we have a management tool but it doesn't feel as flexible because some features are not provided. Although the feature looks simple, it plays such an important role in any infrastructure management process that a long list of provided features doesn't look attractive anymore.

This chapter is about how to expand NNMi features by simply designing and creating additional features within NNMi customization.

NNMi inventory queries and stores, inside NNMi database, a lot of information about our network object (devices, interfaces, and so on). However, there are always cases when specific needs appear and inventory data customization is handy.

Another example is providing our NNMi console users with information to create additional actions, which are simple to implement, but for some reasons are not included in NNMi functionality. So, creating our own action menu gives freedom to adjust the system and adapt it according to our specific needs.

This chapter provides information on the following topics:

- Object custom attributes
- Action menu configuration
- Expanding system capabilities using URLs

Object custom attributes

Custom attributes are used to expand inventory data stored in NNMi. This expansion can be done by the NNMi administrator. Custom attributes may help integrate NNMi with other management tools or may help replace other management tools responsible for performing small functionality (for example, a small, limited functionality inventory database, and so on).

What is a custom attribute?

Custom attributes in NNMi are custom fields that can be added or modified by the NNMi administrator. For example, we want to maintain device serial numbers within NNMi, so we could have them handy if we needed to provide such information to the support team or suppliers.

Another good example could be managing customer data such as the customer name and SLA name on a node's interfaces.

Having such data inside NNMi makes it more comfortable and allows us to reduce the number of external tools.

Custom attributes are provided for nodes, interfaces, and incidents (refer the next diagram).

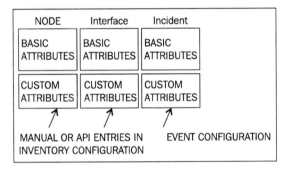

This section describes only node and interface custom attributes because they can be set for a particular device or interface. Incident custom attributes are configured in incident configuration, and configuration provides templates only for custom attribute values. Specific values for the incident custom attributes are set by the incident source, for example, the SNMP trap is one of the OID instances.

Accessing custom attributes

To access node custom attributes, complete the following steps:

1. Open a node. One of the few ways to do so is to select the **Inventory** workspace, and then select **Interfaces | Open** to open the selected interface.

2. Select the **Custom Attributes** tab.

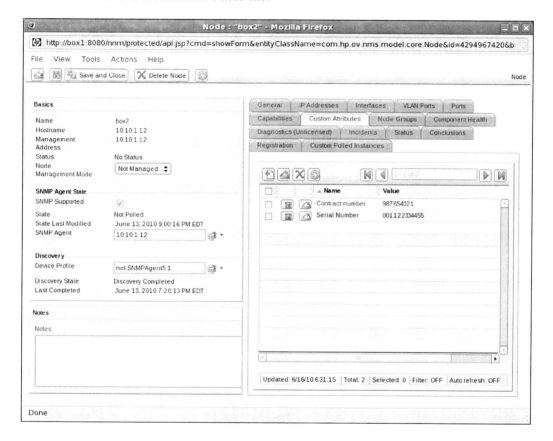

To access interface custom attributes, complete the following steps:

1. Open an interface. One of the few ways to do so is to select the **Inventory** workspace, then select **Interfaces**, and open the selected interface.

2. Select the **Custom Attributes** tab.

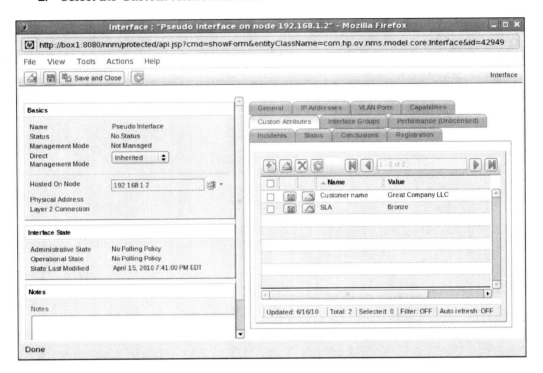

Modifying custom attributes

Modification is done on the selected node or interface. The created or modified custom attribute will be carried in all views and tables where the node or object will be used.

 Note: Only administrator role users can edit custom attributes.

To modify the node's custom attributes, open a **Custom Attribute** tab as described in the preceding section and complete the following steps:

1.   Select **New**.

2.   Enter name and value for the custom attribute (refer to the next screenshot).

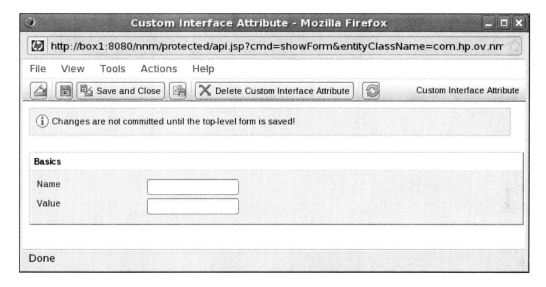

Let's consider the following example, where we will set a new attribute for the **box2** node, where the owner of the node would be recorded. To complete this task, follow the steps given here:

1.   Select **Inventory** workspace.

2.   Open a node named **box2**.

3.   Select the **Custom Attributes** tab.

4.   Select **New**.

5.   Enter **Owner** in the **Name** field.

6.   Enter **John Smith** in the **Value** field.

7. Click **Save and Close.**

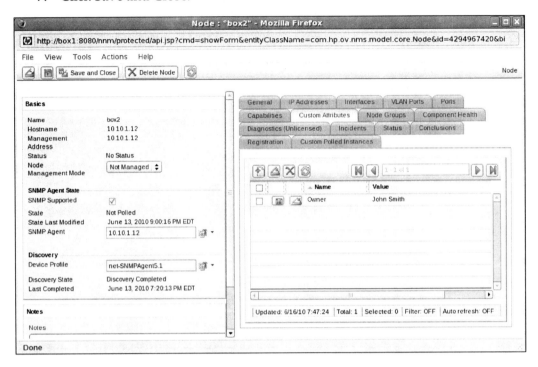

Action menu configuration

NNMi allows system administrators to create new additional action menus. Such NNMi flexibility allows NNMi administrators to easily create additional action menus that can improve NNMi user efficiency and NNMi functionality, to adopt a system for specific needs.

About an action menu

An action menu on the NNMi console provides the ability to initiate configured actions by the NNMi console user. For example, the ping selected node, the open communications configuration window, or the open management console of a third-party management tool.

The **Actions** menu is located on the main menu bar of the NNMi console (refer to the following screenshot).

The NNMi administrator can configure new menus, or modify existing action menus, using the action menu configuration window (**Configuration** workspace | **URL actions**).

Action menus can be configured to be active only for certain conditions, such as depending on the selected object type, number of selected objects, matching criteria for custom attributes, and so on. For example, the ping command can be launched only when the following conditions are fulfilled:

- The node, interface, or object that has an IP address is selected
- Only one object is selected

Another example of using the actions menu can be the status poll of the selected object. This action can be configured to be launched when the following criteria are fulfilled:

- The node or incident is selected (as both of these objects can pass a hostname or IP address to the status poll action).
- At least one, but not more than 10 objects, are selected. This limitation applies to the default configuration. The number can be changed at any time in the **URL actions** configuration.

The administrator can also change the maximum number of allowed object selections.

Configuring URL action

URL actions may be created for different purposes, such as running a command or opening a specific window. Also, a different context can be applied as well, for example, an action will be performed when a router is selected, or the action would be applied only for Juniper routers from 10.10.1.x subnet, and so on.

The following diagram shows the high-level picture of the action menu configuration. As showed in the diagram, the action menu configuration consists of the **Basic Configuration** part, including the **Selection** configuration and **URL Object Types** configuration, which can be treated as configuration within configuration.

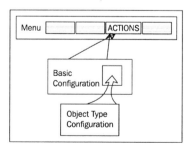

The following section describes, in more detail, how to configure URL action menus.

Configuring URL action basics

To configure basic parameters is a simple and straightforward task. We need to complete following fields for basic configuration (refer to the left-hand side of the configuration window in the following screenshot):

- **Menu Label**: This is a name that will appear on the menu, when the action menu is created.

- **Unique key**: The name for the menu action, which should be unique across all menus. Once it is created, this value cannot be changed. HP recommends using Java naming conventions when we create menu actions, for example, `com.my_company.nnm.urlAction.My_Newly_Created_Action`. Note that the name for the menu action should not exceed 80 characters.

- **Author**: Add an author, either using **Lookup** across existing users or select **New** to create a new author.

- **Ordering**: The value of ordering the number field defines how the action menu will be ordered in a menu. The lowest number goes first. Valid numbers are 1-100.

- **Browser Width**: Defines the width of the browser window. This is optional.

- **Browser Height**: Defines the height of the browser window. This is optional.

- **Add Browser Decorations**: Select checkbox if we want the browser window to have toolbars and menus when the URL is launched.

- **Path View Only**: Select checkbox if we want the created menu action to appear only when the **Path View** window is opened.

- **Requires Remote Management Station**: Select checkbox if we want this menu action to appear only when remote management stations are configured (NNM 6.x/7.x).

- **Description**: We can add our own description.

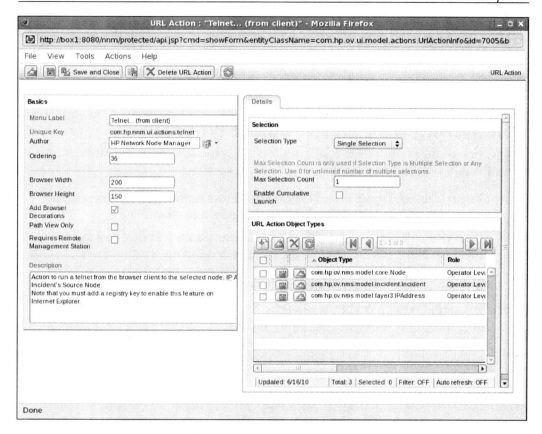

Configuring selection

To configure the action details tab, we need to configure the following (refer to the right-hand side of the configuration window in the preceding screenshot):

- **Selection Type**: Defines whether any objects need to be selected. Possible values are:
    ○ **Any Selection**
    ○ **Single Selection** (default value)
    ○ **Multiple Selections**
    ○ **No Selection**

- **Max Selection Count**: The maximum number of nodes that are allowed to be selected for a menu action to be enabled. Valid only if **Selection Type** is set to **Any Selection** or **Multiple Selections**. If set to **0** (zero), then an unlimited selection count is taken.

- **Enable Cumulative Launch**: If checkbox is enabled, then attributes to URL are passed from all selected objects, comma separated. For example, if the attribute is Name, then the following attributes would be passed: name1,name2,name3. If no checkbox is selected, then a new window is opened for each of the selected object's attributes.

Configuring URL action object types

This section of the menu action configuration holds the key to configuration scope. It stores the following information:

- When (**Object Type**): When to make an action menu active. For example, when the selected object is an interface, node, and so on.

- Who (**Role**): This field describes the minimum user role that has access to this role. Here, we can control the security level of each action menu, so that we needn't have to worry about a user with lower permissions accessing mission-critical action menus.

- What (**Full URL**): A URL is provided that needs to be launched when the action menu is selected. URL supports the NNMi variables, which makes URL building more flexible and dynamic. For example, passing the IP address of the selected node to the URL.

The next section describes URL syntax and NNMi provided views. Also, we are free to build our own URLs, which are outside NNMi. For example, creating a trouble ticket, passing through URL parameters needed for ticket creation.

Expanding system capabilities using URLs

Most of the companies I worked with have been expanding NNMi capabilities according to their specific needs, implementing extra features in or out of NNMi. One of the ways to expand is to use built-in URL syntax support, in order to reach particular areas of NNMi that lie outside the NNMi console. This section describes the following topics:

- Short description about URLs in NNMi

- How URLs works in NNMi

- Description of URL access to particular areas

After completion of this section, we will be familiar with what views, forms, or objects we can reach using URLs, and we will be able to build our own URLs.

URLs in NNMi

NNMi provides the ability to externally open some views, forms, and menu items using URL. It gives flexibility to integrate NNMi with third-party tools, or create our own custom add-ons without breaking into a code.

We can integrate our network topology map, with a real-time status from the NNMi workspace into the existing company's intranet portal with just one URL action. Or we can launch the **Status Poll** tool on NNMi when it has been initiated from our custom application.

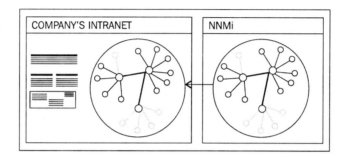

The following sections provide detailed information on how URLs in NNMi works.

Using URLs in NNMi

To build a URL string, we need to know a list of available parameters and their syntax. A username/password is also needed in order to be authenticated in NNMi.

Authentication

In order to use URL, queries need to be authenticated. A username and password need to be passed together with a query. The username and password needs to be configured for the NNMi role that is supposed to be assigned to a user.

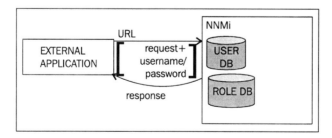

Depending on the role that is assigned to the user, the URL query will be accepted or rejected (refer to the following three tables).

The following parameters are used for transferring the username and password within the URL: j_username and j_password.

Consider this example. There is a URL that passes guest as the username as well as the password, along with the following URL query:

```
https://<server_name>:<port_number>/nnm/launch?j_username=guest&j_
password=guest
```

It is recommended to follow a few security considerations to increase the security level of the NNMi tool.

- Configure NNMi for https (SSL) communication, as there is a security vulnerability when passing the username and password in URL. NNMi 9.x, by default, is already configured for secure communication using https.
- Use guest as the username for URL integrations, unless we need a user to have less restrictions.

Security permissions

Several NNMi management console elements may be launched using URLs. The following table provides information on the permissions to forms each role.

Forms name	Guest	Level 1 operator	Level 2 operator	Administrator
Node Forms	R/O	R/W*	R/W	R/W
Interface Forms	R/O	R/W*	R/W	R/W
IP address forms	R/O	R/W*	R/W	R/W
IP subnet forms	R/O	R/W*	R/W	R/W
Incident Forms	R/O	R/O	R/W	R/W
Node Group forms	R/O	R/O	R/W	R/W
Configuration forms				R/W

* Read/write permissions, except for read-only permissions for the Management Mode field.

The following table provides the information on the limitation of URL access to workspaces by role:

Forms name	Guest	Level 1 operator	Level 2 operator	Administrator
Views in the incident workspaces	YES	YES	YES	YES
Views in the topology workspaces	YES	YES	YES	YES
Views in the monitoring workspaces	YES	YES	YES	YES
Views in the troubleshooting workspaces	YES	YES	YES	YES
Views in the inventory workspaces	YES	YES	YES	YES
Views in the management mode workspaces			YES	YES
Views in the configuration workspaces				YES

The following table provides information about URL access to commands depending on roles:

Forms name	Guest	Level 1 operator	Level 2 operator	Administrator
Actions | Ping		YES	YES	YES
Actions | Trace Route		YES	YES	YES
Actions | Communication Settings				YES
Actions | Monitoring Settings		YES	YES	YES
Actions | Status Poll			YES	YES
Actions | Configuration Poll			YES	YES
Actions | Status Details Command		YES	YES	YES
Tools | NNMi Status		YES	YES	YES
Tools | Sign In/Out Audit Log		YES	YES	YES
File | Sign Out	YES	YES	YES	YES

Using URLs to access NNMi objects

NNMi provides a list of URLs that can be used for accessing most NNMi console objects. This standardized list of URLs and their syntax helps us build the right URL, in order to get the right data object integrated in our selected third-party application.

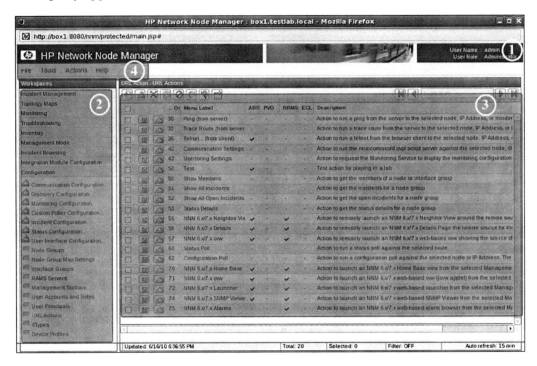

URLs that are listed in this section can be grouped into a few groups (refer to the preceding screenshot):

- Generic URLs.

- Workspace-related URLs.

- Form-related URLs.

- Menu item-related URLs. As an example, we can provide a quick access to menu items for our team. For example, building a smart-phone application that displays critical events and allows user to run ping, trace route, or other commands for faster troubleshooting (refer to the next diagram).

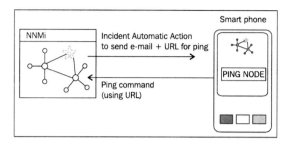

The following section lists these URLs and provides tables of parameters, which can be used for building URLs.

 Note: If our NNMi is configured to use the https protocol, we need to modify our URLs in this chapter accordingly, as URLs here are provided for http access.

Generic URLs

Generic URLs that can be used for obtaining information about NNMi are:

- **View launching URL:** To launch the NNMi console, use the following URL: `http://<server_name>:<port_number>/nnm/launch?cmd=showMain`.

  If we are passing by using a username and password within the URL, we need to use the following syntax: `http://<server_name>:<port_number>/nnm/launch?cmd=showMain&j_username=<account_name>&j_password=<account_password>`.

  Read the *Authentication* section on how to configure NNMi, in order to avoid plain text username and password transfer in URLs.

- **To confirm whether NNMi is running**: The following URL should be used: `http://<serverName>:<portNumber>/nnm/launch?cmd=isRunning`.

  Using this URL, we will receive a confirmation response on whether or not NNMi is running.

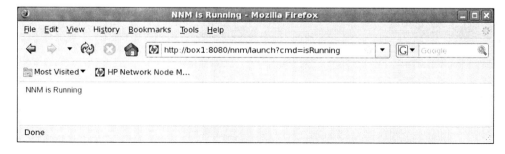

Otherwise, a browser error message will be sent saying that the URL is unreachable.

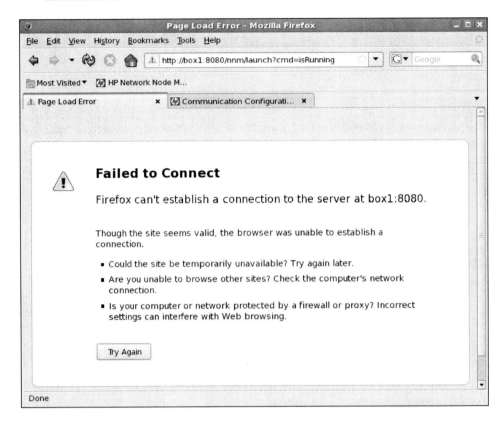

Workspace-related URLs

This URL group is related to NNMi views (refer to the first screenshot under the *URLs to access NNMi objects* section). Here is a list of available URLs.

Launching view

The following table presents the required attributes and their values for launching views.

Attributes	Values	Description
Use the following URL to show the general view: `http://<serverName>:<portNumber>/nnm/launch?cmd=showView&objtype=<x>`		
`objtype`	Incident Node Interface IP Address IP Subnet NodeGroup InterfaceGroup	Incidents workspace, All Incidents table view. Inventory workspace, Nodes table view. Inventory workspace, Interfaces table view. Inventory workspace, IP Addresses table view. Inventory workspace, IP Subnets table view. Inventory workspace, Node Groups table view. Inventory workspace, Interface Groups table view.
Use the following URL to show the general view for a specific node group, filtered by node group name, ID, or UUID: `http://<serverName>:<portNumber>/nnm/launch?cmd= showView&objtype= <x>&nodegroup=<Name>`		
nodegroup	• nodegroup • nodegroupid • nodegroupuuid	• The Name attribute value of Node Group.* • The ID number of node group. This ID is unique across all NNMi databases. Use nnmconfigexport.ovpl tool to see ID number of node group. • Universally Unique Object ID of the node group. Use nnmconfigexport.ovpl tool to see ID number of node group.
Use the following URL to show the general view for a specific node group, filtered by interface group name or ID: `http://<serverName>:<portNumber>/nnm/launch?cmd= showView&objtype= <x>&ifgroup= <Name>`		

Attributes	Values	Description
ifgroup	• ifgroup	• The name attribute value of the interface group.*
	• ifgroupid	• The ID number of the interface group. This ID is unique across all NNMi databases. Use nnmconfigexport.ovpl tool to see the ID number of the interface group.
	• ifgroupduuid	• Universally Unique Object ID of the interface group. Use nnmconfigexport.ovpl tool to see the ID number of the interface group.

Use the following URL to show the general view with custom window settings:

`http://<serverName>:<portNumber>/nnm/launch?cmd= showView&objtype= <x>&menus= <true|false>&newWindow= <true|false>&envattrs= <name1= value>;<name2= value>`

menus	[true|false]	• True: Show the view menus. • False: Hide the view menus. The default value is true.
newWindow	[true|false]	• True: To display view in new window. • False: To display view within same browser window. Default value is false.
envattrs		These are session-specific attributes and are stored by the following syntax: <name=value>.

* If the node group name has spaces in it, use one of the following symbols to represent a "space" character (without brackets): "%20", "+", or " " (space symbol).

Consider the following example. To open a window with incidents, which are related to the node group **Europe**, run the following URL (assuming, that NNMi is installed on node "box1" and uses port number "8080"): `http://box1:8080/nnm/launch?cmd=showView&objtype=Incident&nodegroup=Europe`

Launching an Incident view

The following table presents the required attributes and their values for launching incident-specific views.

Attributes	Values	Description
\multicolumn{3}{}{Use the following URL to show Incident view, filtered by specific incident attributes:}		
\multicolumn{3}{}{`http://<serverName>:<portNumber>/nnm/launch?cmd= showView&view= <x>`}		
view	• `allIncidentsTableView` • `allOpenIncidentsTableView` • `closedKeyIncidentsTableView` • `closedRCIncidentTableView` • `customIncidentTableView` • `incidentsByNatureTableView` • `incidentsByFamilyTableView` • `keyIncidentsByLifecycleStateTableView` • `myIncidentTableView` • `nnm6x7xIncidentTableView` • `nnm6x7xIncidentByCategoryTableView` • `openKeyIncidentsTableView` • `openKeyIncidentsByCategoryTableView` • `openKeyIncidentsByFamilyTableView` • `openKeyIncidentsByPriorityTableView` • `openKeyIncidentsBySeverityTableView` • `openRCIncidentsByCategoryTableView` • `openRCIncidentsByFamilyTableView` • `openRCIncidentsByPriorityTableView` • `openRCIncidentsBySeverityTableView` • `openRCIncidentTableView` • `allRCIncidentTableView` • `RCIncidentsByLifecycleStateTableView` • `serviceImpactIncidentTableView` • `snmpTrapsIncidentTableView` • `snmpTrapsIncidentByFamilyTableView` • `streamCorrelationIncidentTableView` • `unassignedKeyIncidentsTableView` • `unassignedIncidentTableView`	• All incidents • All open incidents • Closed Key Incidents • Closed Root Cause Incidents • Custom Incidents • Incidents by Correlation Nature • Incidents by Family • Key Incidents by Lifecycle State • My Open Incidents • NNM 6.x / 7.x Events • NNM 6.x/7.x Event by Category • Open Key Incidents • Open Key Incidents by Category • Open Key Incidents by Family • Open Key Incidents by Priority • Open Key Incidents by Severity • Open Root Cause by Category • Open Root Cause by Family • Open Root Cause by Priority • Open Root Cause by Severity • Open Root Cause Incidents • Root Cause Incidents • Root Cause by Lifecycle State • Service Impact Incidents • SNMP Traps • SNMP Traps by Family • Stream Correlation Incidents • Unassigned Open Key Incidents • Unassigned Root Cause Incidents

Attributes	Values	Description
Use the following URL to show Incident view, filtered for a specific node group: `http://<serverName>:<portNumber>/nnm/launch?cmd= showView&view= <x>&nodegroup_var= <Name>` See the preceding table for attribute description.		
Use the following URL to show Incident view with custom window settings: `http://<serverName>:<portNumber>/nnm/launch?cmd= showView&view= <x>&menus_var= <true|false>&newWindow= <true|false>&envattrs= <name1= value>;<name2= value>` See the preceding table for attribute description.		

Launching a Topology Maps Workspace view

Here is a list of Topology Maps that can be opened using the following URLs:

Topology Map	URL	Optional parameters
Node group overview map	`http:/<serverName>: <portNumber>/nnm/launch?cmd= showNodeGroupOverview`	`http:/<serverName>: <portNumber>/nnm/launch?cmd= showNodeGroupOverview&menus= <true/false>&newWindow= <true/false>&envattrs= <name1=value>;<name2= value>`
Network overview map	`http:/<serverName>: <portNumber>/nnm/launch?cmd= showNetworkOverview`	`http:/<serverName>: <portNumber>/nnm/launch?cmd= showNodeGroupOverview&menus= <true/false>&newWindow= <true/false>&envattrs= <name1= value>;<name2= value>`
Network infrastructure devices node group map	`http:/<serverName>: <portNumber>/nnm/launch?cmd= showView&objtype= Node&nodegroup= Networking%20 Infrastructure%20Devices`	`http:/<serverName>: <portNumber>/nnm/launch?cmd= showView&objtype= Node&nodegroup= Networking%20Infrastructure% 20Devices&menus= <true/false>& newWindow= <true/false>&envattrs= <name1=value>;<name2=value>`
Routers node group map	`http:/<serverName>: <portNumber>/nnm/launch?cmd= showNodeGroup&name= Routers`	`http:/<serverName>: <portNumber>/nnm/launch?cmd= showNodeGroup&name= Routers&menus= <true/false>&newWindow= <true/false>&envattrs= <name1=value>;<name2=value>`

Topology Map	URL	Optional parameters
Switches node group map	`http:/<serverName>:<portNumber>/nnm/launch?cmd=showNodeGroup&name= Switches`	`http://<serverName>:<portNumber>/nnm/launch?cmd=showNodeGroup&name= Switches&menus=<true/false>&newWindow=<true/false>&envattrs=<name1=value>;<name2=value>`

Consider the following example. Here are the links to open a few groups on NNMi server "box1" (port number 8080):

- Open Routers node groups:

  `http://box1:8080/nnm/launch?cmd=showNodeGroup&name=Routers`

- Open Networking Infrastructure devices:

  `http://box1:8080/nnm/launch?cmd=showView&objtype= Node&nodegroup=Networking%20Infrastructure%20Devices`

Launching a Monitoring Workspace view

The following table presents the required attributes and their values for launching Monitoring workspace-specific views.

Attributes	Values	Description
Use the following URL to show Monitoring view, filtered by specific attributes: `http://<serverName>:<portNumber>/nnm/launch?cmd=showView&view=<x>`		
view	• `criticalComponentHealthTableView`	• Critical Component Health
	• `criticalInterfaceTableView`	• Critical Interfaces
	• `criticalNodeTableView`	• Critical Nodes
	• `nonNormalInterfaceTableView`	• Non-Normal Interfaces
	• `nonNormalNodeTableView`	• Non-Normal Nodes
	• `notRespondingIPAddressTableView`	• Not Responding Addresses
	• `nodesByStatusTableView`	• Nodes by Status
	• `componentHealthByStatusTableView`	• Component Health by Status
	• `interfacesByStatusTableView`	• Interfaces by Status
	• `interfacesByAdministrativeStateTableView`	• Interfaces by Administrative State
	• `interfacesByOperationalStateTableView`	• Interfaces by Operational State
	• `IPAddressesByStateTableView` `interfacePerformanceTableView`	• IP Addresses by State
	• `routerRedundancyGroupsTableView`	• Interface Performance
		• Router Redundancy Groups
	• `nodeGroupsStatusTableView`	• Node Groups

Attributes	Values	Description

Use the following URL to show monitoring view, filtered by node group:
 	
`http://<serverName>:<portNumber>/nnm/launch?cmd=showView&view=`
`<x>&nodegroup=<Name>`
 	
Refer to the table under the *Launching view* section for attribute description.		

Use the following URL to show the Monitoring view, filtered by interface group:
`http://<serverName>:<portNumber>/nnm/launch?cmd=showView&view=`
`<x>&ifgroup=<Name>`
Refer to the table under the *Launching view* section for attribute description.		

Use the following URL to show Monitoring view with custom window settings:
`http://<serverName>:<portNumber>/nnm/launch?cmd= showView&view= <x>&menus=`
`<true|false>&newWindow= <true|false>&envattrs= <name1= value>;<name2= value>`
Refer to the table under the *Launching view* section for attribute description.		

The launching a Troubleshooting Workspace view

Troubleshooting workspace contains the following four different views:

- Layer 2 Neighbor view
- Layer 3 Neighbor view
- Path view
- Node Group Map view

Use the following URL to show the Layer 2 Neighbor view:

`http://<serverName>:<portNumber>/nnm/launch?cmd=showLayer2Neighbors.`

Attributes	Values	Description

Use the following URL to show Layer 2 Neighbor view by specified number of hops:
 	
`http://<serverName>:<portNumber>/nnm/launch?cmd= showLayer2Neighbor`
`s&nodename=<x>&hops=<#>`		

nodename	nodename	The source node's name or IP address
hops	1 - 9	Number of hops

Use the following URL to show Layer 2 Neighbor view with custom window parameters:
 	
`http://<serverName>:<portNumber>/nnm/launch?cmd=showLayer2Neighbors`
`& menus=<true/false>&newWindow=<true/false>&envattrs= <name1=value>`
`;<name2=value>`
Refer to the table under the *Launching view* section for attribute description.		

Use the following URL to show Layer 3 Neighbor view:

`http://<serverName>:<portNumber>/nnm/launch?cmd= showLayer3Neighbors.`

Attributes	Values	Description
Use the following URL to show Layer 3 Neighbor view for specified node by specified number of hops: `http://<serverName>:<portNumber>/nnm/launch?cmd=showLayer3Neighbors &nodename=<x>&hops=<#>`		
`nodename`	See previous table for attribute description.	
`hops`	See previous table for attribute description.	
`menus`	`[true|false]`	Show (true) or hide (false) menu and window toolbar. Default value is `true`.

Use the following URL to show Layer 3 Neighbor view with the specified window parameters: `http://<serverName>:<portNumber>/nnm/launch?cmd=showLayer3 Neighbors&menus= <true/false>&newWindow=<true/false>&envattrs= <name1 =value>;<name2=value>.`

Use the following URL to show Path view: `http://<serverName>:<portNumber>/ nnm/launch?cmd= showPath.`

Attributes	Values	Description
Use the following URL to show Path view by specified source and destination nodes: `http://<serverName>:<portNumber>/nnm/launch?cmd=showPath&src=<x>& dest=<y>`		
`src`	`src`	Source node's hostname or IPv4 address.
`dest`	`dest`	Destination node's hostname or IPv4 address.

Use the following URL to show Path view with custom window parameters:
`http://<serverName>:<portNumber>/nnm/launch?cmd=showPath&menus=<true/ false>&newWindow=<true/false>&envattrs=<name1=value>;<name2= value>`

Attributes	Values	Description
Use the following URL to list nodes belonging to a specified node group: `http://<serverName>:<portNumber>/nnm/launch?cmd=showNodeGroup&name= <x>`		
`name`	`name`	Name attribute value from the Node Group form.

Use the following URL to list nodes belonging to a specified node group with custom window parameters: `http://<serverName>:<portNumber>/nnm/launch?cmd=showNodeGroup&name=<x>&menus= <true/false>&newWindow= <true/false>&envattrs=<name1=value>;<name2= value>.`

Launching an Inventory Workspace view

The following table presents the required attributes and their values for launching Inventory workspace-specific views.

Attributes	Values	Description
	Use the following URL to show a view, specified in the view list below in this table: `http://<serverName>:<portNumber>/nnm/launch?cmd=showView&view=<x>`
view	• `allNodesTableView` • `allInterfacesTableView` • `allIPAddressTableView` • `allIPSubnetsTableView` • `allVlansTableView` • `allLayer2ConnectionsTableView` • `nodesByDeviceCategoryTableView` • `interfacesByIfTypeTableView` • `customNodeTableView` • `customInterfaceTableView` • `customIPAddressTableView` • `routerRedundancyGroupsTableView` • `nodeGroupsTableView` • `interfaceGroupsTableView` • `allManagementStationsTableView`	• Nodes • Interfaces • IP Addresses • IP Subnets • VLANs • Layer 2 Connections • Nodes by Device Category • Interfaces by IfType • Custom Nodes • Custom Interfaces • Custom IP Addresses • Router Redundancy Groups • Node Groups • Interface Groups • Management Stations
	Use the following URL to show a view, specified in the view list below for specified node group: `http://<serverName>:<portNumber>/nnm/launch?cmd=showView&view=<x>&nodegroup=<Name>.` Refer to the table under the *Launching view* section for attribute description.
nodegroup	• nodegroup • nodegroupid • nodegroupuuid	Refer to the table under the *Launching view* section for attribute description.

Attributes	Values	Description
Use the following URL to show a view, specified in the view list below for specified interface group: `http://<serverName>:<portNumber>/nnm/launch?cmd= showView&view= <x>&int erfacegroup=<Name>`		
`interfacegroup`	• `ifgroup` • `ifgroupid` • `ifgroupuuid`	Refer to the table under the *Launching view* section for attribute description.

Use the following URL to show a view, specified in the view list above in a table with custom window settings: `http://<serverName>:<portNumber>/nnm/launch?cmd= showView&view=<x>&menus= <true/false>&newWindow=<true/false>&envattrs =<name1=value>;<name2=value>`.

Launching Management Mode Workspace views

The following table presents the required attributes and their values for launching Management Mode workspace-specific views:

Attributes	Values	Description
Use the following URL to show a view from Management Mode workspace, specified by the view name listed in the table. `http://<serverName>:<portNumber>/nnm/launch?cmd= showView&view= <x>`		
`view`	• `managedNodeTableView` • `managedInterfaceTableView` • `managedIPAddressTableView` • `notManagedNodeTableView` • `notManagedInterfaceTableView` • `notManagedIPAddressTableView` • `outOfServiceNodeTableView` • `outOfServiceInterfaceTableView` • `outOfServiceIPAddressTableView` • `managementModeNodeTableView` • `managementModeInterfaceTableView` • `managementModeIPAddressTableView`	• Managed Nodes • Managed Interfaces • Managed IP Addresses • Not Managed Nodes • Not Managed Interfaces • Not Managed IP Addresses • Out of Service Nodes • Out of Service Interfaces • Out of Service IP Addresses • Nodes • Interfaces • IP Addresses

Attributes	Values	Description
Use the following URL to show a view from Management Mode workspace for specified node group: `http://<serverName>:<portNumber>/nnm/launch?cmd=showView&view=<x> &nodegroup=<Name>.`		
nodegroup	• nodegroup • nodegroupid • nodegroupuuid	Refer to the table under the *Launching view* section for attribute description.
Use the following URL to show a view from Management Mode workspace for specified interface group: `http://<serverName>:<portNumber>/nnm/launch?cmd=showView&v iew=<x>&ifgroup=<Name>.`		
interfacegroup	• ifgroup • ifgroupid • ifgroupuuid	Refer to the table under the *Launching view* section for attribute description.

Use the following URL to show a view, from the Management Mode workspace, with specified window settings: `http://<serverName>:<portNumber>/nnm/launc h?cmd=showView&view=<x>&menus=<true/false>&newWindow=<true/false>&env attrs=<name1=value>;<name2=value>.`

Launching a Configuration Workspace view

The following table presents the required attributes and their values for launching the Configuration workspace-specific views:

Attributes	Values	Description
Use the following URL to show a view from Configuration workspace for a specified view: `http://<serverName>:<portNumber>/nnm/launch?cmd=showView&view=<x>.`		
view	• nodeGroupsTableView • allNodeGroupMapSettingsTableView • interfaceGroupsTableView • allManagementStationsTableView • ramsServerTableView • allURLActionInfosTableView • allAccountsTableView • allIfTypesTableView • allDeviceProfilesTableView	• Node Groups • Node Group Map Settings • Interface Groups • Management Stations • RAMS Servers • URL Actions • User Accounts and Roles • IfTypes • Device Profiles

Use the following URL to show a view, from Configuration workspace, with specified window parameters: `http://<serverName>:<portNumber>/nnm/launch ?cmd=showView&view=<x>&menus=<true/false>&newWindow=<true/false>&enva ttrs=<name1=value>;<name2=value>.`

Form-related URLs

This URL group is related to NNMi forms (refer to the screenshot under the *Using URLs to assess NNMi objects* section). This form should be used to obtain information about a particular node, interface, incident, address, or subnet.

 Note: If attributes provided in the URL find more than one object, the first object found in the database is displayed.

Multiple attributes should be separated by the semicolon symbol.

Here is a URL to launch a particular form:

`http://<serverName>:<portNumber>/nnm/launch?cmd=showForm....`

Launching a Node Form

The following table presents the required attributes and their values for launching views related to the Node Form:

Attributes	Values	Description
Use the following URL to show Node Form for a specified node: `http://<serverName>:<portNumber>/nnm/launch?cmd=showForm&objtype=Node&nodename=<x>`		
nodename	nodename	IP address: FQDN or short name of the host. Short name should be used if one is working in the same DNS zone as the target. Also, short name should be resolvable by the server receiving the request.
Use the following URL to show Node Form for a specified node and object attribute name: `http://<serverName>:<portNumber>/nnm/launch?cmd=showForm&objtype=Node&objattrs=name=<x>`		
Objattrs	name	The Name attribute value from the Node Form.
Use the following URL to show the Node Form for a specified node and the hostname's object attribute: `http://<serverName>:<portNumber>/nnm/launch?cmd=showForm&objtype= Node&objattrs=hostname=<x>`.		

Attributes	Values	Description
hostname	hostname	The hostname of the node is selected by the following rules: • FQDN name in lowercase characters. • If more than one address is associated with a name, loopback address is selected. • If multiple loopback addresses are associated, lowest IP number address is selected. • If no loopback address is associated, NNMi tries to associate name provided by SNMP. • If no response using SNMP is received, the IP address is associated, unless DNS name is found during rediscovery cycle.
Use the following URL to show Node Form for a specified node and specified management address: `http://<serverName>:<portNumber>/nnm/launch?cmd=showForm&objtype=Node&objattrs=snmpAgent.agentSettings.managementAddress=<x>`.		
snmpAgent. agentSettings. managementAddress	• snmpAgent. agentSettings. • managementAddress	The IP address received by SNMP from SNMP agent form assigned to a specified node.
Use the following URL to show Node Form for a specified node and system name: `http://<serverName>:<portNumber>/nnm/launch?cmd=showForm&objtype=Node&objattrs=systemName=<x>`.		
systemName	systemName	System name attribute value.

Use the following URL to show Node Form for a specified node with specified window parameters: `http://<serverName>:<portNumber>/nnm/launch?cmd=showForm&objtype=Node&nodename=<x>&menus=<true/false>&envattrs=<name1=value>;<name2=value>`.

Launching an Interface Form

The following table presents the required attributes and their values for launching views related to Interface Form:

Attributes	Values	Description
Use the following URL to show Interface Form hosted on specified node: `http://<serverName>:<portNumber>/nnm/launch?cmd=showForm&objtype= Interface&objattrs=hostedOn.hostname=<x>;name=<y>.`		

`hostedOn.hostname`
 	
`name`
	• Hostname of the host where interface resides
	
	• Name attribute value
		Value is taken from Node Form

Use the following URL to show Interface Form for specified interface name, hosted on specified node: `http://<serverName>:<portNumber>/nnm/launch?cmd=showForm&objtype= Interface&objattrs=hostedOn.hostname=<x>;ifName=<y>.`		
`ifName`	ifName attribute value	Value is taken from Interface Form
Use the following URL to show Interface Form for specified interface alias, hosted on specified node: `http://<serverName>:<portNumber>/nnm/launch?cmd=showForm&objtype= Interface&objattrs=hostedOn.hostname=<x>;ifAlias=<y>.`		
`ifAlias`	ifAlias attribute value	Value is taken from Interface Form
Use the following URL to show Interface Form for specified interface index, hosted on specified node: `http://<serverName>:<portNumber>/nnm/launch?cmd=showForm&objtype= Interface&objattrs=hostedOn.hostname=<x>;ifIndex=<y>.`		
`ifIndex`	ifIndex attribute value	Value is taken from Interface Form

Use the following URL to show Interface Form for specified interface name, hosted on specified node, with custom window parameters: `http://<serverName>:<portNumber>/nnm/launch?cmd=showForm&objtype= Interface&objattrs=hostedOn.hostname=<x>;name=<y>&menus=<true/false>&envattrs=<name1=value>;<name2=value>.`

Launching an IP address form

The following table presents the required attributes and their values for launching views related to the IP address form:

Attributes	Values	Description
Use the following URL to show IP address form for IP address value: `http:// <serverName>:<portNumber>/nnm/launch?cmd=showForm&objtype= IPAddress&ob jattrs=value=<y>.`		
`value`	IP address attribute value	Value taken from IP address form

Use the following URL to show IP address form for IP address value with custom window parameters: `http://<serverName>:<portNumber>/nnm/launch?cmd=sho wForm&objtype= IPAddress&objattrs=value=<y>&menus=<true/false>&envatt rs=<name1=value>; <name2=value>.`

Launching a Subnet form

The following table presents the required attributes and their values for launching views related to the Subnet form:

Attributes	Values	Description
Use the following URL to show a Subnet form for specified Subnet name: `http:// <serverName>:<portNumber>/nnm/launch?cmd=showForm&objtype= IPSubnet&obj attrs=name=<x>.`		
`name`	Name attribute value	Value taken from IP Subnet form
Use the following URL to show a Subnet form for specified Subnet prefix: `http:// <serverName>:<portNumber>/nnm/launch?cmd=showForm&objtype= IPSubnet&obj attrs=prefix=<x>.`		
`prefix`	Prefix attribute value	Value is taken from IP Subnet form
Use the following URL to show a Subnet form for specified Subnet prefix length: `http:// <serverName>:<portNumber>/nnm/launch?cmd=showForm&objtype= IPSubnet&obj attrs=prefix=<x>;prefixLength=<y>.`		
`prefixLength`	Prefix length attribute value	Value taken from IP Subnet form

Use the following URL to show a Subnet form for specified Subnet name with custom window attributes: `http://<serverName>:<portNumber>/nnm/laun ch?cmd=showForm&objtype= IPSubnet&objattrs=name=<x>&menus=<true/ false>&envattrs= <name1=value>;<name2=value>.`

Launching an Incident Form

The following table presents the required attributes and their values for launching views related to the Incident Form:

Attributes	Values	Description
Use the following URL to show an Incident Form for specified incident ID: `http:/ /<serverName>:<portNumber>/nnm/launch?cmd=showForm&objtype= Incident&objid=<x>.`		
`objid`	Object ID	Unique value across NNMi database.
Use the following URL to show an Incident Form for specified incident UUID: `http:/ /<serverName>:<portNumber>/nnm/launch?cmd=showForm&objtype= Incident&objuuid=<x>.`		
`objuuid`	Universally Unique Object ID	Unique value across all NNMi databases. Use nnmconfigexport.ovpl to find this value.

Use the following URL to show an Incident Form for specified incident ID with custom window settings: `http://<serverName>:<portNumber>/nnm/launc h?cmd=showForm&showForm&objtype=Incident&objid=<x>&menus=<true/ false>&envattrs= <name1=value>;<name2=value>.`

Launching a Node Group form

The following table presents required attributes and their values for launching views related to Node Group form:

Attributes	Values	Description
Use the following URL to show Node Group form for specified group name: `http:// <serverName>:<portNumber>/nnm/launch?cmd=showForm&objtype=NodeGroup&nam e=<y>.`		
`name`	Name	Name attribute value in Node Group form. (If spaces need to be used, replace with "%20" symbols. For some browsers "+" or "space" symbol may work as well.
Use the following URL to show Node Group form for specified group ID: `http:// <serverName>:<portNumber>/nnm/launch?cmd=showForm&objtype=NodeGroup&nod egroupid=<y>.`		
`nodegroupid`	`nodegroupid`	Refer to the table under the *Launching view* section for attribute description.

Attributes	Values	Description
Use the following URL to show Node Group form for specified group UUID: `http://<serverName>:<portNumber>/nnm/launch?cmd=showForm&objtype=NodeGroup&nodegroupuuid=<y>`.		
`nodegroupid`	`nodegroupuuid`	Refer to the table under the *Launching view* section for attribute description.

Use the following URL to show Node Group form for specified group name with custom window parameters: `http://<serverName>:<portNumber>/nnm/launch?cmd=showForm&objtype= NodeGroup&name-<y>&menus=<true/false>&envattrs= <name1=value>;<name2= value>`.

Launching a Configuration form

The following table presents the required attributes and their values for launching Configuration workspace-related views:

Attributes	Values	Description
Use the following URL to show Configuration form views, listed below: `http:// <serverName>:<portNumber>/nnm/launch?cmd=showConfigForm&name=<y>`.		
name	• `communication` • `custompoller` • `discovery` • `monitoring` • `incident` • `status` • `ui`	• Communication Configuration Form • Custom Poller Configuration Form • Discovery Configuration Form • Monitoring Configuration Form • Incident Configuration Form • Status Configuration Form • User Interface Configuration Form

Use the following URL to show Configuration form views with specified window settings: `http://<serverName>:<portNumber>/nnm/launch?cmd=showConfigForm&name= lt;y>&menus=<true/false>&envattrs=<name1=value>;<name2=value>`.

Menu item-related URLs

This URL group is related to the NNMi menu. Here is the available URL:

`http://<serverName>:<portNumber>/nnm/launch?cmd=runTool&tool=<x>`

Consider the following example. To open the Communication Configuration of node 10.10.1.11, enter following URL: `http://box1:8080/nnm/launch?cmd=runTool&tool=commconf&nodename=10.10.1.11`.

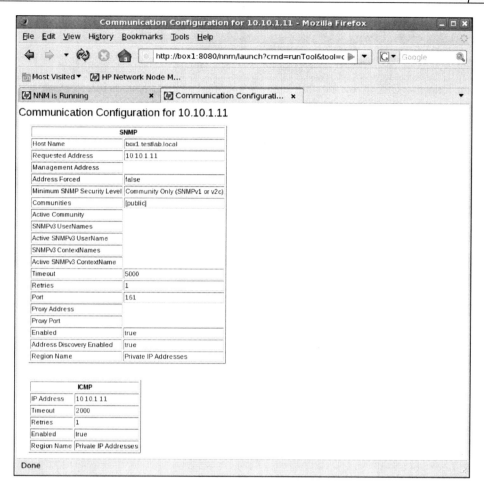

Launching the Ping command

The same action we used in NNMi console, **Tools | Ping (from server)**, can be initiated using the URL in two ways:

- To run a URL, which opens a window and asks for the node name or IP address of the object you want to ping:

    ```
    http://<serverName>:<portNumber>/nnm/launch?cmd=
    runTool&tool=ping
    ```

- Run a URL, which opens a window with ping to node results, follow the table given here:

Attributes	Values	Description
Use the following URL to run the ping tool with specified ping parameters listed below: `http://<serverName>:<portNumber>/nnm/launch?cmd=run-Tool&tool=ping&timeoutSecs=<x>&numPings=<x>&nodename=<x>.`		
`nodename`	DNS resolvable name, or IP address	
`timeoutSecs`	seconds	The number of seconds the command waits for a response before it times out
`numPings`	number	The number of retries

Launching the Trace Route command

The same action we used in NNMi console, **Tools | Trace Route (from server)**, can be initiated using a URL in two ways:

- To run a URL, which opens a window and asks you to enter the node name or IP address of the object you want to make a trace route:

  `http://<serverName>:<portNumber>/nnm/launch?cmd=runTool&tool=traceroute`

- To run a URL, which opens a window with trace route results to node, follow the table given here:

Attributes	Values	Description
Use the following URL to run the Trace Route tool with specified destination node name: `http://<serverName>:<portNumber>/nnm/launch?cmd=runTool&tool=traceroute&nodename=<x>`		
`nodename`	DNS resolvable name, or IP address	

Launching the Communication Configuration command

The same action we used in NNMi console, **Tools | Communication Settings**, can be initiated using the URL in two ways:

- To run a URL, which opens the Communication Settings window:

  `http://<serverName>:<portNumber>/nnm/launch?cmd=runTool&tool=commconf`

- To run a URL, which opens the Communication Settings window for a specified node, follow this table:

Attributes	Values	Description
Use the following URL to run the Communication Configuration tool for a specified node name: `http://<serverName>:<portNumber>/nnm/launch?cmd=runTool&tool=commconf&nodename=<x>`.		
`nodename`	DNS resolvable name, or IP address	

Launching Monitoring Settings command

The same action of opening the **Monitoring Settings** screen that you perform in NNMi console (**Tools | Monitoring Settings**), can be initiated using a URL. There are a few views, which can be shown in Monitoring Settings:

- On node
- On interface
- On IP Address
- On Router Redundancy Group
- On Tracked Object
- On Node component

To run the Monitoring Settings report on a selected node, use one of the following URLs:

Attributes	Values	Description
Use the following URL to run the Monitoring Setting window for a specified node name: `http://<serverName>:<portNumber>/nnm/launch?cmd=run- ool&tool=monitoringconf&objtype=SnmpAgent&nodename=<x>`.		
`nodename`	DNS resolvable name or IP address	

To run the **Monitoring Settings** report on a selected interface, use one of the following URLs:

Attributes	Values	Description
Use the following URL to run the Monitoring Setting window for the specified interface name, with the specified node name where interface is hosted: `http://<serverName>:<portNumber>/nnm/launch?cmd=run- Tool&tool=monitoringconf&objtype=Interface&objattrs=hostedOn.hostname=<x>;name=<x>`.		
• `hostedOn.hostname` • `name`	• The hostname of the Node on which the interface resides • The Name attribute value	• Value from Node Form • Value from Interface Form
Use the following URL to run the Monitoring Setting window for a specified interface name, with a specified node name where interface is hosted: `http://<serverName>:<portNumber>/nnm/launch?cmd-=runTool&tool=monitoringconf&objtype=Interface&objattrs=hostedOn.hostname=<x>;ifName=<x>`.		
`ifName`	The ifName attribute value	Value from Interface form
Use the following URL to run the Monitoring Setting window for a specified interface name, with a specified node name where interface is hosted: `http://<serverName>:<portNumber>/nnm/launch?cmd-=runTool&tool=monitoringconf&objtype=Interface&objattrs=hostedOn.hostname=<x>;ifAlias=<x>`.		
`ifAlias`	The ifAlias attribute value	Value from Interface form
Use the following URL to run the Monitoring Setting window for a specified interface number, with a specified node name where interface is hosted: `http://<serverName>:<portNumber>/nnm/launch?cmd- runTool&tool=monitoringconf&objtype=Interface&objattrs=hostedOn.hostname=<x>;ifIndex=<x>`.		
`ifIndex`	The ifIndex attribute value	Value from Interface form

Use the following URL to run the Monitoring Settings report for the selected IP address:

Attributes	Values	Description
`http://<serverName>:<portNumber>/nnm/launch?cmd=run-Tool&tool=monitoringconf&objtype=IPAddress&objattrs=value=<x>`		
`value`	IP address	Value taken from IP address form

Use the following URL to run the Monitoring Settings report on the Router Redundancy Member:

Attributes	Values	Description
`http://<serverName>:<portNumber>/nnm/launch?cmd=runTool&` `tool=monitoringconf&objtype=RouterRedundancyInstance&objid=<x>`		
`objid`	Object ID	Unique Object ID across the NNMi database.
`objuuid`	Universally Unique Object ID	Unique value across all NNMi databases. Use nnmconfigexport.ovpl to find this value.

Use the following URL to run the Monitoring Settings report on a Tracked Object:

Attributes	Values	Description
`http://<serverName>:<portNumber>/nnm/launch?cmd=runTool&tool=monitoring` `conf&objtype=TrackedObject&objid=<x>`		
`objid`	Object ID	Unique Object ID across the NNMi database.
`objuuid`	Universally Unique Object ID	Unique value across all NNMi databases. Use nnmconfigexport.ovpl to find this value.

Use the following URL to run the Monitoring Settings report on a Node Component:

Attributes	Values	Description
`http://<serverName>:<portNumber>/nnm/launch?cmd=runTool&tool=monitoring` `conf&objtype=ComponentHealth&objid=<x>`		
`objid`	Object ID	Unique Object ID across the NNMi database
`objuuid`	Universally Unique Object ID	Unique value across all NNMi databases. Use nnmconfigexport.ovpl to find this value.

Launching Status Poll command

The same action we used to open the **Status Poll** window in NNMi console (**Tools |
Status Poll**), can be initiated using URL in two ways:

- Launch the **Status Poll** report, where you are prompted to specify a node in a
  window:

  ```
  http://<serverName>:<portNumber>/nnm/launch?cmd=runTool&tool=st
  atuspoll
  ```

- To launch the **Status Poll** report for a particular node, which is provided
  within the URL, follow the next table:

Attributes	Values	Description
`http://<serverName>:<portNumber>/nnm/launch?cmd=runTool&tool=statuspoll` `&nodename=<x>`		
nodename	DNS resolvable name or IP address	The following sequence for checking a nodename value is used: • Hostname field on the Node Form • Address column in IP Address tab of Node Form • System Name field on General tab of the Node Form • Name field of the Node Form

Launching Configuration Poll command

The same action of opening the **Configuration Poll** window in NNMi console (**Tools
| Configuration Poll**), can be initiated using URL in two ways:

- Launch the **Configuration Poll** report, where you are prompted to specify a
  node in a window:

  ```
  http://<serverName>:<portNumber>/nnm/launch?cmd=runTool&tool=co
  nfigurationpoll
  ```

- Launch the **Configuration Poll** report for a particular node, which is
  provided within the URL:

Attributes	Values	Description
`http://<serverName>:<portNumber>/nnm/launch?cmd=run-Tool&tool=confi gurationpoll&nodename=<x>`		
`nodename`	DNS resolvable name or IP address	The following sequence for checking a nodename value is used: • Hostname field on the Node Form • Address column in IP Address tab of Node Form • System Name field on General tab of the Node Form • Name field of the Node Form

Launching Status Details command

The same action we used to open the **Status Details** window in NNMi console (**Tools | Status Details**), can be initiated using URL in two ways:

- Launch the **Status Details** report, where we are prompted to specify a node group name in a window:

  `http://<serverName>:<portNumber>/nnm/launch?cmd=runTool&tool=no degroupstatus`

- Launch the **Status Details** report for a particular node group, which is provided within the URL:

Attributes	Values	Description
`http://<serverName>:<portNumber>/nnm/launch?cmd=run-Tool&tool=nodeg roupstatus&nodegroup=<x>`		
`nodegroup`	• `nodegroup` • `nodegroupid` • `nodegroupuuid`	Refer to the table under the *Launching view* section for attribute description

Launching NNMi Status command

The same action we used to open the NNMi Status window in NNMi console (**Tools | NNMi Status**), can be initiated using URL: `http://<serverName>:<portNumber>/nnm/launch?cmd=runTool&tool=nnmstatus.`

Launching Sign In/Out Audit Log command

The same action as we used in NNMi console (**Tools | Sign In/Out Audit Log**) can be initiated using URL: `http://<serverName>:<portNumber>/nnm/launch?cmd=runTool&tool=signinaudit`.

This URL displays the output of the Sign In/Out Audit Log file.

Launching Sign Out command

The same action as we used in NNMi console (**Tools | Sign Out**), can be initiated using URL: `http://<serverName>:<portNumber>/nnm/launch?cmd=signOut`.

This URL closes the user session and frees up memory associated with the session.

Summary

Now we have completed this chapter, we are able to make design decisions about NNMi extensions and implement such solutions. We are ready to boost NNMi with our custom extensions. Examples provided in this chapter should switch on our imagination and allow us to create our own customizations so that it looks like NNMi was adapted exactly for our environment.

The next chapter describes NNMi integration with major management tools. It will describe how to insert the NNMi puzzle piece into a whole picture, which is called the Network Operations Center or Consolidated Data Management Center.

11
Integrating NNMi with Other Management Tools

There is no management tool that would fit into all customer needs. Also, there is no management tool that would cover all of the infrastructure devices or objects. In most cases, organizations use more than one management tool, and you have to face challenging situations when you try to integrate the tools to improve the overall management process, but it ends in a bottleneck.

Most of the Enterprise-level management tools have integration capabilities. This chapter describes NNMi integration with the following management tools listed in the NNMi integration configuration workspace window (refer to the following screenshot):

- **HP BAC...**
- **CiscoWorks LMS...**
- **HP NA...**
- **Northbound Interface...**
- **HPOM...**
- **HP SIM...**
- **HP UCMDB...**

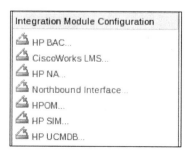

This chapter is a perfect source, if one is looking for a source, which would provide him/her with high-level integration architecture, and give more details on how to implement each of the described integration.

Solution architects, who are looking for expansion and integration opportunities, will find this chapter a perfect source for NNMi integration ideas and solutions.

Integrating NNMi with HP Software BAC

This section describes NNMi integration with HP Business Availability Center management tool.

What is HP Business Availability Center?

HP BAC (Business Availability Center) is a tool that does the monitoring and reporting of your infrastructure from a business point of view. There are business service definitions configured that allow mapping of **CIs (Configuration Items)** and their incidents with a service.

HP BAC family tools can poll objects for status; external tools can seed with monitoring data as well.

HP BAC includes a reporting portal named MyBSM that displays real-time reports and performance information.

How integration works

Integration between NNMi and HP BAC enables BAC to provide NNMi-specific views in MyBSM portal. The following views are included after NNMi and BAC integration:

- Topology map of the selected node group
- Node group status view
- Node group inventory view

If NNMi has iSPI for Performance Smart Plugin installed, the following additional views are provided:

- Top 10 memory utilization report view
- Top 10 CPU utilization report view
- Top 5 node exception report view (by CPU and memory)

The following diagram displays high-level NNMi and BAC integration:

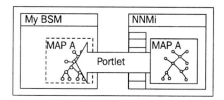

Requirements

The following table provides NNMi and BAC tool-supported versions for NNMi and BAC integration:

Management tool	Supported version
HP BAC	7.50 or higher
NNMi	8.11 or higher

Installation instructions

NNMi integration into MyBSM is based on the portlets.

Configuring portlets

HP BAC provides a few out of the box portlets for integration with NNMi. To configure these portlets, complete the following steps:

1. Select **HP NNMi – HP MyBSM Portal Configuration** on **Integration Module Configuration** workspace.
2. Select one of the listed XML files for customization.
   - i. Select `NOC_Demo_Portal.xml` for NNMi without iSPI for Performance installed.

     ii. Select `NOC_Demo_Portal_iSPIPerf.xml` for NNMi with iSPI for Performance installed.

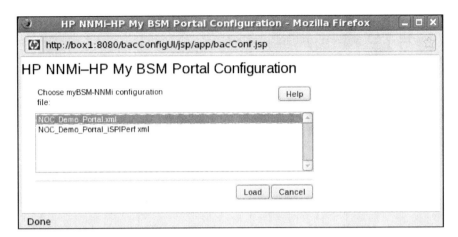

3. Click on **Load**.

4. Fill in the required fields and click on **Next**.

5. Navigate through all pages of the **HP NNMi – HP MyBSM Portal Configuration** form and click on **Finish**. Save the XML file to a known location.

6. Import module configuration to HP BAC by completing the following steps on the HP BAC console:

    i. Select the **Import portlets and modules** option on the **Administration** tab.

    ii. Select the **Browse** option on **Import My BSM Objects** page to import the XML configuration file you just saved.

7. Check the **Replace same Portlet Definitions** and **Replace same Modules** checkboxes.

8. Select the **Import** option. Note that if you receive an error on the **Import Status** window, you need to make sure that the checkboxes mentioned in the preceding step are selected, and then retry the import.

Congratulations!!! You have just created the default portlet provided by the manufacturer. You can make sure the portlet works by opening MyBSM portal and comparing the NNMi-specific view on MyBSM and same view on the NNMi console. Additionally, complete the following tasks:

- Make sure that the portlets display views that you expected
- Modify user access to the portlets using MyBSM administration tools

If you understand how this portlet works, you are ready to create your own portlets. The easiest way to do so is by using the existing MyBSM portlets as templates.

Configuring single sign-on

Single sign-on (SSO) for NNMi-BAC integration supports only username mapping. This means you can use the same username to sign into NNMi or BAC, but passwords and profiles cannot be mapped between these two tools. Also, passwords and profiles are not shared between these tools.

For such single sign-on configuration, you need to configure some initialization string on both the tools. You can copy initialization string from any one of these tools to the other.

 Note: If iSPI for Performance is used, it also needs to be configured to unify initialization strings.

Here is a procedure to find initialization strings:

- With HP BAC:

    i. Open the JMX console by initiating the following URL:

        `http://<bac_hostname>:<bac_jmx_port>/jmx-console/`

    ii. Select `service=LW-SSO Configuration` and find `InitString` value.

    iii. Click on **Apply** if you have made any changes.

- With HP NNMi:

    Open the `lwssofmconf.xml` file. The file can be found in the following locations:

    Unix: `$NnmInstallDir/nonOV/jboss/nms/server/nms/conf/`

    Windows: `%NnmInstallDir%\nonOV\jboss\nms\server\nms\conf\`

    i. Find the `initString` parameter. The initialization string is a value on this string. For example, in the case of the line `initString="A571 23AB1232D58F654BA2C9B335D1"`, the value would be: `A57123AB1232 D58F654BA2C9B335D1`.

    ii. Restart `ovjoboss` if you have made any changes:

        ```
        ovstop ovjboss
        ovstart ovjboss
        ```

Integrating NNMi with CiscoWorks LMS

This section describes NNMi integration with the CiscoWorks LMS management tool.

What is CiscoWorks LMS?

CiscoWorks **LAN Management Solution (LMS)** is a Cisco proprietary management tool that assists in monitoring, configuration, and troubleshooting of Cisco devices. LMS is not a replacement for HP NNMi, and NNMi is not a replacement for LMS.

First of all, Cisco LMS is designed to manage Cisco equipment. It is a great tool for device backups, and restores centralized configuration and IOS updates. It can also monitor network devices. But if your network has other vendor equipment, then CiscoWorks LMS cannot help. HP Network Automation Services or Orion NCM (from SolarWinds) can be considered as an option for configuration management in your network infrastructure.

Integration of these tools can increase value for monitoring. Default NNMi and CiscoWorks LMS integration provide NNMi with additional links to CiscoWorks LMS-specific views (check the next diagram):

- **CiscoWorksDeviceCenter**: Opens the DeviceCenter window based on the context of the selected node in NNMi

- **CiscoWorks CiscoView**: Opens the Cisco View window based on the context of the selected node in NNMi

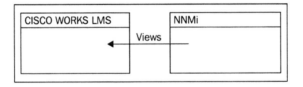

You may also want to send Cisco LMS events to NNMi, and this can be configured by the administrator at any time, without having default NNMi and CiscoWorks LMS integration package.

One may think, why do you need to forward traps from CiscoWorks LMS to NNMi but not vice versa? This is because the NNMi tool is chosen majorly as a centralized management console.

This chapter doesn't provide instructions on how to configure CiscoWorks LMS to forward SNMP traps to NNMi. You can refer to *CiscoWorks LMS Administrator's Guide* for instructions on how to configure SNMP trap forward to third-party systems.

How integration works

As depicted in the preceding diagram, NNMi has the ability to open CiscoWorks LMS-specific views. This helps troubleshoot Cisco equipment.

The NNMi menu is added by CiscoWorks LMS-specific actions, which are context-sensitive and provide the following URL-based actions: CiscoWorksDeviceCenter and CiscoWorks Cisco View.

Node-specific view is opened when the Cisco node is selected in NNMi.

Requirements

The following table provides a list of supported versions for CiscoWorks LMS and NNMi integration:

Management tool	Supported version
CiscoWorks LMS	3.1 or higher
NNMi	8.13 or higher

 Note: According to deployment instructions, CiscoWorks LMS and NNMi must be installed on separate computers.

Installation instructions

This section describes how to implement NNMi-CiscoWorks LMS integration and covers the following topics:

- Enabling integration
- Disabling integration
- Modifying integration

Enabling integration

To enable HP NNMi-CiscoWorks LMS integration, complete the following steps:

1. Select the **HP NNMi – CiscoWorks LMS Integration Configuration** form on the **Integration Module Configuration** workspace.
2. Check the **Enable Integration** option in the configuration window.

3. Fill in the integration configuration fields. The next table in this section describes fields from the NNMi-CiscoWorks LMS integration form.

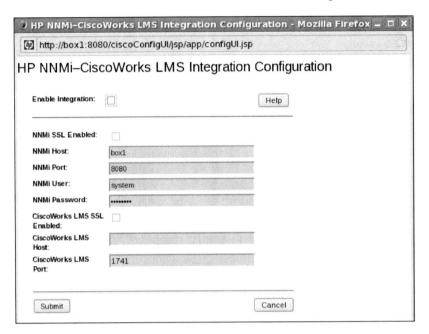

4. Click on **Submit** to save changes.

 Note: A new window opens with status message. If an error message is displayed, repeat steps 1 through 4 to repeat the configuration.

Field name	Description
NNMi SSL Enabled	Select the checkbox if your NNMi is enabled for SSL.
NNMi Host	NNMi server's FQDN. If NNMi and LMS are in the same domain, a short server name can be provided instead.
NNMi Port	The port that should be used for connecting to the console.
	By default, port 80 or 8004 is used for a non-SSL environment, and port 443 is used for an SSL environment.
	If you are not sure which port is configured, you need to check the following file: • Unix: $NnmDataDir/shared/nnm/conf/nnm. ports.properties • Windows: %NnmDataDir%\shared\nnm\conf\nnm. ports.properties

Field name	Description
NNMi User	The username that has Administrator or WebService Client role and will be used to connect to the NNMi console.
NNMi Password	The password for the specified user.
CiscoWorks LMS SSL Enabled	Select the checkbox if your CiscoWorks LMS is enabled for SSL.
CiscoWorks LMS Host	CiscoWorks LMS server's FQDN. If NNMi and LMS are in the same domain, a short server name can be provided instead.
CiscoWorks LMS Port	The port that should be used for connecting to CiscoWorks LMS webservices.
	By default, port 1741 is used for a non-SSL connection and port 443 is used for an SSL connection.

Disabling integration

To disable HP NNMi-CiscoWorks LMS integration, perform the following steps:

1. Select the **HP NNMi – CiscoWorks LMS Integration Configuration** form on the **Integration Module Configuration** workspace.

2. Uncheck the **Enable Integration** checkbox.

3. Click on **Submit** to save changes.

Modifying integration

To modify HP NNMi-CiscoWorks LMS integration, perform the following steps:

1. Select the **HP NNMi – CiscoWorks LMS Integration Configuration** form on the **Integration Module Configuration** workspace.

2. Modify the integration window fields according to your needs. Make sure that the **Enable Integration** checkbox remains checked.

3. Click on **Submit** to save changes.

Integrating NNMi with HP Software Network Automation

This section describes NNMi integration with the HP Network Automation management tool.

What is HP Network Automation?

HP NA is designed to take care of network device configuration management. It backs up and restores configurations, automates configuration changes, and takes care of updates and device troubleshooting.

HP NA is a multi-vendor platform, so it works with a long list of network devices.

Integrating HP NA and NNMi is useful for both the management tools. Starting from viewing detailed device information on NNMi by pulling down information from HP NA, to receiving events about any configuration change and viewing configuration changes, to comparing configurations or notifying about new device discovery—both tools would have a synchronized list of managed nodes.

How integration works

When HP NA and NNMi are integrated, two-way activities are involved:

- **Alarms sent from HP NA to NNMi**: Alarms are sent based on the configuration changes HP NA recognizes. This empowers the NNMi operator to correlate the root cause of the problem, for example, failure because of configuration changes.

- **Access to HP NA views from NNMi**: A few additional views are installed on NNMi, which allows accessing HP NA-specific information.

  The following table lists views that are added into NNMi tools during integration installation:

View	Description
Launch HP NA	Opens the NA user interface.
Launch HP NA command scripts	Opens the **New Task – Run Command Script** page in NA with already prefilled fields from a selected incident or node on NNMi.
Launch NA Diagnostics	Opens the **New Task – Run Diagnostics** page in NA with already prefilled fields from a selected incident or node on NNMi.
Rerun HP NA Diagnostics	Runs an NA action that is configured for a device in an NNMi incident.
Show HP NA Diagnostic Results	Displays a list of tasks in an incident that are scheduled for a device.
View HP NA Device Configuration	Opens NA Device Configuration view for a selected node.
View HP NA Device Configuration Differences	Opens NA Compare Device Configuration view for a selected node.

View	Description
View HP NA Device Configuration History	Opens NA Device Configuration History view for a selected node.
View HP NA Device Information	Opens NA Device Details view for a selected node.
View HP NA Policy Compliance Report	Opens NA Policy, Rule and Compliance Search Results view for a selected device.
Show mismatched connections (NNM iSPI NET)	Lists all Layer 2 connections that have speed or duplex configuration differences.
SSH to HP NA Device	Opens an SSH window for a selected node.
Telnet to HP NA Device	Opens a telnet window for a selected node.

- **Notification about new discovered nodes in NNMi**: NNMi can import its node inventory database to HP NA. By default, NNMi doesn't synchronize the list of nodes with HP NA; instead, manual synchronization is suggested. You, as an NNMi administrator, can automate node import to HP NA in the following ways:

  - Configure node import as a scheduled action on the NNMi server (cron on Unix or Scheduled task on Windows), which would invoke import script:

    In Unix: `/opt/NA/nnmimport.sh`

    In Windows: `C:\NA\nnmimport.bat`

    This solution is preferable because it runs on a regular basis. The only disadvantage is that you will see new nodes only after a script is launched. For example, if you schedule script to run once a day, you may not receive a new node in HP NA for up to one day.

  - Run the import script as the automatic action with new node discovery incident. This solution updates HP NA immediately. You can use this solution if you really know what impact this script may have on your system, and if you know how often new nodes may be discovered. If you have a large number of new nodes discovered, you may have troubles running the import script too often.

- **Notification about SNMP configuration changes**: If a new node has been added into HP NA, or an existing one has changed its SNMP name, HP NA sends a notification message to NNMi about the SNMP community change and it is changed on NNMi's SNMP configuration.

- **Disabling the monitored node in NNMi while it's configured by HP NA**: While some of the configuration actions are made, HP NA can trigger to disable the node on NNMi. This disallows NNMi to receive incidents from devices that are under maintenance. Also, HP NA sends a maintenance cancelation event that triggers nodes on NNMi back to operational status.

Requirements

The following table lists supported versions of official HP NA and NNMi integration:

Management tool	Supported version
HP Network Automation	7.5 or higher with consolidated patch
NNMi	8.11 or higher
	On following OS: Linux, Windows, Solaris

There is no difference between HP NA and NNMi integration. Irrespective of whether management tools are installed on the same or different servers, both configurations are supported.

Also, both management tools may be run on different OS.

Installation instructions

This section describes how to implement NNM-HP NA integration and covers the following topics:

- Enabling integration
- Disabling integration
- Modifying integration

Enabling integration

To enable NNMi-HP NA integration, complete the following steps:

1. Install the NNMi connector on the NNMi server. This software is provided with HP NA's consolidated patch or HP NA's installation CD (following directory inside installation CD: `\add-ons\connectors\hp_network_node_ manager_connector\`). The installation file, which needs to be launched, depends on whether NNMi and HP NA run on the same box or separate ones:

     ° If NNMi and HP NA are installed on separate machines, run the following installation script:

        ° For Linux: `na_nnm_connector_linux.bin`

        ° For Windows: `na_nnm_connector_windows.exe`

        ° For Solaris: `na_nnm_connector_solaris.bin`

- ° If NNMi and HP NA are installed on the same machine, run the following installation script:
    - ° For Linux: `na_nnm_coresidency_linux.bin`
    - ° For Windows: `na_nnm_ coresidency _windows.exe`
    - ° For Solaris: `na_nnm_ coresidency _solaris.bin`

2. Configure integration settings on the NNMi console:

    i. Select the **HP NNMi-HP NA Integration Configuration** form on the **Integration Module Configuration** workspace.

    ii. Check the **Enable integration** checkbox to enable integration.

    iii. Fill in the fields in configuration window. The next table provides description of field names.

    iv. Click **Submit** to confirm settings. New window will show the configuration status. If, for some reason you receive an error, complete the HP NNMi-HP NA Integration Configuration steps one more time.

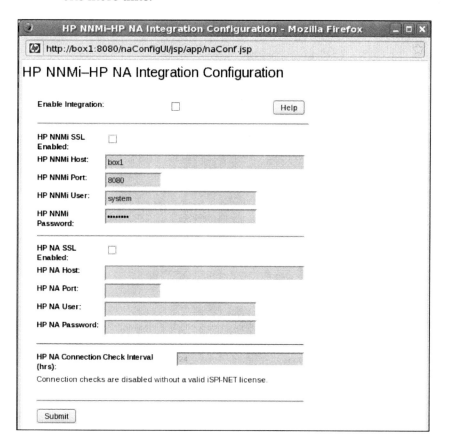

3. Configure a connection to NNMi on the HP NA server. To configure HP NA for connecting to NNMi server, perform the following steps on the HP NA server. This step is optional.

   i. Select **Admin | Administrative Settings | 3rd party integrations**.

   ii. Select the conditions of when the NNMi nodes will be switched to **Out of order** mode during HP NA activity. The following HP NA tasks may trigger node disablement on NNMi:

      ° Running command script

      ° Run diagnostics

      ° Updating device software

      ° Deploying passwords

      ° Deleting ACLs

      ° Configuring syslog

      ° Rebooting device

      ° Discovering driver

      ° Running ICMP test

      ° Taking snapshot

      ° Synchronizing startup and running

      ° OS analysis

   iii. Select SNMP community string propagation behavior. By default, propagation behavior is not enabled. When enabled, HP NA sends an update to NNMi, when HP NA changes SNMP community string to communicate to a device. If a new device has been added, NNMi will also be informed about SNMP community name changes. HP NA informs only SNMP community names that are configured inside HP NA. It doesn't inform if NA changes SNMP community name in device configuration.

   iv. Click on **Save**.

Field name	Description
HP NNMi SSL Enabled	Check this box if your NNMi is configured for SSL communication. Otherwise, leave the checkbox unchecked.
HP NNMi Host	FQDN of NNMi server.
	Run `nnmofficialfqdn.ovpl -t` on the NNMi management server if you are not sure about the name.
HP NNMi Port	The port that is configured to connect to console.
	By default, port 80 or 8004 is used for non-SSL connections and port 443 is used for SSL connections.
	Check the following file to make sure what is configured in your NNMi: • Unix: `$NnmDataDir/shared/nnm/conf/nnm.ports.properties` • Windows: `%NnmDataDir%\shared\nnm\conf\nnm.ports.properties`
HP NNMi User	The username which has an administrator or web service client role.
HP NNMi Password	The password for the user.
HP NA SSL Enabled	Check this box if HP NA is configured for SSL communication, otherwise leave the checkbox unchecked.
HP NA Host	FQDN of HP NA server.
HP NA Port	The port that is configured to NA web services.
	By default, port 80 is used if NA is installed on a separate computer, or port 8080 is used if NA is installed on the same machine as NNMi.
HP NA User	Username that has NA administrator role.
HP NA Password	A password for the user.
HP NA Connection Check Interval (hrs)	Interval, in hours, when the connection should be checked.

Disabling integration

To disable NNMi-HP NA integration, complete the following steps:

1. Select the **HP NNMi – HP NA Integration Configuration** form on the **Integration Module Configuration** workspace.

2. Uncheck the **Enable Integration** checkbox.

3. Click on **Submit**.

Modifying integration

To modify HP NNMi-HP NA integration, perform the following steps:

1. Select the **HP NNMi – HP NA Integration Configuration** form on the **Integration Module Configuration** workspace.

2. Modify values according to your needs, and make sure that the **Enable Integration** checkbox remains enabled.

3. Click on **Submit** to save changes.

Integrating NNMi with Northbound Interface

This section describes the integration of NNMi with third-party tools using Northbound Integration interface.

What is Northbound Interface?

NNMi can be configured to forward incidents to external management tools, for which Northbound Interface is used. Northbound Interface usually forwards NNMi incidents as SNMP v2 traps. So, speaking in general terms, NNMi can be integrated into any other system that has SNMP trap receiver.

How integration works?

Northbound Interface forwards management event and SNMP trap source incidents to a configured destination. Incidents are forwarded as UDP packets. If packet was lost, it will not be resent.

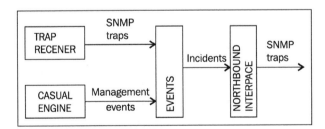

The preceding diagram shows how incident forwarding works using
Northbound Interface:

- Only traps and management events will be picked by Northbound Interface;
  no NNM 6.x/7.x events will be forwarded

- Events are forwarded as SNMP v2 traps

- Only one destination can be configured

Northbound Interface is a good solution if your NNMi has no NNM 6.x/7.x
connected as management stations and you plan to forward incidents only to one
destination. Otherwise, custom solution should be considered.

The following are a few suggestions if one decides to make custom solution instead
of using built-in features:

- If you have NNM 6.x/7.x management station and one forwarding
  destination address, you could make an automatic action, which sends an
  incident as an SNMP trap to your defined destination. The advantage here is
  that you can forward any incident, and the disadvantage is that you have to
  configure automatic action on every single incident that you want to forward.

- If you have more than one destination, you should consider making more
  advanced scripting than just running an SNMP trap from an automatic action
  field. You can run a script as an automatic action, which reads the forwarding
  destination list from your created destination configuration file and sends an
  SNMP trap to all destinations.

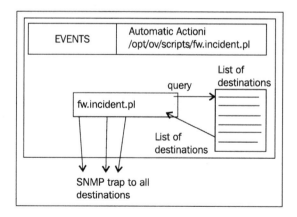

If you have experience writing a code, you will be able to expand your incident
forwarding to a more advanced level; for example, triggering incidents by source,
family, date and time received, or some other attribute.

In the process of incident forwarding using Northbound Interface, SNMP traps are generated based on the following rules:

- SNMP trap source incidents are forwarded with same OID (object identifier) as they were received, but additional varbinds (variable bindings) are added during forwarding. OIDs identify managed objects in an MIB hierarchy. Varbinds are a set of of name-value pairs identifying the MIB objects in PDU, and in the case of messages other than requests, containing their values. To read more about MIBs, OIDs, and varbinds, visit `http://en.wikipedia.org/wiki/Simple_Network_Management_Protocol`. The next diagram displays how NNMi Northbound Interface adds varbind on top of existing SNMP trap:

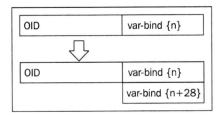

The following table describes varbinds used by NNMi Northbound Interface:

Position	Name	Description
	OID	**ASN type**
	sysUptime	Time since the last start of Northbound Interface
	1.3.6.1.2.1.1.3.0	`ASN TIMETICKS`
	trapOid	`Trap OID`
	1.3.6.1.6.3.1.1.4.1.0	`ASN OBJECT ID`
n	{0-n} original trap varbinds	If varbind is missing from original trap, NULL value is inserted by NNMi.
n+1	Application ID	Always value "NNMi"
	1.3.6.1.4.1.11.2.17.19.2.2.1	ASN Octet String
n+2	NmsUrl	
	1.3.6.1.4.1.11.2.17.19.2.2.2	ASN Octet String
n+3	OriginatingNmsUrl	
	1.3.6.1.4.1.11.2.17.19.2.2.3	ASN Octet String
n+4	OriginatingTrapIpAddress	
	1.3.6.1.4.1.11.2.17.19.2.2.4	ASN Octet String

Position	Name OID	Description ASN type
n+5	IncidentName	
	1.3.6.1.4.1.11.2.17.19.2.2.5	ASN Octet String
n+6	IncidentUuid	ASN Octet String
	1.3.6.1.4.1.11.2.17.19.2.2.6	
n+7	IncidentCategory	ASN Octet String
	1.3.6.1.4.1.11.2.17.19.2.2.7	
n+8	IncidentFamily	
	1.3.6.1.4.1.11.2.17.19.2.2.8	ASN Octet String
n+9	IncidentOrigin	
	1.3.6.1.4.1.11.2.17.19.2.2.9	ASN Octet String
n+10	IncidentNature	
	1.3.6.1.4.1.11.2.17.19.2.2.10	ASN Integer
n+11	IncidentFmtMsg	
	1.3.6.1.4.1.11.2.17.19.2.2.11	ASN Octet String
n+12	IncidentSeverity	
	1.3.6.1.4.1.11.2.17.19.2.2.12	ASN Integer
n+13	IncidentPriority	
	1.3.6.1.4.1.11.2.17.19.2.2.13	ASN Integer
n+14	IncidentLifecycleState	
	1.3.6.1.4.1.11.2.17.19.2.2.14	ASN Integer
n+15	IncidentOriginTime	
	1.3.6.1.4.1.11.2.17.19.2.2.15	ASN Octet String
n+16	IncidentDbCreateTime	
	1.3.6.1.4.1.11.2.17.19.2.2.16	ASN Octet String
n+17	IncidentDbMofidiedTime	
	1.3.6.1.4.1.11.2.17.19.2.2.17	ASN Octet String
n+18	IncidentDupCount	
	1.3.6.1.4.1.11.2.17.19.2.2.18	ASN Integer
n+19	IncidentAssignedTo	
	1.3.6.1.4.1.11.2.17.19.2.2.19	ASN Octet String
n+20	IncidentCias	
	1.3.6.1.4.1.11.2.17.19.2.2.20	ASN Octet String

Position	Name	Description
	OID	ASN type
n+21	IncidentNodeHostname	
	1.3.6.1.4.1.11.2.17.19.2.2.21	ASN Octet String
n+22	IncidentNodeUuid	
	1.3.6.1.4.1.11.2.17.19.2.2.22	ASN Octet String
n+23	IncidentNodeUcmdbId	
	1.3.6.1.4.1.11.2.17.19.2.2.23	ASN Octet String
n+24	IncidentNodeMgmtAddr	
	1.3.6.1.4.1.11.2.17.19.2.2.24	ASN Octet String
n+25	IncidentSourceName	
	1.3.6.1.4.1.11.2.17.19.2.2.25	ASN Octet String
n+26	IncidentSourceType	
	1.3.6.1.4.1.11.2.17.19.2.2.26	ASN Octet String
n+27	IncidentSourceUuid	
	1.3.6.1.4.1.11.2.17.19.2.2.27	ASN Octet String
n+28	IncidentSourceUcmdbId	
	1.3.6.1.4.1.11.2.17.19.2.2.28	ASN Octet String

- Management incidents are defined in SNMP traps on reserved branch
  nnmiMgmtEventNotification (1.3.6.1.4.1.11.2.17.19.2.0.x), where
  x is management event OID. Varbinds for management events are defined
  on the nnmiMgmtEventDescriptions (1.3.6.1.4.1.11.2.17.19.2.2.x)
  branch where x is the varbind number.

  The following table lists all of the varbinds used in a management event trap:

Position	Name	Description
	OID	ASN type
	sysUptime	Time since the last start of Northbound Interface
	1.3.6.1.2.1.1.3.0	ASN TIMETICKS
	trapOid	Trap OID
	1.3.6.1.6.3.1.1.4.1.0	ASN OBJECT ID
n	{0-n} original trap varbinds	If varbind is missing from original trap, NULL value is inserted by NNMi

Position	Name	Description
	OID	ASN type
n+1	Application ID	Always value "NNMi"
	1.3.6.1.4.1.11.2.17.19.2.2.1	ASN Octet String
n+2	NmsUrl	
	1.3.6.1.4.1.11.2.17.19.2.2.2	ASN Octet String
n+3	OriginatingNmsUrl	
	1.3.6.1.4.1.11.2.17.19.2.2.3	ASN Octet String
n+4	OriginatingTrapIpAddress	
	1.3.6.1.4.1.11.2.17.19.2.2.4	ASN Octet String
n+5	IncidentName	
	1.3.6.1.4.1.11.2.17.19.2.2.5	ASN Octet String
n+6	IncidentUuid	
	1.3.6.1.4.1.11.2.17.19.2.2.6	ASN Octet String
n+7	IncidentCategory	
	1.3.6.1.4.1.11.2.17.19.2.2.7	ASN Octet String
n+8	IncidentFamily	
	1.3.6.1.4.1.11.2.17.19.2.2.8	ASN Octet String
n+9	IncidentOrigin	
	1.3.6.1.4.1.11.2.17.19.2.2.9	ASN Octet String
n+10	IncidentNature	
	1.3.6.1.4.1.11.2.17.19.2.2.10	ASN Integer
n+11	IncidentFmtMsg	
	1.3.6.1.4.1.11.2.17.19.2.2.11	ASN Octet String
n+12	IncidentSeverity	
	1.3.6.1.4.1.11.2.17.19.2.2.12	ASN Integer
n+13	IncidentPriority	
	1.3.6.1.4.1.11.2.17.19.2.2.13	ASN Integer
n+14	IncidentLifecycleState	
	1.3.6.1.4.1.11.2.17.19.2.2.14	ASN Integer
n+15	IncidentOriginTime	
	1.3.6.1.4.1.11.2.17.19.2.2.15	ASN Octet String
n+16	IncidentDbCreateTime	
	1.3.6.1.4.1.11.2.17.19.2.2.16	ASN Octet String

Position	Name	Description
	OID	ASN type
n+17	IncidentDbMofidiedTime	
	1.3.6.1.4.1.11.2.17.19.2.2.17	ASN Octet String
n+18	IncidentDupCount	
	1.3.6.1.4.1.11.2.17.19.2.2.18	ASN Integer
n+19	IncidentAssignedTo	
	1.3.6.1.4.1.11.2.17.19.2.2.19	ASN Octet String
n+20	IncidentCias	
	1.3.6.1.4.1.11.2.17.19.2.2.20	ASN Octet String
n+21	IncidentNodeHostname	
	1.3.6.1.4.1.11.2.17.19.2.2.21	ASN Octet String
n+22	IncidentNodeUuid	
	1.3.6.1.4.1.11.2.17.19.2.2.22	ASN Octet String
n+23	IncidentNodeUcmdbId	
	1.3.6.1.4.1.11.2.17.19.2.2.23	ASN Octet String
n+24	IncidentNodeMgmtAddr	
	1.3.6.1.4.1.11.2.17.19.2.2.24	ASN Octet String
n+25	IncidentSourceName	
	1.3.6.1.4.1.11.2.17.19.2.2.25	ASN Octet String
n+26	IncidentSourceType	
	1.3.6.1.4.1.11.2.17.19.2.2.26	ASN Octet String
n+27	IncidentSourceUuid	
	1.3.6.1.4.1.11.2.17.19.2.2.27	ASN Octet String
n+28	IncidentSourceUcmdbId	
	1.3.6.1.4.1.11.2.17.19.2.2.28	ASN Octet String
n+29	IncidentIfName	
	1.3.6.1.4.1.11.2.17.19.2.2.29	ASN Octet String
n+30	IncidentIfAlias	
	1.3.6.1.4.1.11.2.17.19.2.2.30	ASN Octet String
n+31	IncidentIfDescr	
	1.3.6.1.4.1.11.2.17.19.2.2.31	ASN Octet String
n+32	IncidentIfIndex	
	1.3.6.1.4.1.11.2.17.19.2.2.32	ASN Integer

Position	Name	Description
	OID	ASN type
n+33	IncidentRd	
	1.3.6.1.4.1.11.2.17.19.2.2.33	ASN Octet String
n+34	IncidentOtherNodeHostname	
	1.3.6.1.4.1.11.2.17.19.2.2.34	ASN Octet String
n+35	IncidentOtherNodeUuid	
	1.3.6.1.4.1.11.2.17.19.2.2.35	ASN Octet String
n+36	IncidentOtherNodeUcmdbId	
	1.3.6.1.4.1.11.2.17.19.2.2.36	ASN Octet String
n+37	IncidentOtherNodeMgmtAddr	
	1.3.6.1.4.1.11.2.17.19.2.2.37	ASN Octet String
n+38	IncidentOtherIfName	
	1.3.6.1.4.1.11.2.17.19.2.2.38	ASN Octet String
n+39	IncidentOtherIfAlias	
	1.3.6.1.4.1.11.2.17.19.2.2.39	ASN Octet String
n+40	IncidentOtherIfDescr	
	1.3.6.1.4.1.11.2.17.19.2.2.40	ASN Octet String
n+41	IncidentOtherIfIndex	
	1.3.6.1.4.1.11.2.17.19.2.2.41	ASN Integer
n+42	IncidentOtherRd	
	1.3.6.1.4.1.11.2.17.19.2.2.42	ASN Octet String

When an SNMP trap is forwarded on NNMi to external tool, NNMi cannot check whether the managed device also sends an SNMP trap directly to the external system, which results in double events coming to the management tool. The following actions should be considered in order to avoid incident duplicates:

- External tool should be configured for event correlation to ignore duplicate events

- The source node should be configured, eliminating SNMP trap destination duplication

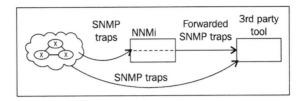

When incident changes the state to CLOSE inside the NNMi tool, an SNMP trap is sent, indicating a state change.

Requirements

The third table under the *How integration works* section provides information about supported versions for Northbound Interface usage as an integration solution.

The following table represents the support matrix for Northbound Interface:

Management tool	Supported version
NNMi	8.12 or higher

Installation instructions

This section describes how to implement Northbound Interface integration and covers the following topics:

- Enabling integration
- Disabling integration
- Modifying integration

Enabling integration

To enable Northbound Interface, perform the following steps:

1. Configure the NNMi server to forward incidents:
    i. Select the **HP NNMi-Northbound Interface Configuration** form on the **Integration Module Configuration** workspace.
    ii. Check the **Enable Integration** checkbox.

iii. Fill-in the configuration window fields. The next table provides a configuration window fields description.

iv. Click on **Submit**.

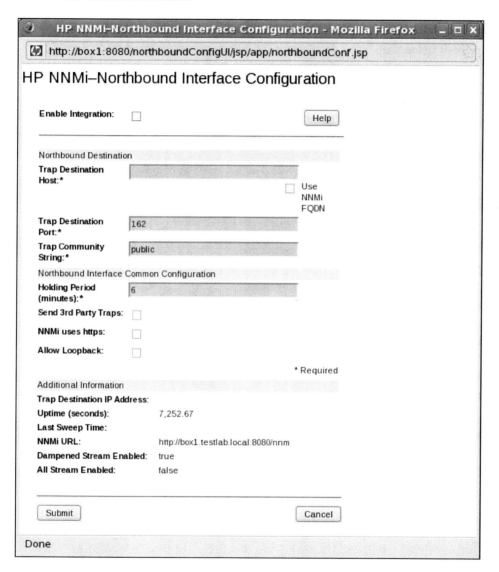

2. Configure trap receiver, to which traps will be sent in order to understand the NNMi definitions.

Field name	Description
Trap Destination Host	FQDN or IP address of node where traps are sent.
Trap Destination Port	UDP port of SNMP trap receiver (by default, port 162 is used).
Trap Community String	SNMP read-only community string for the SNMP agent, which receives traps.
Holding Period (minutes)	Number of minutes to wait the before management event is forwarded. This period applies for management events only.
	This holding period allows a causal engine to process incidents and avoid sending flapping incidents, which are opened and closed within the waiting period.
Send 3rd Party Traps	If you prefer forward all the SNMP traps which NNMi receives, you should enable this checkbox. If you want to forward only NNMi-generated incidents, this checkbox should be cleared.
NNMi uses https	Select this checkbox if NNMi is configured for HTTPS communication.
Allow Loopback	Select this checkbox if your trap receiving application can receive traps on a loopback address.
Trap Destination IP Address	The IP address to which the trap destination host name resolves.
Uptime (seconds)	Time in seconds when Northbound Interface was last enabled.
Last Sweep Time	Time since the last management event query of the NNMi database.
NNMi URL	NNMi URL address.
Dampened Stream Enabled	This value should be `true`.
All Stream Enabled	This value should be `false`.

Disabling integration

To disable NNMi incident forwarding via Northbound Interface, perform the following steps:

1. Select the **HP NNMi-Northbound Interface Configuration** form on the **Integration Module Configuration** workspace.

2. Uncheck the **Enable Integration** checkbox.

3. Click **Submit**.

Modifying integration

To modify Northbound Interface Integration configuration on the HP NNMi server, complete the following steps:

1. Select the **HP NNMi-Northbound Interface Configuration** from the **Integration Module Configuration** workspace.

2. Modify the fields according to your needs. For example, if the SNMP trap community has changed, or you need to forward the SNMP traps to another destination, then the trap destination host should be changed, and so on. Make sure that the **Enable Integration** checkbox remains enabled.

3. Click on **Submit**.

Integrating NNMi with HP Software Operations Manager

This section describes integration of NNMi with the HP Operations Manager Management tool.

What is OM?

HP Software Operations Manager (HP OM) is a systems monitoring tool designed to monitor servers, including OS, middleware, and applications. HP OM works based on server-agent architecture, so that each managed node has to have an HP OM agent installed (refer to the next diagram).

 Note: There are cases when nodes can be monitored without an agent.

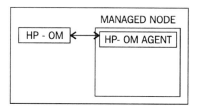

If multiple monitoring tools that monitor separate pieces of your infrastructure are used in the environment, in most cases, HP Operation Manager will be chosen as the centralized monitoring tool. For example, an organization that has HP NNMi for network monitoring, HP System Insight Manager for HP server hardware monitoring, APC InfrastruXure central for monitoring the room environment (APC UPS and PDU devices, temperature, humidity, water leaks and noise ratio sensors), CiscoWorks LMS for Cisco device configuration, and HP Operations Manager for server and services in data room monitoring. Using these tools as standalone would require a long list of dedicated monitors to monitor everything. Instead, all tools can be integrated into one *umbrella* solution. In these circumstances, HP Operations Manager would be the best choice as a centralized management tool. This is because HP OM can accept and display messages from external tools. Some external tools can provide two-way communication and, most importantly, display all messages in one console, including message correlation capability.

If NNMi and HP OM are deployed in the same infrastructure, HP OM is chosen as the primary monitoring tool, where NNMi feeds HP OM with incidents and provides access to NNMi views (maps, neighbors, path views, and so on). Depending on the OS where the HP OM server is installed, HP OM is divided as two separate products:

- HP Software Operations for Windows (HP OMW)
- HP Software Operations for Unix/Linux (HP OMU/HP OML)

This naming has nothing to do with the OS of a managed node. In other words, both HP OMW and HP OMU can manage Windows, Unix, Linux, or Solaris boxes. HP OM names depend on the OS on which an OM server is installed — HP Operations Manager for Windows is installed on Windows OS, whereas HP Operations Manager for Unix is installed on Unix.

This section provides information on how to integrate NNMi and HP OM (Windows or Unix). When you integrate NNMi and HP OM using built-in integration, the following features are provided:

- **Messages from NNMi to HP OM are sent**: Depending on the integration method you choose (both are described in this chapter), incident status changes may be synchronized between NNMi and HP OM management tools.
- NNMi views can be launched from HP OM for more detailed troubleshooting (maps, neighbor, path views, and so on).

- **NNMi actions can be launched from HP OM management console**: *Chapter 10, Extending NNMi* describes how to create your own URL action if you decide to expand your list of NNMi actions on the HP OM, or if you want to implement integration on your own.

How integration works

NNMi and HP OM tools can be integrated in the following two ways:

- Forwarding NNMi messages to HP OM agent as SNMP traps
- Forwarding NNMi messages to HP OM message browser using web services

Forwarding NNMi messages to HP OM agent as SNMP traps

NNMi is configured to forward incidents using SNMP traps via Northbound Interface. Messages are forwarded to an HP OM agent, which is controlled by the HP OM server. The HP OM server administrator has configured templates (policies) that decide which incidents should be sent to the HP OM server. This works as an incident filter and helps limit the number of incidents that are deployed on HP OM.

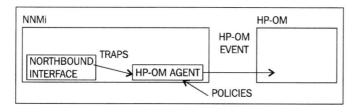

Note: If you have a limited budget or, for some other reasons, you cannot install an HP OM agent on the NNMi server, you can configure sending NNMi incidents to another server that has an HP OM agent installed (for example, the HP OM server, as it always has its own agent installed). The following table compares two integration approaches—sending incidents to an HP OM agent locally on the NNMi server and forwarding to an external server with an HP OM agent installed (agent-less solution).

Basic	Agent-less
If the connection between NNMi and the HP OM server is lost, the HP OM agent buffers messages until the connection is restored.	Messages are forwarded as UDP packets over the network. If packets are lost, the message will not be resent. If the connection between the NNMi server and the forwarded node is lost, incidents sent during that time will be lost.
The amount of incidents sent to the HP OM server are controlled on the HP OM agent by configuring monitoring policies. Incident type and amount can be used for configuration. In case of an incident storm, only configured to pass incidents will be sent to the HP OM server over the network.	All incidents are sent over the network and agent-receiver will take care of applying HP OM policies, which may limit incident type and number. In case of an incident storm, additional network overload may appear.

 It is recommended that you prefer a basic integration solution instead of agent-less.

Forwarding NNMi messages to HP OM message browser using web services

Integration using web services implementation allows the sending of NNMi messages to HP OM, and synchronizes their status on both management tools at the same time using web services. This type of integration uses the following modules:

- NNMi: OM integration module
- HP OM incident web service
- HP OM applications for contextual access to the NNMi console

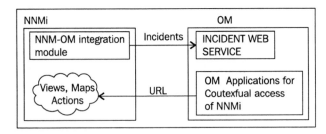

The following table lists the main features of both integration methods. This table should provide an answer to any main question that arises during integration method selection stage:

Feature	Forwarding to HP OM agent	Web Services Implementation
Incident forward to HP OM	✓	✓
Incident state synchronization		✓
Access to NNMi console from HP OM	✓	✓
Filter incidents to forward	✓	✓

As you can see, the main difference between integration methods is incident state synchronization. It is a key factor if both NNMi and HP OM consoles are used by operators. Both consoles have to show an up-to-date incident state, otherwise overlapping may occur.

For example, an incident that appeared on an NNMi console is sent to HP OM. The operator, who works with the NNMi console, started an investigation and changed the incident status to **In progress** on the NNMi console. No changes are synchronized on the same event, which is forwarded to HP OM. The other operator, who works using the HP OM console, also started an investigation. None of these operators know about each other's activity. So, double the effort was invested into this issue. Even worse more damage could be done to the business. Think about the consequences:

- The operator who picked the incident on NNMi spent effort working on the solution. On the other hand, the other operator who picked an incident on Operations Manager has already solved an issue. So, the first operator has been disappointed about the accuracy of the incidents, and so if same incident occurs in the future, the first operator may take an ignorance approach, as either way the incident wasn't accurate last time. There is also the chance that the "somebody else will fix it" approach will be taken by both the NNMi and HP OM operators at a same time, and none of them actually puts effort in to fix the incident.

- If external resources were involved in the troubleshooting process (providers or customer), the opinion about the operations center by third-party users or business partners may be painted in negative colors. This may have a direct impact on future business.

- If external subcontractors were involved in the "double" effort, it results in the company being billed twice, and money is therefore wasted.

Because of more control over the incidents, it is recommended that you use the web service integration method. For example, in case of incident status synchronization between the NNMi and HP OM consoles, if it was changed for one tool, then it will be changed for other tools as well.

So, if possible, you need to consider the web services integration solution.

Requirements

The following table provides a list of the supported versions for integration:

Management tool	Forwarding to HP OM agent	Web Services Implementation
NNMi	8.12 or higher	8.10 or higher
HP Operations Manager for Unix	8.30 or higher	8.30 or higher
HP Operations Manager for Windows	8.10 or higher	8.10 or higher

 Note: NNMi and HP OM installation on the same server is not supported.

Installation instructions

This section describes how to implement NNM-HP Operations Manager integration and covers the following topics:

- Enabling integration
- Disabling integration
- Modifying integration

Enabling integration

This section describes the integration enabling process for both integration modes.

- **Forwarding SNMP traps to an HP OM agent:**

  NNMi integration with HP OM using incident forwarding to HP OM agent consists of the following steps:

  1. SNMP trap policy template needs to be created, or may be generated based on Incident Configuration on NNMi, using `nnmopcexport.ovpl` script and imported to HP OM.

  2. Identify the available SNMP port and configure it on HP OM agent.

3. Configure incident forwarding on the NNMi server using Northbound Interface.

4. On the HP OM console, add custom message attributes from NNMi incidents.

5. Enable contextual launching of the NNMi tools. This step is optional.

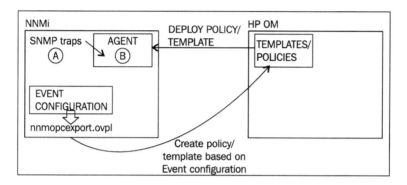

- **Forwarding using web services**:

  NNMi integration with HP OM using Web Services Implementation consists of the following steps:

  1. If you integrate with HP OM-U 8.x, then you need to install HP OM incident web service (IWS) and the latest consolidated patches.

  2. Configure and customize incident forwarding on NNMi console (refer to the next screenshot).

  3. If you are integrating with HP OM-W, you need to configure NNMi adapter.

  4. Add monitored nodes into HP OM, which will be incident sources.

  5. Install the base set of NNMi applications on HP OM. Optionally, you can install additional applications.

6. Add custom attributes, related to NNMi incidents, to the HP OM Java console.

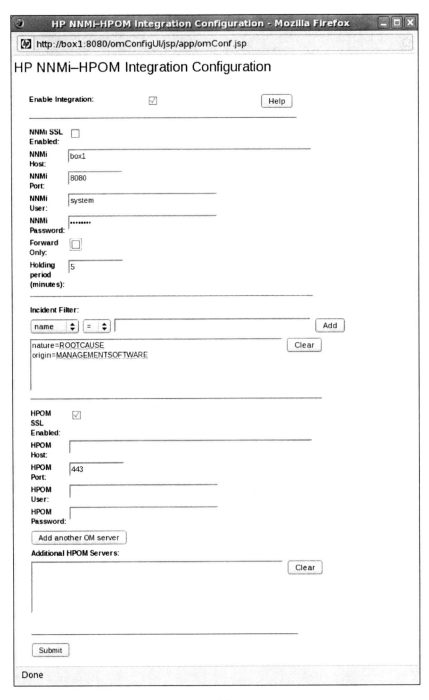

Disabling integration

To disable configuration for integration using SNMP trap forwarding to the HP OM agent, you can take one of the following ways:

- Stop incident forwarding on the NNMi server. This would stop NNMi sending SNMP traps to the HP OM agent.

- Disable or uninstall HP OM templates. Here, you can configure which events should be stopped by receiving to HP OM. You have the flexibility to configure custom list of events that need to be passed to HP OM as events.

To disable configuration for integration using web services integration, perform the following steps:

1. Select **HP OM...** on **Integration Module Configuration**.
2. Uncheck the **Enable Integration** checkbox.
3. Click on **Submit**.

Modifying integration

Depending on which integration solution you have chosen, you can make the following modifications.

- **Incident forwarding as SNMP traps:**

  Here are a few places where you can make modifications:

  ° In the NNMi-HP OM integration configuration window on the NNMi console, you can change the integration-specific parameters such as SNMP trap destination address or port, incident filter, and so on.

  ° Modify templates where you can customize which particular traps to pass as OM events.

- **Incident forwarding using web services**

  You can modify integration configuration by modifying the integration configuration window on the NNMi console:

  i. Select **HP OM...** on **Integration Module Configuration**.
  ii. Modify the fields according to your needs. Make sure the **Enable Integration** checkbox remains checked.
  iii. Click on **Submit**.

Integrating NNMi with HP System Insight Manager

This section describes NNMi integration with the HP System Insight Manager management tool.

What is HP Systems Insight Manager?

HP SIM (System Insight Manager) is a HP server and storage management tool that collects inventory data and proactively monitors hardware issues.

HP SIM is an excellent tool for system administrators, where they can cover the following management areas:

- Keeping track of the HP server and storage hardware inventory
- Monitoring and detecting hardware failures
- Keeping track of hardware drivers, and updating them at regular intervals

HP SIM integration into NNMi adds more information into NNMi while administrators are troubleshooting issues, as HP SIM forwards HP hardware-specific events to NNMi. NNMi users can also open HP SIM console views from NNMi on context-based link integration.

 Please refer to `http://h18013.www1.hp.com/products/servers/ management/hpsim/index.html?jumpid=ex_r163_us/en/esn/ eb/isb_sim60bmm_googlesemaw/&s_kwcid=TC|14803|%2Bsyst ems%20%2Binsight%20%2Bmanager||S|b|5865130404` for the HP System Insight Manager screenshot.

HP SIM integration into NNMi is a good idea if NNMi is the main monitoring console for your users, that is, if NNMi is not forwarding its own incidents to some other central monitoring tool.

For example, if you have NNMi that is used directly by your staff to monitor your infrastructure, integrating HP SIM with NNMi would give additional value. But if you have an additional monitoring tool, say HP OM where NNMi forwards its incidents and operators are using HP OM console as a primary monitoring source, then HP SIM integration into NNMi would create just another hop for your message delivery. Instead, integration between HP SIM and HP OM should be considered.

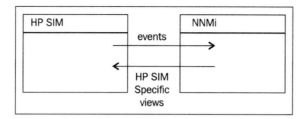

How integration works

After HP SIM and NNMi integration is configured, the following features are added:

- HP SIM events are forwarded into NNMi
- The following features of HP SIM console can be opened from NNMi:
    - ○ HP System Manager's homepage
    - ○ HP System Insight Manager's homepage
    - ○ HP SIM node details

> **Note:** HP SIM and NNMi have separate authentications, and no username/password is passed when the HP SIM console is opened from NNMi. So, the HP SIM username and password needs to be entered when HP SIM-specific windows are opened.

Requirements

HP SIM and NNMi integration is supported by the following versions:

Management tool	Supported version
HP Systems Insight Manager	5.30 or higher
NNMi	8.13 or higher

Note that HP SIM and NNMi must be installed on separate servers.

Installation instructions

This section describes how to implement NNM-HP SIM integration and covers the following topics:

- Enabling integration
- Disabling integration
- Modifying integration

Enabling integration

To configure integration, perform the following steps:

1. Select **HP SIM ...** on **Integration Module Configuration** workspace.

2. Check the **Enable integration** checkbox.

3. Fill in fields that appear in the next screenshot and that are described in the following table:

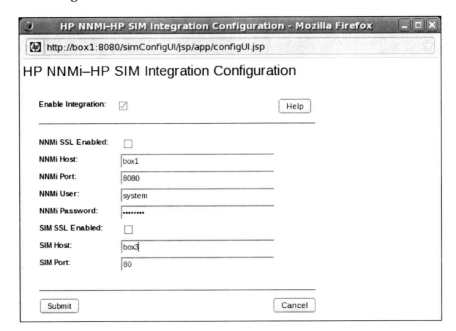

Field name	Description
NNMi SSL Enabled	Check this box if your NNMi is enabled for SSL.
NNMi Host	NNMi server's FQDN.
NNMi Port	Port that should be used for connecting to the console.
	By default, port 80 or 8004 is used for a non-SSL environment, and port 443 for SSL environment.
	Note that if you are not sure which port is configured, you need to check the following file: • Unix: `$NnmDataDir/shared/nnm/conf/nnm.ports.properties` • Windows: `%NnmDataDir%\shared\nnm\conf\nnm.ports.properties`

Field name	Description
NNMi User	The username that has Administrator or WebService Client role and will be used to connect to NNMi console.
NNMi Password	The password for the specified user.
SIM SSL Enabled	Select the checkbox if your HP SIM is enabled for SSL.
SIM Host	HP SIM server's FQDN.
SIM Port	Port that should be used for connecting to the console.
	By default, if the SSL connection is enabled, provide port number as 50000.

4. Click on **Submit**.

Congratulations!!! The HP SIM and NNMi integration is complete.

Disabling integration

To disable HP SIM and NNMi integration, perform the following steps:

1. Select **HP SIM ...** on **Integration Module Configuration** workspace.

2. Uncheck the **Enable integration** option.

3. Click on **Submit**.

Modifying integration

To modify HP SIM and NNMi integration, perform the following steps:

1. Select **HP SIM ...** on the **Integration Module Configuration** workspace.

2. Modify the integration configuration window's fields accordingly.

3. Click on **Submit**.

Integrating NNMi with HP Software uCMDB

This section describes the integration of NNMi with the HP Software Universal CMDB management tool.

What is HP Universal CMDB?

HP uCMDB is a software designed to help in configuration management, and in finding, storing, and creating relationships for infrastructure configuration. For example, assuming your company has a few branch offices, how do you plan to handle the following issues:

- **Inventory**: Network devices, computers, UPS devices, software, and so on.

- **Relationships**: How do you know which monitor is connected to a selected computer, or what software is installed on computers A, B, and C?

- **Impact**: How do you know which of your services will be impacted, and how will they be impacted if you switch off router A?

It's obvious that tracking on inventory needs to be done. Most of monitoring tools have their own inventory DB—NNMi has its managed devices' inventory database.

So, what is the problem? That's the question I have often been asked. The problem is that each monitoring or management tool has its own database, and is limited by the boundaries of its management domain. For example, NNMi has information about all discovered network devices and maybe nodes (if they have been discovered). HP RADIA or MS System Center Configuration Manager stores data about all discovered PCs, including software, hardware, and even patches applied to each node. Looks like you have all you need with these tools, but you have no idea about how network device impacts PCs and vice versa.

How integration works

Integration of HP uCMDB and NNMi allows uCMDB to receive a list of configuration items from NNMi discovered objects, where uCMDB adds its own **discovery and dependency mapping (DDM)** information. Also, NNMi is provided by additional actions, which allow the following functionality:

- Finding impacted CIs
- Opening a CI in uCMDB

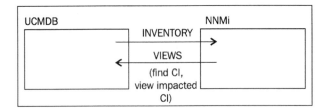

Impacted CI is determined in uCMDB by dependency mapping, where dependency can be made as a physical and logical entity. For example, if Router A is turned down, Router B and Router C would be impacted directly. At the same time, uCMDB can tell that same outage would also impact Services A, B, and C in a network.

Requirements

The next table provides a list of supported management tool versions for uCMDB and NNMi integration:

Management tool	Supported version
HP uCMDB	8.00 or higher
NNMi	8.10 or higher

 Note: There are two things you need to remember:
- uCMDB and NNMi cannot be installed on the same machine
- uCMDB and NNMi can be installed on different OS

Installation instructions

This section describes how to implement NNM-HP uCMDB integration and covers the following topics:

- Enabling integration
- Disabling integration
- Modifying integration

Enabling integration

To enable uCMDB-NNMi integration, the following steps need to be completed:

1. Deploy uCMDB – NNMi integration discovery package on uCMDB server.
2. Set up and start the DDM probe for NNMi topology data.
3. Set up Network-NNMi Layer 2 jobs.
4. Configure the NNMi-uCMDB connection on the NNMi server:
    i. Select the **HP NNMi – HP uCMDB Integration Configuration** form on the **Integration Module Configuration** on workspace.
    ii. Select the **Enable Integration** option.

iii. Fill in the fields in the enabled window (refer to the next screenshot):

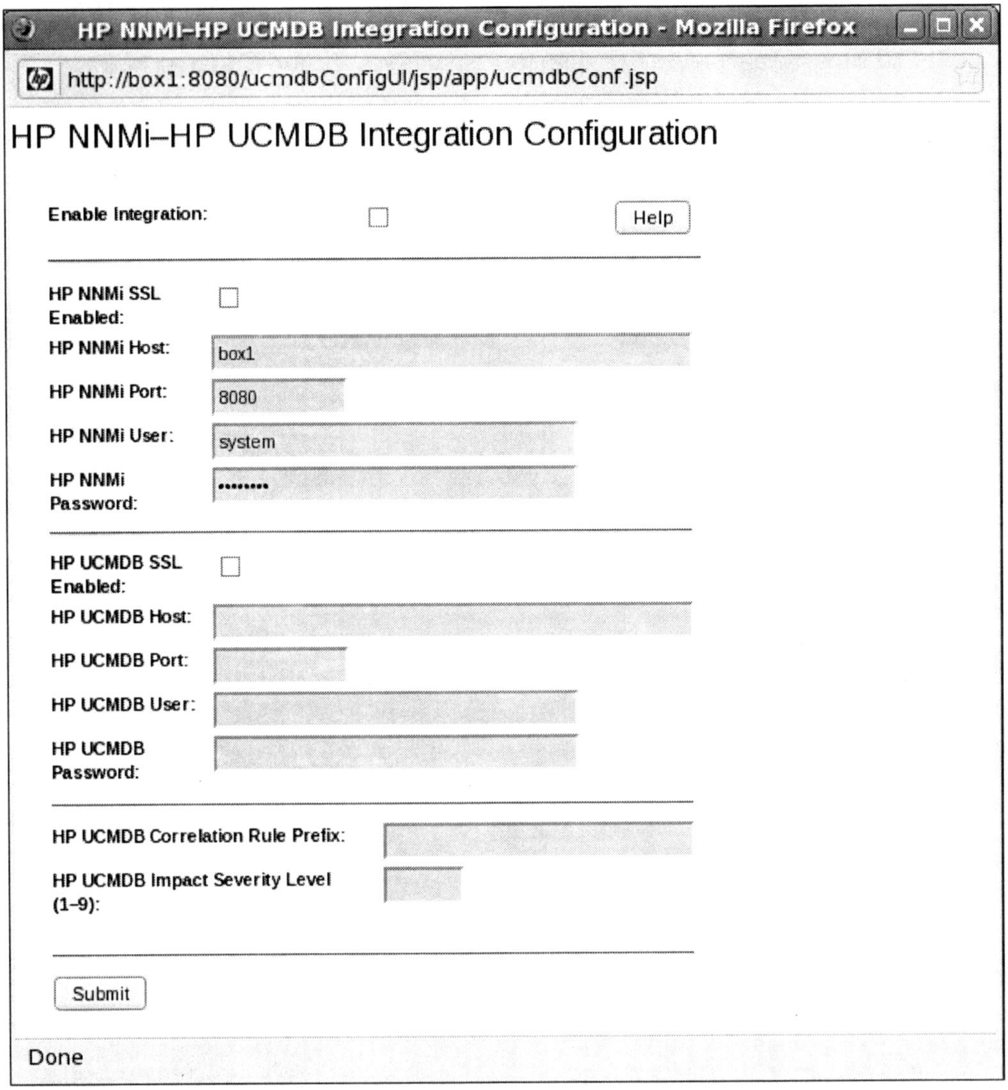

iv. Click on **Submit**.

Note that after you click on the **Submit** button, new status window opens displaying the status of configuration. If you receive an error, perform all four substeps (i to iv) of step 4 once again.

5. Customize the integration on the NNMi server:

i. Select the **HP NNMi – HP uCMDB Integration Configuration** form on **Integration Module Configuration** workspace.

ii. Fill in the **HP uCMDB Correlation Rule Prefix** and **HP UCMDB Impact Severity Level (1-9)** fields.

iii. Click on **Submit**.

The following table describes the fields available on the HP NNMi-uCMDB integration configuration screen:

Field name	Description
HP NNMi SSL Enabled	Check this box if your NNMi is enabled for SSL.
HP NNMi Hostname	NNMi server's FQDN.
HP NNMi Port	Port that should be used for connecting to the console.
	By default, port 80 or 8004 is used for a non-SSL environment and port 443 for an SSL environment.
	Note that if you are not sure which port is configured, you need to check the following file: • Unix: `$NnmDataDir/shared/nnm/conf/nnm.ports.properties` • Windows: `%NnmDataDir%\shared\nnm\conf\nnm.ports.properties`
HP NNMi User	The username that has the Administrator or WebService Client role and will be used to connect to the NNMi console.
HP NNMi Password	The password for the specified user.
HP uCMDB SSL Enabled	Check this box if uCMDB is enabled for SSL.
HP uCMDB Host	HP uCMDB server's FQDN.
HP uCMDB Port	Port that is used for connecting to web services.
	By default, 8080 is used.
HP uCMDB User	The username that has uCMDB Administrator role assigned.
HP uCMDB Password	The password for the specified user.
HP uCMDB Connection Rule Prefix	UCMDB correlation rules' prefix that runs the "Find uCMDB Impacted CIs" action to calculate impact.
HP uCMDB Impact Severity Level	The severity level that should be applied by uCMDB impact correlation rules. The higher number, the higher the severity. HP recommends using severity 9 in this case.

Disabling integration

To disable NNMi-uCMDB integration, perform the following steps:

1. Select the **HP NNMi – HP uCMDB Integration Configuration** form on the **Integration Module Configuration** workspace.

2. Uncheck the **Enable Integration** checkbox.

3. Click on **Submit**.

Modifying integration

To modify the NNMi-uCMDB integration configuration, follow these steps:

1. Select the **HP NNMi – HP uCMDB Integration Configuration** form on the **Integration Module Configuration** workspace.

2. Modify the fields according to your needs. Make sure that the **Enable Integration** checkbox is selected.

3. Click on **Submit** to save changes.

Summary

Congratulations! You have finished the last chapter of this book—a chapter that covered NNMi integration with a list of monitoring tools such as:

- HP Business Availability Center
- CiscoWorks LMS
- HP Network Automation Services
- HP Operations Manager
- HP System Insight Manager
- HP Universal CMDB

The chapter also included Northbound Interface as an integration solution, which in many cases, is universal while integrating NNMi with many other monitoring tools that are not described in this chapter.

If you understand the basics of integration, what integration is and why it needs to take place, then you can think about the integration of NNMi with some other tools as well. Now that NNMi integration possibilities are understood, only a single thing is missing—to read the documentation of a monitoring tool that you plan to integrate with NNMi. Once you are done with that, you are ready to implement your own custom integration solution.

Next in this book will come appendices that describe how to upgrade NNMi from previous 6.x/7.x versions. The appendices also cover some thoughts and recommendations on what the next steps should be in order to improve the network operations center.

Upgrading from NNM 6.x/7.x

This appendix describes how to upgrade NNMi from the 6.x/7.x version to the 8.x/9.x version. Specifically, the following areas will be covered:

- Overview about NNM's upgrade process
- Upgrade path description

Overview

Because of architectural differences, the upgrade from NNM 6.x/7.x to NNMi 8.x/9.x cannot be done by installing upgrade software on NNM 6.x/7.x.

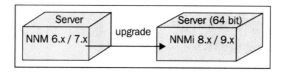

Consider installing NNMi on a new server and either transferring configuration data using provided scripts, or configuring new NNMi installation manually from scratch.

The following table provides some keynotes about each upgrade opportunity:

New installation	Upgrade using tools
You want to improve a new installation, optimizing configuration when upgrading to NNM	You need to upgrade in exact configuration what you had on NNM
Want to re-evaluate the monitoring approach	

A custom upgrade path can be selected as well, upgrading only some configuration parts (For example, transferring SNMP configuration, transferring a list of seeded nodes, and so on).

If you chose fresh installation with configuration from scratch, please refer to *Chapter 1, Before we Manage with NNMi* with the new installation instructions.

The next section describes the upgrade path.

The upgrade path

If you chose the upgrade transferring configuration data from the NNM management server to the newly installed NNMi server, then this section will provide you with a migration path, which is recommended by the HP Software team. Also, read the latest upgrade documentation, as HP Software constantly improves their upgrade tools.

Install the latest patches, especially if you are running the NNMi 8.0x version, as the early versions of NNMi had only a few upgrade tools, which made upgrading inconvenient.

The following upgrade path is recommended by the HP Software team:

- Data Collection from NNM
- SNMP configuration upgrade
- Discovery configuration upgrade
- Status monitoring upgrade
- Event configuration and Event Reduction upgrade
- Map upgrade
- Custom script transfer
- Tools reference upgrade

Data collection from NNM

The first few NNMi versions had no automated tools for the upgrade process. Starting from NNMi 8.10 Path 1, upgrade tools were provided for data migration from NNM to NNMi. Later, patch 3 included the `nnmetmapmigration.ovpl` tool in addition to the existing tools, which can be found in the following directory:

Unix:$NnmInstallDir/migration/bin/

Windows:`%NnmInstallDir%\migration\bin\`

Please consider the latest NNMi version when you start your upgrade, as HP Software continuously improves upgrades by providing new tools or features for an upgrade.

This section provides you with instructions on how to start the upgrade of the data collection tool. Complete the following steps for collecting data from the NNM system:

1. Make a full backup of the NNM system by running ovbackup.ovpl on the NNM server from the following directory:

   Unix: `/opt/OV/bin/`

   Windows: `c:\Program Files\HP OpenView\bin\`

2. Copy the `migration.zip` file from NNMi, which is located in the following directory:

   Unix: `$NnmInstallDir/migration/`

   Windows: `%NnmInstallDir%\migration\`

   to the following directory on NNM:

   Unix: `/opt/OV`

   Windows: `C:\Program Files\HP OpenView`

3. Unzip the `migration.zip` file on the NNM server using any ZIP file extraction tool.

4. Change to the `migration` directory and launch the following scripts to collect NNM data:

   ○ `createMigrationDirs.ovpl`: This tool creates the directory structure for upgrade

   ○ `nnmmigration.ovpl`: This tool collects data from NNM for upgrade

> This script also includes Home Base Container Views, which are configured on NNM. If you need the OVW map location hierarchy included in your upgrade script, run the nnmmapmigration.ovpl tool before you launch the archive script mentioned in the next step.

Run archive `Migration.ovpl` to archive the data, and this will be archived to the file `<hotname>.tar`.

5. Create the following directories on the NNMi server and change them to:

   Unix:`$NnmDataDir/tmp/migration/<hostname>`

   Windows:`%NnmDataDir%\tmp\migration\<hostname>`

6. Run the following script, which will unpack an archive:

   Unix:`$NnmInstallDir/migration/bin/restoreMigration.ovpl -source <hostname>.tar`

   Windows:`%NnmInstallDir%\migration\bin\restoreMigration.ovpl -source <hostname>.tar`

SNMP configuration upgrade

SNMP configuration upgrade from NNM6.x/7.x to NNMi 8.x/9.x covers the following areas:

- **SNMP configuration**: This configuration is used to tell NNM/NNMi which SNMP community name should be used for communicating with a device.

- **Name lookup resolution exception configuration**: This configuration is used to list nodes to NNM, which should not be looked up in DNS.

- **Device profile customization**: This is used to define which profile should be assigned to a node on NNM/NNMi.

SNMP configuration

SNMP configuration can be upgraded in two ways:

- **Upgrade tool approach**: The upgrade tool approach uses the `nnmmigration.ovpl` tool on NNM to collect all configured community strings and store them in the `snmpCapture.out` file.

  To replicate configuration to NNMi, complete the following steps:

  1. Change to the SNMP upgrade directory in the NNM server:

     Unix:`$NnmDataDir/tmp/migration/<hostname>/SNMP/`

     Windows:`%NnmDataDir%\tmp\migration\<hostname>\SNMP\`

2. Create SNMP community file on the NNM server by running the following script:

   Unix: `$NnmInstallDir/migration/bin/snmpCapture.ovpl \`
   `snmpCapture.out > snmpout.txt`

   Windows:`%NnmInstallDir%\migration\bin\snmpCapture.ovpl \`
   `snmpCapture.out > snmpout.txt`

3. To upgrade SNMP configuration, use one of the described manual upgrade options.

   When you are done with the upgrade, you can modify the following additional SNMP parameters in NNMi: timeout, retries, and port (**Configuration** workspace | **Communication configuration** view).

- **Upgrading manually**: Complete the following steps to upgrade configuration:

  1. Export SNMP configuration from the NNM server by running the following command:

     Unix: `$OV_BIN/xnmsnmpconf –export > snmpout.txt`

     Windows:`%OV_BIN%\xnmsnmpconf –export > snmpout.txt`

     For example, if the NNM server IP address is 10.10.10.1 and the original `ipNoLookup.conf` file looks as follows:

     ```
     # ipNoLookup.conf file, which list addresses which should
     not be resolved
     10.10.1.*
     10.10.5.2-25
     10.10.10.1
     10.10.10.2
     192.168.1.*
     ```

     After modification, the line with the NNM server's IP address should be removed or commented out (the pound sign is inserted in front of a line):

     ```
     # ipNoLookup.conf file, which list addresses which should
     not be resolved
     10.10.1.*
     10.10.5.2-25
     # 10.10.10.1 # sign at the beginning of line means that
     this line is treated as comment
     10.10.10.2
     192.168.1.*
     ```

     Or, you can also export it using the NNM console by selecting **SNMP configuration** in the **Options** menu and clicking **Export**.

It also assumes you named the file snmpout.txt and provides you with instructions on how to replicate information to NNMi.

2. Change to the SNMP upgrade directory on the NNM server:

   Unix:$NnmDataDir/tmp/migration/<hostname>/SNMP/

   Windows:%NnmDataDir%\tmp\migration\<hostname>\SNMP\

3. Run a command:

   Unix: $NnmInstallDir/migration/bin/snmpCapture.ovpl \ snmp-Capture.out > snmpout.txt

   Windows: %NnmInstallDir%\migration\bin\snmpCapture.ovpl \ snmpCapture.out > snmpout.txt

4. Load the SNMP configuration into NNMi by selecting **Communication Configuration** from the **Configuration** workspace.

When you are done with the SNMP community upgrade, you can modify other SNMP configuration parameters, such as timeout, retries, and ports.

Name lookup resolution

Please review this section if you have nodes which shouldn't be resolved on DNS. Such nodes are included in the following files:

- ipNoLookup.conf file on NNM
- hostNoLookup.conf file on NNMi

There are two ways to make a name resolution limitation configuration:

- **Using upgrade tool**: If you chose to use the upgrade tool, then it automatically creates ipNoLookup.conf and hostNoLookup.conf files on the NNM server during the upgrade process, which is described in the *SNMP Configuration Upgrade* section.

  To replicate data in NNMi, complete the following steps:

  1. Delete any lines in the ipNoLookup.conf and hostNoLookup.conf files that refer to the NNMi server. Files are located in:

     Unix:$NnmDataDir/tmp/migration/<hostname>/CONFIG/ipNo-Lookup.conf

     $NnmDataDir/tmp/migration/<hostname>/DNS/hostNoLookup.conf

Windows:%NnmDataDir%\tmp\migration\<hostname>\CONFIG\
ipNoLookup.conf

%NnmDataDir%\tmp\migration\<hostname>\DNS\ hostNoLookup.
conf

2. Locate a file in the following directory on the NNMi server:

    Unix:$NnmDataDir/shared/nnm/conf/

    Windows:%NnmDataDir%\conf\

- **Upgrading manually**: If you prefer manual upgrade, complete the following steps:

    1. Check whether the ipNoLookup.conf file exists on the NNM server:

        Unix:$OV_CONF/ipNoLookup.conf

        Windows:%OV_CONF%\ipNoLookup.conf

        If the file doesn't exist or the file is empty, then you don't have any exceptions for the name resolution configured on your NNM server and you can skip the upgrade of the name resolution exception.

    2. Copy the IP addresses from the ipNoLookup.conf file on NNM to the ipNoLookup.conf file on NNMi:

        Unix:$NnmDataDir/shared/nnm/conf/ipNoLookup.conf

        Windows:%NnmDataDir%\conf\ipNoLookup.conf

Device profiles

Device profiles are used to group nodes for monitoring, viewing, and some other grouping. Profile is assigned to a node by mapping a node's system Object ID to a profile.

NNMi is shipped with a long list of device profiles, and in most cases no upgrade is needed at this point.

It is recommended that you allow NNMi to discover your nodes and then decide whether you need to upgrade any profile. In most cases, only selected profiles may need to be upgraded.

If you need to upgrade device profiles, complete the following steps:

1. Use the nnmmigration.ovpl tool to copy profile files from NNM configuration to the CONFIG directory on the NNM server.

2. On the NNMi console, select **Device Profiles** from the **Configuration** workspace and compare configuration on NNMi against NNM. If you are missing any profile, add it.

Discovery configuration upgrade

Before you start upgrading discovery configuration, please remember that the discovery process in NNMi starts when you save your discovery configuration. To have the most accurate discovered objects, make sure you have configured the SNMP community names for your devices.

Some of the topology in NNMi may be presented by manual connection configuration. So when your discovery on NNMi is over, configure such connections on NNMi as well.

Scheduling discovery

When you are upgrading the discovery schedule configuration, you can upgrade only the node discovery interval. There is a list of areas which are not upgraded during an upgrade:

- Topology checks on connector devices. NNMi makes a topology check on any occasion when an indication of change occurs.
- Configuration check, which is launched with a schedule discovery, or any trigger in NNMi.
- Auto-adjusting the discovery polling interval. This feature is not provided in NNMi.
- Layer 2 discovery, if Extended Topology is launched. NNMi makes such a discovery instantly when a node is discovered.

To upgrade the discovery schedule, complete the following steps:

1. Open **Network Polling Configuration** on NNM by selecting **Options | Network Polling Configuration**.
2. Review **Discovery Polling Interval** for transferring it to NNMi.

 If none of the *auto-adjusting* periods were enabled, you will need to decide your own period.

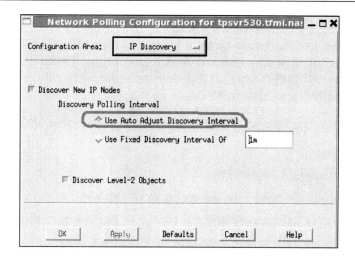

3. On the NNMi console, enter the polling schedule period by selecting **Configuration | Discovery Configuration | Rediscovery Interval**.

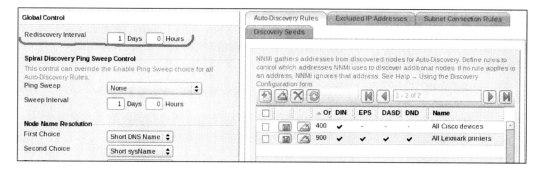

Discovery method selection

Before you proceed further with the upgrade, you need to decide which discovery method you plan to use. You can use one of the following methods:

- **Auto-discovery**: If you use this method, you need to complete the *Configuring Auto-discovery* section and the *Add seeds into NNMi discovery* section

- **Seeded discovery**: Complete the *Add seeds into NNMi discovery* section

Licensing policy between NNM and NNMi is different. NNM counts monitored nodes, and NNMi counts discovered nodes, which means that NNM doesn't count against licensing policy unmanaged nodes. NNMi counts all the nodes discovered, regardless of their monitoring status.

Configuring auto-discovery

If you selected the auto-discovery method instead of manual node seed, please review your infrastructure map carefully before you proceed with the auto-discovery upgrade. In some cases, you may find the new auto-discovery rule configuration is easier than a transfer from existing NNM.

Therefore, the following discovery features are not supported on NNMi:

- IPX discovery
- Discover beyond license limits
- Layer 2 object discovery disablement, as NNMi has it always enabled
- Limit of Layer 2 discovery using the `bridge.NoDiscover` file
- Limit of Layer 2 discovery based on CDP protocol area
- `network.interfaceNoDiscover`
- Discovery exclusion other than IP address and `systemObjectID`
- Extended Topology zones

To configure spiral auto-discovery, you need to configure auto-discovery rules. Otherwise, you can configure spiral discovery using seeds (refer to the section entitled *Add seed into NNMi discovery*).

For the auto-discovery rule configuration, complete the following steps:

1. Locate which filter it is used on NNM by selecting the **Options | Network Polling Configuration | General | Use filter** field.

   [If nothing is selected, then no filter was used and you may proceed by loading nodes using a seed.]

2. Open a filter file on the following location:

   Unix:`$OV_CONF/C/filters`

   Windows:`%OV_CONF%\C\fitlers`

3. Capture the applied filter.
4. Configure the discovery filter on NNMi by filling in a filter configuration window on the **Configuration** workspace | **Discovery configuration**.

Excluding addresses from discovery

Excluded IP addresses in NNM are configured in the `netmon.noDiscover` file. If that file doesn't exist, you can skip this section. Otherwise, you can upgrade it using upgrade script or by doing it manually.

If you choose an upgrade tool, complete the following steps:

1. Change to the following directory:

    Unix:`$NnmDataDir/tmp/migration/<hostname>/CONFIG/conf`

    Windows:`%NnmDataDir%\tmp\migration\<hostname>\CONFIG\conf`

2. Import excluded IP addresses into NNMi by running the following command:

    Unix:`$NnmInstallDir/bin/nnmdiscocfg.ovpl -excludeIpAddrs -f netmon.noDiscover`

    Windows:`%NnmInstallDir%\bin\nnmdiscocfg.ovpl -excludeIpAddrs -f netmon.noDiscover`

If you choose the manual approach, enter IP addresses into the **Excluded IP addresses** field manually (**Configuration | Discovery Configuration | Excluded IP addresses** tab).

Adding seeds into NNMi discovery

Seeds can be added into NNMi using either the manual way, or by using the upgrade tool.

If you selected the upgrade tool approach, complete the following steps:

1. Copy the `topology.out` file from NNM to NNMi. The file location on NNM is as follows:

    Unix:`$NnmDataDir/tmp/migration/<hostname>/TOPO/topology.out`

    Windows:`%NnmDataDir%\tmp\migration\<hostname>\TOPO\topology.out`

2. Modify the file, so that it has only one IP address or hostname per line. No subnet mask is needed in NNMi.

3. Run the following command:

    ```
    nnmloadseeds.ovpl -f <seedfile>
    ```

    where `<seedfile>` is your seed filename.

If you choose the manual approach, complete the following steps:

1. Export NNM topology by running the following command on NNM:

   ```
   ovtopodump > topology.out
   ```

2. Copy the `topology.out` file into the NNMi server.

3. Modify the file, so that it has only one IP address or hostname per line. No subnet mask is needed in NNMi.

4. Run the following command:

   ```
   nnmloadseeds.ovpl -f <seedfile>
   ```

   where `<seedfile>` is your seed filename.

Customizing connectivity

If you have configured a manual connection on NNM Extended Topology, you need to upgrade these connections as well. To upgrade such connections, complete the following steps:

1. Review the `connectionEdits` file on the NNM server in the following location:

   Unix: `$OV_CONF/nnmet/connectionEdits`

   Windows: `%OV_CONF%\nnmet\connectionEdits`

2. Run the following command to generate a connection template file:

   ```
   nnmconnedit.ovpl -t addconn
   ```

3. Modify the template file adding connections from the `connectionEdits` file to the `addconn.xml` template file.

   For example, if the NNM file has the following connection configured:

   ```
   box1.testlab.local[ifAlias:ConnectionToLondon], \
   box2.testlab.local[ifAlias:ConnectionToParis]
   box3.testlab.local[ 0 [ 123 ]], box4.testlab.local[ 0 [ 456 ]]
   ```

   The `addconn.xml` file would look as follows:

   ```
   <connectionedits>
   <connection>
   <operation>add</operation>
   <node> box1.testlab.local</node>
   <interface> ConnectionToLondon</interface>
   <node> box2.testlab.local</node>
   <interface> ConnectionToLondon</interface>
   </connection>
   ```

```
<connection>
<operation>add</operation>
<node> box3.testlab.local</node>
<interface>123</interface>
<node> box4.testlab.local</node>
<interface>456</interface>
</connection>
</connectionedits>
```

4. Load the connection configuration file into NNMi by running:

    nnmconnedit.ovpl -f addconn.xml

5. Verify the results in NNMi by opening the Layer 2 connections window from the **Inventory** workspace.

Status monitoring upgrade

In NNM, the status monitoring was organized using netmon or **APA (Active Problem Analyzer)**. NNMi can be configured for status monitoring at the node, interface, or address level.

The following areas can be upgraded in status monitoring:

*   Polling intervals
*   Polling protocol selection
*   Critical Node configuration
*   Excluding Objects from Status Polling

Polling intervals

If you are using netmon, complete the following steps to upgrade polling intervals:

1. Find the polling intervals configured on the OVW console of NNM.
2. Manually transfer the configuration to NNMi using the console:

    i.   Select **Monitoring Configuration** from the **Configuration** workspace.

    ii. Open Node Group.

    iii. Select **Node Settings**.

    iv. Set value on the **Fault Polling Interval** field.

If you are using APA, complete the following steps:

1. Determine the current configuration in the `paConfig.xml` file on the NNM server.

2. Transfer data to NNMi, as described on the netmon upgrade case in this section.

Polling protocol selection

Depending on whether netmon or APA was used on NNM, different Polling Protocol usage is supported:

*   If netmon was used, then, by default, netmon uses ICMP to make status polling, unless SNMP mode is specified for the specific IP addresses or address ranges on the `netmon.snmpStatus` file in the following directory:

    Unix: `$OV_CONF/netmon.snmpStatus`

    Windows: `%OV_CONF%\netmon.snmpStatus`

     Netmon cannot be configured to use both ICMP and SNMP for the same IP address.

*   If APA is used, ICMP and SNMP protocol combination can be configured on the `TopoFitlers.xml` and `paConfig.xml` files.

In contrast to netmon, where polling is configured for nodes, APA polling policies can be applied for nodes or interfaces.

Polling policies on NNMi can be applied on groups of nodes or interfaces. To upgrade the polling protocol, complete the following steps:

1. Depending on the polling type, review the preceding described polling configurations on the NNM server.

2. Configure the polling protocol for the selected objects (nodes or interfaces) on NNMi using the console (**Monitoring** workspace).

Critical node configuration

Critical nodes can be upgraded from NNM to NNMi if you are using APA. Netmon doesn't support critical node configuration.

Critical nodes in NNMi are called **Important Nodes**.

To upgrade critical node monitoring configuration, complete the following steps:

1. Review the critical Node configuration file in NNMi:

   Unix: `$OV_CONF/nnmet/topology/filter/CriticalNodes.xml`

   Windows: `%OV_CONF%\nnmet\topology\filter\CriticalNodes.xml`

2. Add Important Nodes into the NNMi configuration using the console:

   i. Select **Node Groups** in the **Configuration** workspace.

   ii. Open the **Important Nodes** group.

   ii. Add important nodes manually. Nodes can be added as a specific name, hostname wildcard, or device filter.

Excluding objects from Status Polling

There is no upgrade procedure for excluding objects from status polling. To stop a node being polled in NNM, the node can be switched to **Unmanaged** mode manually by selecting a node and setting it to the unmanaged state (**Edit | Unmanaged**).

NNMi has the ability to set the objects polling mode to one of the following modes:

- Managed
- Not managed
- Out of service

Management mode can be set for nodes or interfaces.

Event configuration and event reduction upgrade

You should know the main differences for event processing in NNM and NNMi before you make an upgrade.

All events in NNM have their OID, while NNMi doesn't have OID for some incidents (that is, within NNMi-created incidents).

Another difference is if NNM has no definition for the incoming event, it will be shown in a browser as a **NO FORMAT DEFINED** event. NNMi ignores events that are not defined in incident configuration.

Also, NNM has the ability to set how events should be processed:

- Display
- Log only
- Don't log or display

Unless **don't log or display** is set for a particular event, that event will be stored in the event DB, while NNMi stores only incidents configured to display in the incident browser.

So, when you plan an event configuration upgrade, consider the following upgrade areas:

- Block, ignore, or disable traps
- Trap display
- Custom display of management events on NNMi
- Automatic actions
- Event correlation

Block, ignore, or disable traps

NNM provided the ability to block, ignore, or disable events, by configuring them in **Event Configuration** and setting the **IGNORE** or **LOG ONLY** mode. If the trap wasn't configured in **Event Configuration**, it would appear as a **NO FORMAT DEFINED** event.

NNMi has only **Enabled** or **Disabled** modes for incidents. Only **Enabled** incidents are stored in the incident database.

You may choose to make an upgrade by selecting either using an upgrade tool or by upgrading manually.

Upgrading using upgrade tool: The `nnmmigration.ovpl` tool collects the `ovtrapd.conf` file while processing. To upgrade it to NNMi, complete the following steps:

1. Change to the following directory:

   Unix: `$NnmDataDir/tmp/migration/<hostname>/CONFIG/conf/`

   Windows: `%NnmDataDir%\tmp\migration\<hostname>\CONFIG\conf\`

2. Run the following tool to copy non commented lines from the `ovtrapd.conf` file to the `nnmtrapd.conf` file:

Unix: `$NnmInstallDir/migration/bin/nnmtrapdMerge.ovpl ovtrapd.conf`

Windows: `%NnmInstallDir%\migration\bin\nnmtrapdMerge.ovpl ovtrapd.conf`

 Note: The upgrade tool doesn't process or convert any trap definitions. So you have to deal manually with **LOG ONLY** events and it's up to you to decide whether they should be enabled or disabled on NNMi.

Upgrading manually: Observe an event configuration on NNM and manually configure events on NNMi by completing the following steps:

1. Disable incidents that you don't want to receive in NNMi:

   Select **Incident Configuration** from the **Configuration** workspace, locate the incident that you want to disable, and clear the **Enable** checkbox option.

2. If you need to block incidents sent from specific IP addresses, edit the following file:

   Unix: `$NnmDataDir/shared/nnm/conf/nnmtrapd.conf`

   Windows: `%NnmDataDir%\shared\nnm\conf\nnmtrapd.conf`

3. Enable trap blocking, include rates and thresholds for trap blocking, and run the nnmtrapconfig.ovpl tool.

Trap display

NNMi has a long list of already configured SNMP traps and they can be modified. Here are the procedures provided for both approaches—using upgrade tool and configuring manually.

- **Upgrade tool approach**: If you prefer to do an upgrade using upgrade tool, complete the following steps:

  1. Go to the following directory:

     Unix: `$NnmDataDir/tmp/migration/<hostname>/CONFIG/conf/`

     Windows: `%NnmDataDir%\tmp\migration\<hostname>\CONFIG\conf\`

2. Load MIBs to NNMi by running:

   Unix: `$NnmInstallDir/migration/bin/nnmmibmigration.ovpl \ -file snmpmib -u <user> -p <password>`

   Windows: `%NnmInstallDir%\migration\bin\nnmmibmigration. ovpl \ -file snmpmib -u <user> -p <password>`

3. Load the `trapd.conf` file on NNMi, which contains custom event definitions:

   Unix: `$NnmInstallDir/migration/bin/nnmtrapdload.ovpl \ -loadTrapd <lang>/trapd.conf -authorLabel NNM_migration \ -authorKey com.domain.nnmUpgrade -u <user> -p <password>`

   Windows: `%NnmInstallDir%\migration\bin\nnmtrapdload.ovpl \ -loadTrapd <lang>\trapd.conf -authorLabel NNM_migration \ -authorKey com.domain.nnmUpgrade -u <user> -p <password>`

   Please make sure that you provide a unique author for this operation.

- **Configuring manually**: Manual approach is used to visually compare events configured on an NNM event `config` with the NNMi incident configuration.

  1. Explore **Event configuration** on NNM to see if you have your custom events. This is not an easy task, as you may need to find custom events where only the severity or category is modified.

     NNMi may need to load some MIB files that can be loaded by running the following command:

     `nnmincidentcfg.ovpl -loadTraps mibfile`

  2. Modify incident configuration on the NNMi management console by completing the following steps:

     i. Select **Incident Configuration** in the **Configuration** workspace.

     ii. Select the **SNMP trap definition** tab.

     iii. Customize the incident in a way to match the incident configuration which was on NNM.

Custom display of management events

Management events in NNMi are like internal messages, which are completely different from NNM, where such events have their own OID. There is no upgrade feature from NNM.

The only thing you can do in this area is to modify NNMi management incidents so that they would appear as an event in NNM. To modify management incidents, complete the following steps:

1. Select **Incident Configuration** in the **Configuration** workspace.

2. Select the **Management event configuration** tab.

3. Locate **Incident Configuration**.

4. Modify according to your needs.

5. Click **Save and close**.

For example, the incident **Interface down** should be modified, and as a result, it was dampened for the next ten minutes before it is displayed in the incident browser. Complete the following steps to modify the incident:

1. Select **Incident Configuration** in the **Configuration** workspace.

2. Select the **Management Event Configuration** tab.

3. Locate the **Interface Down** incident and select **Open**.

4. Select the **Dampening** tab.

5. Make sure that the **Enabled** checkbox is checked.

6. Enter 10 in the **Minutes** field.

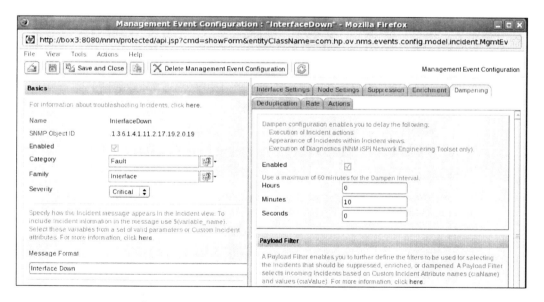

7. Click **Save and close**. If you haven't modified this incident before, you may receive the following error message:

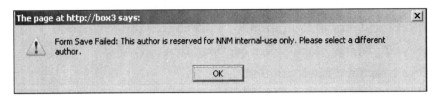

8. Click **Save and close**.

Automatic actions

There are two types of actions used in NNM:

- **Automatic actions**: Actions that are launched automatically when an event occurs.
- **User action**: The ones that are launched by a user from the event browser menu.

In both cases, actions on NNM can only be manually upgraded. There is no automated upgrade tool provided for it.

Here are the generic steps for an action upgrade:

1. Find actions that are used in NNM.
2. Copy scripts to the NNMi server.
3. (For automatic actions only). Configure each incident in **Incident Management** to include scripts that need to be launched:
    i. Select **Incident Management** in the **Configuration** workspace.
    ii. Select an incident to which you want to include an action.
    iii. Configure automatic action on the **Action Configuration** tab.
4. (For operator initiated action only). These actions can be created as a URL menu on NNMi. To do so, determine which actions are used in NNM and create appropriate URL actions on NNMi:
    i. Select **URL actions** on the **Configuration** workspace.
    ii. Select **New**.

iii. Fill-in the menu action fields as required for menu action configuration (check the previous chapters in this book for a detailed description).

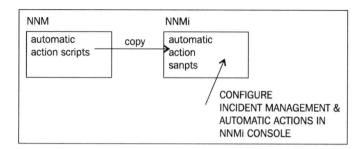

 You can choose on which incident the lifecycle stage action should be launched.

5. To reflect the NNM situation, set **Lifecycle state** to **Registered**. Then automatic action will be launched as soon as the incident is received in NNMi.

Event correlation

Event correlation is not upgraded automatically from NNM to NNMi. Only manual approach is possible, where you have to observe existing configuration on NNM and configure correlation behavior on NNMi accordingly (using **Incident Configuration** on the **Configuration** workspace).

The following correlation types are used:

- Scheduled maintenance
- Repeated/duplicated events
- Rate-based event correlation
- Pairwise-based event correlation

If scheduled maintenance is used in NNM, you can configure NNMi to ignore incidents during maintenance windows by setting node group to the **Out of Service** mode. The difference between NNM and NNMi scheduled maintenance configuration is that the start and end of the maintenance window in NNMi has to be enabled/disabled manually:

1. Select **Node Group Configuration** from the **Configuration** workspace.
2. Create node groups which will be used for the maintenance window.
3. When the maintenance window comes, select nodes by applying the node group filter (**Management Mode** | select nodes | filter nodes using **Set node group filter** | select nodes).
4. Set nodes to the **OUT OF SERVICE** mode (**Actions** | **OUT OF SERVICE**).

When the maintenance window is over, use the same sequence to configure nodes back to the managed mode (**Actions** | **Manage**).

Other event correlations can be configured on the **Incident Configuration** window in NNMi:

1. Select **Incident Configuration** from the **Configuration** workspace.
2. Select an event that needs to be configured for correlation.
3. Select one of the provided correlation tabs (**Deduplication configuration, Rate Configuration,** or **Action Configuration**).
4. Configure an incident according to your needs.

Map upgrade

Because NNM has two map types (OVW and Home Base), there are separate upgrade procedures for these maps.

OVW map upgrade

Upgrade from OVW map to NNMi includes only location icons and does not provide node or network symbol layout.

To upgrade the OVW map, complete the following steps:

1. Create an environment variable PERL5LIB, setting it to the following value:

    Unix: /opt/OV/migration/lib

    Windows: install_dir\migration\lib

If you are using Unix, run the following:

```
export PATH=$PATH: /opt/OV/migration/lib
```

If you are using Windows, complete the following steps to create such a variable:

    i.   Right click on **My computer** | **Properties** | **Advanced** | **Environment variables**.

    ii.   Select **New** on the **System variables** window | Enter `PERL5LI` in the **Variable name** field | enter `%install_dir%\migration\lib` in the **Variable value** field.

    iii. Select **OK**.

2. Open the map you want to export and select **File** | **Export** on the NNM console.

3. Save the file to the following location:

    Unix: `/opt/OV/migration/ipmap.out`

    Windows: `install_dir\migration\ipmap.out`

4. Change to the following directory:

    Unix: `/opt/OV/migration/`

    Windows: `install_dir\migration\`

5. Launch the map processing script:

    Unix: `/opt/OV/migration/bin/nnmmapmigration.ovpl ipmap.out`

    Windows: `install_dir\migration\bin\nnmmapmigration.ovpl ipmap.out`

6. Copy the `nnmnodegrouplist.csv` and `backgrounds.tar` files created in the previous step from the NNM server location:

    Unix: `/opt/OV/migration/<hostname>/MAPS`

    Windows: `install_dir\migration\<hostname>\MAPS`

    To the following location of the NNMi server:

    Unix: `$NnmDataDir/tmp/migration/<hostname>/MAPS/`

    Windows: `%NnmDataDir%\tmp\migration\<hostname>\MAPS\`

7. Run the `nnmloadnodegroups.ovpl` tool to import the node group definitions into the NNMi:

    Unix: `$NnmInstallDir/bin/nnmloadnodegroups.ovpl \ -u <user> -p <password> -r false -f nnmnodegrouplist.csv`

Windows: `%NnmInstallDir%\bin\nnmloadnodegroups.ovpl \ -u <user>`
`-p <password> -r false -f nnmnodegrouplist.csv`

8. Unpack the `backgrounds.tar` file and copy to the following location:

Unix: `$NnmDataDir/shared/nnm/www/htdocs/images/`

Windows: `%NnmDataDir%\shared\nnm\www\htdocs\images\`

9. Apply the background on the NNMi console by completing the following steps:

   i. Select **Node Groups** from the **Configuration** workspace.

   ii. Select a node group.

   iii. Select **Actions | Node Group Map**.

   iv. Select **File | Open Node Group Map Settings**.

   v. Specify the name of the background in the **Node Group Map Settings** form (**Background image** tab) using the following format:

   `/nnmbg/images/<custom_directory>/<background_filename>`

10. For the lowest topology map, add at least one node group. Higher level topology maps don't have to have a node group assigned. See the example in the following figure:

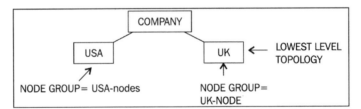

Home Base map upgrade

NNM Advanced Edition Home Base has maps which can include logical containers for map enhancement. Visually, NNMi maps may look similar to Home Base, but from a technical perspective, they are different. Also, there is no tool for maps upgrade so far.

However, the NNMi upgrade tool can upgrade container view into the NNMi map. All files are collected during the `nnmmigration.ovpl` tool execution. There is no manual upgrade procedure.

To replicate container views into NNMi, complete the following steps:

1. On the NNM server, change to the NNMET upgrade directory:

   Unix:`$NnmDataDir/tmp/migration/<hostname>/NNMET/`

   Windows:`%NnmDataDir%\tmp\migration\<hostname>\NNMET\`

2. Run the `nnmet` map migration tool to create a comma separated node group list:

   Unix: `$NnmInstallDir/migration/bin/nnmetmapmigration.ovpl \ con-tainers.xml nnmcontainerlist.csv`

   Windows: `%NnmInstallDir%\migration\bin\nnmetmapmigration.ovpl \ containers.xml nnmcontainerlist.csv.txt`

3. On the NNMi server, run the map migration tool, which imports node group definitions into the NNMi database:

   Unix: `$NnmInstallDir/bin/nnmloadnodegroups.ovpl -u <user> \ -p <password> -r false -f nnmcontainerlist.csv`

   Windows: `%NnmInstallDir%\bin\nnmloadnodegroups.ovpl -u <user> \ -p <password> -r false -f nnmcontainerlist.csv.txt`

4. Add at least one node group to the lowest-level topology map using the NNMi console.

Custom script transfer

When you are upgrading to NNMi, you should upgrade your custom scripts as well. This is because NNMi has enhanced some command line tools, namely, `nnmtopodump.ovpl`.

To upgrade your custom scripts from NNM to the NNMi server, complete the following steps:

1. Copy all custom scripts from NNM to the NNMi server.
2. Each script which is using any of the following commands needs to be examined on the NNMi server as the syntax may be changed:
    - `ovdwquery`
    - `ovet_topodump.ovpl`
    - `ovobjprint`
    - `ovtopodump`

And script needs to be updated to call the `nnm topodump.ovpl` command instead of any one on the list above.

The output of previous scripts and enhanced `ovtopodump.ovpl` may differ, so make sure your scripts are working properly.

Summary

Congratulations if you decided to make an upgrade instead of a new deployment and you succeeded with your upgrade following this appendix.

As you can see, NNMi has a completely new architecture and cannot be compared with NNM side-by-side. Either way, part of configuration data can be upgraded and this appendix listed all the features that can be upgraded. After completing this appendix, you should now be able to make system upgrades and make decisions on which features/areas should be selected for an upgrade, and which you should configure manually from scratch.

This appendix finished explaining any technical data on this book. The next appendix provides you with some guidelines on where you should consider moving with your NNMi in your organization and it doesn't contain any specific technical data.

B
Upgrading from NNMi 8.1x

This appendix describes NNMi 8.1x upgrade NNMi 9.00 process. This appendix covers the following topics:

- Upgrade overview
- Upgrading from NNMi 8.1x on the same server
- Upgrading from NNMi 8.1x on a different server
- Upgrading NNMi from Red Hat 4.6 to 5.2 or 5.3
- Migrating Oracle data in NNMi

Overview

Upgrade to NNMi 9.00 can be started only from NNMi version 8.1x. If the NNMi 8.0x version is installed, direct upgrade is not supported. Rather, the upgrade path from NNMi 8.0x to NNMi 8.1x and then to NNMi 9.00 is suggested instead. The following figure represents a graphical upgrade workflow, depending on the NNMi version.

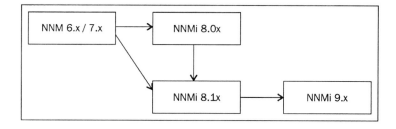

The upgrade to NNMi 9.00 is supported from NNMi 8.10 with any patch level installed. However, for best results, it is recommended to install Patch Level 7 or higher on NNMi 8.1x before you start upgrading.

If NNMi 8.1x is running on Application Failover or High Availability configuration, the supported way is to unconfigure Application Failover or High Availability configuration, upgrade the NNMi to version 9.00, and then to configure Application Failover or High Availability. *Chapter 7, Application Failover and High Availability Solutions* describes how to unconfigure and configure Application Failover or High Availability solution.

While you are planning your upgrade path, the following scenarios described in this chapter:

- Upgrading on the same server
- Upgrading to a different server
- Moving NNMi from Red Hat 4.6 to 5.2 or 5.3
- Migrating Oracle data in NNMi

Upgrading from NNMi 8.1x on the same server

This section describes how to upgrade the NNMi server from version 8.1x to version 9.00. This is the high level description. Complete the following steps for upgrading NNMi 8.1x to NNMi 9.00:

1. Back up your NNMi 8.x server. For detailed instructions about the backup, see *Chapter 6, Troubleshooting, Security, and Backup*.

2. If Oracle DB is running on NNMi only, back up the Oracle data.

3. If Oracle DB is running on NNMi only, back up the configuration data from NNMi 8.1x using the `nnmconfigexport.ovpl` script. Read *Chapter 6* for detailed instructions about this script.

4. Install NNMi 9.00 Patch 2 (NNMi 9.01) on the management server.

5. If you haven't set the **FLASHBACK ANY TABLE** permission before an upgrade, when you complete the install process, you will see a warning message about that permission.

6. Verify the upgrade information. In this step, check if all processes are running and if you can open an NNMi console. Try to navigate through console menus.

Upgrading from NNMi 8.1x to a different server

This section describes how to upgrade the NNMi server from version 8.1x to version 9.00, if NNMi 9.00 is being installed on a separate server. This is a high level description. Complete the following steps for upgrading NNMi 8.1x to NNMi 9.00:

1. Back up your NNMi 8.x server. For detailed instructions about the backup, see *Chapter 6*.

2. If NNMi 8.1x runs on the Oracle database, back up the Oracle data.

3. Install NNMi 9.00 on a source server (including the latest consolidated patch).

4. Verify that the upgraded NNMi 9.00 is working correctly.

5. Back up the NNMi 9.00 source server. Use the `nnmbackup.ovpl` script.

6. Install NNMi 9.00 with the latest consolidated patch on a target server. Make sure that a new server is running with the same operating system as the target server.

7. Using the `nnmrestore.ovpl` tool, restore a backup on the target server. The backup was created in step 5.

8. It is common that the IP address for the upgraded NNMi server has changed compared to the target NNMi server. In that case, generate a new license on the HP portal, or contact the HP representatives with a request to generate a license key for you. Install a new license on the upgraded NNMi server.

9. Verify that the newly upgraded server is working correctly — check if all processes are running, connect to the management console, navigate through view, run some tools from the menu, and assess nodes monitored by the new NNMi 9.00 server.

Upgrading NNMi from Red Hat 4.6 to 5.2 or 5.3

As NNMi 9.00 does not support Red Hat 4.6, the operating system must be upgraded before upgrading NNMi to version 9.00. For an OS upgrade, there are three servers needed:

- Original NNMi 8.1x (Server 1)
- Backup storage server, where backup files will be saved during an upgrade (Server 2)
- New NNMi 9.00 management server, which will be upgraded (Server 3)

In case you don't have three servers, you can perform an upgrade with two servers. The following instructions provide options for an upgrade with two servers as well.

Complete the following steps to upgrade Red Hat OS from 4.6 to 5.2 or 5.3:

1. NNMi 8.1x must have at least patch level 6 or higher installed. If you have a lower patch level installed, upgrade Server 1 to the required patch level.

2. Make sure you checked which patch level is installed on Server 1. It will be needed to install the very same patch level on the newly installed NNMi 8.1x on Server 3.

3. Make an online backup on Server 1 and run the following command:

   `nnmbackup.ovpl -type online scope all -target /tmp/server_backup/all`

4. Copy backup files from Server 1 (`/tmp/server_backup/all directory`) to Server 2.

5. Install Red Hat 5.2 or 5.3 on Server 3. If only two servers are present for an upgrade, Red Hat 5.2 or 5.3 should be installed on Server 1. The disk format should be made before installing Red Hat 5.2 or 5.3 on Server 1.

6. Install NNMi 8.10 on Server C. If two server migration scenarios were chosen, NNMi 8.10 should be installed on Server 1.

7. NNMi 8.1x patch 6 or later should be installed on Server 3. Patch level must be the same as of that installed on Server 1 before backup. In case two server scenarios were chosen, a patch needs to be installed on Server 1.

8. Copy the backup directory from Server 2 to Server 3. If two server migration scenarios were chosen, copy the backup directory to Server 1.

9. Complete NNM restore on Server 3 by running the following command (if two server migration scenarios were chosen, run the restore command on Server 1):

```
nnmrestore.ovpl -force -source /tmp/server_backup/all
```

 The same restore options as were used in step 3 should be used in case other options were used during NNMi backup.

10. If Server 3's IP address is different from the one on Server 1, a new license key needs to be generated and installed. If two server migration scenarios were chosen, the IP address should be compared with Server 1 before the new Red Hat version is installed, and after it is installed.

The following figure shows the high level upgrade workflow:

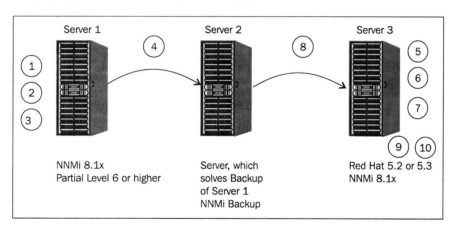

Now, when you have Red Hat 5.2 or 5.3 installed, you can upgrade your NNMi 8.1x to NNMi 9.00. Please refer to the section *Upgrading from NNMi 8.1x on a same server* in this chapter.

Migrating Oracle data in NNMi

This section describes how to migrate data from one Oracle instance to another. For example, the reason for migrating can be:

- NNMi 8.1x, which is connected to Oracle 10g, is being upgraded into NNMi 9.00 with Oracle 11g

Note: NNMi 8.1x connection to Oracle 11g is not supported.

- NNMi 9.00, which is connected to Oracle 10g, needs to be reconnected to Oracle 11g

Migration can be done only to a same or higher version of Oracle. Migration path from Oracle 11g to Oracle 10g cannot be completed.

Complete the following steps to migrate Oracle data in NNMi:

1. Stop NNMi services on NNMi server by running:

   ```
   ovstop -c
   ```

2. Copy or move Oracle data from one server to another using Oracle tools. Consult with your database administrator or refer to the Oracle documentation on how to proceed with this step.

3. Complete this step only if the target Oracle server has a name different from the source server. Reconfigure the NNMi server to point to the new Oracle server by completing the following steps:

   - Edit the nms-ds.xml file, which is located in :

   Unix: `$NNM_JBOSS/server/nms/deploy/nms-ds.xml`

   Windows: `%NNM_JBOSS%\server\nms\deploy\nms-ds.xml`

   - The attribute, which reflects the new server, needs to be changed:

   From the following value:

   ```
   <connection-url>jdbc:oracle:thin:@existing_fqdn:\ existing_ora-
   cle_port:existing_sid</connection-url>
   ```

   To the following value:

   ```
   <connection-url>jdbc:oracle:thin:@new_fqdn:\ new_oracle_port:
   new_sid</connection-url>
   ```

4. If you are upgrading from NNMi 8.1x to NNMi 9.01, complete an upgrade now by following the instructions provided in the section *Upgrading from NNMi 8.1x ...* in this chapter.

5. Start NNMi services by running the following command:

   ```
   ovstart -c
   ```

6. Make sure all processes have started by running the following command:

`ovstatus -c`

Congratulations! You have moved your NNMi Oracle data.

Additional information

From version NNMi 9.00, some files are stored in other locations than NNMi 8.x files. If an upgrade to NNMi 9 is applied, some of the files will be stored in other locations such as the following:

- Properties files are stored in the following locations:

  Unix: `$NNM_DATA/shared/nnm/conf/props`

  `$NNM_DATA/conf/nnm/props`

  Windows: `%NNM_DATA%\shared\nnm\conf\props`

  `%NNM_DATA%\conf\nnm\props`

- `ovjboss` options can be modified in the following file:

  Unix: `$NNM_DATA/shared/nnm/conf/props/ovjboss.jvmargs`

  Windows: `%NNM_DATA%\shared\nnm\conf\props\ovjboss.jvmargs`

- NNMi preserves the `nms-jboss.properties` file contents during an upgrade in the following location. Also, this file contains application failover configuration

  Unix: `$NNM_DATA/shared/nnm/conf/props/nms-jboss.properties`

  Windows: `%NNM_DATA%\shared\nnm\conf\props\nms-jboss.properties`

- SNMP trap services can be modified in the following file:

  Unix: `$NNM_DATA/shared/nnm/conf/props/nnmtrapserver.properties`

  Windows: `%NNM_DATA%/shared/nnm/conf/props/nnmtrapserver.properties`

- The port properties, which used to be configured in the `port.properties` file after an upgrade to NNMi 9.00, is located at the following location:

  Unix: `$NNM_DATA/conf/nnm/props/nms-local.properties`

  Windows: `%NNM_DATA%\conf\nnm\props\nms-local.properties`

Also, there are some functionality differences after an upgrade to NNMi 9.00. The main differences are listed as follows:

- More command line tools in NNMi 9.00; requires a username and password.
- If the Oracle database is used, the `nmsdbmgr` process is not started automatically in NNMi.
- Dampening settings in incident configuration is turned on for most of the incidents. The script `nnmsetdampeninginterval.ovpl` can be used to set the dampening interval for management incidents.
- Management incident **Node Up** is not included in NNMi 9.00, and the root cause analysis does not trigger the **Node Up** incident anymore. In case some notification is needed to notify the **Node Down** incident has ended, there are few ways to make it:
    ◦ Lifecycle action can be associated in the **Node Down** incident, which creates a **Node Up** incident that can be set as **Registered** when **Node Down** is set to the **Closed** state.
    ◦ If integration is used and an incident has to be used, which notifies that **Node Down** has finished, traps can be received. Traps indicate that **Node Down** has been finished.
- Management addresses are being polled by ICMP pings in NNMi 9.0.
- Device profiles might be modified for some devices during the upgrade to NNMi 9.0. The same impact may be done for URL action configurations. If, for some reason, an old profile needs to be used, it is recommended to change the author for that profile. Upgrades, as well as patches, make changes to objects where the author is *HP Network Node Manage*.
- NNMi 9.00 has the **Calculate Status** settings applied for the node group. After an upgrade, all node groups are configured with the status calculation for all node groups. It is recommended to disable status calculation rules for large node groups.

Summary

Now, when you have completed this appendix, you are ready to make an upgrade to NNMi 9.00 and describe the main challenges faced when upgrading NNMi with embedded or external Oracle databases, as well as making an upgrade on the same or different servers. This appendix also describes how to make an NNMi upgrade to version 9.00, if you are running the Red Hat 4.6 operating system.

C

What's Next…

Perfect is the enemy of good enough

These words belong to Francois-Marie Arouet, also known as Voltaire. He lived in the XVII-XVIII century and I'm sure he didn't know anything about any of the NNM versions at that time, but his phrase is true for NNMi as well.

I'm not trying to say that NNMi is the perfect tool, as no management tool is. However, people who work, maintain, and design NNMi, can bring this tool to perfection. I had a lot of demonstrations, trainings, and technical presales of HP Software family products in the last few years. I also participated in many design, implementation, and improvement projects. I've found that there is one common thing to determine the success of a management tool, and that's people's approach to a tool.

This chapter is about how we can make this tool better, and how we can take another step further towards perfection. It doesn't matter whether you are an operator, engineer, analyst, solution architect, or business manager. Everybody's contribution is needed.

Most of this book is about NNMi, but in the real world, we see that other things outside NNMi are also important. No matter how much we love, or would like to love this tool, we have to acknowledge that NNMi is only a part of a successful operations center. Don't forget that there are people, processes, and probably other tools around in your operations center. The same rule of thumb applies here as in an orchestra—all pieces must be tight together. The quality of your operations center is at the same level as the quality of the worst part of your chain.

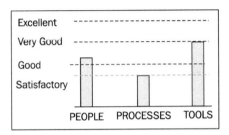

I would divide all activities, which should be considered for your NOC improvement, into the following sections:

- Polishing NNMi
- Making NNMi bigger
- Think outside the box—beyond management tools

Polishing NNMi

Make sure NNMi is working like a Swiss watch before you go anywhere outside NNMi's boundaries. The following questions will help you to find the area you should be concerned with or the area that needs improvement.

Is NNMi delivering the right incidents?

Receiving incidents doesn't mean monitoring your network. Don't forget, your goal is to deliver only meaningful incidents. Meaningful incidents are the ones that give you a hint or information allowing you determine an issue on your network, or, preferably, send you information before the issue occurs so that you could avoid downtimes. Two approaches are used for such activities:

- **Estimating if all incidents are needed in NNMi**: Make an analysis of your incident history. It would show you if any incidents may be filtered out or need modifications. Here are some hints on how to do that:
    - **Making reviews on a regular basis**: In most cases, once a week or once in two weeks would be good enough.

- ° Finding incidents on your incident browser that don't need any attention, and filter them out.

- ° **Finding incidents that need correlation**: Repeated, pair wise, or additional information demanding incidents.

For example, let's say that you found an incident that is needed for monitoring, but it doesn't carry enough information, so your staff puts a lot of additional effort while they gather additional information for decision making (log in to external systems, query data, compare, and make a decision). Why don't you make an automated action that runs a script? The script collects the very same information. The difference is that the staff would spend another one to five minutes, while the script delivers results within a few seconds.

- **Assessing if you can deliver incidents on additional issues**: Find cases in your infrastructure when issue appears or it can be predicted, but no incident appears in NNMi about that issue.

In most cases, system administrators or network engineers provide a good excuse as to why a particular issue cannot be shown in NNMi as an incident is a *device that doesn't send traps for such a case* or *there are no MIB files for such a device*.

But how about spending some extra time on investigating whether we can monitor a particular issue in a custom way? For example, when a router's memory usage exceeds some defined limit, the incident should be created in NNMi. As a solution, the custom poller can be used in that case, configuring NNMi to monitor the SNMP OID value, which represents a router's memory usage. If it goes away from the normal range boundaries, NNMi generates an incident.

Are my maps convenient for the staff?

Observe how your staff monitors the network. How much time do they spend for switching between maps or drilling down inside a map?

Check if you had any cases where an issue was displayed on the NNMi map, but your staff was late to recognize it or missed it all only because the object was located somewhere hard or impossible to recognize.

Let's say you monitor 50 sites that are located in five geographical locations. One possible way to create a map is shown as follows:

In most cases, it is a really nice design. But assume that NOC displays only a map of the initial monitoring. One of the sites in Australia goes down. You start working on this issue, but in the meantime, another issue appears with the other site in Australia. It will be hard to recognize because no other icon change appears on Australia's location. As a solution, redesigning a map would help:

Maybe the map wouldn't be nominated for the best design in a contest, but at least it would do its primary job well—notify an issue.

Am I consuming licenses efficiently?

Always keep track of what you monitor. If you have nodes which are not important to you, why are they in your NNMi? Why did you pay for them to be in NNMi? Don't forget that NNMi is licensed by a number of discovered nodes.

Even if your NNMi has less nodes than the number of licenses you have, check if you really need to monitor these nodes. By reducing number of managed nodes, you may fit into less node license. It means you can save. Here are some hints about maintaining licenses:

- **NNMi is licensed by discovered nodes**: It means that even if you set a node to the **Not managed** mode, the node is still counted against a license.

- **Inventory your network on a regular basis**: The node, which was business critical yesterday, may be a useless license consumer today. Depending on how often you change your network and network monitoring requirements, in most cases, the average inventory period would be 6-12 months. The minimum incremental for HP product support is 12 months, so you should inventory your network at least before extending support or buying additional licenses.

Making NNMi bigger

Don't limit yourself by features, which are provided to you by the NNMi default installation. Here you should remember the 80 by 20 rule, which in NNMi's case says that 80 percent of the features can be achieved by spending 20 percent of time and another 20 percent of features require 80 percent of your time.

So, if you installed an NNMi and are mostly happy with what you have, but still feel it is lacking something, be prepared to spend way more time completing that.

The following are the main areas for improvement:

- Start monitoring custom objects
- Create custom actions and menus
- Integrate NNMi with other tools

Custom object monitors

I'm sure your team wants to monitor more than deliver basic SNMP traps and NNMi's polling engines. If you read a vendor's manuals about your managed equipment, you would find SNMP descriptions with listed parameters, which can be retrieved using SNMP. Another way to list all parameters is to run the `snmpwalk` command on that device through all enterprise branches. SNMP utilities need to be installed on a host where this command is planned to be used.

Some of the object monitoring can be implemented by a custom object poller; some of them may require custom scripting from you outside NNMi and sending SNMP traps from a script. The following diagram represents the Custom scripting diagram:

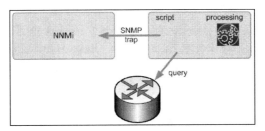

Custom actions and menus

Nobody likes routine tasks. So, follow that rule and try to move all routine tasks from your team members to scripts or other tools. The excuse "why would I need operators then" is not accepted, as you need your operators for decision making. The fewer routine tasks you have for operators, the more space for decision making and communication.

Observe your team's activities. Find out what activities you may automate, so some tasks can be completed faster, and maybe even more accurately. Build custom scripts or menu actions for operators instead.

Example 1: When an issue occurs, your operator opens the configuration management tool for a device configuration check, and then opens the Help Desk window to analyze the history of activities. Why don't you make these tools start from your NNMi's menu?

Example 2: When a particular incident occurs, an operator always connects to a managed device and runs a few commands for further investigation. Why don't you make a custom script that can be launched by the operator using a single click so that output can be provided instantly.

Integrating with NNMi

In most cases, your NOC has more tools than just an NNMi. Check if you can integrate these tools for more efficient management.

Chapter 11, Integrating NNMi with Other Management Tools, describes how to integrate NNMi with management tools and which integration is provided by NNMi integration workspace. But don't limit yourself to that. If you know how to write scripts, and if you are familiar with SQL queries and know how to deal with API, you are just one step away from becoming a superhero in your NOC.

Example: NOC with NNMi for network monitoring, and the Cacti tool for performance collection. These tools are perfect as standalone, but you must be tired of node list synchronization, new graph configuration, or switching between NNMi and Cacti, while you are investigating some issues and want to see graphs for a particular object. Here are a few suggestions on how you can improve this:

- **Synchronize nodes**: When a new node event comes into NNMi, make an automatic action that uses Cacti's command line interface to add a node to Cacti.

- **Configure new graphs**: Cacti also has **Command Line Interface (CLI)** for new graph configurations. If you make a script, which is launched from menu actions and creates a new graph for a selected object, you would bring a lot of convenience to your staff.

- **Open a specific graph from NNMi**: You can create a menu action to open the Cacti console for the specified object and graph almost in the same way as creating a new graph. It is also more convenient than just opening a generic Cacti window and navigating to an object of interest.

Beyond the tools

The shortest way to a successful NOC is by having a working triangle of people, processes, and tools. At the beginning of this chapter, I mentioned the importance of all three parts.

So, it is your job to contribute to this triangle. It doesn't matter which position you are at: operator, engineer, analyst, solution designer, or business manager. It only depends on your role in the contribution process.

Here are the main areas which should be taken into consideration while talking about something other than tools in your NOC:

- Process improvement
- Staff training
- Sharing experience

Improving processes

Process improvement is a never ending story. In most cases, it's boring, but it's a must if you care about efficiency and success.

If you constantly improve your NNMi, you should also participate in process improvement activities as well. If you leave it to others, they may not know your latest improvements and, as a result of that, your changes in NNMi may not make any positive influence in the final success of the whole NOC.

NNMi mainly provides input on the following processes:

- **Configuration management process**: If you have created additional custom attributes on NNMi, you may be an information provider to other management tools or you may need to import data from external tools.
- **Incident management process**: You may find an additional demand for an NNMi to be improved to comply with the latest process, or the opposite, you may provide some input from NNMi for process improvement.
- **Service level management process**: You may be required to determine a customer's name or SLA type while you deliver incidents to operators. Another example of SLM process improvement is that you may find you can create additional **custom attributes (CA)** which would determine a customer for a faster problem resolution, or for reporting expansion purposes.

Training your staff

Once I heard the phrase:

> *The best way to learn is to give a training*

It was said by one successful trainer. Training your staff not only makes others learn, but also forces you to learn yourself. While you train your staff on a regular basis, you achieve the following results:

- Lesser known situations faced by the staff, less enquiries or blames to the administrator or process manager.
- The more discussions you have inside the team, the more the number of new opportunities discovered for tool improvement. Sitting back in an office, away from real life, gives you less opportunity than constantly being inside a NOC kitchen.

Useful links

And finally, I'd like to share with you some useful links, where you can find more information about HP Software NNMi. The following table lists the most useful links, which may help in your work with NNMi.

Link	Description
www.OpenView.hp.com	The official HP Software (legacy HP OpenView) website. In this website, you will find the main descriptions about HP Software products. You will also be pointed to manuals and software trial downloads.
Support.openview.hp.com	Software support online is a website where support issues can be resolved. You need to have the **SAID** (**Support Assurance ID**) number in order to manage your cases. This ID is provided to you by HP sales when you purchase an HP support for your product.
www.ITRC.hp.com	IT Resource Center. Here you can find HP Software patches, manage your cases in HP, or even ask a question in the forum.
	This is one of the best and most visited forums for HP software products. It's free of charge, but registration is needed for posting a question. The only thing you need to remember is to assign points for the guys who are trying to help you with your queries. Points don't cost anything, but do the trick.
http://www.vivit-worldwide.org/	HP Software Users Community. An independent organization, which helps users not to be lost in the HP Software world. You can expect anything from them, from a small article in their website, webinar, to an event in your area.

Index

Symbols

A

HP Virtual Router Redundancy Protocol.
  See **HPVRRP**
HPVRRP 319
HSRP 319

I

Important Nodes 516
incident
  about 130
  attributes 130
  closing, ways 136
  form parameters 133
  source 136
  tuning 158
incident, attributes
  Assigned to 131
  Category 131
  Correlation nature 132
  Correlation notes 132
  Duplicate count 132
  Family 132
  First occurrence time 131
  Last occurrence time 131
  lifecycle state 131
  message 130
  name 131
  Notes 133
  Origin 132
  Origin occurrence time 131
  priority 130
  Root Cause Analysis (RCA) 132
  severity 130
  Source node 131
  Source object 131
incident, source
  Events generated by NNMi 136
  NNM 6.x/7.x events 136
  SNMP traps 136
incident, working with
  assignments, changing 398, 399
  example 398
  lifecycle stages 399
  map, displaying 400
incident details, in NNMi
  Assigned to 392

  category 392, 393
  Correlated Children tab 396
  Correlated Parents tab 396
  correlation nature 395
  Custom attributes tab 397
  Diagnostics tab 397
  family 393-395
  general tab 396
  Lifecycle state 391
  origin 394
  priority 390, 391
  Registration tab 397
  severity 390, 418
incident monitoring, for problems
  about 388
  data, contents 388
  incidents, working with 398
  NNMi, incident details 389
  NNMi sources 388
incidents, tuning
  dampening feature 175
  deduplication 161, 162
  deduplication, configuring 162
  deduplication, restrictions 162
  deduplication configuration, fields 163, 164
  enrichment configuration, screenshot 173, 174
  enrichment settings 173
  first In Pair 161
  interface settings 166
  interface settings, configuring 167, 168
  NNMi, correlation ways 159
  node settings 169
  node settings, configuring 169-171
  pair wise 160, 178
  rate, adding 165
  rate, configuring 164, 165
  rate configuration, fields 166
  scenarios 158
  second In Pair 161
  suppression 171, 172
  suppression, enabling 172
  worst device report 161
  worst event report 161
interface groups
  about 111

Thank you for buying
HP Network Node Manager 9: Getting Started

About Packt Publishing

Packt, pronounced 'packed', published its first book "Mastering phpMyAdmin for Effective MySQL Management" in April 2004 and subsequently continued to specialize in publishing highly focused books on specific technologies and solutions.

Our books and publications share the experiences of your fellow IT professionals in adapting and customizing today's systems, applications, and frameworks. Our solution based books give you the knowledge and power to customize the software and technologies you're using to get the job done. Packt books are more specific and less general than the IT books you have seen in the past. Our unique business model allows us to bring you more focused information, giving you more of what you need to know, and less of what you don't.

Packt is a modern, yet unique publishing company, which focuses on producing quality, cutting-edge books for communities of developers, administrators, and newbies alike. For more information, please visit our website: www.packtpub.com.

About Packt Enterprise

In 2010, Packt launched two new brands, Packt Enterprise and Packt Open Source, in order to continue its focus on specialization. This book is part of the Packt Enterprise brand, home to books published on enterprise software – software created by major vendors, including (but not limited to) IBM, Microsoft and Oracle, often for use in other corporations. Its titles will offer information relevant to a range of users of this software, including administrators, developers, architects, and end users.

Writing for Packt

We welcome all inquiries from people who are interested in authoring. Book proposals should be sent to author@packtpub.com. If your book idea is still at an early stage and you would like to discuss it first before writing a formal book proposal, contact us; one of our commissioning editors will get in touch with you.

We're not just looking for published authors; if you have strong technical skills but no writing experience, our experienced editors can help you develop a writing career, or simply get some additional reward for your expertise.

SOA Patterns with BizTalk Server 2009

ISBN: 978-1-847195-00-5   Paperback: 400 pages

Implement SOA strategies for BizTalk Server solutions

1. Discusses core principles of SOA and shows them applied to BizTalk solutions

2. The most thorough examination of BizTalk and WCF integration in any available book

3. Leading insight into the new WCF SQL Server Adapter, UDDI Services version 3, and ESB Guidance 2.0

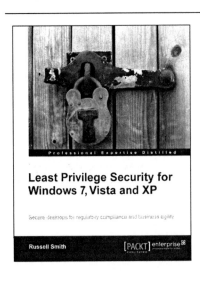

Least Privilege Security for Windows 7, Vista and XP

ISBN: 978-1-849680-04-2   Paperback: 464 pages

Secure desktops for regulatory compliance and business agility

1. Implement Least Privilege Security in Windows 7, Vista and XP to prevent unwanted system changes

2. Achieve a seamless user experience with the different components and compatibility features of Windows and Active Directory

3. Mitigate the problems and limitations many users may face when running legacy applications

Please check **www.PacktPub.com** for information on our titles

Oracle Siebel CRM 8 Installation and Management

ISBN: 978-1-849680-56-1   Paperback: 572 pages

Install, configure, and manage a robust Customer Relationship Management system using Siebel CRM

1. Install and configure the Siebel CRM server and client software on Microsoft Windows and Linux

2. Support development environments and migrate configurations with Application Deployment Manager

3. Understand data security and manage user accounts with LDAP

The Oracle Universal Content Management Handbook

ISBN: 978-1-849680-38-7   Paperback: 356 pages

Practical Knowledge and Breakthrough Shortcuts to Oracle UCM Expertise

1. Build a complete Oracle UCM system from scratch and quickly learn to configure, administer, and operate it efficiently

2. Match and exceed savings and efficiency expectations, and avoid devastating data losses with important tips and tricks

3. Migrate content like a pro — bring mountains of new content in faster than you ever dreamed possible

Please check **www.PacktPub.com** for information on our titles

LaVergne, TN USA
16 February 2011
216775LV00004B/240/P